EVERYMAN'S LIBRARY

EVERYMAN,
I WILL GO WITH THEE,
AND BE THY GUIDE,
IN THY MOST NEED
TO GO BY THY SIDE

ANTON CHEKHOV

My Life and Other Stories

Translated from the Russian by Constance Garnett
with an Introduction by Craig Raine

EVERYMAN'S LIBRARY

120

This book is one of 250 volumes in Everyman's Library
which have been distributed to 4500 state schools
throughout the United Kingdom.
The project has been supported by a grant of £4 million
from the Millennium Commission.

This selection first published in Everyman's Library, 1992

ISBN 1-85715-120-8

A CIP catalogue record for this book is available from the
British Library

Published by David Campbell Publishers Ltd.,
Gloucester Mansions, 140A Shaftesbury Avenue,
London WC2H 8HD

Distributed by Random House (UK) Ltd.,
20 Vauxhall Bridge Road, London SW1V 2SA

MY LIFE AND OTHER STORIES

CONTENTS

Introduction ix
Select Bibliography xxv
Chronology xxvi

A Daughter of Albion (1883) 1
An Incident (1886) 9
A Dreary Story (1889) 19
The Duel (1891) 105
The Chorus Girl (1892) 255
Ward No. 6 (1892) 265
The Teacher of Literature (1894) 345
An Artist's Story (1896) 381
My Life (1896) 409
The Darling (1899) 541
The Lady with the Dog (1899) 561

INTRODUCTION

In *The Middle Years*, Henry James recalls meeting Tennyson at Aldworth, only to discover that 'Tennyson was not Tennysonian'. In the same way, Chekhov is a tougher, more pitiless and less perfect writer than the wryly compassionate connoisseur of heat, doldrums, disappointment and defeat popularly associated with the epithet 'Chekhovian'. Like Joycean or Kafkaesque, Chekhovian is so widely current that we are disinclined to think it might be counterfeit, or have a value markedly different from that generally attributed. 'A Dreary Story' is the testy narrative of an old professor left sleepless by the unsleeping, imminent death lurking in his organism. It was written in 1889, and as early as 1886 Chekhov was apologizing for late copy with this excuse: 'I am ill. Spitting blood and weakness ...' His mother's side of the family was tubercular. In 1889, nursed by Chekhov, his brother Nikolai died of typhoid and tuberculosis. To his friend and mentor, Suvorin, Chekhov wrote: 'there's not a kopek's worth of poetry left in life'. And it is this mood which provides the dismal drive behind the at least quasi-autobiographical 'A Dreary Story'. Chekhov isn't totally dissociated from the professor's withering denunciation of contemporary Russian fiction which, far from being intellectually candid, is set about with debilitating conscientious objections, including the need to have 'a warm attitude to man'. There is a great deal of tonic coldness in Chekhov's report on the professor's coldness as it gradually chills every human contact. The prose is possessed of the arid inanition and unblinking pedantry which we associate with Beckett: 'as regards my present manner of life, I must give a foremost place to the insomnia from which I have suffered of late. If I were asked what constituted the chief and fundamental feature of my existence now, I should answer, insomnia.'

It isn't difficult to find in 'A Dreary Story' observations which manifestly contradict the popular image of Chekhov. The tone is scientific and dispassionate. It is the story of a soul whose central heating has failed, a tale of self-pity and repressed terror: 'is it possible that this old, very stout, ungainly woman, with her dull expression of petty anxiety and alarm about daily bread, with her eyes dimmed by continual brooding over debts and money difficulties, who can talk of nothing but expenses and who smiles at nothing but things getting cheaper – is it possible that this woman is no other than the slender Varya whom I fell in love with so passionately for her fine, clear intelligence, for her pure soul, her beauty ...?' His daughter Liza enacts with him a ritual which has been daily from her childhood. The professor kisses her fingers, pretending each one is a different ice cream flavour: 'but the effect is utterly different. I am cold as ice and ashamed'. It gradually emerges that this menaced egotism isn't entirely the recent result of the professor's ill-health. He has always been inadequate. When his ward, the beloved Katya, is abandoned by her lover, attempts suicide and loses her baby, the professor's testimony is culpably vague: 'Later on, from certain hints, I gathered that there had been an attempt at suicide. I believe Katya tried to poison herself. I imagine that she must have been seriously ill afterwards ...' What a damning trio of verbs: I 'gathered', I 'believe', I 'imagine'. The central heating has never been turned up very high: 'when she wrote to me of her intention of suicide, and then of the death of her baby, every time I lost my head, and all my sympathy for her sufferings found no expression except that, after prolonged reflection, I wrote long, boring letters which I might just as well not have written. And yet I took a father's place with her and loved her like a daughter!' At the story's end, when the troubled Katya follows him all the way to Harkov, she is clearly at the end of her tether, as (brilliantly) is her hat: 'she sinks on a chair and begins sobbing. She flings her head back, wrings her hands, taps with her feet; her hat falls off and hangs bobbing on its elastic ...' And the professor's response? It is two-fold. Inwardly, he feels ashamed because he is happier than she is, despite the proximity of his death and the last-minute realization that he is soulless, a man in whom 'the most skilful analyst could not find what is called a general idea, or the god of a living man'. Outwardly, his response is an invitation to lunch. Unsurprisingly, the offer is rejected.

If Chekhov has a subject, it is the nature of feeling – its failure, its forcing, its fatuity, its pretences, its fickleness. One minute, Trigorin is begging Irina to release him so that he can pursue 'a little provincial miss' who represents for him 'young love, enchanting and magical love that sweeps you off your feet into a make-believe world – can anything else on earth give one happiness?' Two years later, Konstantin reports: 'She had a baby. It died. Trigorin tired of her and returned to his former attachments, as could only be expected.' In 'An Artist's Story', the narrator muses on his declaration to Misuce in a way which suggests the subtle and complex analysis Chekhov brought to bear on the ostensibly simple subject of love: 'I was full of tenderness, peace, and satisfaction with myself – satisfaction at having been able to be carried away by my feelings and having fallen in love ...' In 'The Duel', the susceptible Nadyezhda Fyodorovna can simultaneously luxuriate in the prospect of her continuing an illicit affair with Atchmianov and indulge in a sentimental fantasy about her regular partner, Laevsky: 'she made up her mind to go away that she might not continue this life, shameful for herself, and humiliating for Laevsky. She would beseech him with tears to let her go; and if he opposed her, she would go away secretly. She would not tell him what had happened; let him keep a pure memory of her ... She would live in some far remote place, would work and send Laevsky, "anonymously", money, embroidered shirts, and tobacco, and would return to him only in old age or if he were dangerously ill and needed a nurse. When in his old age he learned what were her reasons for leaving him and refusing to be his wife, he would appreciate her sacrifice and forgive.' In fact, Laevsky is desperate to leave her and is making plans to disappear himself – a sexual irony that looks forward to Milan Kundera, just as his definition of kitsch fits Nadyezhda Fyodorovna's hormonally induced hypothesizing. In *The Art of the Novel*, Kundera formulates what Chekhov shows us in action: 'Kitsch is the translation of the stupidity of received ideas into the language of beauty and feeling. It moves us to tears of compassion for ourselves, for the banality of what we think and feel.'

The curious thing about 'The Duel' is that this kitsch fantasy of transgression and forgiveness actually transpires in the course of the narrative. Atchmianov maliciously leads Laevsky to Muridov's where Laevsky finds Nadyezhda Fyodorovna in bed with Kirilin, the police chief. Then Laevsky fights a duel, narrowly escapes with his life – 'on the right side of his neck was a small swelling, of the length and breadth of his little finger, and he felt a pain, as though someone had passed a hot iron over his neck. The bullet had bruised it' – and is reconciled to his erring partner and his previously wearisome work. His opponent, Von Koren, is so impressed by the moral reformation that, before taking a boat which will carry him away from the Caucasus, he offers his hand. The element of kitsch is purged by Chekhov when he gives us a glimpse of Laevsky's thoughts on seeing the boat which is to ferry Von Koren to the ship. The sea is rough and the boat moves three yards forward only to be sucked two yards back. 'No one knows the real truth ...' thinks Laevsky, 'looking wearily at the dark, restless sea.' It is a pity that Chekhov should make the equation explicit – 'in the search for truth man makes two steps forward and one step back' – when the juxtaposition alone would have told us that the perceived perfection of the remade life was nothing of the kind, but rather a bitter struggle of backsliding and romantic recidivism.

These dark notes are not difficult to hear in 'A Dreary Story' or in 'The Duel', despite the play in both tales of grim comedy. But what of an apparently innocent, slight story like 'An Incident'? Widely regarded as a charming (if callous) humoresque, it is, in fact, a bleak parable of human cruelty and unconsidered indifference. The children, Vanya and Nina, are a mixture of whimsy ('the cat has got puppies!') and casual cruelty. While we may be charmed by their *ingénue* playfulness when they decide that the father of the 'puppies' should be the 'dark-red horse without a tail', we can't help registering the truth of the behaviour presented by Chekhov: 'Vanya is watching its movements, and thrusting first a pencil, then a match into its little mouth ...'; 'he tries to open one kitten's eyes, and spends a long time puffing and breathing hard over it, but his operation is unsuccessful ...' This is recognizable childish behaviour, shrewdly seen by Chekhov, and we readers are charmed by its accuracy into overlooking its lack of proper feeling for the kittens. Subtly, we are compromised and go on being morally compromised when we encounter the expected ending – the consumption of the kittens by the dog, Nero. The laughter of the adults and the footman invites us to join in. We can't take the compassion of children too seriously since we have already witnessed the actions they themselves have visited on the kittens. The whole posture of the story encourages us to read it as comedy. Yet is isn't. We have to take into account the ironic moral peroration near the opening of the story: 'Domestic animals play a scarcely noticed but undoubtedly beneficial part in the education and life of children,' it begins. In the midst of an ostensibly idyllic catalogue, this is the first indication of irony: 'birds dying in captivity', an item which is mildly disconcerting and undeniably familiar. The mood of warm indulgence doesn't quite carry off the reference to treading on the cat's tail 'for fun' either. The peroration ends with the assertion that children learn more from animals – about patience, fidelity, forgiveness and sincerity – than they do from the 'long exhortations' of tutors and governesses. In context, those four qualities are tinged with irony because it is the animals who are required to possess them. By the denouement, Chekhov makes it clear that we have learnt from animals. We have learned the moral sense of animals. We are unperturbed by Nero's action – even amused – and our proper feelings remain immobilized. Basic decency is nowhere in evidence, only the 'snigger' of the footman. In four pages, Chekhov has sketched the moral universe of *Lord of the Flies*, without raising his voice above a deceptively humorous murmur: 'the children expect that all the people in the house will be aghast and fall upon the miscreant Nero. But they all sit calmly in their seats, and only express surprise at the appetite of the huge dog.' *In their seats* is unnecessarily specific – 'they all sit calmly' would have been enough – but taken with 'Nero' it ghosts the proceedings with other, bloodier entertainments, Roman circuses and their equally calm spectators.

In *The Unbearable Lightness of Being*, Milan Kundera touches on this idea of repetition, of eternal recurrence. The unbearable lightness of being is experienced when nothing has weight or importance because nothing is ever repeated: the myth of eternal recurrence is negated. On the other hand, 'if every second of our lives recurs an infinite number of times, we are nailed to eternity as Jesus Christ was nailed to the cross'. This is the unbearable heaviness of being. Chekhov's characters typically suffer from a mixture of these two myths. Their unhappiness arises out of the sense that their lives are infected with futility and insignificance – the eternal repetition of actions whose triviality is suddenly apparent. Life is not life but a shabby simulacrum: 'I have the feeling,' thinks the professor in 'A Dreary Story', 'as though I had once lived at home with a real wife and children and that now I am dining with visitors, in the house of a sham wife who is not the real one, and am looking at a Liza who is not the real Liza.' For these characters, very different in other respects, meaning has seeped out of their lives. Certain protagonists come to terms with their bled existences like, for example, the sterile, cruel egotist Orlov in 'An Anonymous Story', of whom the revolutionist narrator remarks: 'How early your soul has taken to its dressing gown.' The majority, however, rebel against their fate, without necessarily coming any closer to moral redemption. The cry, when it comes, is standard. The narrator's sister, Kleopatra, in 'My Life', explodes to her nurse: 'Haven't I wasted my youth? All the best years of my life to know nothing but keeping accounts, pouring out tea, counting the halfpence, entertaining visitors, and thinking there was nothing better in the world! Nurse, do understand, I have the cravings of a human being, and *I want to live* [my italics] and they have turned me into a housekeeper.' Forty pages on, she is unmarried, ill and pregnant: 'I want to act on the stage, I want to live . . .' Her acting comes to grief in the most brilliant account of stage-fright in the whole of literature. It is only a rehearsal: 'she came forward into the middle of the stage with an expression of horror on her face, looking ugly and angular, and for half a minute stood as though in a trance, perfectly motionless, and only her big ear-rings shook in her ears'.

In 'The Duel', Nadyezhda Fyodorovna shares her plea: 'all this, together with the sultry heat and the soft, transparent waves, excited her and whispered that she must live, live ...' In 'An Anonymous Story', we re-encounter the formulaic plaint, this time in the mouth of a consumptive narrator: ' "I want to live!" I said genuinely. "To live, to live!" ' And it reappears with undiminished sincerity in 'The Lady with the Dog', where Anna Sergeyevna confesses to her new lover, Gurov: 'I have been tormented by curiosity; I wanted something better. "There must be a different sort of life", I said to myself. I wanted to live! To live, to live! ...' Collated thus, these heady resolves, identical down to the repetition and aposiopesis, begin to lose a certain potency – and resemble a different illustration of the doctrine of eternal recurrence.

In fact, Chekhov is more repetitive than any great writer has the right to be. The democratic desire to live, live ... shared among so many characters can be explained as a thematic preoccupation, as can the several discussions of Tolstoyan philosophy which are repeated, more or less unchanged, from story to story to story. 'My Life' and 'An Artist's Story' both address the idea that manual labour should be shared: 'all, without exception, strong and weak, rich and poor, should take part equally in the struggle for existence'. In 'An Artist's Story', this is taken further: the narrator resists social improvement like schools and medical centres, preferring to tackle the 'central' issue of labour. The sharing out of labour would, he argues, free man for his 'highest vocation' – 'the perpetual search for truth and the meaning of life'. This Tolstoyan tosh, advocating communal road-mending as a way to escape from 'this continual, agonizing dread of death, and even from death itself', is thoroughly demolished in 'Ward No. 6' – where Dr Ragin's counsel of philosophic indifference to external circumstances is tested when he finds himself an occupant of Ward 6 for the mentally disturbed. His dressing gown smells of smoked fish; he experiences 'a strange, persistent feeling of irritation', eventually traced to a desire to smoke; beaten up, he survives barely a day: he dies of an apoplectic stroke, in a passage of extraordinarily brilliant writing which utterly transcends the somewhat mechanical debate at the centre of the story. Wittgenstein's irrefutable statement – that death is not an event in life – is somehow refuted by Chekhov: 'At first he had a violent shivering fit and a feeling of sickness; something revolting, as it seemed, penetrating through his whole body, even to his finger-tips, strained from his stomach to his head and flooded his eyes and ears. There was a greenness before his eyes. Andrey Yefimitch understood that his end had come, and remembered that Ivan Dmitritch, Mihail Averyanitch, and millions of people believed in immortality. And what if it really existed? But he did not want immortality, and he thought of it only for one instant. A herd of deer, extraordinarily beautiful and graceful, of which he had been reading the day before, ran by him; then a peasant woman stretched out her hand to him with a registered letter . . . Mihail Averyanitch said something, then it all vanished, and Andrey Yefimitch sank into oblivion for ever.' What an astonishing, lucid, convincing exposition of mental confusion, bringing us, imposing on us with laconic authority, the last illustrations of a brain able, for once, to be above its circumstances. In death, Dr Ragin's theory is ironically validated.

Elsewhere in Chekhov, a brilliant passage or a brilliant phrase is quite likely to be dimmed by its duplication in another corner of the canon. The dog, Nero, has 'a tail as hard as a stick' in 'An Incident' and so has Som in 'A Teacher of Literature': 'Som was a tall black dog with long legs and a tail as hard as a stick.' In the same story, Varya, the elder daughter, is contrary: 'every conversation, even about the weather, she invariably turned into an argument'. In this trait, she is not unlike Pyotr Petrovitch in 'An Artist's Story', 'who had retained from his student days the habit of turning every conversation into an argument'. Both are remarkably similar to Dr Blagovo in 'My Life' who has 'a habit of turning every conversation into an argument'. 'The Chorus Girl' is one of Chekhov's greatest stories: an enraged upper-class wife bursts in on her husband's chorus girl mistress, while the husband overhears everything in the next room. The physical difference is the first thing to make itself felt. Chekhov is as usual brilliantly laconic: 'Pasha felt that on this lady in black with the angry eyes and white slender fingers she produced the impression of something horrid and unseemly, and she felt ashamed of her chubby red cheeks, the pock-mark on her nose, and the fringe on her forehead, which never could be combed back.' What selection. It is as if Chekhov were holding to the prescription Konstantin formulates for Trigorin: 'Trigorin's worked out his methods, it's easy enough for him. He gives you the neck of a broken bottle glittering against a weir and the black-shadow of a mill-wheel – and there's your moonlit night all cut and dried.' Or perhaps he was following the injunction implicit in his story 'The Wolf': 'on the dam, which was covered with moonlight, there was not a trace of shadow; on the middle of it the neck of a broken bottle glittered like a star'. Either way, 'the pock-mark on her nose' is the (beautifully singular) source of the sentence's energy. Both women behave well in the story – the wife according to some consciously noble formula, the tart out of genuine sympathy, tinged with fear. The husband, of course, is more taken by the wife's performance: 'The door from the next room opened and Kolpakov walked in. He was pale and kept shaking his head nervously, as though he had swallowed something very bitter; tears were glistening in his eyes.' *As though he had swallowed something very bitter.* We all recognize the agonized expression of someone trying to hold back tears.

What a pity, then, that, in 'The Duel', Chekhov should recycle the phrase for Von Koren's more conventional, straightforward disgust when he hears that Kirilin and Nadyezhda Fyodorovna have been caught *in flagrante*: 'he walked away from Sheshkovsky, unwilling to hear more, and as though he had accidentally tasted something bitter, spat loudly again, and for the first time that morning looked with hatred at Laevsky'. In 'The Lady with the Dog', Gurov arrives at S— in search of Anna Sergeyevna. The provincial hotel is created with a single stroke. 'On the table was an inkstand, grey with dust and adorned with a figure on horseback, with its hat in its hand and its head broken off.' With this resource on call, why is it that Chekhov should redeploy 'a long grey fence adorned with nails' from its previous situation outside Ward 6? Neither is particularly distinguished. Nor is the phrase used to describe the English governess in 'A Daughter of Albion' and Gnekker in 'A Dreary Story': both have 'prominent eyes like a crab's'. Similarly, Zinaida in 'An Anonymous Story' shares a tic with Liza in 'A Dreary Story': the former 'screwed up her eyes and looked at me', the latter has a 'way of screwing up her eyes whenever there are men in the room'. Occasionally, the repetitions occur in the same story: in 'My Life', Moisey, the agent, is seen uneasily 'crumpling up his cap in his hands'; then an old servant, gripped by emotion, begins 'crumpling up her apron in her agitation'; lastly, Kleopatra, the sister, is shown 'crumpling up the manuscript' before she fails in the rehearsal. Then there is the character who, in several stories, insists on saying the obvious: in 'The Teacher of Literature' it is Ippolit Ippolititch, who dies, 'but even in his delirium' says 'nothing that was not perfectly well known to everyone': 'The Volga flows into the Caspian Sea ... Horses eat oats and hay ...' In 'An Anonymous Story', Zinaida is silenced by Orlov's complaint: 'don't talk of things that everybody knows'.

In the end, oddly enough, these repetitions matter less than they might in another author. It is easy enough to see why if we return to Moisey, the cap-crumpling agent from 'My Life'. This is the full description in which the gesture plays only a part: 'Moisey, a thin pock-marked fellow of twenty-five, with insolent little eyes, who was in the service of the general's widow, stood near him crumpling up his cap in his hands; *one of his cheeks was bigger than the other, as though he had lain too long on it.*' [My italics.] In *ABC of Reading*, Ezra Pound relates: 'It is said that Flaubert taught De Maupassant to write. When De Maupassant returned from a walk Flaubert would ask him to describe someone, say a concierge whom they would both pass in their next walk, and to describe the person so that Flaubert would recognize, say, the concierge and not mistake her for some other concierge and not the one De Maupassant had described.' Chekhov invariably writes as if this precept were before him at his desk. It is these touches, the swift brush strokes of genius, that neutralize the clichés, the artistic lapses and the argumentative longueurs which disfigure Chekhov's work. Is it likely, for instance, that Dr Ragin will receive Gromov's acute and hostile analysis of his own character with such equanimity? Surely a little ruffle would be in order? Isn't the progress of 'The Darling' just a touch too broadly comic and predictable as she moves from partner to partner, first acquiring then shedding her successive consort's opinions? Can we tolerate (in 'A Daughter of Albion') a silence like 'the stillness of the grave'?

'The Darling' is a good test case. The story begins with such sweet authority that the subsequent variants live in the verisimilitude of the first marriage and her life before it: 'she was always fond of someone, and could not exist without loving. In earlier days she had loved her papa, who now sat in a darkened room, breathing with difficulty.' It is completely convincing that darkened room and the difficult breathing – as is the nickname given her by the actors, 'Vanitchka and I'. As is the telegram announcing his sudden death: 'Ivan Petrovitch died suddenly yesterday. Awaiting immate instructions fufuneral Tuesday.' No amount of comically stretched plotting could impair these perfect details. In any case, 'The Darling' is a parable like 'An Incident'. Irina in *Three Sisters* speaks for a great many Chekhovian souls when she says: 'Oh, I've longed for love, dreamed about it so much day and night, but my heart is like a wonderful grand piano that can't be used because it's locked up and the key's lost.' Without love, life is without meaning. In 'The Darling' Chekhov shows us this truth comically. Olga Semyonovna has no opinions, no meaning, when there is no love in her life. Sex isn't the issue either, as Chekhov makes clear when the ten-year-old Sasha enters her life and they do his lessons together: ' "An island is a piece of land," she repeated, and this was the first opinion to which she gave utterance with positive conviction after so many years of silence and dearth of ideas.' She is no longer an island.

In 1970, Vladimir Nabokov replied to the contributors whose essays appeared in a special Nabokov number of *Triquarterly*. Of Simon Karlinsky's contribution he had this to say: 'He is right, I do love Chekhov dearly. I fail, however, to rationalize my feeling for him: I can easily do so in regard to a greater artist, Tolstoy, with the flash of this or that unforgettable passage ('... how sweetly she said: "and even very much" ' – Vronsky recalling Kitty's reply to some trivial question that we will never know), but when I imagine Chekhov with the same detachment all I can make out is a medley of dreadful prosaisms, ready-made epithets, repetitions, doctors, unconvincing vamps, and so forth; yet it is *his* works which I would take on a trip to another planet.' Actually, the prosaic is an intrinsic and essential part of Chekhov's art. There is something akin to Jane Austen in him, the Austen evoked by Virginia Woolf: 'humbly and gaily she collected the twigs and straws out of which the nest was to be made and placed them neatly together. The twigs and straw were a little dry and dusty in themselves. There was a big house and the little house; a tea party, a dinner party, and an occasional picnic; life was hedged in with valuable connections and adequate incomes; by muddy roads, wet feet, and a tendency on the part of ladies to get tired . . . Vice, adventure, passion were left outside. But of all this prosiness, of all this littleness, she evades nothing, and nothing is slurred over.' Of course, 'vice, adventure, passion' show themselves in 'The Duel' but the length of the story brings its own inevitability to the duel, the fornications, the fever and the fret: the sensational is bedded down in the flamboyantly unsensational. There is a picnic which wouldn't be out of place in *Emma*, except that Chekhov displays a certain relish for the sordid details: 'as is always the case at picnics, in the mass of dinner napkins, parcels, useless greasy papers fluttering in the wind, no one knew where was his glass or where his bread'. And earlier, when Von Koren is advocating the extermination of the Laevsky type, Dr Samoylenko interrupts him: '"With pepper, with pepper," he cried in a voice of despair, seeing that the deacon was eating stuffed aubergines without pepper.' For prosaic prose, Chekhov had perfect pitch. As with Jane Austen, the 'Big Bow-wow strain' (as Scott called it) was beyond him.

In *Speak, Memory*, Nabokov includes this bravura sentence as a paragraph on its own: 'the tennis court was a region of great lakes'. No one has caught the aftermath of a rain storm with the same stylistic panache. It is poetry. Chekhov's speciality, though, was touched on earlier when I quoted his comment to Suvorin after his brother's death: 'there's not a kopek's worth of poetry left in life'. Torpor, rather than exaltation, is his forte: 'on the right came the faint, reluctant note of the golden oriole'. *Reluctant.* When Nabokov, in *The Gift*, reports that 'a cuckoo began to call in a copse, listlessly', we note the adverb is perfect and Chekhov's copyright. In the best of these stories, there is a Godot provincialism: nothing happens, not twice, but several times: 'at Dubetchnya they were plastering the inside of the station, and building a wooden upper storey to the pumping shed. It was hot; there was a smell of lime, and workmen sauntered *listlessly* between the heaps of shavings and mortar rubble. The pointsman lay asleep near his sentry-box, and the sun was blazing full on his face. There was not a single tree. The telegraph wire hummed faintly and hawks were perching on it here and there.' [My italics.]

Some critics find the longer stories deficient in shapeliness. This is a totally misdirected criticism. In the short story, long or short, obvious form is precisely to be avoided. The danger is design and clamorous shape of the kind that threatens 'The Darling' with an excess of pattern. There are two solutions – length and a prodigal generosity with detail. In 'My Life', for example, Tcheprakov is as vivid as it is possible for a minor character to be: 'by way of bravado he used to strip and run about the country naked. He used to eat flies and say they were rather sour.' Generous detail, but still Chekhov doesn't make a meal of his meal. The same thing is true of the railway navvies: 'And more than once I had seen these tatterdemalions with a bloodstained countenance being led to the police station, while a samovar or some linen, *wet from the wash*, was carried behind by way of evidence.' [My italics again.] Only four words – with the weight of a world behind them.

Chekhov's skill is, as it were, to make that Russian month in the country a day-trip, to give his readers a concentrate, without ever creating the impression of parsimony or short measure. His endings are almost always open-ended. 'It began to spot with rain.' 'Two minutes later he was sitting on the sand and angling as before.' 'The sheep were pondering, too.' 'She remembered how three years ago a merchant had beaten her for no sort of reason, and she wailed more loudly than ever.' 'And it was clear to both of them that they still had a long, long way to go, and that the most complicated and difficult part of it was only just beginning.' Were one to attempt an encapsulation of Chekhov's genius, it would centre on this gift for distraction, for what appears in the corner of the eye. Two lovers kiss for the first time. Chekhov imagines them and accepts the suggestion from the corner of his mind: 'we were silent for some time, then I put my arms around her and kissed her, scratching my cheek till it bled with her hatpin as I did it'. Another couple, in a different story, kiss for the first time and Chekhov not only captures the kiss at the lips but also its complicated bodily consequences: 'she turned pale, moved her lips, then stepped back from Nikitin and found herself in the corner between the wall and the cupboard ... She threw back her head and he kissed her lips, and that it might last longer he put his fingers to her cheeks; and it somehow happened that he found himself in the corner between the cupboard and the wall, and she put her arms round his neck and pressed her head against his chin.' Exactly.

Craig Raine

SELECT BIBLIOGRAPHY

This is a select bibliography of works in English relating to Chekhov's life and works and is intended principally as a guide to further reading.

BIOGRAPHIES

The best straightforward biography, based mostly on Chekhov's letters, is R. HINGLEY's *A New Life of Chekhov*, Oxford University Press, 1976. It replaces by and large the earlier biographies by D. MAGARSHACK (1952) and E. J. SIMMONS (1970). Among specialized treatments of aspects of Chekhov's life, especially notable are V. LLEWELLYN SMITH's *Anton Chekhov and the Lady with the Dog*, Oxford University Press, 1973, an erudite examination of his relations with women, and H. PITCHER's *Chekhov's Leading Lady,* John Murray, 1979, about his wife, Olga Knipper. The best selection of his letters is *Letters of Anton Chekhov*, translated by Michael Heim and selected, introduced and with a commentary by SIMON KARLINSKY, Bodley Head, 1973, which comprises a scholarly and stimulating biography in its own right.

CRITICISM

Of the critical studies which relate particularly to the stories in this volume, pride of place must go to D. RAYFIELD, *Chekhov: the evolution of his art*, Elek Books, 1975, a well-written and very perceptive study. Also valuable are T. WINNER, *Chekhov and his Prose*, Henry Holt, New York, 1966 and K. D. KRAMER, *The Chameleon and the Dream*, Mouton, The Hague and Paris, 1970. Rich in insights, if fragmentary in its treatment of Chekhov's works, is S. LAFFITTE's *Chekhov, 1860–1904* (translated by Moura Budberg and Gordon Latta), Angus and Robertson, 1974. Scholarly if uninspired is B. HAHN's *Chekhov. A Study of the Major Stories and Plays*, Cambridge University Press, 1977.

Among specialized critical treatments noteworthy are H. PETER STOWELL's *Literary Impressionism, James and Chekhov*, University of Georgia Press, 1980, and CAROLINA DE MAEGD-SOEP's feminist, but erudite, *Chekhov and Women. Women in the Life and Work of Chekhov*, Slavica, Ohio, 1987.

A very early study is W. GERHARDI's *Anton Chekhov. A Critical Study*, Duffield, New York, 1923, still interesting for its attempt to come to grips with Chekhov's 'elusiveness of aim', and V. S. PRITCHETT's *Chekhov: A Spirit Set Free*, Hodder and Stoughton, 1988, a sensitive and beautifully written general treatment.

CHRONOLOGY

DATE	AUTHOR'S LIFE	LITERARY CONTEXT
1859		Goncharov: *Oblomov.* Ostrovsky: *The Storm.*
1860	Anton Pavlovich Chekhov born in Taganrog on the Sea of Azov in southern Russia (16 January), the third of seven children of a small shopkeeper, and grandson of a serf who had bought his freedom.	Turgenev: *On the Eve*; 'First Love'. Dostoevsky: *The House of the Dead* (to 1862). George Eliot: *The Mill on the Floss.*
1861		Herzen publishes *My Past and Thoughts* (to 1866). Dickens: *Great Expectations.*
1862		Turgenev: *Fathers and Children.* Hugo: *Les Misérables.* Flaubert: *Salammbô.*
1863		Tolstoy: *The Cossacks.* Chernyshevsky: *What is to be Done?* Nekrasov: *Red-Nosed Frost.*
1864		Dostoevsky: *Notes from Underground.* Fet: 'Tormented by life ...'.
1865		Leskov: 'Lady Macbeth of the Mtensk District'. Sleptsov: *Hard Times.* Dickens: *Our Mutual Friend.*
1866		Dostoevsky: *Crime and Punishment.* Daudet: *Lettres de mon moulin.*
1867	Enrolled at parish school attached to Greek Orthodox church. Unable to master modern Greek, he leaves at the end of the school year.	Turgenev: *Smoke.* Dostoevsky: *The Gambler.* Zola: *Thérèse Raquin.* Marx: *Das Kapital*, vol. 1.
1868	Joins preparatory class at the Taganrog *gimnazia*. Following the recent reforms of Dmitry Tolstoy, Minister of Education,	Lavrov: *Historical Letters.* Nekrasov: 'Who Can Be Happy and Free in Russia?'

HISTORICAL EVENTS

Alexander II (Tsar since 1855) following a reformist policy, in complete opposition to his predecessor, the reactionary Nicholas I. Port of Vladivostok founded to serve Russia's recent annexations (from China). Huge investment in railway building begins.

Emancipation of the serfs (February), the climax of the Tsar's programme of reform. While his achievement had great moral and symbolic significance, many peasants felt themselves cheated by the terms of the complex emancipation statute. Outbreak of American Civil War. Unification of Italy.
Bismarck Prime Minister of Prussia. 1860s and 70s: 'Nihilism' – rationalist philosophy sceptical of all forms of established authority – becomes widespread amongst young radical intelligentsia in Russia.
Polish rebellion. Poland incorporated into Russia. Itinerant movement formed by young artists, led by Ivan Kramskoi and later joined by Ivan Shishkin: drawing inspiration from the Russian countryside and peasant life, they are also concerned to take art to the people.
The first International. Establishment of the Zemstva, organs of self-government and a significant liberal influence in Tsarist Russia. Legal reforms do much towards removing the class bias from the administration of justice. Trial by jury instituted and a Russian bar established. Russian colonial expansion in Central Asia (to 1868).
Slavery formally abolished in USA.

Young nobleman Dmitry Karakozov tries to assassinate the Tsar. Radical journals *The Contemporary* and *The Russian Word* suppressed. Austro-Prussian war.

St Petersburg section of Moscow Slavonic Benevolent Committee founded (expansion of Pan-Slav movement). Rimsky-Korsakov's symphonic poem *Sadko.*

DATE	AUTHOR'S LIFE	LITERARY CONTEXT
1868 *cont*	Greek and Latin dominate the curriculum and study of 'subversive' subjects such as Russian literature is severely restricted.	
1869	Embarks on 8-year course which he completes in 10, being twice kept down. Obliged to work in his father's shop in the evenings and holidays.	Tolstoy: *War and Peace.* Goncharov: *The Precipice.* Flaubert: *L'Education sentimentale.* Gaboriau: *Monsieur Lecoq.* Verne: *Vingt mille lieues sous les mers.*
1870		Turgenev: 'King Lear of the Steppes'. Death of Herzen and Dickens.
1871	Death of his infant sister, Evgenia.	Dostoevesky: *The Possessed.* Ostrovsky: *The Forest.* Eliot: *Middlemarch* (to 1872).
1872		Turgenev: 'Spring Torrents'; *A Month in the Country* (lst perf.). Leskov: *Cathedral Folk.* Kushchevsky: *Nikolay Negorev, or The Successful Russian.* Nietzsche: *The Birth of Tragedy.*
1873	Goes to the theatre for the first time (Offenbach's *La Belle Hélène*) and is immediately hooked.	Ostrovsky: *The Snow Maiden.*
1874		
1875	His two elder brothers leave for Moscow, Aleksandr to the University, Nikolai to art college. Anton starts a class magazine, *The Hiccup.*	
1876	Facing bankruptcy, his father flees to Moscow, leaving Anton to negotiate with debtors and creditors (April). His mother and the two youngest children, Maria and Mikhail, follow in July.	Eliot: *Daniel Deronda.* Henry James: *Roderick Hudson.*
1877	When his younger brother Ivan joins the rest of the family, Anton is left alone in Taganrog to complete his education. Finances himself by coaching.	Tolstoy: *Anna Karenina.* Turgenev: *Virgin Soil.* Garshin: 'Four Days'. Zola: *L'Assommoir.* Flaubert: *Trois contes.*

CHRONOLOGY

HISTORICAL EVENTS

Chemist D. I. Mendeleyev wins international fame by his periodic table of chemical elements based on atomic weight.

Lenin born. Franco-Prussian war. End of Second Empire in France and establishment of Third Republic. Repin paints *The Volga Boatmen* (to 1873).

Paris Commune set up and suppressed. Fall of Paris ends war. German Empire established.

Three Emperors' League (Germany, Russia and Austria-Hungary) formed in Berlin. During the late 1860s and early 1870s, Narodnik (Populist) 'going to the people' campaign gathers momentum: young intellectuals incite peasantry to rebel against autocracy.

First performance of Rimsky-Korsakov's first opera, *The Maid of Pskov.*

Mussorgsky's *Pictures at an Exhibition*; first performance of *Boris Godunov.*

Bulgarian Atrocities (Bulgarians massacred by Turks). Founding of Land and Freedom, first Russian political party openly to advocate revolution. Death of anarchist Mikhail Bakunin. Official statute for Women's Higher Courses, whereby women able to study at universities of St Petersburg, Moscow, Kiev, Odesssa and Kazan. By 1881 there are 2000 female students. Queen Victoria proclaimed Empress of India.
Russia declares war on Turkey (conflict inspired by Pan-Slav movement).
Tchaikovsky: *Swan Lake.*

DATE	AUTHOR'S LIFE	LITERARY CONTEXT
1878	First attempts to write a play.	Saltykov-Shchedrin: *The Sanctuary of Mon Repos.* Garshin: 'An Incident'. James: 'Daisy Miller'.
1879	Matriculates. Leaves Taganrog for Moscow (August) where he joins his parents and younger siblings in lodgings. Enrols as medical student at Moscow University.	Dostoevsky: *The Brothers Karamazov* (to 1880). Saltykov-Shchedrin: *The Golovlev Family.*
1880	First stories published in *The Dragonfly* under a pseudonym.	Maupassant: 'Boule de suif'. Death of Flaubert and George Eliot.
1881	Possibly writing his first surviving play, *Platonov.* Contributing regularly to *The Spectator.* Affair with Natalia Golden (who later marries his brother Aleksandr).	Tolstoy: 'What Men Live By'. Turgenev: 'The Song of Triumphant Love'. Leskov: 'The Lefthanded Craftsman'. Flaubert: *Bouvard et Pécuchet.* Ibsen: *Ghosts.* Death of Dostoevsky.
1882	Writing regularly for *The Alarm Clock.* First contribution to a St Petersburg paper, *Splinters*, after meeting with the editor, Nikolay Leykin.	Kravchinsky: *Underground Russia* (first chronicle of the revolutionary movement). Uspensky: *The Power of the Soil.*
1883	Spends summer at his brother Ivan's house at Voskresensk, aprovincial town 40 miles from Moscow. Writes 'The Daughter of Albion', his first piece for *Splinters* to win renown. Friendship with Kiseliov family, neighbouring landowners. Beginning of long relationship with Olga Kundasova.	Turgenev: 'Clara Milich'. Garshin: 'The Red Flower'. Fet: *Evening Lights.* Ostrovsky: *The Handsome Man.* Maupassant: *Une Vie*; *Clair de Lune.*
1884	Graduates. Summer at Voskresensk, helping at the hospital. Returns to Moscow to practise medicine. First symptoms of TB. Publishes collection of his best stories, *Tales of Melpomene. A Shooting*	*Tolstoy: Confession.* Leskov: 'The Toupée Artist'. Ostrovsky: *Guilty without Guilt.* Ibsen: *The Wild Duck.* Strindberg: *Getting Married* (to 1885). Maupassant: *Miss Harriet.*

CHRONOLOGY

HISTORICAL EVENTS

Congress of Berlin ends Russo-Turkish war; other European powers compel Russia to give up many of her territorial gains; partition of Bulgaria between Russia and Turkey. Mass trial of Populist agitators in Russia ('The Trial of the 193'). Shishkin, pioneer of the *plein-air* study in the 1870s, paints *Rye*, classic evocation of Russian countryside.
Birth of Stalin. The People's Will, terrorist offshoot of Land and Freedom, founded. Assassination of Prince Kropotkin, governor of Kharkov. Tchaikovsky: *Eugene Onegin*. Death of historian S. M. Solovyov, whose history of Russia had been appearing one volume per year since 1851.

Oil drilling begins in Azerbaidzhan; big programme of railway building commences. Borodin: *In Central Asia*. During 1870s and 1880s the Abramtsevo Colony, drawn together by railway tycoon Mamontov, includes Repin, Serov, Vrubel and Chekhov's friend Levitan. Nationalist in outlook, they draw inspiration from Russian folk art and the Russo-Byzantine tradition.
Assassination of Alexander II by Ignatius Grinevitsky, a member of the People's Will, following which the terrorist movement is crushed by the authorities. Revolutionary opposition goes underground until 1900. 'Epoch of small deeds': intelligentsia work for reform through existing institutions. The new Tsar, Alexander III, is much influenced by his former tutor, the extreme conservative Pobedonostsev, who becomes Chief Procurator of the Holy Synod. Resignation of Loris-Melikov, architect of the reforms of Alexander II's reign. Jewish pogroms.
Censorship laws tightened. Student riots in Kazan and St Petersburg. Reactionary regime of Alexander III characterized by stagnation in agriculture, retrogression in education, russification of non-Russian section of the population and narrow bureacratic paternalism.

First Russian Marxist revolutionary organization, the Liberation of Labour, founded in Geneva by Georgi Plekhanov. Increased persecution of religious minorities.

New education minister Delyanov increases powers of inspectors; university appointments made directly by the ministry rather than academic councils; fees increased. *Fatherland Notes*, edited by Saltykov-Shchedrin, suppressed. During 1880s organizations such as the Moscow Law Society and Committee for the Advancement of Literacy become centres for the discussion of political and social ideas amongst the intelligentsia.

DATE	AUTHOR'S LIFE	LITERARY CONTEXT
1884 *cont*	*Party* serialized in *Daily News* (to 1885). First commission for Khudekov's prestigious *Petersburg Gazette.*	
1885	Produces some 100 pieces this year. First of several summers spent in a dacha on the Kiseliov's estate at Babkino (source of *The Cherry Orchard*). Stories written there include 'The Burbot' and 'The Huntsman', his first big success in the *Petersburg Gazette.* Visits St Petersburg for the first time (December) as a guest of Leykin.	Garshin: 'Nadezhda Nikolaevna'. Leskov: 'The Bogey-Man'. Zola: *Germinal.* Maupassant: *Bel-Ami.*
1886	Short, secret engagement to Dunia Efros. Begins working for Aleksey Suvorin's *New Times*, which becomes his principal outlet; writes under his own name for the first time. Receives letter of praise and encouragement from novelist Dmitry Grigorovich. Publishes the collection *Motley Stories.* Two visits to St Petersburg (April and December) where his stories are winning him considerable renown. Individual tales this year include 'Art', 'Easter Eve', 'Difficult People' and 'On the Road'.	Tolstoy: *The Power of Darkness*; *The Death of Ivan Illych.* James: *The Bostonians*; *The Princess Casamassima.* Stevenson: *Dr Jekyll and Mr Hyde.*
1887	Two visits to St Petersburg (March and November). Deepening friendship with Suvorin family. Vacation in Taganrog; trip to the Don Steppe (April). Writes 'Happiness' (summer). Publishes collection *In the Twilight* (September). First play, *Ivanov*, performed in Moscow (November). 'The Kiss' appears in *New Times* (December).	Saltykov-Shchedrin: *Old Days in Poshekhone.* Sluchevsky: *Thirty-three Stories.* Garshin: 'The Signal'. Leskov: 'The Sentry'. Fofanov: *Poems.* Strindberg: *The Father*; *The Dwellers of Hemsö.* Maupassant: *Mont-Oriol*; *Le Horla.*

CHRONOLOGY

HISTORICAL EVENTS

Students hold a demonstration to commemorate the 50th anniversary of the birth of Dobrolyubov. Several of them, disgusted by the brutal way in which the demonstration is suppressed, resolve to assassinate the Tsar; the plot is discovered and among those executed is Lenin's brother, Alexander Ulyanov, whose death he swears to avenge.

During the late 1880s Russia begins her industrial revolution.

DATE	AUTHOR'S LIFE	LITERARY CONTEXT
1888	Writes 'The Steppe' (January). The Chekhovs rent a summer dacha at Sumy in the Ukraine; friendship with Lintvariov family. Visits Suvorin in the Crimea; goes to Baku with Suvorin's son. Makes first of several abortive attempts to buy a farm in the Ukraine. Awarded half the Russian Academy's 1888 prize for literature. Stays with Suvorin in St Petersburg (December); meets Tchaikovsky.	Suicide of Vsevolod Garshin. Strindberg: *Miss Julie.* Maupassant: *Pierre et Jean.* James: 'The Aspern Papers'. Hardy: *Wessex Tales.* Kipling: *Plain Tales from the Hills.*
1889	*Ivanov* a success in St Petersburg (January). Death of his brother Nikolai, a talented artist, from tuberculosis (June). Spends the summer in Sumy. Short visit to Odessa where the Moscow Maly Theatre company are on tour; writes 'A Dreary Story' while in the Crimea. *The Wood Demons* produced in Moscow but badly received (November).	Tolstoy: 'The Kreutzer Sonata'. Kravchinksy: *The Career of a Nihilist.* Ertel: *The Gardenins.* Hauptmann: *Before Sunrise.* Maeterlinck: *La Princesse Maleine.*
1890	In April sets off for Sakhalin, a penal colony off the Pacific coast of Siberia, travelling by road and river. Returns via Hong Kong, Singapore and Ceylon, arriving in Moscow in December. Writes 'Gusev'.	Tolstoy: *The Fruits of Enlightenment.* Polonsky: *Evening Bell.* Ibsen: *Hedda Gabler.* Maeterlinck: *Les Aveugles.* Wilde: *The Picture of Dorian Gray.*
1891	To Vienna, Venice, Florence, Rome, Naples, Nice, Monte Carlo and Paris with Suvorin (March–May). Summer spent at Bogimovo, joined by friends including Lika Mizinova (later to provide the inspiration for the character of Nina in *The Seagull*) and the artist Levitan. Writes 'The Duel'. Engaged in fundraising activities for victims of the famine.	Death of Goncharov. Leskov: 'Night Owls'. Ertel: *Change.* Conan Doyle: *The Adventures of Sherlock Holmes.*

CHRONOLOGY

HISTORICAL EVENTS

Rimsky-Korsakov: *Scheherazade.*

Land Captains introduced, powerful administrator magnates who increase control of the gentry over the peasants, undermining previous judicial and local government reforms. Shishkin: *Morning in a Pine Forest.*

First performance of Tchaikovsky's opera *The Queen of Spades* and first (posthumous) performance of Borodin's *Prince Igor.* Peasant representation on Zemstva reduced. Bismarck dismissed. During the 1890s growth rate for industrial output averages *c.* 8% per annum. Important development of coal mines in southern European Russia. Industrial expansion sustained by growth of banking and joint stock companies, which begin to attract foreign, later native, investment.

Harvest failure in central Russia causes famine and starvation: up to a million peasants die by the end of the winter. Work commences on Trans-Siberian Railway. 20,000 Jews brutally evicted from Moscow. Rigorously enforced residence restrictions, quotas limiting entry of Jews into high schools and universities, and other anti-Jewish measures drive over a million Russian Jews to emigrate, mainly to North America.

DATE	AUTHOR'S LIFE	LITERARY CONTEXT
1892	Purchases country house and estate at Melikhovo, 50 miles south of Moscow, where he moves with his parents, Maria and Mikhail. During cholera epidemic helps man the local clinic; acts as unpaid 'cholera superintendant' for 25 villages. Writes 'The Grasshopper'. 'Ward No. 6' appears in *Russian Thought*.	Gorky: 'Makar Chudra'. Fofanov: *Shadows and Secrets*. Hauptmann: *The Weavers*. Maeterlinck: *Pelléas et Mélisande*. Ibsen: *The Master Builder*.
1893	Serial publication of *The Island of Sakhalin* (book version published 1895).	Critic Dmitri Merezkhovsky cites Chekhov, Garshin, Fofanov and Minsky as heralds of new era in Russian literature. Zola: *Le Docteur Pascal*.
1894	Writes 'The Student' (spring). Boat trip down the Volga (August). Travels to Europe with Suvorin (autumn).	Bryusov brings out three collections of *The Russian Symbolists* (to 1895). Balmont: *Under Northern Skies*. Rostand: *Les Romanesques*.
1895	Publishes 'Three Years'. Visits Tolstoy at Yasnaya Polyana (August). Works on *The Seagull*. Writes 'The House with the Mezzanine'.	Tolstoy: 'Master and Man'. Gorky: 'The Song of the Falcon'; *Chelkash*. Bryusov: *Chefs d'Oeuvres*. Balmont: *Beyond All Limits*. Fontane: *Effie Briest*. Wilde: *The Importance of Being Earnest*. Rostand: *La Princesse lointaine*.
1896	Writes 'My Life'. Builds school at Melikhovo. *The Seagull* staged in St Petersburg (October). The first night is a disaster, and Chekhov flees to Melikhovo.	Sologub: First collection of Symbolist poetry. Merezhkovsky: *Christ and Antichrist* (to 1905).
1897	Publishes 'Peasants' (February). Collapse in health; TB diagnosed (March). Convalesces in Biarritz and Nice. Sides with Zola in the Dreyfus affair; ceases to write for *New Times* which takes an anti-Semitic line.	Gorky: 'Creatures that Once were Men'. Bunin: *To the Edge of the World*. Bryusov: *Me eum esse*. Kuprin: *Miniatures*. Wells: *The Invisible Man*. Rostand: *Cyrano de Bergerac*.

CHRONOLOGY

HISTORICAL EVENTS

Tchaikovsky: *The Nutcracker.* Property qualification for franchise raised, reducing number of voters in St Petersburg from 21,176 to 7,152.

Armenian massacres begin. As part of the russification of the Balkans the German University of Dorpat is reopened as the University of Yuryev, with a majority of Russian students. Death of Tchaikovsky.

Death of Alexander II; accession of Nicholas II. Growth in popularity of Marxist ideas amongst university students encouraged by appearance of Struve's *Critical Notes* and Beltov's *Monistic View.*

A. S. Popov, pioneer of wireless telegraphy, gives demonstration and publishes article on his discoveries, coinciding with Marconi's independent discoveries in this field. Establishment of Marxist newspaper *Samarskii Vestnik.* In May, 2000 people crushed to death on Klondynka field when a stand collapses during the coronation ceremony.

Tsar Nicholas II visits President Faure of France: Russo-French alliance. Lenin deported for three years to Siberia. Only systematic census carried out in Imperial Russia reports a population of 128,000,000, an increase of three-and-a-half times over the century. The industrial labour force of three million (3%) is small compared with the West but shows a fifteen-fold increase over the century. 13% of the population now urban as opposed to only 4% a century earlier.

DATE	AUTHOR'S LIFE	LITERARY CONTEXT
1898	Returns from Europe (May). Stories include 'Ionych', 'Gooseberries', 'The Man in the Case' and 'About Love'. Death of his father (October). Buys a plot of land for a new house in Yalta, where he is spending the winter for his health. First performance in Moscow of *The Seagull* by the newly founded Moscow Arts Theatre run by Stanislavsky and Nemirovich-Danchenko: a triumph (December). Meets the actress Olga Knipper.	Tolstoy: *What is Art?* Balmont: *Silence.* Zola: *J'Accuse.* Shaw: *Mrs Warren's Profession.* James: 'The Turn of the Screw', 'In the Cage'. Wells: *The War of the Worlds.*
1899	For 75,000 roubles makes over his copyrights to Adolf Marx, who undertakes to republish his Complete Works (1899–1902). Friendship with young writers Gorky and Bunin. Falls in love with Olga Knipper. She visits him at Melikhovo and later at Yalta. Chekhov sells estate at Melikhovo. *Uncle Vanya* (reworking of *The Wood Demons*) opens in Moscow (October). Writes 'The Lady with the Dog' (autumn).	Tolstoy: *Resurrection.* Gorky: *Foma Gordeev*; *Twenty-six Men and a Girl.* Kropotkin: *Memoirs of a Revolutionist.*
1900	'In the Ravine' published in Gorky's Marxist paper, Life. Chekhov, his mother and sister installed in new house at Yalta. Elected to the Writers' Section of the Academy. Travels to Caucasus with Gorky. Joins Olga on Moscow Arts Theatre tour at Sevastapol. *Three Sisters* completed in October. Attends rehearsals in Moscow.	Freud: *The Interpretation of Dreams.* Solovyov: *Three Conversations on War, Progress, and the End of Human History.* Balmont: *Buildings on Fire.* Bryusov: *Tertia vigilia.* Conrad: *Lord Jim.*
1901	Spends January in Nice. Successful first night of *Three Sisters* (31 January). Marries Olga Knipper in Moscow (25 May). Honeymoon at sanatorium at Aksionovo. Olga returns to	Blok: 'Verses on the Beautiful Lady' (to 1902). Mann: *Buddenbrooks.* Kipling: *Kim.*

HISTORICAL EVENTS

Russian Social Democratic Labour Party founded. Between 1898 and 1901 Caucasian oil production is higher than the rest of the world together. Finns begin to lose their rights as a separate nation within the Empire. Sergey Diaghilev and others found the *World of Art* society, prominent members of which are Benois and Bakst; its most notable production is Diaghilev's Ballet Russe. The magazine, to which 'decadent' writers such as Balmont frequently contribute, opposes the 'provincial naturalism' of the Itinerant school, and advocate a philosophy of art for art's sake.

Student riots. All universities in Russia temporarily closed. Moscow Law Society also closed. Reactionary Sipyagin becomes Minister of the Interior. During 1890s the so-called 'Third Element', consisting of doctors, teachers, statisticians, engineers and other professionals employed by the Zemstva, becomes a recognized focus of Liberal opposition to the Tsarist regime. Russian industry enters a period of depression.

Lenin allowed to leave Russia. Founds paper *Iskra* in Germany. Russia ends 19th century with a total of 17,000 students, spread over nine universities: one hundred years before, the Empire had only one university – Moscow. Nevertheless, the proportion of illiterates in the Empire was recorded at this time as 75% of persons aged between 9 and 49.

Murder of Minister of Education Bogolepov by a student marks beginning of wave of political assassinations. For the authorities the principal menace is the Socialist Revolutionary Party, who look for support from the peasantry, rather than the Social Democrats, who hope to rouse the urban proletariat. First performance of Rachmaninov's piano concerto no. 2 with the composer as soloist. Death of Queen Victoria.

DATE	AUTHOR'S LIFE	LITERARY CONTEXT
1901 *cont*	the theatre for the winter season but Chekhov, unable to stand the climate, remains in Yalta. Health deteriorates. Writes 'The Bishop'.	
1902	Olga visits Yalta (February). Back in St Petersburg she miscarries and has to undergo an operation; continues to suffer from peritonitis. Chekhov travels to Perm and the Urals (June). Stays, with Olga, at Stanislavky's country house at Liubimovka (July). Resigns from the Academy when Gorky's election is revoked (September). Visits Olga in Moscow (October–November) and winters in Yalta.	Gorky: *The Lower Depths.* Bely: *Second Symphony.* Andreev: 'The Abyss', 'In the Fog'. Merezhkovsky: *Tolstoy and Dostoevsky.* James: *The Wings of the Dove.* Conrad: *Heart of Darkness.* Gide: *L'Immoraliste.*
1903	Publishes 'The Bride'. Writing *The Cherry Orchard* (March–October). Attends rehearsals in Moscow (December–January).	Balmont: *Let Us Be Like the Sun.* Bryusov: *Urbi et Orbis.* Shaw: *Man and Superman.* Butler: *The Way of All Flesh.* Mann: *Tonio Kröger.*
1904	First night of *The Cherry Orchard* on 17 January, Chekhov's name day. Public tributes. Goes to Yalta (February) where his health continues to deteriorate. Returns to Moscow (May); leaves with Olga for Black Forest spa of Badenweiler (3 June) where he dies on 2 July. Buried at the Novodevichy Cemetry in Moscow.	Tolstoy completes 'Hadji Murad'. Blok: *The City* (to 1908). Bely: *Gold in Azure.* Annensky: *Quiet Songs.* Zinaida Hippius: *Poems.* Shaw: *John Bull's Other Island.* Conrad: *Nostromo.* James: *The Golden Bowl.*
1905		

HISTORICAL EVENTS

Lenin's *What is to be Done?* provides blueprint for future Bolshevik party. Sipyagin assassinated by Socialist Revolutionaries.

Conflict between Bolsheviks and Mensheviks at second Congress of Russian Social Democratic Labour Party. Assassination of King Alexander and Queen Draga of Serbia.

Russo-Japanese war (to 1905), both unpopular and unsuccessful from the point of view of the Russians. Assassination of V. K. Pleve, Minister of the Interior, and notorious oppressor of minority peoples within the Empire.

First Russian Revolution.

A DAUGHTER OF ALBION

A DAUGHTER OF ALBION

A FINE carriage with rubber tyres, a fat coachman, and velvet on the seats, rolled up to the house of a landowner called Gryabov. Fyodor Andreitch Otsov, the district Marshal of Nobility, jumped out of the carriage. A drowsy footman met him in the hall.

'Are the family at home?' asked the Marshal.

'No, sir. The mistress and the children are gone out paying visits, while the master and mademoiselle are catching fish. Fishing all the morning, sir.'

Otsov stood a little, thought a little, and then went to the river to look for Gryabov. Going down to the river he found him a mile and a half from the house. Looking down from the steep bank and catching sight of Gryabov, Otsov gushed with laughter.... Gryabov, a large stout man, with a very big head, was sitting on the sand, angling, with his legs tucked under him like a Turk. His hat was on the back of his head and his cravat had slipped on one side. Beside him stood a tall thin Englishwoman, with prominent eyes like a crab's, and a big bird-like nose more like a hook than a nose. She was dressed in a white muslin gown through which her scraggy yellow shoulders were very distinctly apparent. On her gold belt hung a little gold watch. She too was angling. The stillness of the grave reigned about them both. Both were motionless as the river upon which their floats were swimming.

'A desperate passion, but deadly dull!' laughed Otsov, 'Good-day, Ivan Kuzmitch.'

'Ah . . . is that you?' asked Gryabov, not taking his eyes off the water. 'Have you come?'

'As you see. . . . And you are still taken up with your crazy nonsense! Not given it up yet?'

'The devil's in it. . . . I begin in the morning and fish all day. . . . The fishing is not up to much to-day. I've caught nothing and this dummy hasn't either. We sit on and on and not a devil of a fish! I could scream!'

'Well, chuck it up then. Let's go and have some vodka!'

'Wait a little, maybe we shall catch something. Towards evening the fish bite better . . . . I've been sitting here, my boy, ever since the morning! I can't tell you how fearfully boring it is. It was the devil drove me to take to this fishing! I know that it is rotten idiocy for me to sit here. I sit here like some scoundrel, like a convict, and I stare at the water like a fool. I ought to go to the hay-making, but here I sit catching fish. Yesterday His Holiness held a service at Haponyevo, but I didn't go. I spent the day here with this . . . with this she-devil.'

'But . . . have you taken leave of your senses?' asked Otsov, glancing in embarrassment at the Englishwoman. 'Using such language before a lady and she . . . .'

'Oh, confound her, it doesn't matter, she doesn't understand a syllable of Russian; whether you praise her or blame her, it is all the same to her! Just look at her nose! Her nose alone is enough to make one faint. We sit here for whole days together and not a single word! She stands like a stuffed image and rolls the whites of her eyes at the water.'

The Englishwoman gave a yawn, put a new worm on, and dropped the hook into the water.

'I wonder at her not a little,' Gryabov went on; 'the great stupid has been living in Russia for ten years and not a word of Russian!... Any little aristocrat among us goes to them and learns to babble away in their lingo, while they ... there's no making them out. Just look at her nose, do look at her nose!'

'Come, drop it ... it's uncomfortable. Why attack a woman?'

'She's not a woman, but a maiden lady.... I bet she's dreaming of suitors. The ugly doll. And she smells of something decaying.... I've got a loathing for her, my boy! I can't look at her with indifference. When she turns her ugly eyes on me it sends a twinge all through me as though I had knocked my elbow on the parapet. She likes fishing too. Watch her: she fishes as though it were a holy rite! She looks upon everything with disdain.... She stands there, the wretch, and is conscious that she is a human being, and that therefore she is the monarch of nature. And do you know what her name is? Wilka Charlesovna Fyce! Tfoo! There is no getting it out!'

The Englishwoman, hearing her name, deliberately turned her nose in Gryabov's direction and scanned him with a disdainful glance; she raised her eyes from Gryabov to Otsov and steeped him in disdain. And all this in silence, with dignity and deliberation.

'Did you see?' said Gryabov chuckling. 'As though to say "take that". Ah, you monster! It's only for the children's sake that I keep that triton. If it weren't for the children, I wouldn't let her come within ten miles of my estate.... She has got a nose like a hawk's... and her figure! That doll makes me think of a long nail, so I could take her, and knock her into the ground, you know. Stay, I believe I have got a bite....'

Gryabov jumped up and raised his rod. The line drew taut.... Gryabov tugged again, but could not pull out the hook.

'It has caught,' he said, frowning, 'on a stone I expect... damnation take it....'

There was a look of distress on Gryabov's face. Sighing, moving uneasily, and muttering oaths, he began tugging at the line.

'What a pity; I shall have to go into the water.'

'Oh, chuck it!'

'I can't.... There's always good fishing in the evening.... What a nuisance. Lord, forgive us, I shall have to wade into the water; I must! And if only you knew, I have no inclination to undress. I shall have to get rid of the Englishwoman.... It's awkward to undress before her. After all, she is a lady, you know!'

Gryabov flung off his hat and his cravat.

'Meess... er, er...' he said, addressing the Englishwoman, 'Meess Fyce, je voo pree...? Well, what am I to say to her? How am I to tell you so that you can understand? I say... over there! Go away over there! Do you hear?'

Miss Fyce enveloped Gryabov in disdain and uttered a nasal sound.

'What? Don't you understand? Go away from here! I tell you, I must undress, you devil's doll! Go over there! Over there!'

Gryabov pulled the lady by her sleeve, pointed her towards the bushes, and made as though he would sit down, as much as to say: Go behind the bushes and hide yourself there.... The Englishwoman, moving her eyebrows vigorously, uttered rapidly a long sentence in English. The gentlemen gushed with laughter.

'It's the first time in my life I've heard her voice.... There's no denying, it is a voice! She does not understand! Well, what am I to do with her?'

'Chuck it, let's go and have a drink of vodka!'

'I can't. Now's the time to fish, the evening....It's evening....Come, what would you have me do? It is a nuisance! I shall have to undress before her....'

Gryabov flung off his coat and his waistcoat and sat on the sand to take off his boots.

'I say, Ivan Kuzmitch,' said the Marshal, chuckling behind his hand. 'It's really outrageous, an insult.'

'Nobody asks her not to understand! It's a lesson for these foreigners!'

Gryabov took off his boots and his trousers, flung off his undergarments and remained in the costume of Adam. Otsov held his sides, he turned crimson both from laughter and embarrassment. The Englishwoman twitched her brows and blinked....A haughty, disdainful smile passed over her yellow face.

'I must cool off,' said Gryabov, slapping himself on the ribs. 'Tell me, if you please, Fyodor Andreitch, why I have a rash on my chest every summer.'

'Oh, do get into the water quickly or cover yourself with something! You beast!'

'And if only she were confused, the nasty thing!' said Gryabov, crossing himself as he waded into the water. 'Brrrr... the water's cold.... Look how she moves her eyebrows! She doesn't go away... she is far above the crowd! He, he, he.... And she doesn't reckon us as human beings!'

Wading knee deep in the water and drawing his huge figure up to its full height, he gave a wink and said:

'This isn't England, you see!'

Miss Fyce coolly put on another worm, gave a yawn, and dropped the hook in. Otsov turned away, Gryabov released his hook, ducked into the water and, spluttering, waded out. Two minutes later he was sitting on the sand and angling as before.

AN INCIDENT

AN INCIDENT

MORNING. Brilliant sunshine is piercing through the frozen lacework on the window-panes into the nursery. Vanya, a boy of six, with a cropped head and a nose like a button, and his sister Nina, a short, chubby, curly-headed girl of four, wake up and look crossly at each other through the bars of their cots.

'Oo-oo-oo! naughty children!' grumbles their nurse. 'Good people have had their breakfast already, while you can't get your eyes open.'

The sunbeams frolic over the rugs, the walls, and nurse's skirts, and seem inviting the children to join in their play, but they take no notice. They have woken up in a bad humour. Nina pouts, makes a grimace, and begins to whine:

'Brea-eakfast, nurse, breakfast!'

Vanya knits his brows and ponders what to pitch upon to howl over. He has already begun screwing up his eyes and opening his mouth, but at that instant the voice of mamma reaches them from the drawing-room, saying: 'Don't forget to give the cat her milk, she has a family now!'

The children's puckered countenances grow smooth again as they look at each other in astonishment. Then both at once begin shouting, jump out of their cots, and filling the air with piercing shrieks, run barefoot, in their nightgowns, to the kitchen.

'The cat has puppies!' they cry. 'The cat has got puppies!'

Under the bench in the kitchen there stands a small box, the one in which Stepan brings coal when he lights the fire. The cat is peeping out of the box. There is an expression of extreme exhaustion on her grey face; her green eyes, with their narrow black pupils, have a languid, sentimental look.... From her face it is clear that the only thing lacking to complete her happiness is the presence in the box of 'him', the father of her children, to whom she had abandoned herself so recklessly! She wants to mew, and opens her mouth wide, but nothing but a hiss comes from her throat; the squealing of the kittens is audible.

The children squat on their heels before the box, and, motionless, holding their breath, gaze at the cat .... They are surprised, impressed, and do not hear nurse grumbling as she pursues them. The most genuine delight shines in the eyes of both.

Domestic animals play a scarcely noticed but undoubtedly beneficial part in the education and life of children. Which of us does not remember powerful but magnanimous dogs, lazy lapdogs, birds dying in captivity, dull-witted but haughty turkeys, mild old tabby cats, who forgave us when we trod on their tails for fun and caused them agonizing pain? I even fancy, sometimes, that the patience, the fidelity, the readiness to forgive, and the sincerity which are characteristic of our domestic animals have a far stronger and more definite effect on the mind of a child than the long exhortations of some dry, pale Karl Karlovitch, or the misty expositions of a governess, trying to prove to children that water is made up of hydrogen and oxygen.

'What little things!' says Nina, opening her eyes wide and going off into a joyous laugh. 'They are like mice!'

'One, two, three,' Vanya counts. 'Three kittens. So there is one for you, one for me, and one for somebody else, too.'

'Murrm . . . murrm . . .' purrs the mother, flattered by their attention. 'Murrm.'

After gazing at the kittens, the children take them from under the cat, and begin squeezing them in their hands, then, not satisfied with this, they put them in the skirts of their nightgowns, and run into the other rooms.

'Mamma, the cat has got pups!' they shout.

Mamma is sitting in the drawing-room with some unknown gentleman. Seeing the children unwashed, undressed, with their nightgowns held up high, she is embarrassed, and looks at them severely.

'Let your nightgowns down, disgraceful children,' she says. 'Go out of the room, or I will punish you.'

But the children do not notice either mamma's threats or the presence of a stranger. They put the kittens down on the carpet, and go off into deafening squeals. The mother walks round them, mewing imploringly. When, a little afterwards, the children are dragged off to the nursery, dressed, made to say their prayers, and given their breakfast, they are full of a passionate desire to get away from these prosaic duties as quickly as possible, and to run to the kitchen again.

Their habitual pursuits and games are thrown completely into the background.

The kittens throw everything into the shade by making their appearance in the world, and supply the great sensation of the day. If Nina or Vanya had been offered forty pounds of sweets or ten thousand kopecks for each kitten, they would have rejected such a barter without the slightest hesitation. In spite of the heated protests of the nurse and the cook, the children persist in sitting by the cat's box in the kitchen, busy with the kittens till dinner-time. Their faces are earnest and concentrated and express anxiety. They are worried not so much by the present as by the future of the kittens. They decide that one kitten shall remain at home with the old cat to be a comfort to her mother, while the second shall go to their summer villa, and the third shall live in the cellar, where there are ever so many rats.

'But why don't they look at us?' Nina wondered. 'Their eyes are blind like the beggars'.'

Vanya, too, is perturbed by this question. He tries to open one kitten's eyes, and spends a long time puffing and breathing hard over it, but his operation is unsuccessful. They are a good deal troubled, too, by the circumstance that the kittens obstinately refuse the milk and the meat that is offered to them. Everything that is put before their little noses is eaten by their grey mamma.

'Let's build the kittens little houses,' Vanya suggests. 'They shall live in different houses, and the cat shall come and pay them visits. . .'

Carboard hat-boxes are put in the different corners of the kitchen and the kittens are installed in them. But this division turns out to be premature: the cat, still wearing an imploring and sentimental expression on her face, goes the round of all the hat-boxes, and carries off her children to their original position.

'The cat's their mother,' observed Vanya, 'but who is their father?'

'Yes, who is their father?' repeats Nina.

'They must have a father.'

Vanya and Nina are a long time deciding who is to be the kittens' father, and, in the end, their choice falls on a big dark-red horse without a tail, which is lying in the store-cupboard under the stairs, together with other relics of toys that have outlived their day. They drag him up out of the store-cupboard and stand him by the box.

'Mind now!' they admonish him, 'stand here and see they behave themselves properly.'

All this is said and done in the gravest way, with an expression of anxiety on their faces. Vanya and Nina refuse to recognize the existence of any world but the box of kittens. Their joy knows no bounds. But they have to pass through bitter, agonizing moments, too.

Just before dinner, Vanya is sitting in his father's study, gazing dreamily at the table. A kitten is moving about by the lamp, on stamped note paper. Vanya is watching its movements, and thrusting first a pencil, then a match into its little mouth.... All at once, as though he has sprung out of the floor, his father is beside the table.

'What's this?' Vanya hears, in an angry voice.

'It's . . . it's the kitty, papa. . . .'

'I'll give it you; look what you have done, you naughty boy! You've dirtied all my paper!'

To Vanya's great surprise his papa does not share his partiality for the kittens, and, instead of being moved to enthusiasm and delight, he pulls Vanya's ear and shouts:

'Stepan, take away this horrid thing.'

At dinner, too, there is a scene. . . . During the second course there is suddenly the sound of a shrill mew. They begin to investigate its origin, and discover a kitten under Nina's pinafore.

'Nina, leave the table!' cries her father angrily. 'Throw the kittens in the cesspool! I won't have the nasty things in the house! . . .'

Vanya and Nina are horrified. Death in the cesspool, apart from its cruelty, threatens to rob the cat and the wooden horse of their children, to lay waste the cat's box, to destroy their plans for the future, that fair future in which one cat will be a comfort to its old mother, another will live in the country, while the third will catch rats in the cellar. The children begin to cry and entreat that the kittens may be spared. Their father consents, but on the condition that the children do not go into the kitchen and touch the kittens.

After dinner, Vanya and Nina slouch about the rooms, feeling depressed. The prohibition of visits to the kitchen has reduced them to dejection. They refuse sweets, are naughty, and are rude to their mother. When their uncle Petrusha comes in the evening, they draw him aside, and complain to him of their father, who wanted to throw the kittens into the cesspool.

'Uncle Petrusha, tell mamma to have the kittens taken to the nursery,' the children beg their uncle, 'do-o tell her.'

'There, there... very well,' says their uncle, waving them off. 'All right.'

Uncle Petrusha does not usually come alone. He is accompanied by Nero, a big black dog of Danish breed, with drooping ears, and a tail as hard as a stick. The dog is silent, morose, and full of a sense of his own dignity. He takes not the slightest notice of the children, and when he passes them hits them with his tail as though they were chairs. The children hate him from the bottom of their hearts, but on this occasion, practical considerations override sentiment.

'I say, Nina,' says Vanya, opening his eyes wide. 'Let Nero be their father, instead of the horse! The horse is dead and he is alive, you see.'

They are waiting the whole evening for the moment when papa will sit down to his cards and it will be possible to take Nero to the kitchen without being observed.... At last, papa sits down to cards, mamma is busy with the samovar and not noticing the children....

The happy moment arrives.

'Come along!' Vanya whispers to his sister.

But, at that moment, Stepan comes in and, with a snigger, announces:

'Nero has eaten the kittens, madam.'

Nina and Vanya turn pale and look at Stepan with horror.

'He really has...' laughs the footman, 'he went to the box and gobbled them up.'

The children expect that all the people in the house will be aghast and fall upon the miscreant Nero. But they all sit calmly in their seats, and only express surprise at the appetite of the huge dog. Papa and mamma laugh. Nero walks about by the table, wags his tail, and licks his lips complacently... the cat is the only one who is uneasy. With her tail in the air she walks about the rooms, looking suspiciously at people and mewing plaintively.

'Children, it's past nine,' cries mamma, 'it's bed-time.'

Vanya and Nina go to bed, shed tears, and spend a long time thinking about the injured cat, and the cruel, insolent, and unpunished Nero.

A DREARY STORY

A DREARY STORY

FROM THE NOTEBOOK OF AN OLD MAN

I

THERE is in Russia an emeritus Professor Nikolay Stepanovitch, a chevalier and privy councillor; he has so many Russian and foreign decorations that when he has occasion to put them on the students nickname him 'The Ikonstand'. His acquaintances are of the most aristocratic; for the last twenty-five or thirty years, at any rate, there has not been one single distinguished man of learning in Russia with whom he has not been intimately acquainted. There is no one for him to make friends with nowadays; but if we turn to the past, the long list of his famous friends winds up with such names as Pirogov, Kavelin, and the poet Nekrasov, all of whom bestowed upon him a warm and sincere affection. He is a member of all the Russian and of three foreign universities. And so on, and so on. All that and a great deal more that might be said makes up what is called my 'name'.

That is my name as known to the public. In Russia it is known to every educated man, and abroad it is mentioned in the lecture-room with the addition 'honoured and distinguished'. It is one of those fortunate names to abuse which or to take which in vain, in public or in print, is considered a sign of bad taste. And that is as it should be. You see, my name is closely associated with the conception of a highly distinguished man of great gifts and unquestionable usefulness. I have the industry and power of endurance of a camel, and that is important, and I have talent, which is even more important. Moreover, while I am on this subject, I am a well-educated, modest, and honest fellow. I have never poked my nose into literature or politics; I have never sought popularity in polemics with the ignorant; I have never made speeches either at public dinners or at the funerals of my friends.... In fact, there is no slur on my learned name, and there is no complaint one can make against it. It is fortunate.

The bearer of that name, that is I, see myself as a man of sixty-two, with a bald head, with false teeth, and with an incurable tic douloureux. I am myself as dingy and unsightly as my name is brilliant and splendid. My head and my hands tremble with weakness; my neck, as Turgenev says of one of his heroines, is like the handle of a double bass; my chest is hollow; my shoulders narrow; when I talk or lecture, my mouth turns down at one corner; when I smile, my whole face is covered with aged-looking, deathly wrinkles. There is nothing impressive about my pitiful figure; only, perhaps, when I have an attack of tic douloureux my face wears a peculiar expression, the sight of which must have roused in everyone the grim and impressive thought, 'Evidently that man will soon die.'

I still, as in the past, lecture fairly well; I can still, as in the past, hold the attention of my listeners for a couple of hours. My fervour, the literary skill of my exposition, and my humour, almost efface the defects of my voice, though it is harsh, dry, and monotonous as a praying beggar's. I write poorly. That bit of my brain which presides over the faculty of authorship refuses to work. My memory has grown weak; there is a lack of sequence in my ideas, and when I put them on paper it always seems to me that I have lost the instinct for their organic connection; my construction is monotonous; my language is poor and timid. Often I write what I do not mean; I have forgotten the beginning when I am writing the end. Often I forget ordinary words, and I always have to waste a great deal of energy in avoiding superfluous phrases and unnecessary parentheses in my letters, both unmistakable proofs of a decline in mental activity. And it is noteworthy that the simpler the letter the more painful the effort to write it. At a scientific article I feel far more intelligent and at ease than at a letter of congratulation or a minute of proceedings. Another point: I find it easier to write German or English than to write Russian.

As regards my present manner of life, I must give a foremost place to the insomnia from which I have suffered of late. If I were asked what constituted the chief and fundamental feature of my existence now, I should answer, Insomnia. As in the past, from habit I undress and go to bed exactly at midnight. I fall asleep quickly, but before two o'clock I wake up and feel as though I had not slept at all. Sometimes I get out of bed and light a lamp. For an hour or two I walk up and down the room looking at the familiar photographs and pictures. When I am weary of walking about, I sit down to my table. I sit motionless, thinking of nothing, conscious of no inclination; if a book is lying before me, I mechanically move it closer and read it without any interest – in that way not long ago I mechanically read through in one night a whole novel, with the strange title 'The Song the Lark was Singing'; or to occupy my attention I force myself to count to a thousand; or I imagine the face of one of my colleagues and begin trying to remember in what year and under what circumstances he entered the service. I like listening to sounds. Two rooms away from me my daughter Liza says something rapidly in her sleep, or my wife crosses the drawing-room with a candle and invariably drops the matchbox; or a warped cupboard creaks; or the burner of the lamp suddenly begins to hum – and all these sounds, for some reason, excite me.

To lie awake at night means to be at every moment conscious of being abnormal, and so I look forward with impatience to the morning and the day when I have a right to be awake. Many wearisome hours pass before the cock crows in the yard. He is my first bringer of good tidings. As soon as he crows I know that within an hour the porter will wake up below, and, coughing angrily, will go upstairs to fetch something. And then a pale light will begin gradually glimmering at the windows, voices will sound in the street....

The day begins for me with the entrance of my wife. She comes in to me in her petticoat, before she has done her hair, but after she has washed, smelling of flower-scented eau-de-Cologne, looking as though she had come in by chance. Every time she says exactly the same thing: 'Excuse me, I have just come for a minute.... Have you had a bad night again?'

Then she puts out the lamp, sits down near the table, and begins talking. I am no prophet, but I know what she will talk about. Every morning it is exactly the same thing. Usually, after anxious enquiries concerning my health, she suddenly mentions our son who is an officer serving at Warsaw. After the twentieth of each month we send him fifty roubles, and that serves as the chief topic of our conversation.

'Of course it is difficult for us,' my wife would sigh, 'but until he is completely on his own feet it is our duty to help him. The boy is among strangers, his pay is small.... However, if you like, next month we won't send him fifty, but forty. What do you think?'

Daily experience might have taught my wife that constantly talking of our expenses does not reduce them, but my wife refuses to learn by experience, and regularly every morning discusses our officer son, and tells me that bread, thank God, is cheaper, while sugar is a halfpenny dearer – with a tone and an air as though she were communicating interesting news.

I listen, mechanically assent, and, probably because I have had a bad night, strange and inappropriate thoughts intrude themselves upon me. I gaze at my wife and wonder like a child. I ask myself in perplexity, is it possible that this old, very stout, ungainly woman, with her dull expression of petty anxiety and alarm about daily bread, with eyes dimmed by continual brooding over debts and money difficulties, who can talk of nothing but expenses and who smiles at nothing but things getting cheaper – is it possible that this woman is no other than the slender Varya whom I fell in love with so passionately for her fine, clear intelligence, for her pure soul, her beauty, and, as Othello his Desdemona, for her 'sympathy' for my studies? Could that woman be no other than the Varya who had once borne me a son?

I look with strained attention into the face of this flabby, spiritless, clumsy old woman, seeking in her my Varya, but of her past self nothing is left but her anxiety over my health and her manner of calling my salary 'our salary', and my cap 'our cap'. It is painful for me to look at her, and, to give her what little comfort I can, I let her say what she likes, and say nothing even when she passes unjust criticisms on other people or pitches into me for not having a private practice or not publishing textbooks.

Our conversation always ends in the same way. My wife suddenly remembers with dismay that I have not had my tea.

'What am I thinking about, sitting here?' she says, getting up. 'The samovar has been on the table ever so long, and here I stay gossiping. My goodness! how forgetful I am growing!'

She goes out quickly, and stops in the doorway to say:

'We owe Yegor five months' wages. Did you know it? You mustn't let the servants' wages run on; how many times I have said it! It's much easier to pay ten roubles a month than fifty roubles every five months!'

As she goes out, she stops to say:

'The person I am sorriest for is our Liza. The girl studies at the Conservatoire, always mixes with people of good position, and goodness knows how she is dressed. Her fur coat is in such a state she is ashamed to show herself in the street. If she were somebody else's daughter it wouldn't matter, but of course everyone knows that her father is a distinguished professor, a privy councillor.'

And having reproached me with my rank and reputation, she goes away at last. That is how my day begins. It does not improve as it goes on.

As I am drinking my tea, my Liza comes in wearing her fur coat and her cap, with her music in her hand, already quite ready to go to the Conservatoire. She is two-and-twenty. She looks younger, is pretty, and rather like my wife in her young days. She kisses me tenderly on my forehead and on my hand, and says:

'Good-morning, papa; are you quite well?'

As a child she was very fond of ice-cream, and I used often to take her to a confectioner's. Ice-cream was for her the type of everything delightful. If she wanted to praise me she would say: 'You are as nice as cream, papa.' We used to call one of her little fingers 'pistachio ice', the next, 'cream ice', the third 'raspberry', and so on. Usually when she came in to say good-morning to me I used to sit her on my knee, kiss her little fingers, and say:

'Creamy ice . . . pistachio . . . lemon. . . .'

And now, from old habit, I kiss Liza's fingers and mutter: 'Pistachio . . . cream . . . lemon . . .' but the effect is utterly different. I am cold as ice and I am ashamed. When my daughter comes in to me and touches my forehead with her lips I start as though a bee had stung me on the head, give a forced smile, and turn my face away. Ever since I have been suffering from sleeplessness, a question sticks in my brain like a nail. My daughter often sees me, an old man and a distinguished man, blush painfully at being in debt to my footman; she sees how often anxiety over petty debts forces me to lay aside my work and to walk up and down the room for hours together, thinking; but why is it she never comes to me in secret to whisper in my ear: 'Father, here is my watch, here are my bracelets, my earrings, my dresses.... Pawn them all; you want money...'? How is it that, seeing how her mother and I are placed in a false position and do our utmost to hide our poverty from people, she does not give up her expensive pleasure of music lessons? I would not accept her watch nor her bracelets, nor the sacrifice of her lessons – God forbid! That isn't what I want.

I think at the same time of my son, the officer at Warsaw. He is a clever, honest, and sober fellow. But that is not enough for me. I think if I had an old father, and if I knew there were moments when he was put to shame by his poverty, I should give up my officer's commission to somebody else, and should go out to earn my living as a workman. Such thoughts about my children poison me. What is the use of them? It is only a narrow-minded or embittered man who can harbour evil thoughts about ordinary people because they are not heroes. But enough of that!

At a quarter to ten I have to go and give a lecture to my dear boys. I dress and walk along the road which I have known for thirty years, and which has its history for me. Here is the big grey house with the chemist's shop; at this point there used to stand a little house, and in it was a beershop; in that beershop I thought out my thesis and wrote my first love-letter to Varya. I wrote it in pencil, on a page headed 'Historia morbi'. Here there is a grocer's shop; at one time it was kept by a little Jew, who sold me cigarettes on credit; then by a fat peasant woman, who liked the students because 'every one of them has a mother'; now there is a red-haired shopkeeper sitting in it, a very stolid man who drinks tea from a copper teapot. And here are the gloomy gates of the University, which have long needed doing up; I see the bored porter in his sheep-skin, the broom, the drifts of snow.... On a boy coming fresh from the provinces and imagining that the temple of science must really be a temple, such gates cannot make a healthy impression. Altogether the dilapidated condition of the University buildings, the gloominess of the corridors, the griminess of the walls, the lack of light, the dejected aspect of the steps, the hatstands and the benches, take a prominent position among predisposing causes in the history of Russian pessimism.... Here is our garden... I fancy it has grown neither better nor worse since I was a student. I don't like it. It would be far more sensible if there were tall pines and fine oaks growing there instead of sickly-looking lime-trees, yellow acacias, and skimpy pollard lilacs. The student, whose state of mind is in the majority of cases created by his surroundings, ought in the place where he is studying to see facing him at every turn nothing but what is lofty, strong, and elegant.... God preserve him from gaunt trees, broken windows, grey walls, and doors covered with torn American leather!

When I go to my own entrance the door is flung wide open, and I am met by my colleague, contemporary, and namesake, the porter Nikolay. As he lets me in he clears his throat and says:

'A frost, your Excellency!'

Or, if my great-coat is wet:

'Rain, your Excellency!'

Then he runs on ahead of me and opens all the doors on my way. In my study he carefully takes off my fur coat, and while doing so manages to tell me some bit of University news. Thanks to the close intimacy existing between all the University porters and beadles, he knows everything that goes on in the four faculties, in the office, in the rector's private room, in the library. What does he not know? When in an evil day a rector or a dean, for instance, retires, I hear him in conversation with the young porters mention the candidates for the post, explain that such a one would not be confirmed by the minister, that another would himself refuse to accept it, then drop into fantastic details concerning mysterious papers received in the office, secret conversations alleged to have taken place between the minister and the trustee, and so on. With the exception of these details, he almost always turns out to be right. His estimates of the candidates, though original, are very correct, too. If one wants to know in what year someone read his thesis, entered the service, retired, or died, then summon to your assistance the vast memory of that soldier, and he will not only tell you the year, the month and the day, but will furnish you also with the details that accompanied this or that event. Only one who loves can remember like that.

He is the guardian of the University traditions. From the porters who were his predecessors he has inherited many legends of University life, has added to that wealth much of his own gained during his time of service, and if you care to hear he will tell you many long and intimate stories. He can tell one about extraordinary sages who knew *everything*, about remarkable students who did not sleep for weeks, about numerous martyrs and victims of science; with him good triumphs over evil, the weak always vanquishes the strong, the wise man the fool, the humble the proud, the young the old. There is no need to take all these fables and legends for sterling coin; but filter them, and you will have left what is wanted: our fine traditions and the names of real heroes, recognized as such by all.

In our society the knowledge of the learned world consists of anecdotes of the extraordinary absent-mindedness of certain old professors, and two or three witticisms variously ascribed to Gruber, to me, and to Babukin. For the educated public that is not much. If it loved science, learned men, and students, as Nikolay does, its literature would long ago have contained whole epics, records of sayings and doings such as, unfortunately, it cannot boast of now.

After telling me a piece of news, Nikolay assumes a severe expression, and conversation about business begins. If any outsider could at such times overhear Nikolay's free use of our terminology, he might perhaps imagine that he was a learned man disguised as a soldier. And, by the way, the rumours of the erudition of the University porters are greatly exaggerated. It is true that Nikolay knows more than a hundred Latin words, knows how to put the skeleton together, sometimes prepares the apparatus and amuses the students by some long, learned quotation, but the by no means complicated theory of the circulation of the blood, for instance, is as much a mystery to him now as it was twenty years ago.

At the table in my study, bending low over some book or preparation, sits Pyotr Ignatyevitch, my demonstrator, a modest and industrious but by no means clever man of five-and-thirty, already bald and corpulent; he works from morning to night, reads a lot, remembers well everything he has read – and in that way he is not a man, but pure gold; in all else he is a carthorse or, in other words, a learned dullard. The carthorse characteristics that show his lack of talent are these: his outlook is narrow and sharply limited by his speciality; outside his special branch he is simple as a child.

'Fancy! what a misfortune! They say Skobelev is dead.'

Nikolay crosses himself, but Pyotr Ignatyevitch turns to me and asks:

'What Skobelev is that?'

Another time – somewhat earlier – I told him that Professor Perov was dead. Good Pyotr Ignatyevitch asked:

'What did he lecture on?'

I believe if Patti had sung in his very ear, if a horde of Chinese had invaded Russia, if there had been an earthquake, he would not have stirred a limb, but screwing up his eye, would have gone on calmly looking through his microscope. What is he to Hecuba or Hecuba to him, in fact? I would give a good deal to see how this dry stick sleeps with his wife at night.

Another characteristic is his fanatical faith in the infallibility of science, and, above all, of everything written by the Germans. He believes in himself, in his preparations; knows the object of life, and knows nothing of the doubts and disappointments that turn the hair of talent grey. He has a slavish reverence for authorities and a complete lack of any desire for independent thought. To change his convictions is difficult, to argue with him impossible. How is one to argue with a man who is firmly persuaded that medicine is the finest of sciences, that doctors are the best of men, and that the traditions of the medical profession are superior to those of any other? Of the evil past of medicine only one tradition has been preserved – the white tie still worn by doctors; for a learned – in fact, for any educated man the only traditions that can exist are those of the University as a whole, with no distinction between medicine, law, etc. But it would be hard for Pyotr Ignatyevitch to accept these facts, and he is ready to argue with you till the day of judgment.

I have a clear picture in my mind of his future. In the course of his life he will prepare many hundreds of chemicals of exceptional purity; he will write a number of dry and very accurate memoranda, will make some dozen conscientious translations, but he won't do anything striking. To do that one must have imagination, inventiveness, the gift of insight, and Pyotr Ignatyevitch has nothing of the kind. In short, he is not a master in science, but a journeyman.

Pyotr Ignatyevitch, Nikolay, and I, talk in subdued tones. We are not quite ourselves. There is always a peculiar feeling when one hears through the doors a murmur as of the sea from the lecture-theatre. In the course of thirty years I have not grown accustomed to this feeling, and I experience it every morning. I nervously button up my coat, ask Nikolay unnecessary questions, lose my temper.... It is just as though I were frightened; it is not timidity, though, but something different which I can neither describe nor find a name for.

Quite unnecessarily, I look at my watch and say: 'Well, it's time to go in.'

And we march into the room in the following order: foremost goes Nikolay, with the chemicals and apparatus or with a chart; after him I come; and then the cart-horse follows humbly, with hanging head; or, when necessary, a dead body is carried in first on a stretcher, followed by Nikolay, and so on. On my entrance the students all stand up, then they sit down, and the sound as of the sea is suddenly hushed. Stillness reigns.

I know what I am going to lecture about, but I don't know how I am going to lecture, where I am going to begin or with what I am going to end. I haven't a single sentence ready in my head. But I have only to look round the lecture-hall (it is built in the form of an amphitheatre) and utter the stereotyped phrase, 'Last lecture we stopped at...' when sentences spring up from my soul in a long string, and I am carried away by my own eloquence. I speak with irresistible rapidity and passion, and it seems as though there were no force which could check the flow of my words. To lecture well – that is, with profit to the listeners and without boring them – one must have, besides talent, experience and a special knack; one must possess a clear conception of one's own powers, of the audience to which one is lecturing, and of the subject of one's lecture. Moreover, one must be a man who knows what he is doing; one must keep a sharp lookout, and not for one second lose sight of what lies before one.

A good conductor, interpreting the thought of the composer, does twenty things at once: reads the score, waves his baton, watches the singer, makes a motion sideways, first to the drum then to the wind-instruments, and so on. I do just the same when I lecture. Before me a hundred and fifty faces, all unlike one another; three hundred eyes all looking straight into my face. My object is to dominate this many-headed monster. If every moment as I lecture I have a clear vision of the degree of its attention and its power of comprehension, it is my power. The other foe I have to overcome is in myself. It is the infinite variety of forms, phenomena, laws, and the multitude of ideas of my own and other people's conditioned by them. Every moment I must have the skill to snatch out of that vast mass of material what is most important and necessary, and, as rapidly as my words flow, clothe my thought in a form in which it can be grasped by the monster's intelligence, and may arouse its attention, and at the same time one must keep a sharp lookout that one's thoughts are conveyed, not just as they come, but in a certain order, essential for the correct composition of the picture I wish to sketch. Further, I endeavour to make my diction literary, my definitions brief and precise, my wording, as far as possible, simple and eloquent. Every minute I have to pull myself up and remember that I have only an hour and forty minutes at my disposal. In short, one has one's work cut out. At one and the same minute one has to play the part of savant and teacher and orator, and it's a bad thing if the orator gets the upper hand of the savant or of the teacher in one, or *vice versa.*

You lecture for a quarter of an hour, for half an hour, when you notice that the students are beginning to look at the ceiling, at Pyotr Ignatyevitch; one is feeling for his handkerchief, another shifts in his seat, another smiles at his thoughts.... That means that their attention is flagging. Something must be done. Taking advantage of the first opportunity, I make some pun. A broad grin comes on to a hundred and fifty faces, the eyes shine brightly, the sound of the sea is audible for a brief moment.... I laugh too. Their attention is refreshed, and I can go on.

No kind of sport, no kind of game or diversion, has ever given me such enjoyment as lecturing. Only at lectures have I been able to abandon myself entirely to passion, and have understood that inspiration is not an invention of the poets, but exists in real life, and I imagine Hercules after the most piquant of his exploits felt just such voluptuous exhaustion as I experience after every lecture.

That was in old times. Now at lectures I feel nothing but torture. Before half an hour is over I am conscious of an overwhelming weakness in my legs and my shoulders. I sit down in my chair, but I am not accustomed to lecture sitting down; a minute later I get up and go on standing, then sit down again.

There is a dryness in my mouth, my voice grows husky, my head begins to go round.... To conceal my condition from my audience I continually drink water, cough, often blow my nose as though I were hindered by a cold, make puns inappropriately, and in the end break off earlier than I ought to. But above all I am ashamed.

My conscience and my intelligence tell me that the very best thing I could do now would be to deliver a farewell lecture to the boys, to say my last word to them, to bless them, and give up my post to a man younger and stronger than me. But, God be my judge, I have not manly courage enough to act according to my conscience.

Unfortunately, I am not a philosopher and not a theologian. I know perfectly well that I cannot live more than another six months; it might be supposed that I ought now to be chiefly concerned with the question of the shadowy life beyond the grave, and the visions that will visit my slumbers in the tomb. But for some reason my soul refuses to recognize these questions, though my mind is fully alive to their importance. Just as twenty, thirty years ago, so now, on the threshold of death, I am interested in nothing but science. As I yield up my last breath I shall still believe that science is the most important, the most splendid, the most essential thing in the life of man; that it always has been and will be the highest manifestation of love, and that only by means of it will man conquer himself and nature. This faith is perhaps naïve and may rest on false assumptions, but it is not my fault that I believe that and nothing else; I cannot overcome in myself this belief.

But that is not the point. I only ask people to be indulgent to my weakness, and to realize that to tear from the lecture-theatre and his pupils a man who is more interested in the history of the development of the bone medulla than in the final object of creation would be equivalent to taking him and nailing him up in his coffin without waiting for him to be dead.

Sleeplessness and the consequent strain of combating increasing weakness leads to something strange in me. In the middle of my lecture tears suddenly rise in my throat, my eyes begin to smart, and I feel a passionate, hysterical desire to stretch out my hands before me and break into loud lamentation. I want to cry out in a loud voice that I, a famous man, have been sentenced by fate to the death penalty, that within some six months another man will be in control here in the lecture-theatre. I want to shriek that I am poisoned; new ideas such as I have not known before have poisoned the last days of my life, and are still stinging my brain like mosquitoes. And at that moment my position seems to me so awful that I want all my listeners to be horrified, to leap up from their seats and to rush in panic terror, with desperate screams, to the exit.

It is not easy to get through such moments.

II

AFTER my lecture I sit at home and work. I read journals and monographs, or prepare my next lecture; sometimes I write something. I work with interruptions, as I have from time to time to see visitors.

There is a ring at the bell. It is a colleague come to discuss some business matter with me. He comes in to me with his hat and his stick, and, holding out both these objects to me, says:

'Only for a minute! Only for a minute! Sit down, *collega*! Only a couple of words.'

To begin with, we both try to show each other that we are extraordinarily polite and highly delighted to see each other. I make him sit down in an easy-chair, and he makes me sit down; as we do so, we cautiously pat each other on the back, touch each other's buttons, and it looks as though we were feeling each other and afraid of scorching our fingers. Both of us laugh, though we say nothing amusing. When we are seated we bow our heads towards each other and begin talking in subdued voices. However affectionately disposed we may be to one another, we cannot help adorning our conversation with all sorts of Chinese mannerisms, such as 'As you so justly observed', or 'I have already had the honour to inform you'; we cannot help laughing if one of us makes a joke, however unsuccessfully. When we have finished with business my colleague gets up impulsively and, waving his hat in the direction of my work, begins to say good-bye. Again we paw one another and laugh. I see him into the hall; then I assist my colleague to put on his coat, while he does all he can to decline this high honour. Then when Yegor opens the door my colleague declares that I shall catch cold, while I make a show of being ready to go even into the street with him. And when at last I go back into my study my face still goes on smiling, I suppose from inertia.

A little later another ring at the bell. Somebody comes into the hall, and is a long time coughing and taking off his things. Yegor announces a student. I tell him to ask him in. A minute later a young man of agreeable appearance comes in. For the last year he and I have been on strained relations; he answers me disgracefully at the examinations, and I mark him one. Every year I have some seven such hopefuls whom, to express it in the students' slang, I 'chivy' or 'floor'. Those of them who fail in their examination through incapacity or illness usually bear their cross patiently and do not haggle with me; those who come to the house and haggle with me are always youths of sanguine temperament, broad natures, whose failure at examinations spoils their appetites and hinders them from visiting the opera with their usual regularity. I let the first class off easily, but the second I chivy through a whole year.

'Sit down,' I say to my visitor; 'what have you to tell me?'

'Excuse me, professor, for troubling you,' he begins, hesitating, and not looking me in the face. 'I would not have ventured to trouble you if it had not been... I have been up for your examination five times, and have been ploughed.... I beg you, be so good as to mark me for a pass, because....'

The argument which all the sluggards bring forward on their own behalf is always the same; they have passed well in all their subjects and have only come to grief in mine, and that is the more surprising because they have always been particularly interested in my subject and knew it so well; their failure has always been entirely owing to some incomprehensible misunderstanding.

'Excuse me, my friend,' I say to the visitor; 'I cannot mark you for a pass. Go and read up the lectures and come to me again. Then we shall see.'

A pause. I feel an impulse to torment the student a little for liking beer and the opera better than science, and I say, with a sigh:

'To my mind, the best thing you can do now is to give up medicine altogether. If, with your abilities, you cannot succeed in passing the examination, it's evident that you have neither the desire nor the vocation for a doctor's calling.'

The sanguine youth's face lengthens.

'Excuse me, professor,' he laughs, 'but that would be odd of me, to say the least of it. After studying for five years, all at once to give it up.'

'Oh, well! Better to have lost your five years than have to spend the rest of your life in doing work you do not care for.'

But at once I feel sorry for him, and I hasten to add:

'However, as you think best. And so read a little more and come again.'

'When?' the idle youth asks in a hollow voice.

'When you like. To-morrow if you like.'

And in his good-natured eyes I read:

'I can come all right, but of course you will plough me again, you beast!'

'Of course,' I say, 'you won't know more science for going in for my examination another fifteen times, but it is training your character, and you must be thankful for that.'

Silence follows. I get up and wait for my visitor to go, but he stands and looks towards the window, fingers his beard, and thinks. It grows boring.

The sanguine youth's voice is pleasant and mellow, his eyes are clever and ironical, his face is genial, though a little bloated from frequent indulgence in beer and overlong lying on the sofa; he looks as though he could tell me a lot of interesting things about the opera, about his affairs of the heart, and about comrades whom he likes. Unluckily, it is not the thing to discuss these subjects, or else I should have been glad to listen to him.

'Professor, I give you my word of honour that if you mark me for a pass I. . . I'll. . . .'

As soon as we reach the 'word of honour' I wave my hands and sit down to the table. The student ponders a minute longer, and says dejectedly:

'In that case, good-bye. . . . I beg your pardon.'

'Good-bye, my friend. Good luck to you.'

He goes irresolutely into the hall, slowly puts on his outdoor things, and, going out into the street, probably ponders for some time longer; unable to think of anything, except 'old devil', inwardly addressed to me, he goes into a wretched restaurant to dine and drink beer, and then home to bed. 'Peace be to thy ashes, honest toiler.'

A third ring at the bell. A young doctor, in a pair of new black trousers, gold spectacles, and of course a white tie, walks in. He introduces himself. I beg him to be seated, and ask what I can do for him. Not without emotion, the young devotee of science begins telling me that he has passed his examination as a doctor of medicine, and that he has now only to write his dissertation. He would like to work with me under my guidance, and he would be greatly obliged to me if I would give him a subject for his dissertation.

'Very glad to be of use to you, colleague,' I say, 'but just let us come to an understanding as to the meaning of a dissertation. That word is taken to mean a composition which is a product of independent creative effort. Is that not so? A work written on another man's subject and under another man's guidance is called something different. . . .'

The doctor says nothing. I fly into a rage and jump up from my seat.

'Why is it you all come to me?' I cry angrily. 'Do I keep a shop? I don't deal in subjects. For the thousand and oneth time I ask you all to leave me in peace! Excuse my brutality, but I am quite sick of it!'

The doctor remains silent, but a faint flush is apparent on his cheek-bones. His face expresses a profound reverence for my fame and my learning, but from his eyes I can see he feels a contempt for my voice, my pitiful figure, and my nervous gesticulation. I impress him in my anger as a queer fish.

'I don't keep a shop,' I go on angrily. 'And it is a strange thing! Why don't you want to be independent? Why have you such a distaste for independence?'

I say a great deal, but he still remains silent. By degrees I calm down, and of course give in. The doctor gets a subject from me for his theme not worth a halfpenny, writes under my supervision a dissertation of no use to anyone, with dignity defends it in a dreary discussion, and receives a degree of no use to him.

The rings at the bell may follow one another endlessly, but I will confine my description here to four of them. The bell rings for the fourth time, and I hear familiar footsteps, the rustle of a dress, a dear voice....

Eighteen years ago a colleague of mine, an oculist, died leaving a little daughter Katya, a child of seven, and sixty thousand roubles. In his will he made me the child's guardian. Till she was ten years old Katya lived with us as one of the family, then she was sent to a boarding-school, and only spent the summer holidays with us. I never had time to look after her education. I only superintended it at leisure moments, and so I can say very little about her childhood.

The first thing I remember, and like so much in remembrance, is the extraordinary trustfulness with which she came into our house and let herself be treated by the doctors, a trustfulness which was always shining in her little face. She would sit somewhere out of the way, with her face tied up, invariably watching something with attention; whether she watched me writing or turning over the pages of a book, or watched my wife bustling about, or the cook scrubbing a potato in the kitchen, or the dog playing, her eyes invariably expressed the same thought – that is, 'Everything that is done in this world is nice and sensible.' She was curious, and very fond of talking to me. Sometimes she would sit at the table opposite me, watching my movements and asking questions. It interested her to know what I was reading, what I did at the University, whether I was not afraid of the dead bodies, what I did with my salary.

'Do the students fight at the University?' she would ask.

'They do, dear.'

'And do you make them go down on their knees?'

'Yes, I do.'

And she thought it funny that the students fought and I made them go down on their knees, and she laughed. She was a gentle, patient, good child. It happened not infrequently that I saw something taken away from her, saw her punished without reason, or her curiosity repressed; at such times a look of sadness was mixed with the invariable expression of trustfulness on her face – that was all. I did not know how to take her part; only when I saw her sad I had an inclination to draw her to me and to commiserate with her like some old nurse: 'My poor little orphan one!'

I remember, too, that she was fond of fine clothes and of sprinkling herself with scent. In that respect she was like me. I, too, am fond of pretty clothes and nice scent.

I regret that I had not time nor inclination to watch over the rise and development of the passion which took complete possession of Katya when she was fourteen or fifteen. I mean her passionate love for the theatre. When she used to come from boarding-school and stay with us for the summer holidays, she talked of nothing with such pleasure and such warmth as of plays and actors. She bored us with her continual talk of the theatre. My wife and children would not listen to her. I was the only one who had not the courage to refuse to attend to her. When she had a longing to share her transports, she used to come into my study and say in an imploring tone:

'Nikolay Stepanitch, do let me talk to you about the theatre!'

I pointed to the clock, and said:

'I'll give you half an hour – begin.'

Later on she used to bring with her dozens of portraits of actors and actresses which she worshipped; then she attempted several times to take part in private theatricals, and the upshot of it all was that when she left school she came to me and announced that she was born to be an actress.

I had never shared Katya's inclinations for the theatre. To my mind, if a play is good there is no need to trouble the actors in order that it may make the right impression; it is enough to read it. If the play is poor, no acting will make it good.

In my youth I often visited the theatre, and now my family takes a box twice a year and carries me off for a little distraction. Of course, that is not enough to give me the right to judge of the theatre. In my opinion the theatre has become no better than it was thirty or forty years ago. Just as in the past, I can never find a glass of clean water in the corridors or foyers of the theatre. Just as in the past, the attendants fine me twenty kopecks for my fur coat, though there is nothing reprehensible in wearing a warm coat in winter. As in the past, for no sort of reason, music is played in the intervals, which adds something new and uncalled-for to the impression made by the play. As in the past, men go in the intervals and drink spirits in the buffet. If no progress can be seen in trifles, I should look for it in vain in what is more important. When an actor wrapped from head to foot in stage traditions and conventions tries to recite a simple ordinary speech, 'To be, or not to be', not simply, but invariably with the accompaniment of hissing and convulsive movements all over his body, or when he tries to convince me at all costs that Tchatsky, who talks so much with fools and is so fond of folly, is a very clever man, and that 'Woe from Wit' is not a dull play, the stage gives me the same feeling of conventionality which bored me so much forty years ago when I was regaled with the classical howling and beating on the breast. And every time I come out of the theatre more conservative than I go in.

The sentimental and confiding public may be persuaded that the stage, even in its present form, is a school; but anyone who is familiar with a school in its true sense will not be caught with that bait. I cannot say what will happen in fifty or a hundred years, but in its actual condition the theatre can serve only as an entertainment. But this entertainment is too costly to be frequently enjoyed. It robs the state of thousands of healthy and talented young men and women, who, if they had not devoted themselves to the theatre, might have been good doctors, farmers, schoolmistresses, officers; it robs the public of the evening hours – the best time for intellectual work and social intercourse. I say nothing of the waste of money and the moral damage to the spectator when he sees murder, fornication, or false witness unsuitably treated on the stage.

Katya was of an entirely different opinion. She assured me that the theatre, even in its present condition, was superior to the lecture-hall, to books, or to anything in the world. The stage was a power that united in itself all the arts, and actors were missionaries. No art nor science was capable of producing so strong and so certain an effect on the soul of man as the stage, and it was with good reason that an actor of medium quality enjoys greater popularity than the greatest savant or artist. And no sort of public service could provide such enjoyment and gratification as the theatre.

And one fine day Katya joined a troupe of actors, and went off, I believe to Ufa, taking away with her a good supply of money, a store of rainbow hopes, and the most aristocratic views of her work.

Her first letters on the journey were marvellous. I read them, and was simply amazed that those small sheets of paper could contain so much youth, purity of spirit, holy innocence, and at the same time subtle and apt judgments which would have done credit to a fine masculine intellect. It was more like a rapturous pæan of praise she sent me than a mere description of the Volga, the country, the towns she visited, her companions, her failures and successes; every sentence was fragrant with that confiding trustfulness I was accustomed to read in her face – and at the same time there were a great many grammatical mistakes, and there was scarcely any punctuation at all.

Before six months had passed I received a highly poetical and enthusiastic letter beginning with the words, 'I have come to love . . .'. This letter was accompanied by a photograph representing a young man with a shaven face, a wide-brimmed hat, and a plaid flung over his shoulder. The letters that followed were as splendid as before, but now commas and stops made their appearance in them, the grammatical mistakes disappeared, and there was a distinctly masculine flavour about them. Katya began writing to me how splendid it would be to build a great theatre somewhere on the Volga, on a cooperative system, and to attract to the enterprise the rich merchants and the steamer owners; there would be a great deal of money in it; there would be vast audiences; the actors would play on cooperative terms.... Possibly all this was really excellent, but it seemed to me that such schemes could only originate from a man's mind.

However that may have been, for a year and a half everything seemed to go well: Katya was in love, believed in her work, and was happy; but then I began to notice in her letters unmistakable signs of falling off. It began with Katya's complaining of her companions – this was the first and most ominous symptom; if a young scientific or literary man begins his career with bitter complaints of scientific and literary men, it is a sure sign that he is worn out and not fit for his work. Katya wrote to me that her companions did not attend the rehearsals and never knew their parts; that one could see in every one of them an utter disrespect for the public in the production of absurd plays, and in their behaviour on the stage; that for the benefit of the Actors' Fund, which they only talked about, actresses of the serious drama demeaned themselves by singing chansonettes, while tragic actors sang comic songs making fun of deceived husbands and the pregnant condition of unfaithful wives, and so on. In fact, it was amazing that all this had not yet ruined the provincial stage, and that it could still maintain itself on such a rotten and unsubstantial footing.

In answer I wrote Katya a long and, I must confess, a very boring letter. Among other things, I wrote to her:

'I have more than once happened to converse with old actors, very worthy men, who showed a friendly disposition towards me; from my conversations with them I could understand that their work was controlled not so much by their own intelligence and free choice as by fashion and the mood of the public. The best of them had had to play in their day in tragedy, in operetta, in Parisian farces, and in extravaganzas, and they always seemed equally sure that they were on the right path and that they were of use. So, as you see, the cause of the evil must be sought, not in the actors, but, more deeply, in the art itself and in the attitude of the whole of society to it.'

This letter of mine only irritated Katya. She answered me:

'You and I are singing parts out of different operas. I wrote to you, not of the worthy men who showed a friendly disposition to you, but of a band of knaves who have nothing worthy about them. They are a horde of savages who have got on the stage simply because no one would have taken them elsewhere, and who call themselves artists simply because they are impudent. There are numbers of dull-witted creatures, drunkards, intriguing schemers and slanderers, but there is not one person of talent among them. I cannot tell you how bitter it is to me that the art I love has fallen into the hands of people I detest; how bitter it is that the best men look on at evil from afar, not caring to come closer, and, instead of intervening, write ponderous commonplaces and utterly useless sermons....' And so on, all in the same style.

A little time passed, and I got this letter: 'I have been brutally deceived. I cannot go on living. Dispose of my money as you think best. I loved you as my father and my only friend. Good-bye.'

It turned out that *he*, too, belonged to the 'horde of savages'. Later on, from certain hints, I gathered that there had been an attempt at suicide. I believe Katya tried to poison herself. I imagine that she must have been seriously ill afterwards, as the next letter I got was from Yalta, where she had most probably been sent by the doctors. Her last letter contained a request to send her a thousand roubles to Yalta as quickly as possible, and ended with these words:

'Excuse the gloominess of this letter; yesterday I buried my child.' After spending about a year in the Crimea, she returned home.

She had been about four years on her travels, and during those four years, I must confess, I had played a rather strange and unenviable part in regard to her. When in earlier days she had told me she was going on the stage, and then wrote to me of her love; when she was periodically overcome by extravagance, and I continually had to send her first one and then two thousand roubles; when she wrote to me of her intention of suicide, and then of the death of her baby, every time I lost my head, and all my sympathy for her sufferings found no expression except that, after prolonged reflection, I wrote long, boring letters which I might just as well not have written. And yet I took a father's place with her and loved her like a daughter!

Now Katya is living less than half a mile off. She has taken a flat of five rooms, and has installed herself fairly comfortably and in the taste of the day. If anyone were to undertake to describe her surroundings, the most characteristic note in the picture would be indolence. For the indolent body there are soft lounges, soft stools; for indolent feet soft rugs; for indolent eyes faded, dingy, or flat colours; for the indolent soul the walls are hung with a number of cheap fans and trivial pictures, in which the originality of the execution is more conspicuous than the subject; and the room contains a multitude of little tables and shelves filled with utterly useless articles of no value, and shapeless rags in place of curtains.... All this, together with the dread of bright colours, of symmetry, and of empty space, bears witness not only to spiritual indolence, but also to a corruption of natural taste. For days together Katya lies on the lounge reading, principally novels and stories. She only goes out of the house once a day, in the afternoon, to see me.

I go on working while Katya sits silent not far from me on the sofa, wrapping herself in her shawl, as though she were cold. Either because I find her sympathetic or because I was used to her frequent visits when she was a little girl, her presence does not prevent me from concentrating my attention. From time to time I mechanically ask her some question; she gives very brief replies; or, to rest for a minute, I turn round and watch her as she looks dreamily at some medical journal or review. And at such moments I notice that her face has lost the old look of confiding trustfulness. Her expression now is cold, apathetic, and absentminded, like that of passengers who have had to wait too long for a train. She is dressed, as in old days, simply and beautifully, but carelessly; her dress and her hair show visible traces of the sofas and rocking-chairs in which she spends whole days at a stretch. And she has lost the curiosity she had in old days. She has ceased to ask me questions now, as though she had experienced everything in life and looked for nothing new from it.

Towards four o'clock there begin to be sounds of movement in the hall and in the drawing-room. Liza has come back from the Conservatoire, and has brought some girl-friends in with her. We hear them playing on the piano, trying their voices and laughing; in the dining-room Yegor is laying the table, with the clatter of crockery.

'Good-bye,' said Katya. 'I won't go in and see your people to-day. They must excuse me. I haven't time. Come and see me.'

While I am seeing her to the door, she looks me up and down grimly, and says with vexation:

'You are getting thinner and thinner! Why don't you consult a doctor? I'll call at Sergey Fyodorovitch's and ask him to have a look at you.'

'There's no need, Katya.'

'I can't think where your people's eyes are! They are a nice lot, I must say!'

She puts on her fur coat abruptly, and as she does so two or three hairpins drop unnoticed on the floor from her carelessly arranged hair. She is too lazy and in too great a hurry to do her hair up; she carelessly stuffs the falling curls under her hat, and goes away.

When I go into the dining-room my wife asks me:

'Was Katya with you just now? Why didn't she come in to see us? It's really strange. . . .'

'Mamma,' Liza says to her reproachfully, 'let her alone, if she doesn't want to. We are not going down on our knees to her.'

'It's very neglectful, anyway. To sit for three hours in the study without remembering our existence! But of course she must do as she likes.'

Varya and Liza both hate Katya. This hatred is beyond my comprehension, and probably one would have to be a woman in order to understand it. I am ready to stake my life that of the hundred and fifty young men I see every day in the lecture-theatre, and of the hundred elderly ones I meet every week, hardly one could be found capable of understanding their hatred and aversion for Katya's past – that is, for her having been a mother without being a wife, and for her having had an illegitimate child; and at the same time I cannot recall one woman or girl of my acquaintance who would not consciously or unconsciously harbour such feelings. And this is not because woman is purer or more virtuous than man: why, virtue and purity are not very different from vice if they are not free from evil feeling. I attribute this simply to the backwardness of woman. The mournful feeling of compassion and the pang of conscience experienced by a modern man at the sight of suffering is, to my mind, far greater proof of culture and moral elevation than hatred and aversion. Woman is as tearful and as coarse in her feelings now as she was in the Middle Ages, and to my thinking those who advise that she should be educated like a man are quite right.

My wife also dislikes Katya for having been an actress, for ingratitude, for pride, for eccentricity, and for the numerous vices which one woman can always find in another.

Besides my wife and daughter and me, there are dining with us two or three of my daughter's friends and Alexandr Adolfovitch Gnekker, her admirer and suitor. He is a fair-haired young man under thirty, of medium height, very stout and broad-shouldered, with red whiskers near his ears, and little waxed moustaches which make his plump smooth face look like a toy. He is dressed in a very short reefer jacket, a flowered waistcoat, breeches very full at the top and very narrow at the ankle, with a large check pattern on them, and yellow boots without heels. He has prominent eyes like a crab's, his cravat is like a crab's neck, and I even fancy there is a smell of crab-soup about the young man's whole person. He visits us every day, but no one in my family knows anything of his origin nor of the place of his education, nor of his means of livelihood. He neither plays nor sings, but has some connection with music and singing, sells somebody's pianos somewhere, is frequently at the Conservatoire, is acquainted with all the celebrities, and is a steward at the concerts; he criticizes music with great authority, and I have noticed that people are eager to agree with him.

Rich people always have dependents hanging about them; the arts and sciences have the same. I believe there is not an art nor a science in the world free from 'foreign bodies' after the style of this Mr. Gnekker. I am not a musician, and possibly I am mistaken in regard to Mr. Gnekker, of whom, indeed, I know very little. But his air of authority and the dignity with which he takes his stand beside the piano when anyone is playing or singing strike me as very suspicious.

You may be ever so much of a gentleman and a privy councillor, but if you have a daughter you cannot be secure of immunity from that petty bourgeois atmosphere which is so often brought into your house and into your mood by the attentions of suitors, by matchmaking and marriage. I can never reconcile myself, for instance, to the expression of triumph on my wife's face every time Gnekker is in our company, nor can I reconcile myself to the bottles of Lafitte, port, and sherry which are only brought out on his account, that he may see with his own eyes the liberal and luxurious way in which we live. I cannot tolerate the habit of spasmodic laughter Liza has picked up at the Conservatoire, and her way of screwing up her eyes whenever there are men in the room. Above all, I cannot understand why a creature utterly alien to my habits, my studies, my whole manner of life, completely different from the people I like, should come and see me every day, and every day should dine with me. My wife and my servants mysteriously whisper that he is a suitor, but still I don't understand his presence; it rouses in me the same wonder and perplexity as if they were to set a Zulu beside me at the table. And it seems strange to me, too, that my daughter, whom I am used to thinking of as a child, should love that cravat, those eyes, those soft cheeks....

In old days I used to like my dinner, or at least was indifferent about it; now it excites in me no feeling but weariness and irritation. Ever since I became an 'Excellency' and one of the Deans of the Faculty my family has for some reason found it necessary to make a complete change in our menu and dining habits. Instead of the simple dishes to which I was accustomed when I was a student and when I was in practice, now they feed me with a purée with little white things like circles floating about in it, and kidneys stewed in madeira. My rank as a general and my fame have robbed me for ever of cabbage-soup and savoury pies, and goose with apple-sauce, and bream with boiled grain. They have robbed me of our maid-servant Agasha, a chatty and laughter-loving old woman, instead of whom Yegor, a dull-witted and conceited fellow with a white glove on his right hand, waits at dinner. The intervals between the courses are short, but they seem immensely long because there is nothing to occupy them. There is none of the gaiety of the old days, the spontaneous talk, the jokes, the laughter; there is nothing of mutual affection and the joy which used to animate the children, my wife, and me when in old days we met together at meals. For me, the celebrated man of science, dinner was a time of rest and reunion, and for my wife and children a fête – brief indeed, but bright and joyous – in which they knew that for half an hour I belonged, not to science, not to students, but to them alone. Our real exhilaration from one glass of wine is gone for ever, gone is Agasha, gone the bream with boiled grain, gone the uproar that greeted every little startling incident at dinner, such as the cat and dog fighting under the table, or Katya's bandage falling off her face into her soup-plate.

To describe our dinner nowadays is as uninteresting as to eat it. My wife's face wears a look of triumph and affected dignity, and her habitual expression of anxiety. She looks at our plates and says, 'I see you don't care for the joint. Tell me; you don't like it, do you?' and I am obliged to answer: 'There is no need for you to trouble, my dear; the meat is very nice.' And she will say: 'You always stand up for me, Nikolay Stepanovitch, and you never tell the truth. Why is Alexandr Adolfovitch eating so little?' And so on in the same style all through dinner. Liza laughs spasmodically and screws up her eyes. I watch them both, and it is only now at dinner that it becomes absolutely evident to me that the inner life of these two has slipped away out of my ken. I have a feeling as though I had once lived at home with a real wife and children and that now I am dining with visitors, in the house of a sham wife who is not the real one, and am looking at a Liza who is not the real Liza. A startling change has taken place in both of them; I have missed the long process by which that change was effected, and it is no wonder that I can make nothing of it. Why did that change take place? I don't know. Perhaps the whole trouble is that God has not given my wife and daughter the same strength of character as me. From childhood I have been accustomed to resisting external influences, and have steeled myself pretty thoroughly. Such catastrophes in life as fame, the rank of a general, the transition from comfort to living beyond our means, acquaintance with celebrities, etc., have scarcely affected me, and I have remained intact and unashamed; but on my wife and Liza, who have not been through the same hardening process and are weak, all this has fallen like an avalanche of snow, overwhelming them. Gnekker and the young ladies talk of fugues, of counterpoint, of singers and pianists, of Bach and Brahms, while my wife, afraid of their suspecting her of ignorance of music, smiles to them sympathetically and mutters: 'That's exquisite . . . really! You don't say so! . . .' Gnekker eats with solid dignity, jests with solid dignity, and condescendingly listens to the remarks of the young ladies. From time to time he is moved to speak in bad French, and then, for some reason or other, he thinks it necessary to address me as '*Votre Excellence*'.

And I am glum. Evidently I am a constraint to them and they are a constraint to me. I have never in my earlier days had a close knowledge of class antagonism, but now I am tormented by something of that sort. I am on the lookout for nothing but bad qualities in Gnekker; I quickly find them, and am fretted at the thought that a man not of my circle is sitting here as my daughter's suitor. His presence has a bad influence on me in other ways, too. As a rule, when I am alone or in the society of people I like, I never think of my own achievements, or, if I do recall them, they seem to me as trivial as though I had only completed my studies yesterday; but in the presence of people like Gnekker my achievements in science seem to be a lofty mountain the top of which vanishes into the clouds, while at its foot Gnekkers are running about scarcely visible to the naked eye.

After dinner I go into my study and there smoke my pipe, the only one in the whole day, the sole relic of my old bad habit of smoking from morning till night. While I am smoking my wife comes in and sits down to talk to me. Just as in the morning, I know beforehand what our conversation is going to be about.

'I must talk to you seriously, Nikolay Stepanovitch,' she begins. 'I mean about Liza.... Why don't you pay attention to it?'

'To what?'

'You pretend to notice nothing. But that is not right. We can't shirk responsibility.... Gnekker has intentions in regard to Liza.... What do you say?'

'That he is a bad man I can't say, because I don't know him, but that I don't like him I have told you a thousand times already.'

'But you can't... you can't!'

She gets up and walks about in excitement.

'You can't take up that attitude to a serious step,' she says. 'When it is a question of our daughter's happiness we must lay aside all personal feeling. I know you do not like him.... Very good... if we refuse him now, if we break it all off, how can you be sure that Liza will not have a grievance against us all her life? Suitors are not plentiful nowadays, goodness knows, and it may happen that no other match will turn up.... He is very much in love with Liza, and she seems to like him.... Of course, he has no settled position, but that can't be helped. Please God, in time he will get one. He is of good family and well off.'

'Where did you learn that?'

'He told us so. His father has a large house in Harkov and an estate in the neighbourhood. In short, Nikolay Stepanovitch, you absolutely must go to Harkov.'

'What for?'

'You will find out all about him there.... You know the professors there; they will help you. I would go myself, but I am a woman. I cannot....'

'I am not going to Harkov,' I say morosely.

My wife is frightened, and a look of intense suffering comes into her face.

'For God's sake, Nikolay Stepanovitch,' she implores me, with tears in her voice – 'for God's sake, take this burden off me! I am so worried!'

It is painful for me to look at her.

'Very well, Varya,' I say affectionately, 'if you wish it, then certainly I will go to Harkov and do all you want.'

She presses her handkerchief to her eyes and goes off to her room to cry, and I am left alone.

A little later lights are brought in. The arm-chair and the lamp-shade cast familiar shadows that have long grown wearisome on the walls and on the floor, and when I look at them I feel as though the night had come and with it my accursed sleeplessness. I lie on my bed, then get up and walk about the room, then lie down again. As a rule it is after dinner, at the approach of evening, that my nervous excitement reaches its highest pitch. For no reason I begin crying and burying my head in the pillow. At such times I am afraid that someone may come in; I am afraid of suddenly dying; I am ashamed of my tears, and altogether there is something insufferable in my soul. I feel that I can no longer bear the sight of my lamp, of my books, of the shadows on the floor. I cannot bear the sound of the voices coming from the drawing-room. Some force unseen, uncomprehended, is roughly thrusting me out of my flat. I leap up hurriedly, dress, and cautiously, that my family may not notice, slip out into the street. Where am I to go?

The answer to that question has long been ready in my brain. To Katya.

III

AS a rule she is lying on the sofa or in a lounge-chair, reading. Seeing me, she raises her head languidly, sits up, and shakes hands.

'You are always lying down,' I say, after pausing and taking breath. 'That's not good for you. You ought to occupy yourself with something.'

'What?'

'I say you ought to occupy yourself in some way.'

'With what? A woman can be nothing but a simple workwoman or an actress.'

'Well, if you can't be a workwoman, be an actress.'

She says nothing.

'You ought to get married,' I say, half in jest.

'There is no one to marry. There's no reason to, either.'

'You can't live like this.'

'Without a husband? Much that matters; I could have as many men as I like if I wanted to.'

'That's ugly, Katya.'

'What is ugly?'

'Why, what you have just said.'

Noticing that I am hurt and wishing to efface the disagreeable impression, Katya says:

'Let us go; come this way.'

She takes me into a very snug little room, and says, pointing to the writing-table:

'Look . . . I have got that ready for you. You shall work here. Come here every day and bring your work with you. They only hinder you there at home. Will you work here? Will you like to?'

Not to wound her by refusing, I answer that I will work here, and that I like the room very much. Then we both sit down in the snug little room and begin talking.

The warm, snug surroundings and the presence of a sympathetic person does not, as in old days, arouse in me a feeling of pleasure, but an intense impulse to complain and grumble. I feel for some reason that if I lament and complain I shall feel better.

'Things are in a bad way with me, my dear – very bad. . . .'

'What is it?'

'You see how it is, my dear; the best and holiest right of kings is the right of mercy. And I have always felt myself a king, since I have made unlimited use of that right. I have never judged, I have been indulgent, I have readily forgiven everyone, right and left. Where others have protested and expressed indignation, I have only advised and persuaded. All my life it has been my endeavour that my society should not be a burden to my family, to my students, to my colleagues, to my servants. And I know that this attitude to people has had a good influence on all who have chanced to come into contact with me. But now I am not a king. Something is happening to me that is only excusable in a slave; day and night my brain is haunted by evil thoughts, and feelings such as I never knew before are brooding in my soul. I am full of hatred, and contempt, and indignation, and loathing, and dread. I have become excessively severe, exacting, irritable, ungracious, suspicious. Even things that in old days would have provoked me only to an unnecessary jest and a good-natured laugh now arouse an oppressive feeling in me. My reasoning, too, has undergone a change: in old days I despised money; now I harbour an evil feeling, not towards money, but towards the rich, as though they were to blame: in old days I hated violence and tyranny, but now I hate the men who make use of violence, as though they were alone to blame, and not all of us who do not know how to educate each other. What is the meaning of it? If these new ideas and new feelings have come from a change of convictions, what is that change due to? Can the world have grown worse and I better, or was I blind before and indifferent? If this change is the result of a general decline of physical and intellectual powers – I am ill, you know, and every day I am losing weight – my position is pitiable; it means that my new ideas are morbid and abnormal; I ought to be ashamed of them and think them of no consequence. . . .'

'Illness has nothing to do with it,' Katya interrupts me; 'it's simply that your eyes are opened, that's all. You have seen what in old days, for some reason, you refused to see. To my thinking, what you ought to do, first of all, is to break with your family for good, and go away.'

'You are talking nonsense.'

'You don't love them; why should you force your feelings? Can you call them a family? Nonentities! If they died to-day, no one would notice their absence to-morrow.'

Katya despises my wife and Liza as much as they hate her. One can hardly talk at this date of people's having a right to despise one another. But if one looks at it from Katya's standpoint and recognizes such a right, one can see she has as much right to despise my wife and Liza as they have to hate her.

'Nonentities,' she goes on. 'Have you had dinner to-day? How was it they did not forget to tell you it was ready? How is it they still remember your existence?'

'Katya,' I say sternly, 'I beg you to be silent.'

'You think I enjoy talking about them? I should be glad not to know them at all. Listen, my dear: give it all up and go away. Go abroad. The sooner the better.'

'What nonsense! What about the University?'

'The University, too. What is it to you? There's no sense in it, anyway. You have been lecturing for thirty years, and where are your pupils? Are many of them celebrated scientific men? Count them up! And to multiply the doctors who exploit ignorance and pile up hundreds of thousands for themselves, there is no need to be a good and talented man. You are not wanted.'

'Good heavens! how harsh you are!' I cry in horror. 'How harsh you are! Be quiet or I will go away! I don't know how to answer the harsh things you say!'

The maid comes in and summons us to tea. At the samovar our conversation, thank God, changes. After having had my grumble out, I have a longing to give way to another weakness of old age, reminiscences. I tell Katya about my past, and to my great astonishment tell her incidents which, till then, I did not suspect of being still preserved in my memory, and she listens to me with tenderness, with pride, holding her breath. I am particularly fond of telling her how I was educated in a seminary and dreamed of going to the University.

'At times I used to walk about our seminary garden...' I would tell her. 'If from some far-away tavern the wind floated sounds of a song and the squeaking of an accordion, or a sledge with bells dashed by the garden-fence, it was quite enough to send a rush of happiness, filling not only my heart, but even my stomach, my legs, my arms.... I would listen to the accordion or the bells dying away in the distance and imagine myself a doctor, and paint pictures, one better than another. And here, as you see, my dreams have come true. I have had more than I dared to dream of. For thirty years I have been the favourite professor, I have had splendid comrades, I have enjoyed fame and honour. I have loved, married from passionate love, have had children. In fact, looking back upon it, I see my whole life as a fine composition arranged with talent. Now all that is left to me is not to spoil the end. For that I must die like a man. If death is really a thing to dread, I must meet it as a teacher, a man of science, and a citizen of a Christian country ought to meet it, with courage and untroubled soul. But I am spoiling the end; I am sinking, I fly to you, I beg for help, and you tell me "Sink; that is what you ought to do."'

But here there comes a ring at the front-door. Katya and I recognize it, and say:

'It must be Mihail Fyodorovitch.'

And a minute later my colleague, the philologist

Mihail Fyodorovitch, a tall, well-built man of fifty, clean-shaven, with thick grey hair and black eyebrows, walks in. He is a good-natured man and an excellent comrade. He comes of a fortunate and talented old noble family which has played a prominent part in the history of literature and enlightenment. He is himself intelligent, talented, and very highly educated, but has his oddities. To a certain extent we are all odd and all queer fish, but in his oddities there is something exceptional, apt to cause anxiety among his acquaintances. I know a good many people for whom his oddities completely obscure his good qualities.

Coming in to us, he slowly takes off his gloves and says in his velvety bass:

'Good-evening. Are you having tea? That's just right. It's diabolically cold.'

Then he sits down to the table, takes a glass, and at once begins talking. What is most characteristic in his manner of talking is the continually jesting tone, a sort of mixture of philosophy and drollery as in Shakespeare's gravediggers. He is always talking about serious things, but he never speaks seriously. His judgments are always harsh and railing, but, thanks to his soft, even, jesting tone, the harshness and abuse do not jar upon the ear, and one soon grows used to them. Every evening he brings with him some five or six anecdotes from the University, and he usually begins with them when he sits down to table.

'Oh, Lord!' he sighs, twitching his black eyebrows ironically. 'What comic people there are in the world!'

'Well?' asks Katya.

'As I was coming from my lecture this morning I met that old idiot N. N— on the stairs.... He was going along as usual, sticking out his chin like a horse, looking for someone to listen to his grumblings at his migraine, at his wife, and his students who won't attend his lectures. "Oh," I thought, "he has seen me – I am done for now; it is all up...." '

And so on in the same style. Or he will begin like this:

'I was yesterday at our friend Z. Z—'s public lecture. I wonder how it is our alma mater – don't speak of it after dark – dare display in public such noodles and patent dullards as that Z. Z—. Why, he is a European fool! Upon my word, you could not find another like him all over Europe! He lectures – can you imagine? – as though he were sucking a sugar-stick – sue, sue, sue;... he is in a nervous funk; he can hardly decipher his own manuscript; his poor little thoughts crawl along like a bishop on a bicycle, and, what's worse, you can never make out what he is trying to say. The deadly dulness is awful, the very flies expire. It can only be compared with the boredom in the assembly-hall at the yearly meeting when the traditional address is read – damn it!'

And at once an abrupt transition:

'Three years ago – Nikolay Stepanovitch here will remember it – I had to deliver that address. It was hot, stifling, my uniform cut me under the arms – it was deadly! I read for half an hour, for an hour, for an hour and a half, for two hours.... "Come," I thought; "thank God, there are only ten pages left!" And at the end there were four pages that there was no need to read, and I reckoned to leave them out. "So there are only six really," I thought; "that is, only six pages left to read." But, only fancy, I chanced to glance before me, and, sitting in the front row, side by side, were a general with a ribbon on his breast and a bishop. The poor beggars were numb with boredom; they were staring with their eyes wide open to keep awake, and yet they were trying to put on an expression of attention and to pretend that they understood what I was saying and liked it. "Well," I thought, "since you like it you shall have it! I'll pay you out"; so I just gave them those four pages too.'

As is usual with ironical people, when he talks nothing in his face smiles but his eyes and eyebrows. At such times there is no trace of hatred or spite in his eyes, but a great deal of humour, and that peculiar fox-like slyness which is only to be noticed in very observant people. Since I am speaking about his eyes, I notice another peculiarity in them. When he takes a glass from Katya, or listens to her speaking, or looks after her as she goes out of the room for a moment, I notice in his eyes something gentle, beseeching, pure....

The maid-servant takes away the samovar and puts on the table a large piece of cheese, some fruit, and a bottle of Crimean champagne – a rather poor wine of which Katya had grown fond in the Crimea. Mihail Fyodorovitch takes two packs of cards off the whatnot and begins to play patience. According to him, some varieties of patience require great concentration and attention, yet while he lays out the cards he does not leave off distracting his attention with talk. Katya watches his cards attentively, and more by gesture than by words helps him in his play. She drinks no more than a couple of wine-glasses of wine the whole evening; I drink four glasses, and the rest of the bottle falls to the share of Mihail Fyodorovitch, who can drink a great deal and never get drunk.

Over our patience we settle various questions, principally of the higher order, and what we care for most of all – that is, science and learning – is more roughly handled than anything.

'Science, thank God, has outlived its day,' says Mihail Fyodorovitch emphatically. 'Its song is sung. Yes, indeed. Mankind begins to feel impelled to replace it by something different. It has grown on the soil of superstition, been nourished by superstition, and is now just as much the quintessence of superstition as its defunct granddames, alchemy, metaphysics, and philosophy. And, after all, what has it given to mankind? Why, the difference between the learned Europeans and the Chinese who have no science is trifling, purely external. The Chinese know nothing of science, but what have they lost thereby?'

'Flies know nothing of science, either,' I observe, 'but what of that?'

'There is no need to be angry, Nikolay Stepanovitch. I only say this here between ourselves. . . . I am more careful than you think, and I am not going to say this in public – God forbid! The superstition exists in the multitude that the arts and sciences are superior to agriculture, commerce, superior to handicrafts. Our sect is maintained by that superstition, and it is not for you and me to destroy it. God forbid!'

After patience the younger generation comes in for a dressing too.

'Our audiences have degenerated,' sighs Mihail Fyodorovitch. 'Not to speak of ideals and all the rest of it, if only they were capable of work and rational thought! In fact, it's a case of "I look with mournful eyes on the young men of to-day." '

'Yes; they have degenerated horribly,' Katya agrees. 'Tell me, have you had one man of distinction among them for the last five or ten years?'

'I don't know how it is with the other professors, but I can't remember any among mine.'

'I have seen in my day many of your students and young scientific men and many actors – well, I have never once been so fortunate as to meet – I won't say a hero or a man of talent, but even an interesting man. It's all the same grey mediocrity, puffed up with self-conceit.'

All this talk of degeneration always affects me as though I had accidentally overheard offensive talk about my own daughter. It offends me that these charges are wholesale, and rest on such worn-out commonplaces, on such wordy vapourings as degeneration and absence of ideals, or on references to the splendours of the past. Every accusation, even if it is uttered in ladies' society, ought to be formulated with all possible definiteness, or it is not an accusation, but idle disparagement, unworthy of decent people.

I am an old man, I have been lecturing for thirty years, but I notice neither degeneration nor lack of ideals, and I don't find that the present is worse than the past. My porter Nikolay, whose experience of this subject has its value, says that the students of to-day are neither better nor worse than those of the past.

If I were asked what I don't like in my pupils of to-day, I should answer the question, not straight off and not at length, but with sufficient definiteness. I know their failings, and so have no need to resort to vague generalities. I don't like their smoking, using spirituous beverages, marrying late, and often being so irresponsible and careless that they will let one of their number be starving in their midst while they neglect to pay their subscriptions to the Students' Aid Society. They don't know modern languages, and they don't express themselves correctly in Russian; no longer ago than yesterday my colleague, the professor of hygiene, complained to me that he had to give twice as many lectures, because the students had a very poor knowledge of physics and were utterly ignorant of meteorology. They are readily carried away by the influence of the last new writers, even when they are not first-rate, but they take absolutely no interest in classics such as Shakespeare, Marcus Aurelius, Epictetus, or Pascal, and this inability to distinguish the great from the small betrays their ignorance of practical life more than anything. All difficult questions that have more or less a social character (for instance the migration question) they settle by studying monographs on the subject, but not by way of scientific investigation or experiment, though that method is at their disposal and is more in keeping with their calling. They gladly become ward-surgeons, assistants, demonstrators, external teachers, and are ready to fill such posts till they are forty, though independence, a sense of freedom and personal initiative, are no less necessary in science than, for instance, in art or commerce. I have pupils and listeners, but no successors and helpers, and so I love them and am touched by them, but am not proud of them. And so on, and so on....

Such shortcomings, however numerous they may be, can only give rise to a pessimistic or fault-finding temper in a faint-hearted and timid man. All these failings have a casual, transitory character, and are completely dependent on conditions of life; in some ten years they will have disappeared or given place to other fresh defects, which are all inevitable and will in their turn alarm the faint-hearted. The students' sins often vex me, but that vexation is nothing in comparison with the joy I have been experiencing now for the last thirty years when I talk to my pupils, lecture to them, watch their relations, and compare them with people not of their circle.

Mihail Fyodorovitch speaks evil of everything. Katya listens, and neither of them notices into what depths the apparently innocent diversion of finding fault with their neighbours is gradually drawing them. They are not conscious how by degrees simple talk passes into malicious mockery and jeering, and how they are both beginning to drop into the habits and methods of slander.

'Killing types one meets with,' says Mihail Fyodorovitch. 'I went yesterday to our friend Yegor Petrovitch's, and there I found a studious gentleman, one of your medicals in his third year, I believe. Such a face!... in the Dobrolubov style, the imprint of profound thought on his brow; we got into talk. "Such doings, young man," said I. "I've read," said I, "that some German – I've forgotten his name – has created from the human brain a new kind of alkaloid, idiotine." What do you think? He believed it, and there was positively an expression of respect on his face, as though to say, "See what we fellows can do!" And the other day I went to the theatre. I took my seat. In the next row directly in front of me were sitting two men: one of "us fellows" and apparently a law student, the other a shaggy-looking figure, a medical student. The latter was as drunk as a cobbler. He did not look at the stage at all. He was dozing with his nose on his shirt-front. But as soon as an actor begins loudly reciting a monologue, or simply raises his voice, our friend starts, pokes his neighbour in the ribs, and asks, "What is he saying? Is it elevating?" "Yes," answers one of our fellows. "B-r-r-ravo!" roars the medical student. "Elevating! Bravo!" He had gone to the theatre, you see, the drunken blockhead, not for the sake of art, the play, but for elevation! He wanted noble sentiments.'

Katya listens and laughs. She has a strange laugh; she catches her breath in rhythmically regular gasps, very much as though she were playing the accordion, and nothing in her face is laughing but her nostrils. I grow depressed and don't know what to say. Beside myself, I fire up, leap up from my seat, and cry:

'Do leave off! Why are you sitting here like two toads, poisoning the air with your breath? Give over!'

And without waiting for them to finish their gossip I prepare to go home. And, indeed, it is high time: it is past ten.

'I will stay a little longer' says Mihail Fyodorovitch. 'Will you allow me, Ekaterina Vladimirovna?'

'I will,' answers Katya.

'*Bene!* In that case have up another little bottle.'

They both accompany me with candles to the hall, and while I put on my fur coat, Mihail Fyodorovitch says:

'You have grown dreadfully thin and older looking, Nikolay Stepanovitch. What's the matter with you? Are you ill?'

'Yes; I am not very well.'

'And you are not doing anything for it...' Katya puts in grimly.

'Why don't you? You can't go on like that! God helps those who help themselves, my dear fellow. Remember me to your wife and daughter, and make my apologies for not having been to see them. In a day or two, before I go abroad, I shall come to say good-bye. I shall be sure to. I am going away next week.'

I come away from Katya, irritated and alarmed by what has been said about my being ill, and dissatisfied with myself. I ask myself whether I really ought not to consult one of my colleagues. And at once I imagine how my colleague, after listening to me, would walk away to the window without speaking, would think a moment, then would turn round to me and, trying to prevent my reading the truth in his face, would say in a careless tone: 'So far I see nothing serious, but at the same time, *collega*, I advise you to lay aside your work....' And that would deprive me of my last hope.

Who is without hope? Now that I am diagnosing my illness and prescribing for myself, from time to time I hope that I am deceived by my own illness, that I am mistaken in regard to the albumen and the sugar I find, and in regard to my heart, and in regard to the swellings I have twice noticed in the mornings; when with the fervour of the hypochondriac I look through the textbooks of therapeutics and take a different medicine every day, I keep fancying that I shall hit upon something comforting. All that is petty.

Whether the sky is covered with clouds or the moon and the stars are shining, I turn my eyes towards it every evening and think that death is taking me soon. One would think that my thoughts at such times ought to be deep as the sky, brilliant, striking.... But no! I think about myself, about my wife, about Liza, Gnekker, the students, people in general; my thoughts are evil, petty, I am insincere with myself, and at such times my theory of life may be expressed in the words the celebrated Araktcheev said in one of his intimate letters: 'Nothing good can exist in the world without evil, and there is more evil than good.' That is, everything is disgusting; there is nothing to live for, and the sixty-two years I have already lived must be reckoned as wasted. I catch myself in these thoughts, and try to persuade myself that they are accidental, temporary, and not deeply rooted in me, but at once I think:

'If so, what drives me every evening to those two toads?'

And I vow to myself that I will never go to Katya's again, though I know I shall go next evening.

Ringing the bell at the door and going upstairs, I feel that I have no family now and no desire to bring it back again. It is clear that the new Araktcheev thoughts are not casual, temporary visitors, but have possession of my whole being. With my conscience ill at ease, dejected, languid, hardly able to move my limbs, feeling as though tons were added to my weight, I get into bed and quickly drop asleep.

And then – insomnia!

IV

SUMMER comes on and life is changed.

One fine morning Liza comes in to me and says in a jesting tone:

'Come, your Excellency! We are ready.'

My Excellency is conducted into the street, and seated in a cab. As I go along, having nothing to do, I read the signboards from right to left. The word 'Traktir' reads 'Ritkart'; that would just suit some baron's family: Baroness Ritkart. Farther on I drive through fields, by the graveyard, which makes absolutely no impression on me, though I shall soon lie in it; then I drive by forests and again by fields. There is nothing of interest. After two hours of driving, my Excellency is conducted into the lower storey of a summer villa and installed in a small, very cheerful little room with light blue hangings.

At night there is sleeplessness as before, but in the morning I do not put a good face upon it and listen to my wife, but lie in bed. I do not sleep, but lie in the drowsy, half-conscious condition in which you know you are not asleep, but dreaming. At midday I get up and from habit sit down at my table, but I do not work now; I amuse myself with French books in yellow covers, sent me by Katya. Of course, it would be more patriotic to read Russian authors, but I must confess I cherish no particular liking for them. With the exception of two or three of the older writers, all our literature of to-day strikes me as not being literature, but a special sort of home industry, which exists simply in order to be encouraged, though people do not readily make use of its products. The very best of these home products cannot be called remarkable and cannot be sincerely praised without qualification. I must say the same of all the literary novelties I have read during the last ten or fifteen years; not one of them is remarkable, and not one of them can be praised without a 'but'. Cleverness, a good tone, but no talent; talent, a good tone, but no cleverness; or talent, cleverness, but not a good tone.

I don't say the French books have talent, cleverness, and a good tone. They don't satisfy me, either. But they are not so tedious as the Russian, and it is not unusual to find in them the chief element of artistic creation – the feeling of personal freedom which is lacking in the Russian authors. I don't remember one new book in which the author does not try from the first page to entangle himself in all sorts of conditions and contracts with his conscience. One is afraid to speak of the naked body; another ties himself up hand and foot in psychological analysis; a third must have a 'warm attitude to man'; a fourth purposely scrawls whole descriptions of nature that he may not be suspected of writing with a purpose.... One is bent upon being middle-class in his work, another must be a nobleman, and so on. There is intentionalness, circumspection, and self-will, but they have neither the independence nor the manliness to write as they like, and therefore there is no creativeness.

All this applies to what is called belles-lettres.

As for serious treatises in Russian on sociology, for instance, on art, and so on, I do not read them simply from timidity. In my childhood and early youth I had for some reason a terror of doorkeepers and attendants at the theatre, and that terror has remained with me to this day. I am afraid of them even now. It is said that we are only afraid of what we do not understand. And, indeed, it is very difficult to understand why doorkeepers and theatre attendants are so dignified, haughty, and majestically rude. I feel exactly the same terror when I read serious articles. Their extraordinary dignity, their bantering lordly tone, their familiar manner to foreign authors, their ability to split straws with dignity – all that is beyond my understanding; it is intimidating and utterly unlike the quiet, gentlemanly tone to which I am accustomed when I read the works of our medical and scientific writers. It oppresses me to read not only the articles written by serious Russians, but even works translated or edited by them. The pretentious, edifying tone of the preface; the redundancy of remarks made by the translator, which prevent me from concentrating my attention; the question marks and 'sic' in parenthesis scattered all over the book or article by the liberal translator, are to my mind an outrage on the author and on my independence as a reader.

Once I was summoned as an expert to a circuit court; in an interval one of my fellow-experts drew my attention to the rudeness of the public prosecutor to the defendants, among whom there were two ladies of good education. I believe I did not exaggerate at all when I told him that the prosecutor's manner was no ruder than that of the authors of serious articles to one another. Their manners are, indeed, so rude that I cannot speak of them without distaste. They treat one another and the writers they criticize either with superfluous respect, at the sacrifice of their own dignity, or, on the contrary, with far more ruthlessness than I have shown in my notes and my thoughts in regard to my future son-in-law Gnekker. Accusations of irrationality, of evil intentions, and, indeed, of every sort of crime, form an habitual ornament of serious articles. And that, as young medical men are fond of saying in their monographs, is the *ultima ratio*! Such ways must infallibly have an effect on the morals of the younger generation of writers, and so I am not at all surprised that in the new works with which our literature has been enriched during the last ten or fifteen years the heroes drink too much vodka and the heroines are not over-chaste.

I read French books, and I look out of the window which is open; I can see the spikes of my garden-fence, two or three scraggy trees, and beyond the fence the road, the fields, and beyond them a broad stretch of pine-wood. Often I admire a boy and girl, both flaxen-headed and ragged, who clamber on the fence and laugh at my baldness. In their shining little eyes I read, 'Go up, go up, thou baldhead!' They are almost the only people who care nothing for my celebrity or my rank.

Visitors do not come to me every day now. I will only mention the visits of Nikolay and Pyotr Ignatyevitch. Nikolay usually comes to me on holidays, with some pretext of business, though really to see me. He arrives very much exhilarated, a thing which never occurs to him in the winter.

'What have you to tell me?' I ask, going out to him in the hall.

'Your Excellency!' he says, pressing his hand to his heart and looking at me with the ecstasy of a lover – 'your Excellency! God be my witness! Strike me dead on the spot! *Gaudeamus egitur juventus!*'

And he greedily kisses me on the shoulder, on the sleeve, and on the buttons.

'Is everything going well?' I ask him.

'Your Excellency! So help me God! . . .'

He persists in grovelling before me for no sort of reason, and soon bores me, so I send him away to the kitchen, where they give him dinner.

Pyotr Ignatyevitch comes to see me on holidays, too, with the special object of seeing me and sharing his thoughts with me. He usually sits down near my table, modest, neat, and reasonable, and does not venture to cross his legs or put his elbows on the table. All the time, in a soft, even, little voice, in rounded bookish phrases, he tells me various, to his mind, very interesting and piquant items of news which he has read in the magazines and journals. They are all alike and may be reduced to this type: 'A Frenchman has made a discovery; someone else, a German, has denounced him, proving that the discovery was made in 1870 by some American; while a third person, also a German, trumps them both by proving they both had made fools of themselves, mistaking bubbles of air for dark pigment under the microscope. Even when he wants to amuse me, Pyotr Ignatyevitch tells me things in the same lengthy, circumstantial manner as though he were defending a thesis, enumerating in detail the literary sources from which he is deriving his narrative, doing his utmost to be accurate as to the date and number of the journals and the name of everyone concerned, invariably mentioning it in full – Jean Jacques Petit, never simply Petit. Sometimes he stays to dinner with us, and then during the whole of dinner-time he goes on telling me the same sort of piquant anecdotes, reducing everyone at table to a state of dejected boredom. If Gnekker and Liza begin talking before him of fugues and counterpoint, Brahms and Bach, he drops his eyes modestly, and is overcome with embarrassment; he is ashamed that such trivial subjects should be discussed before such serious people as him and me.

In my present state of mind five minutes of him is enough to sicken me as though I had been seeing and hearing him for an eternity. I hate the poor fellow. His soft, smooth voice and bookish language exhaust me, and his stories stupefy me.... He cherishes the best of feelings for me, and talks to me simply in order to give me pleasure, and I repay him by looking at him as though I wanted to hypnotize him, and think, 'Go, go, go!...' But he is not amenable to thought-suggestion, and sits on and on and on....

While he is with me I can never shake off the thought, 'It's possible when I die he will be appointed to succeed me', and my poor lecture-hall presents itself to me as an oasis in which the spring is dried up; and I am ungracious, silent, and surly with Pyotr Ignatyevitch, as though he were to blame for such thoughts, and not I myself. When he begins, as usual, praising up the German savants, instead of making fun of him good-humouredly, as I used to do, I mutter sullenly:

'Asses, your Germans! . . .'

That is like the late Professor Nikita Krylov, who once, when he was bathing with Pirogov at Revel and vexed at the water being very cold, burst out with, 'Scoundrels, these Germans!' I behave badly with Pyotr Ignatyevitch, and only when he is going away, and from the window I catch a glimpse of his grey hat behind the garden-fence, I want to call out and say, 'Forgive me, my dear fellow!'

Dinner is even drearier than in the winter. Gnekker, whom now I hate and despise, dines with us almost every day. I used to endure his presence in silence, now I aim biting remarks at him which make my wife and daughter blush. Carried away by evil feeling, I often say things that are simply stupid, and I don't know why I say them. So on one occasion it happened that I stared a long time at Gnekker, and, *à propos* of nothing, I fired off:

'An eagle may perchance swoop down below a cock,
But never will the fowl soar upwards to the clouds. . . .'

And the most vexatious thing is that the fowl Gnekker shows himself much cleverer than the eagle professor. Knowing that my wife and daughter are on his side, he takes up the line of meeting my gibes with condescending silence, as though to say:

'The old chap is in his dotage; what's the use of talking to him?'

Or he makes fun of me good-naturedly. It is wonderful how petty a man may become! I am capable of dreaming all dinner-time of how Gnekker will turn out to be an adventurer, how my wife and Liza will come to see their mistake, and how I will taunt them

– and such absurd thoughts at the time when I am standing with one foot in the grave!

There are now, too, misunderstandings of which in the old days I had no idea except from hearsay. Though I am ashamed of it, I will describe one that occurred the other day after dinner.

I was sitting in my room smoking a pipe; my wife came in as usual, sat down, and began saying what a good thing it would be for me to go to Harkov now while it is warm and I have free time, and there find out what sort of person our Gnekker is.

'Very good; I will go,' I assented.

My wife, pleased with me, got up and was going to the door, but turned back and said:

'By the way, I have another favour to ask of you. I know you will be angry, but it is my duty to warn you. . . . Forgive my saying it, Nikolay Stepanovitch, but all our neighbours and acquaintances have begun talking about your being so often at Katya's. She is clever and well-educated; I don't deny that her company may be agreeable; but at your age and with your social position it seems strange that you should find pleasure in her society. . . . Besides, she has such a reputation that . . . .'

All the blood suddenly rushed to my brain, my eyes flashed fire, I leaped up and, clutching at my head and stamping my feet, shouted in a voice unlike my own:

'Let me alone! let me alone! let me alone!'

Probably my face was terrible, my voice was strange, for my wife suddenly turned pale and began shrieking aloud in a despairing voice that was utterly unlike her own. Liza, Gnekker, then Yegor, came running in at our shouts....

'Let me alone!' I cried; 'let me alone! Go away!'

My legs turned numb as though they had ceased to exist; I felt myself falling into someone's arms; for a little while I still heard weeping, then sank into a swoon which lasted two or three hours.

Now about Katya; she comes to see me every day towards evening, and of course neither the neighbours nor our acquaintances can avoid noticing it. She comes in for a minute and carries me off for a drive with her. She has her own horse and a new chaise bought this summer. Altogether she lives in an expensive style; she has taken a big detached villa with a large garden, and has brought all her town retinue with her – two maids, a coachman.... I often ask her:

'Katya, what will you live on when you have spent your father's money?'

'Then we shall see,' she answers.

'That money, my dear, deserves to be treated more seriously. It was earned by a good man, by honest labour.'

'You have told me that already. I know it.'

At first we drive through the open country, then through the pine-wood which is visible from my window. Nature seems to me as beautiful as it always has been, though some evil spirit whispers to me that these pines and fir trees, birds, and white clouds on the sky, will not notice my absence when in three or four months I am dead. Katya loves driving, and she is pleased that it is fine weather and that I am sitting beside her. She is in good spirits and does not say harsh things.

'You are a very good man, Nikolay Stepanovitch,' she says. 'You are a rare specimen, and there isn't an actor who would understand how to play you. Me or Mihail Fyodorovitch, for instance, any poor actor could do, but not you. And I envy you, I envy you horribly! Do you know what I stand for? What?'

She ponders for a minute, and then asks me:

'Nikolay Stepanovitch, I am a negative phenomenon! Yes?'

'Yes,' I answer.

'H'm! what am I to do?'

What answer was I to make her? It is easy to say 'work', or 'give your possessions to the poor', or 'know yourself', and because it is so easy to say that, I don't know what to answer.

My colleagues when they teach therapeutics advise 'the individual study of each separate case'. One has but to obey this advice to gain the conviction that the methods recommended in the textbooks as the best and as providing a safe basis for treatment turn out to be quite unsuitable in individual cases. It is just the same in moral ailments.

But I must make some answer, and I say:

'You have too much free time, my dear; you absolutely must take up some occupation. After all, why shouldn't you be an actress again if it is your vocation?'

'I cannot!'

'Your tone and manner suggest that you are a victim. I don't like that, my dear; it is your own fault. Remember, you began with falling out with people and methods, but you have done nothing to make either better. You did not struggle with evil, but were cast down by it, and you are not the victim of the struggle, but of your own impotence. Well, of course you were young and inexperienced then; now it may all be different. Yes, really, go on the stage. You will work, you will serve a sacred art.'

'Don't pretend, Nikolay Stepanovitch,' Katya interrupts me. 'Let us make a compact once for all; we will talk about actors, actresses, and authors, but we will let art alone. You are a splendid and rare person, but you don't know enough about art sincerely to think it sacred. You have no instinct or feeling for art. You have been hard at work all your life, and have not had time to acquire that feeling. Altogether . . . I don't like talk about art,' she goes on nervously. 'I don't like it! And, my goodness, how they have vulgarized it!'

'Who has vulgarized it?'

'They have vulgarized it by drunkenness, the newspapers by their familiar attitude, clever people by philosophy.'

'Philosophy has nothing to do with it.'

'Yes, it has. If anyone philosophizes about it, it shows he does not understand it.'

To avoid bitterness I hasten to change the subject, and then sit a long time silent. Only when we are driving out of the wood and turning towards Katya's villa I go back to my former question, and say:

'You have still not answered me, why you don't want to go on the stage.'

'Nikolay Stepanovitch, this is cruel!' she cries, and suddenly flushes all over. 'You want me to tell you the truth aloud? Very well, if . . . if you like it! I have no talent! No talent and . . . and a great deal of vanity! So there!'

After making this confession she turns her face away from me, and to hide the trembling of her hands tugs violently at the reins.

As we are driving towards her villa we see Mihail Fyodorovitch walking near the gate, impatiently awaiting us.

'That Mihail Fyodorovitch again!' says Katya with vexation. 'Do rid me of him, please! I am sick and tired of him... bother him!'

Mihail Fyodorovitch ought to have gone abroad long ago, but he puts off going from week to week. Of late there have been certain changes in him. He looks, as it were, sunken, has taken to drinking until he is tipsy, a thing which never used to happen to him, and his black eyebrows are beginning to turn grey. When our chaise stops at the gate he does not conceal his joy and his impatience. He fussily helps me and Katya out, hurriedly asks questions, laughs, rubs his hands, and that gentle, imploring, pure expression, which I used to notice only in his eyes, is now suffused all over his face. He is glad and at the same time he is ashamed of his gladness, ashamed of his habit of spending every evening with Katya. And he thinks it necessary to explain his visit by some obvious absurdity such as: 'I was driving by, and I thought I would just look in for a minute.'

We all three go indoors; first we drink tea, then the familiar packs of cards, the big piece of cheese, the fruit, and the bottle of Crimean champagne are put upon the table. The subjects of our conversation are not new; they are just the same as in the winter. We fall foul of the University, the students, and literature and the theatre; the air grows thick and stifling with evil speaking, and poisoned by the breath, not of two toads as in the winter, but of three. Besides the velvety baritone laugh and the giggle like the gasp of a concertina, the maid who waits upon us hears an unpleasant cracked 'He, he!' like the chuckle of a general in a vaudeville.

V

THERE are terrible nights with thunder, lightning, rain, and wind, such as are called among the people 'sparrow nights'. There has been one such night in my personal life....

I woke up after midnight and leaped suddenly out of bed. It seemed to me for some reason that I was just immediately going to die. Why did it seem so? I had no sensation in my body that suggested my immediate death, but my soul was oppressed with terror, as though I had suddenly seen a vast menacing glow of fire.

I rapidly struck a light, drank some water straight out of the decanter, then hurried to the open window. The weather outside was magnificent. There was a smell of hay and some other very sweet scent. I could see the spikes of the fence, the gaunt, drowsy trees by the window, the road, the dark streak of woodland; there was a serene, very bright moon in the sky and not a single cloud, perfect stillness, not one leaf stirring. I felt that everything was looking at me and waiting for me to die....

It was uncanny. I closed the window and ran to my bed. I felt for my pulse, and not finding it in my wrist, tried to find it in my temple, then in my chin, and again in my wrist, and everything I touched was cold and clammy with sweat. My breathing came more and more rapidly, my body was shivering, all my inside was in commotion; I had a sensation on my face and on my bald head as though they were covered with spiders' webs.

What should I do? Call my family? No; it would be no use. I could not imagine what my wife and Liza would do when they came in to me.

I hid my head under the pillow, closed my eyes, and waited and waited.... My spine was cold; it seemed to be drawn inwards, and I felt as though death were coming upon me stealthily from behind....

'Kee-vee! kee-vee!' I heard a sudden shriek in the night's stillness, and did not know where it was – in my breast or in the street. 'Kee-vee! kee-vee!'

'My God, how terrible!' I would have drunk some more water, but by then I was fearful to open my eyes and I was afraid to raise my head. I was possessed by unaccountable animal terror, and I cannot understand why I was so frightened: was it that I wanted to live, or that some new unknown pain was in store for me?

Upstairs, overhead, someone moaned or laughed.... I listened. Soon afterwards there was a sound of footsteps on the stairs. Someone came hurriedly down, then went up again. A minute later there was a sound of steps downstairs again; someone stopped near my door and listened.

'Who is there?' I cried.

The door opened. I boldly opened my eyes, and saw my wife. Her face was pale and her eyes were tear-stained.

'You are not asleep, Nikolay Stepanovitch?' she asked.

'What is it?'

'For God's sake, go up and have a look at Liza; there is something the matter with her. . . .'

'Very good, with pleasure,' I muttered, greatly relieved at not being alone. 'Very good, this minute. . . .'

I followed my wife, heard what she said to me, and was too agitated to understand a word. Patches of light from her candle danced about the stairs, our long shadows trembled. My feet caught in the skirts of my dressing-gown; I gasped for breath, and felt as though something were pursuing me and trying to catch me from behind.

'I shall die on the spot, here on the staircase,' I thought. 'On the spot. . . .' But we passed the staircase, the dark corridor with the Italian windows, and went into Liza's room. She was sitting on the bed in her nightdress, with her bare feet hanging down, and she was moaning.

'Oh, my God! Oh, my God!' she was muttering, screwing up her eyes at our candle. 'I can't bear it.'

'Liza, my child,' I said, 'what is it?'

Seeing me, she began crying out, and flung herself on my neck.

'My kind papa! . . .' she sobbed – 'my dear, good papa . . . my darling, my pet, I don't know what is the matter with me. . . . I am miserable!'

She hugged me, kissed me, and babbled fond words I used to hear from her when she was a child.

'Calm yourself, my child. God be with you,' I said. 'There is no need to cry. I am miserable, too.'

I tried to tuck her in; my wife gave her water, and we awkwardly stumbled by her bedside; my shoulder jostled against her shoulder, and meanwhile I was thinking how we used to give our children their bath together.

'Help her! help her!' my wife implored me. 'Do something!'

What could I do? I could do nothing. There was some load on the girl's heart; but I did not understand, I knew nothing about it, and could only mutter:

'It's nothing, it's nothing; it will pass. Sleep, sleep!'

To make things worse, there was a sudden sound of dogs howling, at first subdued and uncertain, then loud, two dogs howling together. I had never attached significance to such omens as the howling of dogs or the shrieking of owls, but on that occasion it sent a pang to my heart, and I hastened to explain the howl to myself.

'It's nonsense,' I thought, 'the influence of one organism on another. The intensely strained condition of my nerves has infected my wife, Liza, the dog – that is all.... Such infection explains presentiments, forebodings....'

When a little later I went back to my room to write a prescription for Liza, I no longer thought I should die at once, but only had such a weight, such a feeling of oppression in my soul that I felt actually sorry that I had not died on the spot. For a long time I stood motionless in the middle of the room, pondering what to prescribe for Liza. But the moans overhead ceased, and I decided to prescribe nothing, and yet I went on standing there....

There was a deathlike stillness, such a stillness, as some author has expressed it, 'it rang in one's ears'. Time passed slowly; the streaks of moonlight on the window-sill did not shift their position, but seemed as though frozen.... It was still some time before dawn.

But the gate in the fence creaked, someone stole in and, breaking a twig from one of those scraggy trees, cautiously tapped on the window with it.

'Nikolay Stepanovitch,' I heard a whisper. 'Nikolay Stepanovitch.'

I opened the window, and fancied I was dreaming: under the window, huddled against the wall, stood a woman in a black dress, with the moonlight bright upon her, looking at me with great eyes. Her face was pale, stern, and weird-looking in the moonlight, like marble, her chin was quivering.

'It is I,' she said – 'I... Katya.'

In the moonlight all women's eyes look big and black, all people look taller and paler, and that was probably why I had not recognized her for the first minute.

'What is it?'

'Forgive me!' she said. 'I suddenly felt unbearably miserable... I couldn't stand it, so came here. There was a light in your window and... and I ventured to knock.... I beg your pardon.... Ah! if you knew how miserable I am! What are you doing just now?'

'Nothing.... I can't sleep.'

'I had a feeling that there was something wrong, but that is nonsense.'

Her brows were lifted, her eyes shone with tears, and her whole face was lighted up with the familiar look of trustfulness which I had not seen for so long.

'Nikolay Stepanovitch,' she said imploringly, stretching out both hands to me, 'my precious friend, I beg you, I implore you.... If you don't despise my affection and respect for you, consent to what I ask of you.'

'What is it?'

'Take my money from me!'

'Come! what an idea! What do I want with your money?'

'You'll go away somewhere for your health.... You ought to go for your health. Will you take if? Yes? Nikolay Stepanovitch darling, yes?'

She looked greedily into my face and repeated: 'Yes, you will take it?'

'No, my dear, I won't take it...' I said. 'Thank you.'

She turned her back upon me and bowed her head. Probably I refused her in a tone which made further conversation about money impossible.

'Go home to bed,' I said. 'We will see each other to-morrow.'

'So you don't consider me your friend?' she asked dejectedly.

'I don't say that. But your money would be no use to me now.'

'I beg your pardon...' she said, dropping her voice a whole octave. 'I understand you... to be indebted to a person like me... a retired actress.... But, good-bye....'

And she went away so quickly that I had not time even to say good-bye.

VI

I AM in Harkov.

As it would be useless to contend against my present mood and, indeed, beyond my power, I have made up my mind that the last days of my life shall at least be irreproachable externally. If I am unjust in regard to my wife and daughter, which I fully recognize, I will try and do as she wishes; since she wants me to go to Harkov, I go to Harkov. Besides, I have become of late so indifferent to everything that it is really all the same to me where I go, to Harkov, or to Paris, or to Berditchev.

I arrived here at midday, and have put up at the hotel not far from the cathedral. The train was jolting, there were draughts, and now I am sitting on my bed, holding my head and expecting tic douloureux. I ought to have gone to-day to see some professors of my acquaintance, but I have neither strength nor inclination.

The old corridor attendant comes in and asks whether I have brought my bed-linen. I detain him for five minutes, and put several questions to him about Gnekker, on whose account I have come here. The attendant turns out to be a native of Harkov; he knows the town like the fingers of his hand, but does not remember any household of the surname of Gnekker. I question him about the estate – the same answer.

The clock in the corridor strikes one, then two, then three.... These last months in which I am waiting for death seem much longer than the whole of my life. And I have never before been so ready to resign myself to the slowness of time as now. In the old days, when one sat in the station and waited for a train, or presided in an examination-room, a quarter of an hour would seem an eternity. Now I can sit all night on my bed without moving, and quite unconcernedly reflect that to-morrow will be followed by another night as long and colourless, and the day after to-morrow.

In the corridor it strikes five, six, seven.... It grows dark.

There is a dull pain in my cheek, the tic beginning. To occupy myself with thoughts, I go back to my old point of view when I was not so indifferent and ask myself why I a distinguished man, a privy councillor, am sitting in this little hotel room on this bed with the unfamiliar grey quilt. Why am I looking at that cheap tin washing-stand and listening to the whirr of the wretched clock in the corridor? Is all this in keeping with my fame and my lofty position? And I answer these questions with a jeer. I am amused by the naïveté with which I used in my youth to exaggerate the value of renown and of the exceptional position which celebrities are supposed to enjoy. I am famous, my name is pronounced with reverence, my portrait has been both in the *Niva* and in the *Illustrated News of the World*; I have read my biography even in a German magazine. And what of all that? Here I am sitting utterly alone in a strange town, on a strange bed, rubbing my aching cheek with my hand.... Domestic worries, the hard-heartedness of creditors, the rudeness of the railway servants, the inconveniences of the passport system, the expensive and unwholesome food in the refreshment-rooms, the general rudeness and coarseness in social intercourse – all this, and a great ideal more which would take too long to reckon up, affects me as much as any working man who is famous only in his alley. In what way does my exceptional position find expression? Admitting that I am celebrated a thousand times over, that I am a hero of whom my country is proud. They publish bulletins of my illness in every paper, letters of sympathy come to me by post from my colleagues, my pupils, the general public; but all that does not prevent me from dying in a strange bed, in misery, in utter loneliness. Of course, no one is to blame for that; but I in my foolishness dislike my popularity, I feel as though it had cheated me.

At ten o'clock I fall asleep, and in spite of the tic I sleep soundly, and should have gone on sleeping if I had not been awakened. Soon after one came a sudden knock at the door.

'Who is there?'

'A telegram.'

'You might have waited till to-morrow,' I say angrily, taking the telegram from the attendant. 'Now I shall not get to sleep again.'

'I am sorry. Your light was burning, so I thought you were not asleep.'

I tear open the telegram and look first at the signature . . . From my wife.

'What does she want?'

'Gnekker was secretly married to Liza yesterday. Return.'

I read the telegram, and my dismay does not last long. I am dismayed, not by what Liza and Gnekker have done, but by the indifference with which I hear of their marriage. They say philosophers and the truly wise are indifferent. It is false: indifference is the paralysis of the soul; it is premature death.

I go to bed again, and begin trying to think of something to occupy my mind. What am I to think about? I feel as though everything had been thought over already and there is nothing which could hold my attention now.

When daylight comes I sit up in bed with my arms round my knees, and to pass the time I try to know myself. 'Know thyself' is excellent and useful advice; it is only a pity that the ancients never thought to indicate the means of following this precept.

When I have wanted to understand somebody or myself, I have considered, not the actions, in which everything is relative, but the desires.

'Tell me what you want, and I will tell you what manner of man you are.'

And now I examine myself: what do I want?

I want our wives, our children, our friends, our pupils, to love in us, not our fame, not the brand and not the label, but to love us as ordinary men. Anything else? I should like to have had helpers and successors. Anything else? I should like to wake up in a hundred years' time and to have just a peep out of one eye at what is happening in science. I should have liked to have lived another ten years.... What further? Why, nothing further. I think and think, and can think of nothing more. And however much I might think, and however far my thoughts might travel, it is clear to me that there is nothing vital, nothing of great importance in my desires. In my passion for science, in my desire to live, in this sitting on a strange bed, and in this striving to know myself – in all the thoughts, feelings, and ideas I form about everything, there is no common bond to connect it all into one whole. Every feeling and every thought exists apart in me; and in all my criticisms of science, the theatre, literature, my pupils, and in all the pictures my imagination draws, even the most skilful analyst could not find what is called a general idea, or the god of a living man.

And if there is not that, then there is nothing.

In a state so poverty-stricken, a serious ailment, the fear of death, the influences of circumstance and men were enough to turn upside down and scatter in fragments all which I had once looked upon as my theory of life, and in which I had seen the meaning and joy of my existence. So there is nothing surprising in the fact that I have over-shadowed the last months of my life with thoughts and feelings only worthy of a slave and barbarian, and that now I am indifferent and take no heed of the dawn. When a man has not in him what is loftier and mightier than all external impressions, a bad cold is really enough to upset his equilibrium and make him begin to see an owl in every bird, to hear a dog howling in every sound. And all his pessimism or optimism with his thoughts great and small have at such times significance as symptoms and nothing more.

I am vanquished. If it is so, it is useless to think, it is useless to talk. I will sit and wait in silence for what is to come.

In the morning the corridor attendant brings me tea and a copy of the local newspaper. Mechanically I read the advertisements on the first page, the leading article, the extracts from the newspapers and journals, the chronicle of events.... In the latter I find, among other things, the following paragraph: 'Our distinguished savant, Professor Nikolay Stepanovitch So-and-so, arrived yesterday in Harkov, and is staying in the So-and-so Hotel.'

Apparently, illustrious names are created to live on their own account, apart from those that bear them. Now my name is promenading tranquilly about Harkov; in another three months, printed in gold letters on my monument, it will shine bright as the sun itself, while I shall be already under the moss.

A light tap at the door. Somebody wants me.

'Who is there? Come in.'

The door opens, and I step back surprised and hurriedly wrap my dressing-gown round me. Before me stands Katya.

'How do you do?' she says, breathless with running upstairs. 'You didn't expect me? I have come here, too.... I have come, too!'

She sits down and goes on, hesitating and not looking at me.

'Why don't you speak to me? I have come, too... to-day.... I found out that you were in this hotel, and have come to you.'

'Very glad to see you,' I say, shrugging my shoulders, 'but I am surprised. You seem to have dropped from the skies. What have you come for?'

'Oh... I've simply come.'

Silence. Suddenly she jumps up impulsively and comes to me.

'Nikolay Stepanovitch,' she says, turning pale and pressing her hands on her bosom – 'Nikolay Stepanovitch, I cannot go on living like this! I cannot! For God's sake, tell me quickly, this minute, what I am to do! Tell me, what am I to do?'

'What can I tell you?' I ask in perplexity. 'I can do nothing.'

'Tell me, I beseech you,' she goes on, breathing hard and trembling all over. 'I swear that I cannot go on living like this. It's too much for me!'

She sinks on a chair and begins sobbing. She flings her head back, wrings her hands, taps with her feet; her hat falls off and hangs bobbing on its elastic; her hair is ruffled.

'Help me! help me!' she implores me. 'I cannot go on!'

She takes her handkerchief out of her travelling-bag, and with it pulls out several letters, which fall from her lap to the floor. I pick them up, and on one of them I recognize the handwriting of Mihail Fyodorovitch and accidentally read a bit of a word 'passion at . . .'.

'There is nothing I can tell you, Katya,' I say.

'Help me!' she sobs, clutching at my hand and kissing it. 'You are my father, you know, my only friend! You are clever, educated; you have lived so long; you have been a teacher! Tell me, what am I to do?'

'Upon my word, Katya, I don't know. . . .'

I am utterly at a loss and confused, touched by her sobs, and hardly able to stand.

'Let us have lunch, Katya,' I say, with a forced smile. 'Give over crying.'

And at once I add in a sinking voice:

'I shall soon be gone, Katya. . . .'

'Only one word, only one word!' she weeps, stretching out her hands to me. 'What am I to do?'

'You are a queer girl, really...' I mutter. 'I don't understand it! So sensible, and all at once...crying your eyes out....'

A silence follows. Katya straightens her hair, puts on her hat, then crumples up the letters and stuffs them in her bag – and all this deliberately, in silence. Her face, her bosom, and her gloves are wet with tears, but her expression now is cold and forbidding. ...I look at her, and feel ashamed that I am happier than she. The absence of what my philosophic colleagues call a general idea I have detected in myself only just before death, in the decline of my days, while the soul of this poor girl has known and will know no refuge all her life, all her life!

'Let us have lunch, Katya,' I say.

'No, thank you,' she answers coldly.

Another minute passes in silence.

'I don't like Harkov,' I say; 'it's so grey here – such a grey town.'

'Yes, perhaps....It's ugly. I am here not for long, passing through. I am going on to-day.'

'Where?'

'To the Crimea...that is, to the Caucasus.'

'Oh! For long?'

'I don't know.'

Katya gets up, and, with a cold smile, holds out her hand without looking at me.

I want to ask her, 'Then, you won't be at my funeral?' but she does not look at me; her hand is cold and, as it were, strange. I escort her to the door in silence. She goes out, walks down the long corridor without looking back; she knows that I am looking after her, and most likely she will look back at the turn.

No, she did not look back. I've seen her black dress for the last time: her steps have died away. Farewell, my treasure!

THE DUEL

THE DUEL

I

IT was eight o'clock in the morning – the time when the officers, the local officials, and the visitors usually took their morning dip in the sea after the hot, stifling night, and then went into the pavilion to drink tea or coffee. Ivan Andreitch Laevsky, a thin, fair young man of twenty-eight, wearing the cap of a clerk in the Ministry of Finance and with slippers on his feet, coming down to bathe, found a number of acquaintances on the beach, and among them his friend Samoylenko, the army doctor.

With his big cropped head, short neck, his red face, his big nose, his shaggy black eyebrows and grey whiskers, his stout puffy figure and his hoarse military bass, this Samoylenko made on every newcomer the unpleasant impression of a gruff bully; but two or three days after making his acquaintance, one began to think his face extraordinarily good-natured, kind, and even handsome. In spite of his clumsiness and rough manner, he was a peaceable man, of infinite kindliness and goodness of heart, always ready to be of use. He was on familiar terms with everyone in the town, lent everyone money, doctored everyone, made matches, patched up quarrels, arranged picnics at which he cooked *shashlik* and an awfully good soup of grey mullets. He was always looking after other people's affairs and trying to interest someone on their behalf, and was always delighted about something. The general opinion about him was that he was without faults of character. He had only two weaknesses: he was ashamed of his own good nature, and tried to disguise it by a surly expression and an assumed gruffness; and he liked his assistants and his soldiers to call him 'Your Excellency', although he was only a civil councillor.

'Answer one question for me, Alexandr Daviditch,' Laevsky began, when both he and Samoylenko were in the water up to their shoulders. 'Suppose you had loved a woman and had been living with her for two or three years, and then left off caring for her, as one does, and began to feel that you had nothing in common with her. How would you behave in that case?'

'It's very simple. "You go where you please, madam" – and that would be the end of it.'

'It's easy to say that! But if she has nowhere to go? A woman with no friends or relations, without a farthing, who can't work. . . .'

'Well? Five hundred roubles down or an allowance of twenty-five roubles a month – and nothing more. It's very simple.'

'Even supposing you have five hundred roubles and can pay twenty-five roubles a month, the woman I am speaking of is an educated woman and proud. Could you really bring yourself to offer her money? And how would you do it?'

Samoylenko was going to answer, but at that moment a big wave covered them both, then broke on the beach and rolled back noisily over the shingle. The friends got out and began dressing.

'Of course, it is difficult to live with a woman if you don't love her,' said Samoylenko, shaking the sand out of his boots. 'But one must look at the thing humanely, Vanya. If it were my case, I should never show a sign that I did not love her, and I should go on living with her till I died.'

He was at once ashamed of his own words; he pulled himself up and said:

'But for aught I care, there might be no females at all. Let them all go to the devil!'

The friends dressed and went into the pavilion. There Samoylenko was quite at home, and even had a special cup and saucer. Every morning they brought him on a tray a cup of coffee, a tall cut glass of iced water, and a tiny glass of brandy. He would first drink the brandy, then the hot coffee, then the iced water, and this must have been very nice, for after drinking it his eyes looked moist with pleasure, he would stroke his whiskers with both hands, and say, looking at the sea:

'A wonderfully magnificent view!'

After a long night spent in cheerless, unprofitable thoughts which prevented him from sleeping, and seemed to intensify the darkness and sultriness of the night, Laevsky felt listless and shattered. He felt no better for the bathe and the coffee.

'Let us go on with our talk, Alexandr Daviditch,' he said. 'I won't make a secret of it; I'll speak to you openly as to a friend. Things are in a bad way with

Nadyezhda Fyodorovna and me . . . a very bad way! Forgive me for forcing my private affairs upon you, but I must speak out.'

Samoylenko, who had a misgiving of what he was going to speak about, dropped his eyes and drummed with his fingers on the table.

'I've lived with her for two years and have ceased to love her,' Laevsky went on; 'or, rather, I realized that I never had felt any love for her. . . . These two years have been a mistake.'

It was Laevsky's habit as he talked to gaze attentively at the pink palms of his hands, to bite his nails, or to pinch his cuffs. And he did so now.

'I know very well you can't help me,' he said. 'But I tell you, because unsuccessful and superfluous people like me find their salvation in talking. I have to generalize about everything I do. I'm bound to look for an explanation and justification of my absurd existence in somebody else's theories, in literary types – in the idea that we, upper-class Russians, are degenerating, for instance, and so on. Last night, for example, I comforted myself by thinking all the time: "Ah, how true Tolstoy is, how mercilessly true!" And that did me good. Yes, really, brother, he is a great writer, say what you like!'

Samoylenko, who had never read Tolstoy and was intending to do so every day of his life, was a little embarrassed, and said:

'Yes, all other authors write from imagination, but he writes straight from nature.'

'My God!' sighed Laevsky; 'how distorted we all are by civilization! I fell in love with a married woman and she with me. . . . To begin with, we had kisses, and calm evenings, and vows, and Spencer, and ideals, and interests in common.... What a deception! We really ran away from her husband, but we lied to ourselves and made out that we ran away from the emptiness of the life of the educated class. We pictured our future like this: to begin with, in the Caucasus, while we were getting to know the people and the place, I would put on the Government uniform and enter the service; then at our leisure we would pick out a plot of ground, would toil in the sweat of our brow, would have a vineyard and a field, and so on. If you were in my place, or that zoologist of yours, Von Koren, you might live with Nadyezhda Fyodorovna for thirty years, perhaps, and might leave your heirs a rich vineyard and three thousand acres of maize; but I felt like a bankrupt from the first day. In the town you have insufferable heat, boredom, and no society; if you go out into the country, you fancy poisonous spiders, scorpions, or snakes lurking under every stone and behind every bush, and beyond the fields – mountains and the desert. Alien people, an alien country, a wretched form of civilization – all that is not so easy, brother, as walking on the Nevsky Prospect in one's fur coat, arm-in-arm with Nadyezhda Fyodorovna, dreaming of the sunny South. What is needed here is a life and death struggle, and I'm not a fighting man. A wretched neurasthenic, an idle gentleman.... From the first day I knew that my dreams of a life of labour and of a vineyard were worthless. As for love, I ought to tell you that living with a woman who has read Spencer and has followed you to the ends of the earth is no more interesting than living with any

Anfissa or Akulina. There's the same smell of ironing, of powder, and of medicines, the same curl-papers every morning, the same self-deception.'

'You can't get on in the house without an iron,' said Samoylenko, blushing at Laevsky's speaking to him so openly of a lady he knew. 'You are out of humour to-day, Vanya, I notice. Nadyezhda Fyodorovna is a splendid woman, highly educated, and you are a man of the highest intellect. Of course, you are not married,' Samoylenko went on, glancing round at the adjacent tables, 'but that's not your fault; and besides . . . one ought to be above conventional prejudices and rise to the level of modern ideas. I believe in free love myself, yes. . . . But to my thinking, once you have settled together, you ought to go on living together all your life.'

'Without love?'

'I will tell you directly,' said Samoylenko. 'Eight years ago there was an old fellow, an agent, here – a man of very great intelligence. Well, he used to say that the great thing in married life was patience. Do you hear, Vanya? Not love, but patience. Love cannot last long. You have lived two years in love, and now evidently your married life has reached the period when, in order to preserve equilibrium, so to speak, you ought to exercise all your patience. . . .'

'You believe in your old agent; to me his words are meaningless. Your old man could be a hypocrite; he could exercise himself in the virtue of patience, and, as he did so, look upon a person he did not love as an object indispensable for his moral exercises; but I have not yet fallen so low. If I want to exercise myself in patience, I will buy dumb-bells or a frisky horse, but I'll leave human beings alone.'

Samoylenko asked for some white wine with ice. When they had drunk a glass each, Laevsky suddenly asked:

'Tell me, please, what is the meaning of softening of the brain?'

'How can I explain it to you?...It's a disease in which the brain becomes softer...as it were, dissolves.'

'Is it curable?'

'Yes, if the disease is not neglected. Cold douches, blisters.... Something internal, too.'

'Oh!...Well, you see my position; I can't live with her: it is more than I can do. While I'm with you I can be philosophical about it and smile, but at home I lose heart completely; I am so utterly miserable, that if I were told, for instance, that I should have to live another month with her, I should blow out my brains. At the same time, parting with her is out of the question. She has no friends or relations; she cannot work, and neither she nor I have any money.... What could become of her? To whom could she go? There is nothing one can think of.... Come, tell me, what am I to do?'

'H'm!...' growled Samoylenko, not knowing what to answer. 'Does she love you?'

'Yes, she loves me in so far as at her age and with her temperament she wants a man. It would be as difficult for her to do without me as to do without her powder or her curl-papers. I am for her an indispensable, integral part of her boudoir.'

Samoylenko was embarrassed.

'You are out of humour to-day, Vanya,' he said. 'You must have had a bad night.'

'Yes, I slept badly.... Altogether, I feel horribly out of sorts, brother. My head feels empty; there's a sinking at my heart, a weakness.... I must run away.'

'Run where?'

'There, to the North. To the pines and the mushrooms, to people and ideas.... I'd give half my life to bathe now in some little stream in the province of Moscow or Tula; to feel chilly, you know, and then to stroll for three hours even with the feeblest student, and to talk and talk endlessly.... And the scent of the hay! Do your remember it? And in the evening, when one walks in the garden, sounds of the piano float from the house; one hears the train passing....'

Laevsky laughed with pleasure; tears came into his eyes, and to cover them, without getting up, he stretched across the next table for the matches.

'I have not been in Russia for eighteen years,' said Samoylenko. 'I've forgotten what it is like. To my mind, there is not a country more splendid than the Caucasus.'

'Vereshtchagin has a picture in which some men condemned to death are languishing at the bottom of a very deep well. Your magnificent Caucasus strikes me as just like that well. If I were offered the choice of a chimney-sweep in Petersburg or a prince in the Caucasus, I should choose the job of chimney-sweep.'

Laevsky grew pensive. Looking at his stooping figure, at his eyes fixed dreamily on one spot, at his pale, perspiring face and sunken temples, at his bitten nails, at the slipper which had dropped off his heel, displaying a badly darned sock, Samoylenko was moved to pity, and probably because Laevsky reminded him of a helpless child, he asked:

'Is your mother living?'

'Yes, but we are on bad terms. She could not forgive me for this affair.'

Samoylenko was fond of his friend. He looked upon Laevsky as a good-natured fellow, a student, a man with no nonsense about him, with whom one could drink, and laugh, and talk without reserve. What he understood in him he disliked extremely. Laevsky drank a great deal and at unsuitable times; he played cards, despised his work, lived beyond his means, frequently made use of unseemly expressions in conversation, walked about the streets in his slippers, and quarrelled with Nadyezhda Fyodorovna before other people – and Samoylenko did not like this. But the fact that Laevsky had once been a student in the Faculty of Arts, subscribed to two fat reviews, often talked so cleverly that only a few people understood him, was living with a well-educated woman – all this Samoylenko did not understand, and he liked this and respected Laevsky, thinking him superior to himself.

'There is another point,' said Laevsky, shaking his head. 'Only it is between ourselves. I'm concealing it from Nadyezhda Fyodorovna for the time.... Don't let it out before her.... I got a letter the day before yesterday, telling me that her husband has died from softening of the brain.'

'The Kingdom of Heaven be his!' sighed Samoylenko. 'Why are you concealing it from her?'

'To show her that letter would be equivalent to "Come to church to be married." And we should first have to make our relations clear. When she understands that we can't go on living together, I will show her the letter. Then there will be no danger in it.'

'Do you know what, Vanya,' said Samoylenko, and a sad and imploring expression came into his face, as though he were going to ask him about something very touching and were afraid of being refused. 'Marry her, my dear boy!'

'Why?'

'Do your duty to that splendid woman! Her husband is dead, and so Providence itself shows you what to do!'

'But do understand, you queer fellow, that it is impossible. To marry without love is as base and unworthy of a man as to perform mass without believing in it.'

'But it's your duty to.'

'Why is it my duty?' Laevsky asked irritably.

'Because you took her away from her husband and made yourself responsible for her.'

'But now I tell you in plain Russian, I don't love her!'

'Well, if you've no love, show her proper respect, consider her wishes....'

' "Show her respect, consider her wishes," ' Laevsky mimicked him. 'As though she were some Mother Superior!... You are a poor psychologist and physiologist if you think that living with a woman one can get off with nothing but respect and consideration. What a woman thinks most of is her bedroom.'

'Vanya, Vanya!' said Samoylenko, overcome with confusion.

'You are an elderly child, a theorist, while I am an old man in spite of my years, and practical, and we shall never understand one another. We had better drop this conversation. Mustapha!' Laevsky shouted to the waiter. 'What's our bill?'

'No, no...' the doctor cried in dismay, clutching Laevsky's arm. 'It is for me to pay. I ordered it. Make it out to me,' he cried to Mustapha.

The friends got up and walked in silence along the sea-front. When they reached the boulevard, they stopped and shook hands at parting.

'You are awfully spoilt, my friend!' Samoylenko sighed. 'Fate has sent you a young, beautiful, cultured woman, and you refuse the gift, while if God were to give me a crooked old woman, how pleased I should be if only she were kind and affectionate! I would live with her in my vineyard and....'

Samoylenko caught himself up and said:

'And she might get the samovar ready for me there, the old hag.'

After parting with Laevsky he walked along the boulevard. When, bulky and majestic, with a stern expression on his face, he walked along the boulevard in his snow-white tunic and superbly polished boots, squaring his chest, decorated with the Vladimir cross on a ribbon, he was very much pleased with himself, and it seemed as though the whole world were looking at him with pleasure. Without turning his head, he looked to each side and thought that the boulevard was extremely well laid out; that the young cypress-trees, the eucalyptuses, and the ugly, anæmic palm-trees were very handsome and would in time give abundant shade; that the Circassians were an honest and hospitable people.

'It's strange that Laevsky does not like the Caucasus,' he thought, 'very strange.'

Five soldiers, carrying rifles, met him and saluted him. On the right side of the boulevard the wife of a local official was walking along the pavement with her son, a schoolboy.

'Good-morning, Marya Konstantinovna,' Samoylenko shouted to her with a pleasant smile. 'Have you been to bathe? Ha, ha, ha!...My respects to Nikodim Alexandritch!'

And he went on, still smiling pleasantly, but seeing an assistant of the military hospital coming towards him, he suddenly frowned, stopped him, and asked:

'Is there anyone in the hospital?'

'No one, your Excellency.'

'Eh?'

'No one, your Excellency.'

'Very well, run along....'

Swaying majestically, he made for the lemonade stall, where sat a full-bosomed old Jewess, who gave herself out to be a Georgian, and said to her as loudly as though he were giving the word of command to a regiment:

'Be so good as to give me some soda-water!'

II

LAEVSKY'S not loving Nadyezhda Fyodorovna showed itself chiefly in the fact that everything she said or did seemed to him a lie, or equivalent to a lie, and everything he read against women and love seemed to him to apply perfectly to himself, to Nadyezhda Fyodorovna and her husband. When he returned home, she was sitting at the window, dressed and with her hair done, and with a preoccupied face was drinking coffee and turning over the leaves of a fat magazine; and he thought the drinking of coffee was not such a remarkable event that she need put on a preoccupied expression over it, and that she had been wasting her time doing her hair in a fashionable style, as there was no one here to attract and no need to be attractive. And in the magazine he saw nothing but falsity. He thought she had dressed and done her hair so as to look handsomer, and was reading in order to seem clever.

'Will it be all right for me to go to bathe to-day?' she said.

'Why? There won't be an earthquake whether you go or not, I suppose....'

'No, I only ask in case the doctor should be vexed.'

'Well, ask the doctor, then; I'm not a doctor.'

On this occasion what displeased Laevsky most in Nadyezhda Fyodorovna was her white open neck and the little curls at the back of her head. And he remembered that when Anna Karenin got tired of her husband, what she disliked most of all was his ears, and thought: 'How true it is, how true!'

Feeling weak and as though his head were perfectly empty, he went into his study, lay down on his sofa, and covered his face with a handkerchief that he might not be bothered by the flies. Despondent and oppressive thoughts always about the same thing trailed slowly across his brain like a long string of waggons on a gloomy autumn evening, and he sank into a state of drowsy oppression. It seemed to him that he had wronged Nadyezhda Fyodorovna and her husband, and that it was through his fault that her husband had died. It seemed to him that he had sinned against his own life, which he had ruined, against the world of lofty ideas, of learning, and of work, and he conceived that wonderful world as real and possible, not on this sea-front with hungry Turks and lazy mountaineers sauntering upon it, but there in the North, where there were operas, theatres, newspapers, and all kinds of intellectual activity. One could only there – not here – be honest, intelligent, lofty, and pure. He accused himself of having no ideal, no guiding principle in life, though he had a dim understanding now what it meant. Two years before, when he fell in love with Nadyezhda Fyodorovna, it seemed to him that he had only to go with her as his wife to the Caucasus, and he would be saved from vulgarity and emptiness; in the same way now, he was convinced that he had only to part from Nadyezhda Fyodorovna and to go to Petersburg, and he would get everything he wanted.

'Run away,' he muttered to himself, sitting up and biting his nails. 'Run away!'

He pictured in his imagination how he would go aboard the steamer and then would have some lunch, would drink some cold beer, would talk on deck with ladies, then would get into the train at Sevastopol and set off. Hurrah for freedom! One station after another would flash by, the air would keep growing colder and keener, then the birches and the fir-trees, then Kursk, Moscow.... In the restaurants cabbage soup, mutton with kasha, sturgeon, beer, no more Asiaticism, but Russia, real Russia. The passengers in the train would talk about trade, new singers, the Franco-Russian *entente*; on all sides there would be the feeling of keen, cultured, intellectual, eager life.... Hasten on, on! At last Nevsky Prospect, and Great Morskaya Street, and then Kovensky Place, where he used to live at one time when he was a student, the dear grey sky, the drizzling rain, the drenched cab-men....

'Ivan Andreitch!' someone called from the next room. 'Are you at home?'

'I'm here,' Laevsky responded. 'What do you want?'

'Papers.'

Laevsky got up languidly, feeling giddy, walked into the other room, yawning and shuffling with his slippers. There, at the open window that looked into the street, stood one of his young fellow-clerks, laying out some Government documents on the window-sill.

'One minute, my dear fellow,' Laevsky said softly, and he went to look for the ink; returning to the window, he signed the papers without looking at them, and said: 'It's hot!'

'Yes. Are you coming to-day?'

'I don't think so.... I'm not quite well. Tell Sheshkovsky that I will come and see him after dinner.'

The clerk went away. Laevsky lay down on his sofa again and began thinking:

'And so I must weigh all the circumstances and reflect on them. Before I go away from here I ought to pay up my debts. I owe about two thousand roubles. I have no money.... Of course, that's not important; I shall pay part now, somehow, and I shall send the rest, later, from Petersburg. The chief point is Nadyezhda Fyodorovna.... First of all we must define our relations.... Yes.'

A little later he was considering whether it would not be better to go to Samoylenko for advice.

'I might go,' he thought, 'but what use would there be in it? I shall only say something inappropriate about boudoirs, about women, about what is honest or dishonest. What's the use of talking about what is honest or dishonest, if I must make haste to save my life, if I am suffocating in this cursed slavery and am killing myself?... One must realize at last that to go on leading the life I do is something so base and so cruel that everything else seems petty and trivial beside it. To run away,' he muttered, sitting down, 'to run away.'

The deserted seashore, the insatiable heat, and the monotony of the smoky lilac mountains, ever the same and silent, everlastingly solitary, overwhelmed him with depression, and, as it were, made him drowsy and sapped his energy. He was perhaps very clever, talented, remarkably honest; perhaps if the sea and the mountains had not closed him in on all sides, he might have become an excellent Zemstvo leader, a statesman, an orator, a political writer, a saint. Who knows? If so, was it not stupid to argue whether it were honest or dishonest when a gifted and useful man – an artist or musician, for instance – to escape from prison, breaks a wall and deceives his jailers? Anything is honest when a man is in such a position.

At two o'clock Laevsky and Nadyezhda Fyodorovna sat down to dinner. When the cook gave them rice and tomato soup, Laevsky said:

'The same thing every day. Why not have cabbage soup?'

'There are no cabbages.'

'It's strange. Samoylenko has cabbage soup and Marya Konstantinovna has cabbage soup, and only I am obliged to eat this mawkish mess. We can't go on like this, darling.'

As is common with the vast majority of husbands and wives, not a single dinner had in earlier days passed without scenes and fault-finding between Nadyezhda Fyodorovna and Laevsky; but ever since Laevsky had made up his mind that he did not love her, he had tried to give way to Nadyezhda Fyodorovna in everything, spoke to her gently and politely, smiled, and called her 'darling'.

'This soup tastes like liquorice,' he said, smiling; he made an effort to control himself and seem amiable, but could not refrain from saying: 'Nobody looks after the housekeeping.... If you are too ill or busy with reading, let me look after the cooking.'

In earlier days she would have said to him, 'Do by all means', or, 'I see you want to turn me into a cook'; but now she only looked at him timidly and flushed crimson.

'Well, how do you feel to-day?' he asked kindly.

'I am all right to-day. There is nothing but a little weakness.'

'You must take care of yourself, darling. I am awfully anxious about you.'

Nadyezhda Fyodorovna was ill in some way. Samoylenko said she had intermittent fever, and gave her quinine; the other doctor, Ustimovitch, a tall, lean, unsociable man, who used to sit at home in the day-time, and in the evenings walk slowly up and down on the sea-front coughing, with his hands folded behind him and a cane stretched along his back, was of opinion that she had a female complaint, and prescribed warm compresses. In old days, when Laevsky loved her, Nadyezhda Fyodorovna's illness had excited his pity and terror; now he saw falsity even in her illness. Her yellow, sleepy face, her lustreless eyes, her apathetic expression, and the yawning that always followed her attacks of fever, and the fact that during them she lay under a shawl and looked more like a boy than a woman, and that it was close and stuffy in her room – all this, in his opinion, destroyed the illusion and was an argument against love and marriage.

The next dish given him was spinach with hard-boiled eggs, while Nadyezhda Fyodorovna, as an invalid, had jelly and milk. When with a preoccupied face she touched the jelly with a spoon and then began languidly eating it, sipping milk, and he heard her swallowing, he was possessed by such an overwhelming aversion that it made his head tingle. He recognized that such a feeling would be an insult even to a dog, but he was angry, not with himself but with Nadyezhda Fyodorovna, for arousing such a feeling, and he understood why lovers sometimes murder their mistresses. He would not murder her, of course, but if he had been on a jury now, he would have acquitted the murderer.

'Merci, darling,' he said after dinner, and kissed Nadyezhda Fyodorovna on the forehead.

Going back into his study, he spent five minutes in walking to and fro, looking at his boots; then he sat down on his sofa and muttered:

'Run away, run away! We must define the position and run away!'

He lay down on the sofa and recalled again that Nadyezhda Fyodorovna's husband had died, perhaps, by his fault.

'To blame a man for loving a woman, or ceasing to love a woman, is stupid,' he persuaded himself, lying down and raising his legs in order to put on his high boots. 'Love and hatred are not under our control. As for her husband, maybe I was in an indirect way one of the causes of his death; but again, is it my fault that I fell in love with his wife and she with me?'

Then he got up, and finding his cap, set off to the lodgings of his colleague, Sheshkovsky, where the Government clerks met every day to play *vint* and drink beer.

'My indecision reminds me of Hamlet,' thought Laevsky on the way. 'How truly Shakespeare describes it! Ah, how truly!'

III

FOR the sake of sociability and from sympathy for the hard plight of newcomers without families, who, as there was not an hotel in the town, had nowhere to dine, Dr. Samoylenko kept a sort of *table d'hôte*. At this time there were only two men who habitually dined with him: a young zoologist called Von Koren, who had come for the summer to the Black Sea to study the embryology of the medusa, and a deacon called Pobyedov, who had only just left the seminary and been sent to the town to take the duty of the old deacon who had gone away for a cure. Each of them paid twelve roubles a month for their dinner and supper, and Samoylenko made them promise to turn up at two o'clock punctually.

Von Koren was usually the first to appear. He sat down in the drawing-room in silence, and taking an album from the table, began attentively scrutinizing the faded photographs of unknown men in full trousers and top-hats, and ladies in crinolines and caps. Samoylenko only remembered a few of them by name, and of those whom he had forgotten he said with a sigh: 'A very fine fellow, remarkably intelligent!' When he had finished with the album, Von Koren took a pistol from the whatnot, and screwing up his left eye, took deliberate aim at the portrait of Prince Vorontsov, or stood still at the looking-glass and gazed a long time at his swarthy face, his big forehead, and his black hair, which curled like a negro's, and his shirt of dull-coloured cotton with big flowers on it like a Persian rug, and the broad leather belt he wore instead of a waistcoat. The contemplation of his own image seemed to afford him almost more satisfaction than looking at photographs or playing with the pistols. He was very well satisfied with his face, and his becomingly clipped beard, and the broad shoulders, which were unmistakable evidence of his excellent health and physical strength. He was satisfied, too, with his stylish get-up, from the cravat, which matched the colour of his shirt, down to his brown boots.

While he was looking at the album and standing before the glass, at that moment, in the kitchen and in the passage near, Samoylenko, without his coat and waistcoat, with his neck bare, excited and bathed in perspiration, was bustling about the tables, mixing the salad, or making some sauce, or preparing meat, cucumbers, and onion for the cold soup, while he glared fiercely at the orderly who was helping him, and brandished first a knife and then a spoon at him.

'Give me the vinegar!' he said. 'That's not the vinegar – it's the salad oil!' he shouted, stamping. 'Where are you off to, you brute?'

'To get the butter, your Excellency,' answered the flustered orderly in a cracked voice.

'Make haste; it's in the cupboard! And tell Daria to put some fennel in the jar with the cucumbers! Fennel! Cover the cream up, gaping laggard, or the flies will get into it!'

And the whole house seemed resounding with his shouts. When it was ten or fifteen minutes to two the deacon would come in; he was a lanky young man of twenty-two, with long hair, with no beard and a hardly perceptible moustache. Going into the drawing-room, he crossed himself before the ikon, smiled, and held out his hand to Von Koren.

'Good-morning,' the zoologist said coldly. 'Where have you been?'

'I've been catching sea-gudgeon in the harbour.'

'Oh, of course. . . . Evidently, deacon, you will never be busy with work.'

'Why not? Work is not like a bear; it doesn't run off into the woods,' said the deacon, smiling and thrusting his hands into the very deep pockets of his white cassock.

'There's no one to whip you!' sighed the zoologist.

Another fifteen or twenty minutes passed and they were not called to dinner, and they could still hear the orderly running into the kitchen and back again, noisily treading with his boots, and Samoylenko shouting:

'Put it on the table! Where are your wits? Wash it first.'

The famished deacon and Von Koren began tapping on the floor with their heels, expressing in this way their impatience like the audience at a theatre. At last the door opened and the harassed orderly announced that dinner was ready! In the dining-room they were met by Samoylenko, crimson in the face, wrathful, perspiring from the heat of the kitchen; he looked at them furiously, and with an expression of horror, took the lid off the soup tureen and helped each of them to a plateful; and only when he was convinced that they were eating it with relish and liked it, he gave a sigh of relief and settled himself in his deep arm-chair. His face looked blissful and his eyes grew moist.... He deliberately poured himself out a glass of vodka and said:

'To the health of the younger generation.'

After his conversation with Laevsky, from early morning till dinner Samoylenko had been conscious of a load at his heart, although he was in the best of humours; he felt sorry for Laevsky and wanted to help him. After drinking a glass of vodka before the soup, he heaved a sigh and said:

'I saw Vanya Laevsky to-day. He is having a hard time of it, poor fellow! The material side of life is not encouraging for him, and the worst of it is all this psychology is too much for him. I'm sorry for the lad.'

'Well, that is a person I am not sorry for,' said Von Koren. 'If that charming individual were drowning, I would push him under with a stick and say, "Drown, brother, drown away." ...'

'That's untrue. You wouldn't do it.'

'Why do you think that?' The zoologist shrugged his shoulders. 'I'm just as capable of a good action as you are.'

'Is drowning a man a good action?' asked the deacon, and he laughed

'Laevsky? Yes.'

'I think there is something amiss with the soup ...' said Samoylenko, anxious to change the conversation.

'Laevsky is absolutely pernicious and is as dangerous to society as the cholera microbe,' Von Koren went on. 'To drown him would be a service.'

'It does not do you credit to talk like that about your neighbour. Tell us: what do you hate him for?'

'Don't talk nonsense, doctor. To hate and despise a microbe is stupid, but to look upon everybody one meets without distinction as one's neighbour, whatever happens – thanks very much, that is equivalent to giving up criticism, renouncing a straightforward attitude to people, washing one's hands of responsibility, in fact! I consider your Laevsky a blackguard; I do not conceal it, and I am perfectly conscientious in treating him as such. Well, you look upon him as your neighbour – and you may kiss him if you like:

you look upon him as your neighbour, and that means that your attitude to him is the same as to me and to the deacon; that is no attitude at all. You are equally indifferent to all.'

'To call a man a blackguard!' muttered Samoylenko, frowning with distaste – 'that is so wrong that I can't find words for it!'

'People are judged by their actions,' Von Koren continued. 'Now you decide, deacon.... I am going to talk to you, deacon. Mr. Laevsky's career lies open before you, like a long Chinese puzzle, and you can read it from beginning to end. What has he been doing these two years that he has been living here? We will reckon his doings on our fingers. First, he has taught the inhabitants of the town to play *vint*: two years ago that game was unknown here; now they all play it from morning till late at night, even the women and the boys. Secondly, he has taught the residents to drink beer, which was not known here either; the inhabitants are indebted to him for the knowledge of various sorts of spirits, so that now they can distinguish Kospelov's vodka from Smirnov's No. 21, blindfold. Thirdly, in former days, people here made love to other men's wives in secret, from the same motives as thieves steal in secret and not openly; adultery was considered something they were ashamed to make a public display of. Laevsky has come as a pioneer in that line; he lives with another man's wife openly.... Fourthly....'

Von Koren hurriedly ate up his soup and gave his plate to the orderly.

'I understood Laevsky from the first month of our acquaintance,' he went on, addressing the deacon.

'We arrived here at the same time. Men like him are very fond of friendship, intimacy, solidarity, and all the rest of it, because they always want company for *vint*, drinking, and eating; besides, they are talkative and must have listeners. We made friends – that is, he turned up every day, hindered me working and indulged in confidences in regard to his mistress. From the first he struck me by his exceptional falsity, which simply made me sick. As a friend I pitched into him, asking him why he drank too much, why he lived beyond his means and got into debt, why he did nothing and read nothing, why he had so little culture and so little knowledge; and in answer to all my questions he used to smile bitterly, sigh, and say: "I am a failure, a superfluous man" or: "What do you expect, my dear fellow, from us, the débris of the serf-owning class?" or: "We are degenerate...." Or he would begin a long rigmarole about Onyegin, Petchorin, Byron's Cain, and Bazarov of whom he would say: "They are our fathers in flesh and in spirit." So we are to understand that it was not his fault that Government envelopes lay unopened in his office for weeks together and that he drank and taught others to drink, but Onyegin, Petchorin, and Turgenev, who had invented the failure and the superfluous man, were responsible for it. The cause of his extreme dissoluteness and unseemliness lies, do you see, not in himself, but somewhere outside in space. And so – an ingenious idea – it is not only he who is dissolute, false, and disgusting, but we... "we men of the eighties", "we the spiritless, nervous offspring of the serf-owning class"; "civilization has crippled us"... in fact, we are to understand that such a great man as Laevsky is great even in his fall; that his dissoluteness, his lack of culture and of moral purity, is a phenomenon of natural history, sanctified by inevitability; that the causes of it are world-wide, elemental; and that we ought to hang up a lamp before Laevsky, since he is the fated victim of the age, of influences, of heredity, and so on. All the officials and their ladies were in ecstasies when they listened to him, and I could not make out for a long time what sort of man I had to deal with, a cynic or a clever rogue. Such types as he, on the surface intellectual with a smattering of education and a great deal of talk about their own nobility, are very clever in posing as exceptionally complex natures.'

'Hold your tongue!' Samoylenko flared up. 'I will not allow a splendid fellow to be spoken ill of in my presence!'

'Don't interrupt, Alexandr Daviditch,' said Von Koren coldly; 'I am just finishing. Laevsky is by no means a complex organism. Here is his moral skeleton: in the morning, slippers, a bathe, and coffee; then till dinner-time, slippers, a constitutional, and conversation; at two o'clock slippers, dinner, and wine; at five o'clock a bathe, tea and wine, then *vint* and lying; at ten o'clock supper and wine; and after midnight sleep and *la femme*. His existence is confined within this narrow programme like an egg within its shell. Whether he walks or sits, is angry, writes, rejoices, it may all be reduced to wine, cards, slippers, and women. Woman plays a fatal, overwhelming part in his life. He tells us himself that at thirteen he was in love; that when he was a student in his first year he was living with a lady who had a good influence over him, and to whom he was indebted for his musical education. In his second year he bought a prostitute from a brothel and raised her to his level – that is, took her as his kept mistress, and she lived with him for six months and then ran away back to the brothel-keeper, and her flight caused him much spiritual suffering. Alas! his sufferings were so great that he had to leave the university and spend two years at home doing nothing. But this was all for the best. At home he made friends with a widow who advised him to leave the Faculty of Jurisprudence and go into the Faculty of Arts. And so he did. When he had taken his degree, he fell passionately in love with his present ... what's her name? ... married lady, and was obliged to flee with her here to the Caucasus for the sake of his ideals, he would have us believe, seeing that ... to-morrow, if not to-day, he will be tired of her and flee back again to Petersburg, and that, too, will be for the sake of his ideals.'

'How do you know?' growled Samoylenko, looking angrily at the zoologist. 'You had better eat your dinner.'

The next course consisted of boiled mullet with Polish sauce. Samoylenko helped each of his companions to a whole mullet and poured out the sauce with his own hand. Two minutes passed in silence.

'Woman plays an essential part in the life of every man,' said the deacon. 'You can't help that.'

'Yes, but to what degree? For each of us woman means mother, sister, wife, friend. To Laevsky she is everything, and at the same time nothing but a mistress. She – that is, cohabitation with her – is the happiness and object of his life; he is gay, sad, bored, disenchanted – on account of woman; his life grows disagreeable – woman is to blame; the dawn of a new life begins to glow, ideals turn up – and again look for the woman.... He only derives enjoyment from books and pictures in which there is woman. Our age is, to his thinking, poor and inferior to the forties and the sixties only because we do not know how to abandon ourselves obliviously to the passion and ecstasy of love. These voluptuaries must have in their brains a special growth of the nature of sarcoma, which stifles the brain and directs their whole psychology. Watch Laevsky when he is sitting anywhere in company. You notice: when one raises any general question in his presence, for instance, about the cell or instinct, he sits apart, and neither speaks nor listens; he looks languid and disillusioned; nothing has any interest for him, everything is vulgar and trivial. But as soon as you speak of male and female – for instance, of the fact that the female spider, after fertilization, devours the male – his eyes glow with curiosity, his face brightens, and the man revives, in fact. All his thoughts, however noble, lofty, or neutral they may be, they all have one point of resemblance. You walk along the street with him and meet a donkey, for instance.... "Tell me, please," he asks, "what would happen if you mated a donkey with a camel?" And his dreams! Has he told you of his dreams? It is magnificent! First, he dreams that he is married to the moon, then that he is summoned before the police and ordered to live with a guitar....'

The deacon burst into resounding laughter; Samoylenko frowned and wrinkled up his face angrily so as not to laugh, but could not restrain himself, and laughed.

'And it's all nonsense!' he said, wiping his tears. 'Yes, by Jove, it's nonsense!'

IV

THE deacon was very easily amused, and laughed at every trifle till he got a stitch in his side, till he was helpless. It seemed as though he only liked to be in people's company because there was a ridiculous side to them, and because they might be given ridiculous nicknames. He had nicknamed Samoylenko 'the tarantula', his orderly 'the drake', and was in ecstasies when on one occasion Von Koren spoke of Laevsky and Nadyezhda Fyodorovna as 'Japanese monkeys'. He watched people's faces greedily, listened without blinking, and it could be seen that his eyes filled with laughter and his face was tense with expectation of the moment when he could let himself go and burst into laughter.

'He is a corrupt and depraved type,' the zoologist continued, while the deacon kept his eyes riveted on his face, expecting he would say something funny. 'It is not often one can meet with such a nonentity. In body he is inert, feeble, prematurely old, while in intellect he differs in no respect from a fat shopkeeper's wife who does nothing but eat, drink, and sleep on a feather-bed, and who keeps her coachman as a lover.'

The deacon began guffawing again.

'Don't laugh, deacon,' said Von Koren. 'It grows stupid, at last. I should not have paid attention to his insignificance,' he went on, after waiting till the deacon had left off laughing; 'I should have passed him by if he were not so noxious and dangerous. His noxiousness lies first of all in the fact that he has great success with women, and so threatens to leave descendants – that is, to present the world with a dozen Laevskys as feeble and as depraved as himself. Secondly, he is in the highest degree contaminating. I have spoken to you already of *vint* and beer. In another year or two he will dominate the whole Caucasian coast. You know how the mass, especially its middle stratum, believe in intellectuality, in a university education, in gentlemanly manners, and in literary language. Whatever filthy thing he did, they would all believe that it was as it should be, since he is an intellectual man, of liberal ideas and university education. What is more, he is a failure, a superfluous man, a neurasthenic, a victim of the age, and that means he can do anything. He is a charming fellow, a regular good sort, he is so genuinely indulgent to human weaknesses; he is compliant, accommodating, easy, and not proud; one can drink with him and gossip and talk evil of people.... The masses, always inclined to anthropomorphism in religion and morals, like best of all the little gods who have the same weaknesses as themselves. Only think what a wide field he has for contamination! Besides, he is not a bad actor and is a clever hypocrite, and knows very well how to twist things round. Only take his little shifts and dodges, his attitude to civilization, for instance. He has scarcely sniffed at civilization, yet: "Ah how we have been crippled by civilization! Ah, how I envy those savages, those children of nature, who know nothing of civilization!" We are to understand, you see, that at one time, in ancient days, he has been devoted to civilization with his whole soul, has served it, has sounded it to its depths, but it has exhausted him, disillusioned him, deceived him; he is a Faust, do you see? – a second Tolstoy.... As for Schopenhauer and Spencer, he treats them like small boys and slaps them on the shoulder in a fatherly way: "Well, what do you say, old Spencer?" He has not read Spencer, of course, but how charming he is when with light, careless irony he says of his lady friend: "She has read Spencer!" And they all listen to him, and no one cares to understand that this charlatan has not the right to kiss the sole of Spencer's foot, let alone speaking about him in that tone! Sapping the foundations of civilization, of authority, of other people's altars, spattering them with filth, winking jocosely at them only to justify and conceal one's own rottenness and moral poverty is only possible for a very vain, base, and nasty creature.'

'I don't know what it is you expect of him, Kolya,' said Samoylenko, looking at the zoologist, not with anger now, but with a guilty air. 'He is a man the same as everyone else. Of course, he has his weaknesses, but he is abreast of modern ideas, is in the service, is of use to his country. Ten years ago there was an old fellow serving as agent here, a man of the greatest intelligence... and he used to say....'

'Nonsense, nonsense!' the zoologist interrupted. 'You say he is in the service; but how does he serve? Do you mean to tell me that things have been done better because he is here, and the officials are more punctual, honest, and civil? On the contrary, he has only sanctioned their slackness by his prestige as an intellectual university man. He is only punctual on the 20th of the month, when he gets his salary; on the other days he lounges about at home in slippers and tries to look as if he were doing the Government a great service by living in the Caucasus. No, Alexandr Daviditch, don't stick up for him. You are insincere from beginning to end. If you really loved him and considered him your neighbour, you would above all not be indifferent to his weaknesses, you would not be indulgent to them, but for his own sake would try to make him innocuous.'

'That is?'

'Innocuous. Since he is incorrigible, he can only be made innocuous in one way. . . .' Von Koren passed his finger round his throat. 'Or he might be drowned . . .' he added. 'In the interests of humanity and in their own interests, such people ought to be destroyed. They certainly ought.'

'What are you saying?' muttered Samoylenko, getting up and looking with amazement at the zoologist's calm, cold face. 'Deacon, what is he saying? Why – are you in your senses?'

'I don't insist on the death penalty,' said Von Koren. 'If it is proved that it is pernicious, devise something else. If we can't destroy Laevsky, why then, isolate him, make him harmless, send him to hard labour.'

'What are you saying!' said Samoylenko in horror. 'With pepper, with pepper,' he cried in a voice of despair, seeing that the deacon was eating stuffed aubergines without pepper. 'You with your great intellect, what are you saying! Send our friend, a proud intellectual man, to penal servitude!'

'Well, if he is proud and tries to resist, put him in fetters!'

Samoylenko could not utter a word, and only twiddled his fingers; the deacon looked at his flabbergasted and really absurd face, and laughed.

'Let us leave off talking of that,' said the zoologist. 'Only remember one thing, Alexandr Daviditch: primitive man was preserved from such as Laevsky by the struggle for existence and by natural selection; now our civilization has considerably weakened the struggle and the selection, and we ought to look after the destruction of the rotten and worthless for ourselves; otherwise, when the Laevskys multiply, civilization will perish and mankind will degenerate utterly. It will be our fault.'

'If it depends on drowning and hanging,' said Samoylenko, 'damnation take your civilization, damnation take your humanity! Damnation take it! I tell you what: you are a very learned and intelligent man and the pride of your country, but the Germans have ruined you. Yes, the Germans! The Germans!'

Since Samoylenko had left Dorpat, where he had studied medicine, he had rarely seen a German and had not read a single German book, but, in his opinion, every harmful idea in politics or science was due to the Germans. Where he had got this notion he could not have said himself, but he held it firmly.

'Yes, the Germans!' he repeated once more. 'Come and have some tea.'

All three stood up, and putting on their hats, went out into the little garden, and sat there under the shade of the light green maples, the pear-trees, and a chestnut-tree. The zoologist and the deacon sat on a bench by the table, while Samoylenko sank into a deep wicker chair with a sloping back. The orderly handed them tea, jam, and a bottle of syrup.

It was very hot, thirty degrees Réaumur in the shade. The sultry air was stagnant and motionless, and a long spider-web, stretching from the chestnut-tree to the ground, hung limply and did not stir.

The deacon took up the guitar, which was constantly lying on the ground near the table, tuned it, and began singing softly in a thin voice:

'Gathered round the tavern were the seminary lads'

but instantly subsided, overcome by the heat, mopped his brow and glanced upwards at the blazing blue sky. Samoylenko grew drowsy; the sultry heat, the stillness and the delicious after-dinner languor, which quickly pervaded all his limbs, made him feel heavy and sleepy; his arms dropped at his sides, his eyes grew small, his head sank on his breast. He looked with almost tearful tenderness at Von Koren and the deacon, and muttered:

'The younger generation.... A scientific star and a luminary of the Church.... I shouldn't wonder if the long-skirted alleluia will be shooting up into a bishop; I dare say I may come to kissing his hand.... Well... please God....'

Soon a snore was heard. Von Koren and the deacon finished their tea and went out into the street.

'Are you going to the harbour again to catch sea-gudgeon?' asked the zoologist.

'No, it's too hot.'

'Come and see me. You can pack up a parcel and copy something for me. By the way, we must have a talk about what you are to do. You must work, deacon. You can't go on like this.'

'Your words are just and logical,' said the deacon. 'But my laziness finds an excuse in the circumstances of my present life. You know yourself that an uncertain position has a great tendency to make people apathetic. God only knows whether I have been sent here for a time or permanently. I am living here in uncertainty, while my wife is vegetating at her father's and is missing me. And I must confess my brain is melting with the heat.'

'That's all nonsense,' said the zoologist. 'You can get used to the heat, and you can get used to being without the deaconess. You mustn't be slack; you must pull yourself together.'

V

NADYEZHDA FYODOROVNA went to bathe in the morning, and her cook, Olga, followed her with a jug, a copper basin, towels, and a sponge. In the bay stood two unknown steamers with dirty white funnels, obviously foreign cargo vessels. Some men dressed in white and wearing white shoes were walking along the harbour, shouting loudly in French, and were answered from the steamers. The bells were ringing briskly in the little church of the town.

'To-day is Sunday!' Nadyezhda Fyodorovna remembered with pleasure.

She felt perfectly well, and was in a gay holiday humour. In a new loose-fitting dress of coarse thick tussore silk, and a big wide-brimmed straw hat which was bent down over her ears, so that her face looked out as though from a basket, she fancied she looked very charming. She thought that in the whole town there was only one young, pretty, intellectual woman, and that was herself, and that she was the only one who knew how to dress herself cheaply, elegantly, and with taste. That dress, for example, cost only twenty-two roubles, and yet how charming it was! In the whole town she was the only one who could be attractive, while there were numbers of men, so they must all, whether they would or not, be envious of Laevsky.

She was glad that of late Laevsky had been cold to her, reserved and polite, and at times even harsh and rude; in the past she had met all his outbursts, all his contemptuous, cold or strange incomprehensible glances, with tears, reproaches, and threats to leave him or to starve herself to death; now she only blushed, looked guiltily at him, and was glad he was not affectionate to her. If he had abused her, or threatened her, it would have been better and pleasanter, since she felt hopelessly guilty towards him. She felt she was to blame, in the first place, for not sympathizing with the dreams of a life of hard work, for the sake of which he had given up Petersburg and had come here to the Caucasus, and she was convinced that he had been angry with her of late for precisely that. When she was travelling to the Caucasus, it seemed that she would find here on the first day a cosy nook by the sea, a snug little garden with shade, with birds, with little brooks, where she could grow flowers and vegetables, rear ducks and hens, entertain her neighbours, doctor poor peasants and distribute little books amongst them. It had turned out that the Caucasus was nothing but bare mountains, forests, and huge valleys, where it took a long time and a great deal of effort to find anything and settle down; that there were no neighbours of any sort; that it was very hot and one might be robbed. Laevsky had been in no hurry to obtain a piece of land; she was glad of it, and they seemed to be in a tacit compact never to allude to a life of hard work. He was silent about it, she thought, because he was angry with her for being silent about it.

In the second place, she had without his knowledge during those two years bought various trifles to the value of three hundred roubles at Atchmianov's shop. She had bought the things by degrees, at one time materials, at another time silk or a parasol, and the debt had grown imperceptibly.

'I will tell him about it to-day...' she used to decide, but at once reflected that in Laevsky's present mood it would hardly be convenient to talk to him of debts.

Thirdly, she had on two occasions in Laevsky's absence received a visit from Kirilin, the police captain: once in the morning when Laevsky had gone to bathe, and another time at midnight when he was playing cards. Remembering this, Nadyezhda Fyodorovna flushed crimson, and looked round at the cook as though she might overhear her thoughts. The long, insufferably hot, wearisome days, beautiful languorous evenings and stifling nights, and the whole manner of living, when from morning to night one is at a loss to fill up the useless hours, and the persistent thought that she was the prettiest young woman in the town, and that her youth was passing and being wasted, and Laevsky himself, though honest and idealistic, always the same, always lounging about in his slippers, biting his nails, and wearying her with his caprices, led by degrees to her becoming possessed by desire, and as though she were mad, she thought of nothing else day and night. Breathing, looking, walking, she felt nothing but desire. The sound of the sea told her she must love; the darkness of evening – the same; the mountains – the same.... And when Kirilin began paying her attentions, she had neither the power nor the wish to resist, and surrendered to him....

Now the foreign steamers and the men in white reminded her for some reason of a huge hall; together with the shouts of French she heard the strains of a waltz, and her bosom heaved with unaccountable delight. She longed to dance and talk French.

She reflected joyfully that there was nothing terrible about her infidelity. Her soul had no part in her infidelity; she still loved Laevsky, and that was proved by the fact that she was jealous of him, was sorry for him, and missed him when he was away. Kirilin had turned out to be very mediocre, rather coarse though handsome; everything was broken off with him already and there would never be anything more. What had happened was over; it had nothing to do with anyone, and if Laevsky found it out he would not believe in it.

There was only one bathing-house for ladies on the sea-front; men bathed under the open sky. Going into the bathing-house, Nadyezhda Fyodorovna found there an elderly lady, Marya Konstantinovna Bityugov, and her daughter Katya, a schoolgirl of fifteen; both of them were sitting on a bench undressing. Marya Konstantinovna was a good-natured, enthusiastic, and genteel person, who talked in a drawling and pathetic voice. She had been a governess until she was thirty-two, and then had married Bityugov, a Government official – a bald little man with his hair combed on to his temples and with a very meek disposition. She was still in love with him, was jealous, blushed at the word 'love', and told everyone she was very happy.

'My dear,' she cried enthusiastically, on seeing Nadyezhda Fyodorovna, assuming an expression which all her acquaintances called 'almond-oily'. 'My dear, how delightful that you have come! We'll bathe together – that's enchanting!'

Olga quickly flung off her dress and chemise, and began undressing her mistress.

'It's not quite so hot to-day as yesterday?' said Nadyezhda Fyodorovna, shrinking at the coarse touch of the naked cook. 'Yesterday I almost died of the heat.'

'Oh yes, my dear; I could hardly breathe myself. Would you believe it? I bathed yesterday three times! Just imagine, my dear, three times! Nikodim Alexandritch was quite uneasy.'

'Is it possible to be so ugly?' thought Nadyezhda Fyodorovna, looking at Olga and the official's wife; she glanced at Katya and thought: 'The little girl's not badly made.'

'Your Nikodim Alexandritch is very charming!' she said. 'I'm simply in love with him.'

'Ha, ha, ha!' cried Marya Konstantinovna, with a forced laugh; 'that's quite enchanting.'

Free from her clothes, Nadyezhda Fyodorovna felt a desire to fly. And it seemed to her that if she were to wave her hands she would fly upwards. When she was undressed, she noticed that Olga looked scornfully at her white body. Olga, a young soldier's wife, was living with her lawful husband, and so considered herself superior to her mistress. Marya Konstantinovna and Katya were afraid of her, and did not respect her. This was disagreeable, and to raise herself in their opinion, Nadyezhda Fyodorovna said:

'At home, in Petersburg, summer villa life is at its height now. My husband and I have so many friends! We ought to go and see them.'

'I believe your husband is an engineer?' said Marya Konstantinovna timidly.

'I am speaking of Laevsky. He has a great many acquaintances. But unfortunately his mother is a proud aristocrat, not very intelligent. . . .'

Nadyezhda Fyodorovna threw herself into the water without finishing; Marya Konstantinovna and Katya made their way in after her.

'There are so many conventional ideas in the world,' Nadyezhda Fyodorovna went on, 'and life is not so easy as it seems.'

Marya Konstantinovna, who had been a governess in aristocratic families and who was an authority on social matters, said:

'Oh yes! Would you believe me, my dear, at the Garatynskys' I was expected to dress for lunch as well as for dinner, so that, like an actress, I received a special allowance for my wardrobe in addition to my salary.'

She stood between Nadyezhda Fyodorovna and Katya as though to screen her daughter from the water that washed the former.

Through the open doors looking out to the sea they could see someone swimming a hundred paces from their bathing-place.

'Mother, it's our Kostya,' said Katya.

'Ach, ach!' Marya Konstantinovna cackled in her dismay. 'Ach, Kostya!' she shouted, 'Come back! Kostya, come back!'

Kostya, a boy of fourteen, to show off his prowess before his mother and sister, dived and swam farther, but began to be exhausted and hurried back, and from his strained and serious face it could be seen that he could not trust his own strength.

'The trouble one has with these boys, my dear!' said Marya Konstantinovna, growing calmer. 'Before you can turn round, he will break his neck. Ah, my dear, how sweet it is, and yet at the same time how difficult, to be a mother! One's afraid of everything.'

Nadyezhda Fyodorovna put on her straw hat and dashed out into the open sea. She swam some thirty feet and then turned on her back. She could see the sea to the horizon, the steamers, the people on the sea-front, the town; and all this, together with the sultry heat and the soft, transparent waves, excited her and whispered that she must live, live. . . . A sailing-boat darted by her rapidly and vigorously, cleaving the waves and the air; the man sitting at the helm looked at her, and she liked being looked at. . . .

After bathing, the ladies dressed and went away together.

'I have fever every alternate day, and yet I don't get thin,' said Nadyezhda Fyodorovna, licking her lips, which were salt from the bathe, and responding with a smile to the bows of her acquaintances. 'I've always been plump, and now I believe I'm plumper than ever.'

'That, my dear, is constitutional. If, like me, one has no constitutional tendency to stoutness, no diet is of any use.... But you've wetted your hat, my dear.'

'It doesn't matter; it will dry.'

Nadyezhda Fyodorovna saw again the men in white who were walking on the sea-front and talking French; and again she felt a sudden thrill of joy, and had a vague memory of some big hall in which she had once danced, or of which, perhaps, she had once dreamed. And something at the bottom of her soul dimly and obscurely whispered to her that she was a petty, common, miserable, worthless woman....

Marya Konstantinovna stopped at her gate and asked her to come in and sit down for a little while.

'Come in, my dear,' she said in an imploring voice, and at the same time she looked at Nadyezhda Fyodorovna with anxiety and hope; perhaps she would refuse and not come in!

'With pleasure,' said Nadyezhda Fyodorovna, accepting. 'You know how I love being with you!'

And she went into the house. Marya Konstantinovna sat her down and gave her coffee, regaled her with milk rolls, then showed her photographs of her former pupils, the Garatynskys, who were by now married. She showed her, too, the examination reports of Kostya and Katya. The reports were very good, but to make them seem even better, she complained, with a sigh, how difficult the lessons at school were now.. ..She made much of her visitor, and was sorry for her, though at the same time she was harassed by the thought that Nadyezhda Fyodorovna might have a corrupting influence on the morals of Kostya and Katya, and was glad that her Nikodim Alexandritch was not at home. Seeing that in her opinion all men are fond of 'women like that', Nadyezhda Fyodorovna might have a bad effect on Nikodim Alexandritch too.

As she talked to her visitor, Marya Konstantinovna kept remembering that they were to have a picnic that evening, and that Von Koren had particularly begged her to say nothing about it to the 'Japanese monkeys' – that is, Laevsky and Nadyezhda Fyodorovna; but she dropped a word about it unawares, crimsoned, and said in confusion:

'I hope you will come too!'

VI

IT was agreed to drive about five miles out of town on the road to the south, to stop near a *duhan* at the junction of two streams – the Black River and the Yellow River – and to cook fish soup. They started out soon after five. Foremost of the party in a char-à-banc drove Samoylenko and Laevsky; they were followed by Marya Konstantinovna, Nadyezhda Fyodorovna, Katya and Kostya, in a coach with three horses, carrying with them the crockery and a basket with provisions. In the next carriage came the police captain, Kirilin, and the young Atchmianov, the son of the shopkeeper to whom Nadyezhda Fyodorovna owed three hundred roubles; opposite them, huddled up on the little seat with his feet tucked under him, sat Nikodim Alexandritch, a neat little man with hair combed on to his temples. Last of all came Von Koren and the deacon; at the deacon's feet stood a basket of fish.

'R-r-right!' Samoylenko shouted at the top of his voice when he met a cart or a mountaineer riding on a donkey.

'In two years' time, when I shall have the means and the people ready, I shall set off on an expedition,' Von Koren was telling the deacon. 'I shall go by the sea-coast from Vladivostok to the Bering Straits, and then from the Straits to the mouth of the Yenisei. We shall make the map, study the fauna and the flora, and make detailed geological, anthropological, and ethnographical researches. It depends upon you to go with me or not.'

'It's impossible,' said the deacon.

'Why?'

'I'm a man with ties and a family.'

'Your wife will let you go; we will provide for her. Better still if you were to persuade her for the public benefit to go into a nunnery; that would make it possible for you to become a monk, too, and join the expedition as a priest. I can arrange it for you.'

The deacon was silent.

'Do you know your theology well?' asked the zoologist.

'No, rather badly.'

'H'm!...I can't give you any advice on that score, because I don't know much about theology myself. You give me a list of books you need, and I will send them to you from Petersburg in the winter. It will be necessary for you to read the notes of religious travellers, too; among them are some good ethnologists and Oriental scholars. When you are familiar with their methods, it will be easier for you to set to work. And you needn't waste your time till you get the books; come to me, and we will study the compass and go through a course of meteorology. All that's indispensable.'

'To be sure...' muttered the deacon, and he laughed. 'I was trying to get a place in Central Russia, and my uncle, the head priest, promised to help me. If I go with you I shall have troubled them for nothing.'

'I don't understand your hesitation. If you go on being an ordinary deacon, who is only obliged to hold a service on holidays, and on the other days can rest from work, you will be exactly the same as you are now in ten years' time, and will have gained nothing but a beard and moustache; while on returning from this expedition in ten years' time you will be a different man, you will be enriched by the consciousness that something has been done by you.'

From the ladies' carriage came shrieks of terror and delight. The carriages were driving along a road hollowed in a literally overhanging precipitous cliff, and it seemed to everyone that they were galloping along a shelf on a steep wall, and that in a moment the carriages would drop into the abyss. On the right stretched the sea; on the left was a rough brown wall with black blotches and red veins and with climbing roots; while on the summit stood shaggy fir-trees bent over, as though looking down in terror and 'curiosity. A minute later there were shrieks and laughter again: they had to drive under a huge overhanging rock.

'I don't know why the devil I'm coming with you,' said Laevsky. 'How stupid and vulgar it is! I want to go to the North, to run away, to escape; but here I am, for some reason, going to this stupid picnic.'

'But look, what a view!' said Samoylenko as the horses turned to the left, and the valley of the Yellow River came into sight and the stream itself gleamed in the sunlight, yellow, turbid, frantic.

'I see nothing fine in that, Sasha,' answered Laevsky. 'To be in continual ecstasies over nature shows poverty of imagination. In comparison with what my imagination can give me, all these streams and rocks are trash, and nothing else.'

The carriages now were by the bank of the stream. The high mountain banks gradually grew closer, the valley shrank together and ended in a gorge; the rocky mountain round which they were driving had been piled together by nature out of huge rocks, pressing upon each other with such terrible weight, that Samoylenko could not help gasping every time he looked at them. The dark and beautiful mountain was cleft in places by narrow fissures and gorges from which came a breath of dewy moisture and mystery; through the gorges could be seen other mountains, brown, pink, lilac, smoky, or bathed in vivid sunlight. From time to time as they passed a gorge they caught the sound of water falling from the heights and splashing on the stones.

'Ach, the damned mountains!' sighed Laevsky. 'How sick I am of them!'

At the place where the Black River falls into the Yellow, and the water black as ink stains the yellow and struggles with it, stood the Tatar Kerbalay's *duhan*, with the Russian flag on the roof and with an inscription written in chalk: 'The Pleasant Duhan.' Near it was a little garden, enclosed in a hurdle fence, with tables and chairs set out in it, and in the midst of a thicket of wretched thorn-bushes stood a single solitary cypress, dark and beautiful.

Kerbalay, a nimble little Tatar in a blue shirt and a white apron, was standing in the road, and, holding his stomach, he bowed low to welcome the carriages, and smiled, showing his glistening white teeth.

'Good-evening, Kerbalay,' shouted Samoylenko. 'We are driving on a little further, and you take along the samovar and chairs! Look sharp!'

Kerbalay nodded his shaven head and muttered something, and only those sitting in the last carriage could hear: 'We've got trout, your Excellency.'

'Bring them, bring them!' said Von Koren.

Five hundred paces from the *duhan* the carriages stopped. Samoylenko selected a small meadow round which there were scattered stones convenient for sitting on, and a fallen tree blown down by the storm with roots overgrown by moss and dry yellow needles. Here there was a fragile wooden bridge over the stream, and just opposite on the other bank there was a little barn for drying maize, standing on four low piles, and looking like the hut on hen's legs in the fairy tale; a little ladder sloped from its door.

The first impression in all was a feeling that they would never get out of that place again. On all sides, wherever they looked, the mountains rose up and towered above them, and the shadows of evening were stealing rapidly, rapidly from the *duhan* and dark cypress, making the narrow winding valley of the Black River narrower and the mountains higher. They could hear the river murmuring and the unceasing chirrup of the grasshoppers.

'Enchanting!' said Marya Konstantinovna, heaving deep sighs of ecstasy. 'Children, look how fine! What peace!'

'Yes, it really is fine,' assented Laevsky, who liked the view, and for some reason felt sad as he looked at the sky and then at the blue smoke rising from the chimney of the *duhan*. 'Yes, it is fine,' he repeated.

'Ivan Andreitch, describe this view,' Marya Konstantinovna said tearfully.

'Why?' asked Laevsky. 'The impression is better than any description. The wealth of sights and sounds which everyone receives from nature by direct impression is ranted about by authors in a hideous and unrecognizable way.'

'Really?' Von Koren asked coldly, choosing the biggest stone by the side of the water, and trying to clamber up and sit upon it. 'Really?' he repeated, looking directly at Laevsky. 'What of "Romeo and Juliet"? Or, for instance, Pushkin's "Night in the Ukraine"? Nature ought to come and bow down at their feet.'

'Perhaps,' said Laevsky, who was too lazy to think and oppose him. 'Though what is "Romeo and Juliet" after all?' he added after a short pause. 'The beauty of poetry and holiness of love are simply the roses under which they try to hide its rottenness.

Romeo is just the same sort of animal as all the rest of us.'

'Whatever one talks to you about, you always bring it round to . . . .' Von Koren glanced round at Katya and broke off.

'What do I bring it round to?' asked Laevsky.

'One tells you, for instance, how beautiful a bunch of grapes is, and you answer: "Yes, but how ugly it is when it is chewed and digested in one's stomach!" Why say that? It's not new, and . . . altogether it is a queer habit.'

Laevsky knew that Von Koren did not like him, and so was afraid of him, and felt in his presence as though everyone were constrained and someone were standing behind his back. He made no answer and walked away, feeling sorry he had come.

'Gentlemen, quick march for brushwood for the fire!' commanded Samoylenko.

They all wandered off in different directions, and no one was left but Kirilin, Atchmianov, and Nikodim Alexandritch. Kerbalay brought chairs, spread a rug on the ground, and set a few bottles of wine.

The police captain, Kirilin, a tall, good-looking man, who in all weathers wore his great-coat over his tunic, with his haughty deportment, stately carriage, and thick, rather hoarse voice, looked like a young provincial chief of police; his expression was mournful and sleepy, as though he had just been waked against his will.

'What have you brought this for, you brute?' he asked Kerbalay, deliberately articulating each word. 'I ordered you to give us *kvarel*, and what have you brought, you ugly Tatar? Eh? What?'

'We have plenty of wine of our own, Yegor Alekseitch,' Nikodim Alexandritch observed, timidly and politely.

'What? But I want us to have my wine, too; I'm taking part in the picnic and I imagine I have full right to contribute my share. I im-ma-gine so! Bring ten bottles of *kvarel*.'

'Why so many?' asked Nikodim Alexandritch, in wonder, knowing Kirilin had no money.

'Twenty bottles! Thirty!' shouted Kirilin.

'Never mind, let him,' Atchmianov whispered to Nikodim Alexandritch; 'I'll pay.'

Nadyezhda Fyodorovna was in a light-hearted, mischievous mood; she wanted to skip and jump, to laugh, to shout, to tease, to flirt. In her cheap cotton dress with blue pansies on it, in her red shoes and the same straw hat, she seemed to herself little, simple, light, ethereal as a butterfly. She ran over the rickety bridge and looked for a minute into the water, in order to feel giddy; then, shrieking and laughing, ran to the other side to the drying-shed, and she fancied that all the men were admiring her, even Kerbalay. When in the rapidly falling darkness the trees began to melt into the mountains and the horses into the carriages, and a light gleamed in the windows of the *duhan*, she climbed up the mountain by the little path which zigzagged between stones and thorn-bushes and sat on a stone. Down below, the camp-fire was burning. Near the fire, with his sleeves tucked up, the deacon was moving to and fro, and his long black shadow kept describing a circle round it; he put on wood, and with a spoon tied to a long stick he stirred the cauldron. Samoylenko, with a copper-red face, was fussing round the fire just as though he were in his own kitchen, shouting furiously:

'Where's the salt, gentlemen? I bet you've forgotten it. Why are you all sitting about like lords while I do all the work?'

Laevsky and Nikodim Alexandritch were sitting side by side on the fallen tree looking pensively at the fire. Marya Konstantinovna, Katya, and Kostya were taking the cups, saucers, and plates out of the baskets. Von Koren, with his arms folded and one foot on a stone, was standing on a bank at the very edge of the water, thinking about something. Patches of red light from the fire moved together with the shadows over the ground near the dark human figures, and quivered on the mountain, on the trees, on the bridge, on the drying-shed; on the other side the steep, scooped-out bank was all lighted up and glimmering in the stream, and the rushing turbid water broke its reflection into little bits.

The deacon went for the fish which Kerbalay was cleaning and washing on the bank, but he stood still half-way and looked about him.

'My God, how nice it is!' he thought. 'People, rocks, the fire, the twilight, a monstrous tree – nothing more, and yet how fine it is!'

On the further bank some unknown persons made their appearance near the drying-shed. The flickering light and the smoke from the camp-fire puffing in that direction made it impossible to get a full view of them all at once, but glimpses were caught now of a shaggy hat and a grey beard, now of a blue shirt, now of a figure, ragged from shoulder to knee, with a dagger across the body; then a swarthy young face with black eyebrows, as thick and bold as though they had been drawn in charcoal. Five of them sat in a circle on the ground, and the other five went into the drying-shed. One was standing at the door with his back to the fire, and with his hands behind his back was telling something, which must have been very interesting, for when Samoylenko threw on twigs and the fire flared up, and scattered sparks and threw a glaring light on the shed, two calm countenances with an expression on them of deep attention could be seen, looking out of the door, while those who were sitting in a circle turned round and began listening to the speaker. Soon after, those sitting in a circle began softly singing something slow and melodious, that sounded like Lenten Church music.... Listening to them, the deacon imagined how it would be with him in ten years' time, when he would come back from the expedition: he would be a young priest and monk, an author with a name and a splendid past; he would be consecrated an archimandrite, then a bishop; and he would serve mass in the cathedral; in a golden mitre he would come out into the body of the church with the ikon on his breast, and blessing the mass of the people with the triple and the double candelabra, would proclaim: 'Look down from Heaven, O God, behold and visit this vineyard which Thy Hand has planted,' and the children with their angel voices would sing in response: 'Holy God....'

'Deacon, where is that fish?' he heard Samoylenko's voice.

As he went back to the fire, the deacon imagined the Church procession going along a dusty road on a hot July day; in front the peasants carrying the banners and the women and children the ikons, then the boy choristers and the sacristan with his face tied up and a straw in his hair, then in due order himself, the deacon, and behind him the priest wearing his *calotte* and carrying a cross, and behind them, tramping in the dust, a crowd of peasants – men, women, and children; in the crowd his wife and the priest's wife with kerchiefs on their heads. The choristers sing, the babies cry, the corncrakes call, the lark carols.... Then they make a stand and sprinkle the herd with holy water.... They go on again, and then kneeling pray for rain. Then lunch and talk....

'And that's nice too...' thought the deacon.

VII

KIRILIN and Atchmianov climbed up the mountain by the path. Atchmianov dropped behind and stopped, while Kirilin went up to Nadyezhda Fyodorovna.

'Good-evening,' he said, touching his cap.

'Good-evening.'

'Yes!' said Kirilin, looking at the sky and pondering.

'Why "yes"?' asked Nadyezhda Fyodorovna after a brief pause, noticing that Atchmianov was watching them both.

'And so it seems,' said the officer, slowly, 'that our love has withered before it has blossomed, so to speak. How do you wish me to understand it? Is it a sort of coquetry on your part, or do you look upon me as a nincompoop who can be treated as you choose?'

'It was a mistake! Leave me alone!' Nadyezhda Fyodorovna said sharply, on that beautiful, marvellous evening, looking at him with terror and asking herself with bewilderment, could there really have been a moment when that man attracted her and had been near to her?

'So that's it!' said Kirilin; he thought in silence for a few minutes and said: 'Well, I'll wait till you are in a better humour, and meanwhile I venture to assure you I am a gentleman, and I don't allow anyone to doubt it. Adieu!'

He touched his cap again and walked off, making his way between the bushes. After a short interval Atchmianov approached hesitatingly.

'What a fine evening!' he said with a slight Armenian accent.

He was nice-looking, fashionably dressed, and behaved unaffectedly like a well-bred youth, but Nadyezhda Fyodorovna did not like him because she owed his father three hundred roubles; it was displeasing to her, too, that a shopkeeper had been asked to the picnic, and she was vexed at his coming up to her that evening when her heart felt so pure.

'The picnic is a success altogether,' he said, after a pause.

'Yes,' she agreed, and as though suddenly remembering her debt, she said carelessly: 'Oh, tell them in your shop that Ivan Andreitch will come round in a day or two and will pay three hundred roubles.... I don't remember exactly what it is.'

'I would give another three hundred if you would not mention that debt every day. Why be prosaic?'

Nadyezhda Fyodorovna laughed; the amusing idea occurred to her that if she had been willing and sufficiently immoral she might in one minute be free from her debt. If she, for instance, were to turn the head of this handsome young fool! How amusing, absurd, wild it would be really! And she suddenly felt a longing to make him love her, to plunder him, throw him over, and then to see what would come of it.

'Allow me to give you one piece of advice,' Atchmianov said timidly. 'I beg you to beware of Kirilin. He says horrible things about you everywhere.'

'It doesn't interest me to know what every fool says of me,' Nadyezhda Fyodorovna said coldly, and the amusing thought of playing with handsome young Atchmianov suddenly lost its charm.

'We must go down,' she said; 'they're calling us.'

The fish soup was ready by now. They were ladling it out by platefuls, and eating it with the religious solemnity with which this is only done at a picnic; and everyone thought the fish soup very good, and thought that at home they had never eaten anything so nice. As is always the case at picnics, in the mass of dinner napkins, parcels, useless greasy papers fluttering in the wind, no one knew where was his glass or where his bread. They poured the wine on the carpet and on their own knees, spilt the salt, while it was dark all round them and the fire burnt more dimly, and everyone was too lazy to get up and put wood on. They all drank wine, and even gave Kostya and Katya half a glass each. Nadyezhda Fyodorovna drank one glass and then another, got a little drunk and forgot about Kirilin.

'A splendid picnic, an enchanting evening,' said Laevsky, growing lively with the wine. 'But I should prefer a fine winter to all this. "His beaver collar is silver with hoar-frost." '

'Everyone to his taste,' observed Von Koren.

Laevsky felt uncomfortable; the heat of the camp-fire was beating upon his back, and the hatred of Von Koren upon his breast and face: this hatred on the part of a decent, clever man, a feeling in which there probably lay hid a well-grounded reason, humiliated him and enervated him, and unable to stand up against it, he said in a propitiatory tone:

'I am passionately fond of nature, and I regret that I'm not a naturalist. I envy you.'

'Well, I don't envy you, and don't regret it,' said Nadyezhda Fyodorovna. 'I don't understand how anyone can seriously interest himself in beetles and ladybirds while the people are suffering.'

Laevsky shared her opinion. He was absolutely ignorant of natural science, and so could never reconcile himself to the authoritative tone and the learned and profound air of the people who devoted themselves to the whiskers of ants and the claws of beetles, and he always felt vexed that these people, relying on these whiskers, claws, and something they called protoplasm (he always imagined it in the form of an oyster), should undertake to decide questions involving the origin and life of man. But in Nadyezhda Fyodorovna's words he heard a note of falsity, and simply to contradict her he said: 'The point is not the ladybirds, but the deductions made from them.

VIII

IT was late, eleven o'clock, when they began to get into the carriages to go home. They took their seats, and the only ones missing were Nadyezhda Fyodorovna and Atchmianov, who were running after one another, laughing, the other side of the stream.

'Make haste, my friends,' shouted Samoylenko.

'You oughtn't to give ladies wine,' said Von Koren in a low voice.

Laevsky, exhausted by the picnic, by the hatred of Von Koren, and by his own thoughts, went to meet Nadyezhda Fyodorovna, and when, gay and happy, feeling light as a feather, breathless and laughing, she took him by both hands and laid her head on his breast, he stepped back and said dryly:

'You are behaving like a ... cocotte.'

It sounded horribly coarse, so that he felt sorry for her at once. On his angry, exhausted face she read hatred, pity and vexation with himself, and her heart sank at once. She realized instantly that she had gone too far, had been too free and easy in her behaviour, and overcome with misery, feeling herself heavy, stout, coarse, and drunk, she got into the first empty carriage together with Atchmianov. Laevsky got in with Kirilin, the zoologist with Samoylenko, the deacon with the ladies, and the party set off.

'You see what the Japanese monkeys are like,' Von Koren began, rolling himself up in his cloak and shutting his eyes. 'You heard she doesn't care to take an interest in beetles and ladybirds because the people are suffering. That's how all the Japanese monkeys look upon people like us. They're a slavish, cunning race, terrified by the whip and the fist for ten generations; they tremble and burn incense only before violence; but let the monkey into a free state where there's no one to take it by the collar, and it relaxes at once and shows itself in its true colours. Look how bold they are in picture galleries, in museums, in theatres, or when they talk of science: they puff themselves out and get excited, they are abusive and critical... they are bound to criticize – it's the sign of the slave. You listen: men of the liberal professions are more often sworn at than pickpockets – that's because three-quarters of society are made up of slaves, of just such monkeys. It never happens that a slave holds out his hand to you and sincerely says "Thank you" to you for your work.'

'I don't know what you want,' said Samoylenko, yawning; 'the poor thing, in the simplicity of her heart, wanted to talk to you of scientific subjects, and you draw a conclusion from that. You're cross with him for something or other, and with her, too, to keep him company. She's a splendid woman.'

'Ah, nonsense! An ordinary kept woman, depraved and vulgar. Listen, Alexandr Daviditch; when you meet a simple peasant woman, who isn't living with her husband, who does nothing but giggle, you tell her to go and work. Why are you timid in this case and afraid to tell the truth? Simply because Nadyezhda Fyodorovna is kept, not by a sailor, but by an official.'

'What am I to do with her?' said Samoylenko, getting angry. 'Beat her or what?'

'Not flatter vice. We curse vice only behind its back, and that's like making a long nose at it round a corner. I am a zoologist or a sociologist, which is the same thing; you are a doctor; society believes in us; we ought to point out the terrible harm which threatens it and the next generation from the existence of ladies like Nadyezhda Ivanovna.'

'Fyodorovna,' Samoylenko corrected. 'But what ought society to do?'

'Society? That's its affair. To my thinking the surest and most direct method is – compulsion. *Manu militari* she ought to be returned to her husband; and if her husband won't take her in, then she ought to be sent to penal servitude or some house of correction.'

'Ouf!' sighed Samoylenko. He paused and asked quietly: 'You said the other day that people like Laevsky ought to be destroyed.... Tell me, if you... if the State or society commissioned you to destroy him, could you... bring yourself to it?'

'My hand would not tremble.'

IX

WHEN they got home, Laevsky and Nadyezhda Fyodorovna went into their dark, stuffy, dull rooms. Both were silent. Laevsky lighted a candle, while Nadyezhda Fyodorovna sat down, and without taking off her cloak and hat, lifted her melancholy, guilty eyes to him.

He knew that she expected an explanation from him, but an explanation would be wearisome, useless and exhausting, and his heart was heavy because he had lost control over himself and been rude to her. He chanced to feel in his pocket the letter which he had been intending every day to read to her, and thought if he were to show her that letter now, it would turn her thoughts in another direction.

'It is time to define our relations,' he thought. 'I will give it her; what is to be will be.'

He took out the letter and gave it her.

'Read it. It concerns you.'

Saying this, he went into his own room and lay down on the sofa in the dark without a pillow. Nadyezhda Fyodorovna read the letter, and it seemed to her as though the ceiling were falling and the walls were closing in on her. It seemed suddenly dark and shut in and terrible. She crossed herself quickly three times and said:

'Give him peace, O Lord . . . give him peace. . . .'

And she began crying.

'Vanya,' she called. 'Ivan Andreitch!'

There was no answer. Thinking that Laevsky had come in and was standing behind her chair, she sobbed like a child, and said:

'Why did you not tell me before that he was dead? I wouldn't have gone to the picnic; I shouldn't have laughed so horribly. . . . The men said horrid things to me. What a sin, what a sin! Save me, Vanya, save me. . . . I have been mad. . . . I am lost. . . .'

Laevsky heard her sobs. He felt stifled and his heart was beating violently. In his misery he got up, stood in the middle of the room, groped his way in the dark to an easy-chair by the table, and sat down.

'This is a prison . . .' he thought. 'I must get away. . . . I can't bear it.'

It was too late to go and play cards; there were no restaurants in the town. He lay down again and covered his ears that he might not hear her sobbing, and he suddenly remembered that he could go to Samoylenko. To avoid going near Nadyezhda Fyodorovna, he got out of the window into the garden, climbed over the garden fence, and went along the street. It was dark. A steamer, judging by its lights, a big passenger one, had just come in.... He heard the clank of the anchor chain. A red light was moving rapidly from the shore in the direction of the steamer: it was the Customs boat going out to it.

'The passengers are asleep in their cabins...' thought Laevsky, and he envied the peace of mind of other people.

The windows in Samoylenko's house were open. Laevsky looked in at one of them, then in at another; it was dark and still in the rooms.

'Alexandr Daviditch, are you asleep?' he called. 'Alexandr Daviditch!'

He heard a cough and an uneasy shout:

'Who's there? What the devil?'

'It is I, Alexandr Daviditch; excuse me.'

A little later the door opened; there was a glow of soft light from the lamp, and Samoylenko's huge figure appeared, all in white, with a white nightcap on his head.

'What now?' he asked, scratching himself and breathing hard from sleepiness. 'Wait a minute; I'll open the door directly.'

'Don't trouble; I'll get in at the window....'

Laevsky climbed in at the window, and when he reached Samoylenko, seized him by the hand.

'Alexandr Daviditch,' he said in a shaking voice, 'save me! I beseech you, I implore you. Understand me! My position is agonizing. If it goes on for another two days I shall strangle myself like . . . like a dog.'

'Wait a bit. . . . What are you talking about exactly?'

'Light a candle.'

'Oh . . . oh! . . .' sighed Samoylenko, lighting a candle. 'My God! My God! . . . Why, it's past one, brother.'

'Excuse me, but I can't stay at home,' said Laevsky, feeling great comfort from the light and the presence of Samoylenko. 'You are my best, my only friend, Alexandr Daviditch. . . . You are my only hope. For God's sake, come to my rescue, whether you want to or not. I must get away from here, come what may! . . . Lend me the money!'

'Oh, my God, my God! . . .' sighed Samoylenko, scratching himself. 'I was dropping asleep and I hear the whistle of the steamer, and now you . . . . Do you want much?'

'Three hundred roubles at least. I must leave her a hundred, and I need two hundred for the journey. . . . I owe you about four hundred already, but I will send it you all . . . all. . . .'

Samoylenko took hold of both his whiskers in one hand, and standing with his legs wide apart, pondered.

'Yes . . .' he muttered, musing. 'Three hundred. . . . Yes. . . . But I haven't got so much. I shall have to borrow it from someone.'

'Borrow it, for God's sake!' said Laevsky, seeing from Samoylenko's face that he wanted to lend him the money and certainly would lend it. 'Borrow it, and I'll be sure to pay you back. I will send it from

Petersburg as soon as I get there. You can set your mind at rest about that. I'll tell you what, Sasha,' he said, growing more animated; 'let us have some wine.'

'Yes . . . we can have some wine, too.'

They both went into the dining-room.

'And how about Nadyezhda Fyodorovna?' asked Samoylenko, setting three bottles and a plate of peaches on the table. 'Surely she's not remaining?'

'I will arrange it all, I will arrange it all,' said Laevsky, feeling an unexpected rush of joy. 'I will send her the money afterwards and she will join me. . . . Then we will define our relations. To your health, friend.'

'Wait a bit,' said Samoylenko. 'Drink this first. . . . This is from my vineyard. This bottle is from Navaridze's vineyard and this one is from Ahatulov's. . . . Try all three kinds and tell me candidly. . . . There seems a little acidity about mine. Eh? Don't you taste it?'

'Yes. You have comforted me, Alexandr Daviditch. Thank you. . . . I feel better.'

'Is there any acidity?'

'Goodness only knows, I don't know. But you are a splendid, wonderful man!'

Looking at his pale, excited, good-natured face, Samoylenko remembered Von Koren's view that men like that ought to be destroyed, and Laevsky seemed to him a weak, defenceless child, whom anyone could injure and destroy.

'And when you go, make it up with your mother,' he said. 'It's not right.'

'Yes, yes; I certainly shall.'

They were silent for a while. When they had emptied the first bottle, Samoylenko said:

'You ought to make it up with Von Koren too. You are both such splendid, clever fellows, and you glare at each other like wolves.'

'Yes, he's a fine, very intelligent fellow,' Laevsky assented, ready now to praise and forgive everyone. 'He's a remarkable man, but it's impossible for me to get on with him. No! Our natures are too different. I'm an indolent, weak, submissive nature. Perhaps in a good minute I might hold out my hand to him, but he would turn away from me . . . with contempt.'

Laevsky took a sip of wine, walked from corner to corner and went on, standing in the middle of the room:

'I understand Von Koren very well. His is a resolute, strong, despotic nature. You have heard him continually talking of "the expedition", and it's not mere talk. He wants the wilderness, the moonlit night: all around in little tents, under the open sky, lie sleeping his sick and hungry Cossacks, guides, porters, doctor, priest, all exhausted with their weary marches, while only he is awake, sitting like Stanley on a camp-stool, feeling himself the monarch of the desert and the master of these men. He goes on and on and on, his men groan and die, one after another, and he goes on and on, and in the end perishes himself, but still is monarch and ruler of the desert, since the cross upon his tomb can be seen by the caravans for thirty or forty miles over the desert. I am sorry the man is not in the army. He would have made a splendid military genius. He would not have hesitated to drown his cavalry in the river and make a bridge out of dead bodies. And such hardihood is more needed in war than any kind of fortification or strategy. Oh, I understand him perfectly! Tell me: why is he wasting his substance here? What does he want here?'

'He is studying the marine fauna.'

'No, no, brother, no!' Laevsky sighed. 'A scientific man who was on the steamer told me the Black Sea was poor in animal life, and that in its depths, thanks to the abundance of sulphuric hydrogen, organic life was impossible. All the serious zoologists work at the biological station at Naples or Villefranche. But Von Koren is independent and obstinate: he works on the Black Sea because nobody else is working there; he is at loggerheads with the university, does not care to know his comrades and other scientific men because he is first of all a despot and only secondly a zoologist. And you'll see he'll do something. He is already dreaming that when he comes back from his expedition he will purify our universities from intrigue and mediocrity, and will make the scientific men mind their ps and qs. Despotism is just as strong in science as in the army. And he is spending his second summer in this stinking little town because he would rather be first in a village than second in a town. Here he is a king and an eagle; he keeps all the inhabitants under his thumb and oppresses them with his authority. He has appropriated everyone, he meddles in other people's affairs; everything is of use to him, and everyone is afraid of him. I am slipping out of his clutches, he feels that and hates me. Hasn't he told you that I ought to be destroyed or sent to hard labour?'

'Yes,' laughed Samoylenko.

Laevsky laughed too, and drank some wine.

'His ideals are despotic too,' he said, laughing, and biting a peach. 'Ordinary mortals think of their neighbour – me, you, man in fact – if they work for the common weal. To Von Koren men are puppets and nonentities, too trivial to be the object of his life. He works, will go for his expedition and break his neck there, not for the sake of love for his neighbour, but for the sake of such abstractions as humanity, future generations, an ideal race of men. He exerts himself for the improvement of the human race, and we are in his eyes only slaves, food for the cannon, beasts of burden; some he would destroy or stow away in Siberia, others he would break by discipline, would, like Araktcheev, force them to get up and go to bed to the sound of the drum; would appoint eunuchs to preserve our chastity and morality, would order them to fire at anyone who steps out of the circle of our narrow conservative morality; and all this in the name of the improvement of the human race.... And what is the human race? Illusion, mirage... despots have always been illusionists. I understand him very well, brother. I appreciate him and don't deny his importance; this world rests on men like him, and if the world were left only to such men as us, for all our good-nature and good intentions, we should make as great a mess of it as the flies have of that picture. Yes.'

Laevsky sat down beside Samoylenko, and said with genuine feeling: 'I'm a foolish, worthless, depraved man. The air I breathe, this wine, love, life in fact – for all that, I have given nothing in exchange so far but lying, idleness, and cowardice. Till now I have deceived myself and other people; I have been miserable about it, and my misery was cheap and common. I bow my back humbly before Von Koren's hatred because at times I hate and despise myself.'

Laevsky began again pacing from one end of the room to the other in excitement, and said:

'I'm glad I see my faults clearly and am conscious of them. That will help me to reform and become a different man. My dear fellow, if only you knew how passionately, with what anguish, I long for such a change. And I swear to you I'll be a man! I will! I don't know whether it is the wine that is speaking in me, or whether it really is so, but it seems to me that it is long since I have spent such pure and lucid moments as I have just now with you.'

'It's time to sleep, brother,' said Samoylenko.

'Yes, yes.... Excuse me; I'll go directly.'

Laevsky moved hurriedly about the furniture and windows, looking for his cap.

'Thank you,' he muttered, sighing. 'Thank you.... Kind and friendly words are better than charity. You have given me new life.'

He found his cap, stopped, and looked guiltily at Samoylenko.

'Alexandr Daviditch,' he said in an imploring voice.

'What is it?'

'Let me stay the night with you, my dear fellow!'

'Certainly.... Why not?'

Laevsky lay down on the sofa, and went on talking to the doctor for a long time.

X

THREE days after the picnic, Marya Konstantinovna unexpectedly called on Nadyezhda Fyodorovna, and without greeting her or taking off her hat, seized her by both hands, pressed them to her breast and said in great excitement:

'My dear, I am deeply touched and moved: our dear kind-hearted doctor told my Nikodim Alexandritch yesterday that your husband was dead. Tell me, my dear ... tell me, is it true?'

'Yes, it's true; he is dead,' answered Nadyezhda Fyodorovna.

'That is awful, awful, my dear! But there's no evil without some compensation; your husband was no doubt a noble, wonderful, holy man, and such are more needed in Heaven than on earth.'

Every line and feature in Marya Konstantinovna's face began quivering as though little needles were jumping up and down under her skin; she gave an almond-oily smile and said, breathlessly, enthusiastically:

'And so you are free, my dear. You can hold your head high now, and look people boldly in the face. Henceforth God and man will bless your union with Ivan Andreitch. It's enchanting. I am trembling with joy, I can find no words. My dear, I will give you away.... Nikodim Alexandritch and I have been so fond of you, you will allow us to give our blessing to your pure, lawful union. When, when do you think of being married?'

'I haven't thought of it,' said Nadyezhda Fyodorovna, freeing her hands.

'That's impossible, my dear. You have thought of it, you have.'

'Upon my word, I haven't,' said Nadyezhda Fyodorovna, laughing. 'What should we be married for? I see no necessity for it. We'll go on living as we have lived.'

'What are you saying!' cried Marya Konstantinovna in horror. 'For God's sake, what are you saying!'

'Our getting married won't make things any better. On the contrary, it will make them even worse. We shall lose our freedom.'

'My dear, my dear, what are you saying!' exclaimed Marya Konstantinovna, stepping back and flinging up her hands. 'You are talking wildly! Think what you are saying. You must settle down!'

' "Settle down." How do you mean? I have not lived yet, and you tell me to settle down.'

Nadyezhda Fyodorovna reflected that she really had not lived. She had finished her studies in a boarding-school and had been married to a man she did not love; then she had thrown in her lot with Laevsky, and had spent all her time with him on this empty, desolate coast, always expecting something better. Was that life?

'I ought to be married though,' she thought, but remembering Kirilin and Atchmianov she flushed and said:

'No, it's impossible. Even if Ivan Andreitch begged me to on his knees – even then I would refuse.'

Marya Konstantinovna sat on the sofa for a minute in silence, grave and mournful, gazing fixedly into space; then she got up and said coldly:

'Good-bye, my dear! Forgive me for having troubled you. Though it's not easy for me, it's my duty to tell you that from this day all is over between us, and, in spite of my profound respect for Ivan Andreitch, the door of my house is closed to you henceforth.'

She uttered these words with great solemnity and was herself overwhelmed by her solemn tone. Her face began quivering again; it assumed a soft almond-oily expression. She held out both hands to Nadyezhda Fyodorovna, who was overcome with alarm and confusion, and said in an imploring voice:

'My dear, allow me if only for a moment to be a mother or an elder sister to you! I will be as frank with you as a mother.'

Nadyezhda Fyodorovna felt in her bosom warmth, gladness, and pity for herself, as though her own mother had really risen up and were standing before her. She impulsively embraced Marya Konstantinovna and pressed her face to her shoulder. Both of them shed tears. They sat down on the sofa and for a few minutes sobbed without looking at one another or being able to utter a word.

'My dear child,' began Marya Konstantinovna, 'I will tell you some harsh truths, without sparing you.'

'For God's sake, for God's sake, do!'

'Trust me, my dear. You remember of all the ladies here, I was the only one to receive you. You horrified me from the very first day, but I had not the heart to treat you with disdain like all the rest. I grieved over dear, good Ivan Andreitch as though he were my son – a young man in a strange place, inexperienced, weak, with no mother; and I was worried, dreadfully worried. . . . My husband was opposed to our making his acquaintance, but I talked him over . . . persuaded him. . . . We began receiving Ivan Andreitch, and with him, of course, you. If we had not, he would have been insulted. I have a daughter, a son. . . . You understand the tender mind, the pure heart of childhood . . . "whoso offendeth one of these little ones". . . . I received you into my house and trembled for my children. Oh, when you become a mother, you will understand my fears. And everyone was surprised at my receiving you, excuse my saying so, as a respectable woman, and hinted to me . . . well, of course, slanders, suppositions. . . . At the bottom of my heart I blamed you, but you were unhappy, flighty, to be pitied, and my heart was wrung with pity for you.'

'But why, why?' asked Nadyezhda Fyodorovna, trembling all over. 'What harm have I done anyone?'

'You are a terrible sinner. You broke the vow you made your husband at the altar. You seduced a fine young man, who perhaps had he not met you might have taken a lawful partner for life from a good family in his own circle, and would have been like everyone else now. You have ruined his youth. Don't speak, don't speak, my dear! I never believe that man is to blame for our sins. It is always the woman's fault. Men are frivolous in domestic life; they are guided by their minds, and not by their hearts. There's a great deal they don't understand; woman understands it all. Everything depends on her. To her much is given and from her much will be required. Oh, my dear, if she had been more foolish or weaker than man on that side, God would not have entrusted her with the education of boys and girls. And then, my dear, you entered on the path of vice, forgetting all modesty; any other woman in your place would have hidden herself from people, would have sat shut up at home, and would only have been seen in the temple of God, pale, dressed all in black and weeping, and everyone would have said in genuine compassion: "O Lord, this erring angel is coming back again to Thee...." But you, my dear, have forgotten all discretion; have lived openly, extravagantly; have seemed to be proud of your sin; you have been gay and laughing, and I, looking at you, shuddered with horror, and have been afraid that thunder from Heaven would strike our house while you were sitting with us. My dear, don't speak, don't speak,' cried Marya Konstantinovna, observing that Nadyezhda Fyodorovna wanted to speak. 'Trust me, I will not deceive you, I will not hide one truth from the eyes of your soul. Listen to me, my dear.... God marks great sinners, and you have been marked out: only think – your costumes have always been appalling.'

Nadyezhda Fyodorovna, who had always had the highest opinion of her costumes, left off crying and looked at her with surprise.

'Yes, appalling,' Marya Konstantinovna went on. 'Anyone could judge of your behaviour from the elaboration and gaudiness of your attire. People laughed and shrugged their shoulders as they looked at you, and I grieved, I grieved.... And forgive me, my dear; you are not nice in your person! When we met in the bathing-place, you made me tremble. Your outer clothing was decent enough, but your petticoat, your chemise.... My dear, I blushed! Poor Ivan Andreitch! No one ever ties his cravat properly, and from his linen and his boots, poor fellow! one can see he has no one at home to look after him. And he is always hungry, my darling, and of course, if there is no one at home to think of the samovar and the coffee, one is forced to spend half one's salary at the pavilion. And it's simply awful, awful in your home! No one else in the town has flies, but there's no getting rid of them in your rooms: all the plates and dishes are black with them. If you look at the windows and the chairs, there's nothing but dust, dead flies, and glasses.... What do you want glasses standing about for? And, my dear, the table's not cleared till this time in the day. And one's ashamed to go into your bedroom: underclothes flung about everywhere, india-rubber tubes hanging on the walls, pails and basins standing about.... My dear! A husband ought to know nothing, and his wife ought to be as neat as a little angel in his presence. I wake up every morning before it is light, and wash my face with cold water that my Nikodim Alexandritch may not see me looking drowsy.'

'That's all nonsense,' Nadyezhda Fyodorovna sobbed. 'If only I were happy, but I am so unhappy!'

'Yes, yes; you are very unhappy!' Marya Konstantinovna sighed, hardly able to restrain herself from weeping. 'And there's terrible grief in store for you in the future! A solitary old age, ill-health; and then you will have to answer at the dread judgment seat.... It's awful, awful. Now fate itself holds out to you a helping hand, and you madly thrust it from you. Be married, make haste and be married!'

'Yes, we must, we must,' said Nadyezhda Fyodorovna; 'but it's impossible!'

'Why?'

'It's impossible. Oh, if only you knew!'

Nadyezhda Fyodorovna had an impulse to tell her about Kirilin, and how the evening before she had met handsome young Atchmianov at the harbour, and how the mad, ridiculous idea had occurred to her of cancelling her debt for three hundred; it had amused her very much, and she returned home late in the evening feeling that she had sold herself and was irrevocably lost. She did not know herself how it had happened. And she longed to swear to Marya Konstantinovna that she would certainly pay that debt, but sobs and shame prevented her from speaking.

'I am going away,' she said. 'Ivan Andreitch may stay, but I am going.'

'Where?'

'To Russia.'

'But how will you live there? Why, you have nothing.'

'I will do translation, or . . . or I will open a library. . . .'

'Don't let your fancy run away with you, my dear. You must have money for a library. Well, I will leave you now, and you calm yourself and think things over, and to-morrow come and see me, bright and happy. That will be enchanting! Well, good-bye, my angel. Let me kiss you.'

Marya Konstantinovna kissed Nadyezhda Fyodorovna on the forehead, made the sign of the cross over her, and softly withdrew. It was getting dark, and Olga lighted up in the kitchen. Still crying, Nadyezhda Fyodorovna went into the bedroom and lay down on the bed. She began to be very feverish. She undressed without getting up, crumpled up her clothes at her feet, and curled herself up under the bedclothes. She was thirsty, and there was no one to give her something to drink.

'I'll pay it back!' she said to herself, and it seemed to her in delirium that she was sitting beside some sick woman, and recognized her as herself. 'I'll pay it back. It would be stupid to imagine that it was for money I . . . I will go away and send him the money from Petersburg. At first a hundred . . . then another hundred . . . and then the third hundred. . . .'

It was late at night when Laevsky came in.

'At first a hundred . . .' Nadyezhda Fyodorovna said to him, 'then another hundred . . . .'

'You ought to take some quinine,' he said, and thought, 'To-morrow is Wednesday; the steamer goes and I am not going in it. So I shall have to go on living here till Saturday.'

Nadyezhda Fyodorovna knelt up in bed.

'I didn't say anything just now, did I?' she asked, smiling and screwing up her eyes at the light.

'No, nothing. We shall have to send for the doctor to-morrow morning. Go to sleep.'

He took his pillow and went to the door. Ever since he had finally made up his mind to go away and leave Nadyezhda Fyodorovna, she had begun to raise in him pity and a sense of guilt; he felt a little ashamed in her presence, as though in the presence of a sick or old horse whom one has decided to kill. He stopped in the doorway and looked round at her.

'I was out of humour at the picnic and said something rude to you. Forgive me, for God's sake!'

Saying this, he went off to his study, lay down, and for a long while could not get to sleep.

Next morning when Samoylenko, attired, as it was a holiday, in full-dress uniform with epaulettes on his shoulders and decorations on his breast, came out of the bedroom after feeling Nadyezhda Fyodorovna's pulse and looking at her tongue, Laevsky, who was standing in the doorway, asked him anxiously: 'Well? Well?'

There was an expression of terror, of extreme uneasiness, and of hope on his face.

'Don't worry yourself; there's nothing dangerous,' said Samoylenko; 'it's the usual fever.'

'I don't mean that.' Laevsky frowned impatiently. 'Have you got the money?'

'My dear soul, forgive me,' he whispered, looking round at the door and overcome with confusion. 'For God's sake, forgive me! No one has anything to spare, and I've only been able to collect by five- and by ten-rouble notes.... Only a hundred and ten in all. To-day I'll speak to someone else. Have patience.'

'But Saturday is the latest date,' whispered Laevsky, trembling with impatience. 'By all that's sacred, get it by Saturday! If I don't get away by Saturday, nothing's any use, nothing! I can't understand how a doctor can be without money!'

'Lord have mercy on us!' Samoylenko whispered rapidly and intensely, and there was positively a breaking note in his throat. 'I've been stripped of everything; I am owed seven thousand, and I'm in debt all round. Is it my fault?'

'Then you'll get it by Saturday? Yes?'

'I'll try.'

'I implore you, my dear fellow! So that the money may be in my hands by Friday morning!'

Samoylenko sat down and prescribed solution of quinine and kalii bromati and tincture of rhubarb, tincturæ gentianæ, aquæ fœniculi – all in one mixture, added some pink syrup to sweeten it, and went away.

XI

'YOU look as though you were coming to arrest me,' said Von Koren, seeing Samoylenko coming in, in his full-dress uniform.

'I was passing by and thought: "Suppose I go in and pay my respects to zoology,"' said Samoylenko, sitting down at the big table, knocked together by the zoologist himself out of plain boards. 'Good-morning, holy father,' he said to the deacon, who was sitting in the window, copying something. 'I'll stay a minute and then run home to see about dinner. It's time.... I'm not hindering you?'

'Not in the least,' answered the zoologist, laying out over the table slips of paper covered with small writing. 'We are busy copying.'

'Ah!... Oh, my goodness, my goodness!...' sighed Samoylenko. He cautiously took up from the table a dusty book on which there was lying a dead dried spider, and said: 'Only fancy, though; some little green beetle is going about its business, when suddenly a monster like this swoops down upon it. I can fancy its terror.'

'Yes, I suppose so.'

'Is poison given it to protect it from its enemies?'

'Yes, to protect it and enable it to attack.'

'To be sure, to be sure.... And everything in nature, my dear fellows, is consistent and can be explained,' sighed Samoylenko; 'only I tell you what I don't understand. You're a man of very great intellect, so explain it to me, please. There are, you know, little beasts no bigger than rats, rather handsome to look at, but nasty and immoral in the extreme, let me tell you. Suppose such a little beast is running in the woods. He sees a bird; he catches it and devours it. He goes on and sees in the grass a nest of eggs; he does not want to eat them – he is not hungry, but yet he tastes one egg and scatters the others out of the nest with his paw. Then he meets a frog and begins to play with it; when he has tormented the frog he goes on licking himself and meets a beetle; he crushes the beetle with his paw ... and so he spoils and destroys everything on his way.... He creeps into other beasts' holes, tears up the anthills, cracks the snail's shell. If he meets a rat, he fights with it; if he meets a snake or a mouse, he must strangle it; and so the whole day long. Come, tell me: what is the use of a beast like that? Why was he created?'

'I don't know what animal you are talking of,' said Von Koren; 'most likely one of the insectivora. Well, he got hold of the bird because it was incautious; he broke the nest of eggs because the bird was not skilful, had made the nest badly and did not know how to conceal it. The frog probably had some defect in its colouring or he would not have seen it, and so on. Your little beast only destroys the weak, the unskilful, the careless – in fact, those who have defects which nature does not think fit to hand on to posterity. Only the cleverer, the stronger, the more careful and developed survive; and so your little beast, without suspecting it, is serving the great ends of perfecting creation.'

'Yes, yes, yes.... By the way, brother,' said Samoylenko carelessly, 'lend me a hundred roubles.'

'Very good. There are some very interesting types among the insectivorous mammals. For instance, the mole is said to be useful because he devours noxious insects. There is a story that some German sent William I. a fur coat made of moleskins, and the Emperor ordered him to be reproved for having destroyed so great a number of useful animals. And yet the mole is not a bit less cruel than your little beast, and is very mischievous besides, as he spoils meadows terribly.'

Von Koren opened a box and took out a hundred-rouble note.

'The mole has a powerful thorax, just like the bat,' he went on, shutting the box; 'the bones and muscles are tremendously developed, the mouth is extraordinarily powerfully furnished. If it had the proportions of an elephant, it would be an all-destructive, invincible animal. It is interesting when two moles meet underground; they begin at once as though by agreement digging a little platform; they need the platform in order to have a battle more conveniently. When they have made it they enter upon a ferocious struggle and fight till the weaker one falls. Take the hundred roubles,' said Von Koren, dropping his voice, 'but only on condition that you're not borrowing it for Laevsky.'

'And if it were for Laevsky,' cried Samoylenko, flaring up, 'what is that to you?'

'I can't give it to you for Laevsky. I know you like lending people money. You would give it to Kerim, the brigand, if he were to ask you; but, excuse me, I can't assist you in that direction.'

'Yes, it is for Laevsky I am asking it,' said Samoylenko, standing up and waving his right arm. 'Yes! For Laevsky! And no one, fiend or devil, has a right to dictate to me how to dispose of my own money. It doesn't suit you to lend it me? No?'

The deacon began laughing.

'Don't get excited, but be reasonable,' said the zoologist. 'To shower benefits on Mr. Laevsky is, to my thinking, as senseless as to water weeds or to feed locusts.'

'To my thinking, it is our duty to help our neighbours!' cried Samoylenko.

'In that case, help that hungry Turk who is lying under the fence! He is a workman and more useful and indispensable than your Laevsky. Give him that hundred-rouble note! Or subscribe a hundred roubles to my expedition!'

'Will you give me the money or not? I ask you!'

'Tell me openly: what does he want money for?'

'It's not a secret; he wants to go to Petersburg on Saturday.'

'So that is it!' Von Koren drawled out. 'Aha!... We understand. And is she going with him, or how is it to be?'

'She's staying here for the time. He'll arrange his affairs in Petersburg and send her the money, and then she'll go.'

'That's smart!' said the zoologist, and he gave a short tenor laugh. 'Smart, well planned.'

He went rapidly up to Samoylenko, and standing face to face with him, and looking him in the eyes, asked: 'Tell me now honestly: is he tired of her? Yes? tell me: is he tired of her? Yes?'

'Yes,' Samoylenko articulated, beginning to perspire.

'How repulsive it is!' said Von Koren, and from his face it could be seen that he felt repulsion. 'One of two things, Alexandr Daviditch: either you are in the plot with him, or, excuse my saying so, you are a simpleton. Surely you must see that he is taking you in like a child in the most shameless way? Why, it's as clear as day that he wants to get rid of her and abandon her here. She'll be left a burden on you. It is as clear as day that you will have to send her to Petersburg at your expense. Surely your fine friend can't have so blinded you by his dazzling qualities that you can't see the simplest thing?'

'That's all supposition,' said Samoylenko, sitting down.

'Supposition? But why is he going alone instead of taking her with him? And ask him why he doesn't send her off first. The sly beast!'

Overcome with sudden doubts and suspicions about his friend, Samoylenko weakened and took a humbler tone.

'But it's impossible,' he said, recalling the night Laevsky had spent at his house. 'He is so unhappy!'

'What of that? Thieves and incendiaries are unhappy too!'

'Even supposing you are right...' said Samoylenko, hesitating. 'Let us admit it.... Still, he's a young man in a strange place... a student. We have been students, too, and there is no one but us to come to his assistance.'

'To help him to do abominable things, because he and you at different times have been at universities, and neither of you did anything there! What nonsense!'

'Stop; let us talk it over coolly. I imagine it will be possible to make some arrangement. . . .' Samoylenko reflected, twiddling his fingers. 'I'll give him the money, you see, but make him promise on his honour that within a week he'll send Nadyezhda Fyodorovna the money for the journey.'

'And he'll give you his word of honour – in fact, he'll shed tears and believe in it himself; but what's his word of honour worth? He won't keep it, and when in a year or two you meet him on the Nevsky Prospect with a new mistress on his arm, he'll excuse himself on the ground that he has been crippled by civilization, and that he is made after the pattern of Rudin. Drop him, for God's sake! Keep away from the filth; don't stir it up with both hands!'

Samoylenko thought for a minute and said resolutely:

'But I shall give him the money all the same. As you please. I can't bring myself to refuse a man simply on an assumption.'

'Very fine, too. You can kiss him if you like.'

'Give me the hundred roubles, then,' Samoylenko asked timidly.

'I won't.'

A silence followed. Samoylenko was quite crushed; his face wore a guilty, abashed, and ingratiating expression, and it was strange to see this pitiful, childish, shamefaced countenance on a huge man wearing epaulettes and orders of merit.

'The bishop here goes the round of his diocese on horseback instead of in a carriage,' said the deacon, laying down his pen. 'It's extremely touching to see him sit on his horse. His simplicity and humility are full of biblical grandeur.'

'Is he a good man?' asked Von Koren, who was glad to change the conversation.

'Of course! If he hadn't been a good man, do you suppose he would have been consecrated a bishop?'

'Among the bishops are to be found good and gifted men,' said Von Koren. 'The only drawback is that some of them have the weakness to imagine themselves statesmen. One busies himself with Russification, another criticizes the sciences. That's not their business. They had much better look into their consistory a little.'

'A layman cannot judge of bishops.'

'Why so, deacon? A bishop is a man just the same as you or I.'

'The same, but not the same.' The deacon was offended and took up his pen. 'If you had been the same, the Divine Grace would have rested upon you, and you would have been bishop yourself; and since you are not bishop, if follows you are not the same.'

'Don't talk nonsense, deacon,' said Samoylenko dejectedly. 'Listen to what I suggest,' he said, turning to Von Koren. 'Don't give me that hundred roubles. You'll be having your dinners with me for three months before the winter, so let me have the money beforehand for three months.'

'I won't.'

Samoylenko blinked and turned crimson; he mechanically drew towards him the book with the spider on it and looked at it, then he got up and took his hat.

Von Koren felt sorry for him.

'What it is to have to live and do with people like this,' said the zoologist, and he kicked a paper into the corner with indignation. 'You must understand that this is not kindness, it is not love, but cowardice, slackness, poison! What's gained by reason is lost by your flabby good-for-nothing hearts! When I was ill with typhoid as a schoolboy, my aunt in her sympathy gave me pickled mushrooms to eat, and I very nearly died. You, and my aunt too, must understand that love for man is not to be found in the heart or the stomach or the bowels, but here!'

Von Koren slapped himself on the forehead.

'Take it,' he said, and thrust a hundred-rouble note into his hand.

'You've no need to be angry, Kolya,' said Samoylenko mildly, folding up the note. 'I quite understand you, but . . . you must put yourself in my place.'

'You are an old woman, that's what you are.'

The deacon burst out laughing.

'Hear my last request, Alexandr Daviditch,' said Von Koren hotly. 'When you give that scoundrel the money, make it a condition that he takes his lady with him, or sends her on ahead, and don't give it him without. There's no need to stand on ceremony with him. Tell him so, or, if you don't, I give you my word I'll go to his office and kick him downstairs, and I'll break off all acquaintance with you. So you'd better know it.'

'Well! To go with her or send her on beforehand will be more convenient for him,' said Samoylenko. 'He'll be delighted indeed. Well, good-bye.'

He said good-bye affectionately and went out, but before shutting the door after him, he looked round at Von Koren and, with a ferocious face, said:

'It's the Germans who have ruined you, brother! Yes! The Germans!'

XII

NEXT day, Thursday, Marya Konstantinovna was celebrating the birthday of her Kostya. All were invited to come at midday and eat pies, and in the evening to drink chocolate. When Laevsky and Nadyezhda Fyodorovna arrived in the evening, the zoologist, who was already sitting in the drawing-room, drinking chocolate, asked Samoylenko:

'Have you talked to him?'

'Not yet.'

'Mind now, don't stand on ceremony. I can't understand the insolence of these people! Why, they know perfectly well the view taken by this family of their cohabitation, and yet they force themselves in here.'

'If one is to pay attention to every prejudice,' said Samoylenko, 'one could go nowhere.'

'Do you mean to say that the repugnance felt by the masses for illicit love and moral laxity is a prejudice?'

'Of course it is. It's prejudice and hate. When the soldiers see a girl of light behaviour, they laugh and whistle; but just ask them what they are themselves.'

'It's not for nothing they whistle. The fact that girls strangle their illegitimate children and go to prison for it, and that Anna Karenin flung herself under the train, and that in the villages they smear the gates with tar, and that you and I, without knowing why, are pleased by Katya's purity, and that every one of us feels a vague craving for pure love, though he knows there is no such love – is all that prejudice? That is the one thing, brother, which has survived intact from natural selection, and, if it were not for that obscure force regulating the relations of the sexes, the Laevskys would have it all their own way, and mankind would degenerate in two years.'

Laevsky came into the drawing-room, greeted everyone, and shaking hands with Von Koren, smiled ingratiatingly. He waited for a favourable moment and said to Samoylenko:

'Excuse me, Alexandr Daviditch, I must say two words to you.'

Samoylenko got up, put his arm round Laevsky's waist, and both of them went into Nikodim Alexandritch's study.

'To-morrow's Friday,' said Laevsky, biting his nails. 'Have you got what you promised?'

'I've only got two hundred. I'll get the rest to-day or to-morrow. Don't worry yourself.'

'Thank God...' sighed Laevsky, and his hands began trembling with joy. 'You are saving me, Alexandr Daviditch, and I swear to you by God, by my happiness and anything you like, I'll send you the money as soon as I arrive. And I'll send you my old debt too.'

'Look here, Vanya...' said Samoylenko, turning crimson and taking him by the button. 'You must forgive my meddling in your private affairs, but... why shouldn't you take Nadyezhda Fyodorovna with you?'

'You queer fellow. How is that possible? One of us must stay, or our creditors will raise an outcry. You see, I owe seven hundred or more to the shops. Only wait, and I will send them the money. I'll stop their mouths, and then she can come away.'

'I see.... But why shouldn't you send her on first?'

'My goodness, as though that were possible!' Laevsky was horrified. 'Why, she's a woman; what would she do there alone? What does she know about it? That would only be a loss of time and a useless waste of money.'

'That's reasonable...' thought Samoylenko, but remembering his conversation with Von Koren, he looked down and said sullenly: 'I can't agree with you. Either go with her or send her first; otherwise... otherwise I won't give you the money. Those are my last words....'

He staggered back, lurched backwards against the door, and went into the drawing-room, crimson, and overcome with confusion.

'Friday... Friday,' thought Laevsky, going back into the drawing-room. 'Friday...'

He was handed a cup of chocolate; he burnt his lips and tongue with the scalding chocolate and thought: 'Friday... Friday...'

For some reason he could not get the word 'Friday' out of his head; he could think of nothing but Friday, and the only thing that was clear to him, not in his brain but somewhere in his heart, was that he would not get off on Saturday. Before him stood Nikodim

Alexandritch, very neat, with his hair combed over his temples, saying:

'Please take something to eat....'

Marya Konstantinovna showed the visitors Katya's school report and said, drawling:

'It's very, very difficult to do well at school nowadays! So much is expected....'

'Mamma!' groaned Katya, not knowing where to hide her confusion at the praises of the company.

Laevsky, too, looked at the report and praised it. Scripture, Russian language, conduct, fives and fours, danced before his eyes, and all this, mixed with the haunting refrain of 'Friday', with the carefully combed locks of Nikodim Alexandritch and the red cheeks of Katya, produced on him a sensation of such immense overwhelming boredom that he almost shrieked with despair and asked himself: 'Is it possible, is it possible I shall not get away?'

They put two card tables side by side and sat down to play post. Laevsky sat down too.

'Friday...Friday...' he kept thinking, as he smiled and took a pencil out of his pocket. 'Friday....'

He wanted to think over his position, and was afraid to think. It was terrible to him to realize that the doctor had detected him in the deception which he had so long and carefully concealed from himself. Every time he thought of his future he would not let his thoughts have full rein. He would get into the train and set off, and thereby the problem of his life would be solved, and he did not let his thoughts go farther. Like a far-away dim light in the fields, the thought sometimes flickered in his mind that in one of the side-streets of Petersburg, in the remote future, he would have to have recourse to a tiny lie in order to get rid of Nadyezhda Fyodorovna and pay his debts; he would tell a lie only once, and then a completely new life would begin. And that was right: at the price of a small lie he would win so much truth.

Now when by his blunt refusal the doctor had crudely hinted at his deception, he began to understand that he would need deception not only in the remote future, but to-day, and to-morrow, and in a month's time, and perhaps up to the very end of his life. In fact, in order to get away he would have to lie to Nadyezhda Fyodorovna, to his creditors, and to his superiors in the Service; then, in order to get money in Petersburg, he would have to lie to his mother, to tell her that he had already broken with Nadyezhda Fyodorovna; and his mother would not give him more than five hundred roubles, so he had already deceived the doctor, as he would not be in a position to pay him back the money within a short time. Afterwards, when Nadyezhda Fyodorovna came to Petersburg, he would have to resort to a regular series of deceptions, little and big, in order to get free of her; and again there would be tears, boredom, a disgusting existence, remorse, and so there would be no new life. Deception and nothing more. A whole mountain of lies rose before Laevsky's imagination. To leap over it at one bound and not to do his lying piecemeal, he would have to bring himself to stern, uncompromising action; for instance, to getting up without saying a word, putting on his hat, and at once setting off without money and without explanation. But Laevsky felt that was impossible for him.

'Friday, Friday...' he thought. 'Friday....'

They wrote little notes, folded them in two, and put them in Nikodim Alexandritch's old top-hat. When there were a sufficient heap of notes, Kostya, who acted the part of postman, walked round the table and delivered them. The deacon, Katya, and Kostya, who received amusing notes and tried to write as funnily as they could, were highly delighted.

'We must have a little talk,' Nadyezhda Fyodorovna read in a little note; she glanced at Marya Konstantinovna, who gave her an almond-oily smile and nodded.

'Talk of what?' thought Nadyezhda Fyodorovna. 'If one can't tell the whole, it's no use talking.'

Before going out for the evening she had tied Laevsky's cravat for him, and that simple action filled her soul with tenderness and sorrow. The anxiety in his face, his absent-minded looks, his pallor, and the incomprehensible change that had taken place in him of late, and the fact that she had a terrible revolting secret from him, and the fact that her hands trembled when she tied his cravat – all this seemed to tell her that they had not long left to be together. She looked at him as though he were an ikon, with terror and penitence, and thought: 'Forgive, forgive.'

Opposite her was sitting Atchmianov, and he never took his black, love-sick eyes off her. She was stirred by passion; she was ashamed of herself, and afraid that even her misery and sorrow would not prevent her from yielding to impure desire to-morrow, if not to-day – and that, like a drunkard, she would not have the strength to stop herself.

She made up her mind to go away that she might not continue this life, shameful for herself, and humiliating for Laevsky. She would beseech him with tears to let her go; and if he opposed her, she would go away secretly. She would not tell him what had happened; let him keep a pure memory of her.

'I love you, I love you, I love you,' she read. It was from Atchmianov.

She would live in some far remote place, would work and send Laevsky, 'anonymously', money, embroidered shirts, and tobacco, and would return to him only in old age or if he were dangerously ill and needed a nurse. When in his old age he learned what were her reasons for leaving him and refusing to be his wife, he would appreciate her sacrifice and forgive.

'You've got a long nose.' That must be from the deacon or Kostya.

Nadyezhda Fyodorovna imagined how, parting from Laevsky, she would embrace him warmly, would kiss his hand, and would swear to love him all her life, all her life, and then, living in obscurity among strangers, she would every day think that somewhere she had a friend, someone she loved – a pure, noble, lofty man who kept a pure memory of her.

'If you don't give me an interview to-day, I shall take measures, I assure you on my word of honour. You can't treat decent people like this; you must understand that.' That was from Kirilin.

XIII

LAEVSKY received two notes; he opened one and read: 'Don't go away, my darling.'

'Who could have written that?' he thought. 'Not Samoylenko, of course. And not the deacon, for he doesn't know I want to go away. Von Koren, perhaps?'

The zoologist bent over the table and drew a pyramid. Laevsky fancied that his eyes were smiling.

'Most likely Samoylenko . . . has been gossiping,' thought Laevsky.

In the other note, in the same disguised angular handwriting with long tails to the letters, was written: 'Somebody won't go away on Saturday.'

'A stupid gibe,' thought Laevsky. 'Friday, Friday. . . .'

Something rose in his throat. He touched his collar and coughed, but instead of a cough a laugh broke from his throat.

'Ha-ha-ha!' he laughed. 'Ha-ha-ha! What am I laughing at? Ha-ha- ha!'

He tried to restrain himself, covered his mouth with his hand, but the laugh choked his chest and throat, and his hand could not cover his mouth.

'How stupid it is!' he thought, rolling with laughter. 'Have I gone out of my mind?'

The laugh grew shriller and shriller, and became something like the bark of a lap-dog. Laevsky tried to get up from the table, but his legs would not obey him and his right hand was strangely, without his volition, dancing on the table, convulsively clutching and crumpling up the bits of paper. He saw looks of wonder, Samoylenko's grave, frightened face, and the eyes of the zoologist full of cold irony and disgust, and realized that he was in hysterics.

'How hideous, how shameful!' he thought, feeling the warmth of tears on his face. '...Oh, oh, what a disgrace! It has never happened to me....'

They took him under his arms, and supporting his head from behind, led him away; a glass gleamed before his eyes and knocked against his teeth, and the water was spilt on his breast; he was in a little room, with two beds in the middle, side by side, covered by two snow-white quilts. He dropped on one of the beds and sobbed.

'It's nothing, it's nothing,' Samoylenko kept saying; 'it does happen... it does happen....'

Chill with horror, trembling all over and dreading something awful, Nadyezhda Fyodorovna stood by the bedside and kept asking:

'What is it? What is it? For God's sake, tell me.'

'Can Kirilin have written him something?' she thought.

'It's nothing,' said Laevsky, laughing and crying; 'go away, darling.'

His face expressed neither hatred nor repulsion: so he knew nothing; Nadyezhda Fyodorovna was somewhat reassured, and she went into the drawing-room.

'Don't agitate yourself, my dear!' said Marya Konstantinovna, sitting down beside her and taking her hand. 'It will pass. Men are just as weak as we poor sinners. You are both going through a crisis.... One can so well understand it! Well, my dear, I am waiting for an answer. Let us have a little talk.'

'No, we are not going to talk,' said Nadyezhda

Fyodorovna, listening to Laevsky's sobs. 'I feel depressed.... You must allow me to go home.'

'What do you mean, what do you mean, my dear?' cried Marya Konstantinovna in alarm. 'Do you think I could let you go without supper? We will have something to eat, and then you may go with my blessing.'

'I feel miserable...' whispered Nadyezhda Fyodorovna, and she caught at the arm of the chair with both hands to avoid falling.

'He's got a touch of hysterics,' said Von Koren gaily, coming into the drawing-room, but seeing Nadyezhda Fyodorovna, he was taken aback and retreated.

When the attack was over, Laevsky sat on the strange bed and thought.

'Disgraceful! I've been howling like some wretched girl! I must have been absurd and disgusting. I will go away by the back stairs.... But that would seem as though I took my hysterics too seriously. I ought to take it as a joke....'

He looked in the looking-glass, sat there for some time, and went back into the drawing-room.

'Here I am,' he said, smiling; he felt agonizingly ashamed, and he felt others were ashamed in his presence. 'Fancy such a thing happening,' he said, sitting down. 'I was sitting here, and all of a sudden, do you know, I felt a terrible piercing pain in my side... unendurable, my nerves could not stand it, and... and it led to this silly performance. This is the age of nerves; there is no help for it.'

At supper he drank some wine, and, from time to time, with an abrupt sigh rubbed his side as though to suggest that he still felt the pain. And no one, except Nadyezhda Fyodorovna, believed him, and he saw that.

After nine o'clock they went for a walk on the boulevard. Nadyezhda Fyodorovna, afraid that Kirilin would speak to her, did her best to keep all the time beside Marya Konstantinovna and the children. She felt weak with fear and misery, and felt she was going to be feverish; she was exhausted and her legs would hardly move, but she did not go home, because she felt sure that she would be followed by Kirilin or Atchmianov or both at once. Kirilin walked behind her with Nikodim Alexandritch, and kept humming in an undertone:

'I don't al-low people to play with me! I don't allow it.'

From the boulevard they went back to the pavilion and walked along the beach, and looked for a long time at the phosphorescence on the water. Von Koren began telling them why it looked phosphorescent.

XIV

'IT'S time I went to my *vint*. . . . They will be waiting for me,' said Laevsky. 'Good-bye, my friends.'

'I'll come with you; wait a minute,' said Nadyezhda Fyodorovna, and she took his arm.

They said good-bye to the company and went away. Kirilin took leave too, and saying that he was going the same way, went along beside them.

'What will be, will be,' thought Nadyezhda Fyodorovna. 'So be it. . . .'

And it seemed to her that all the evil memories in her head had taken shape and were walking beside her in the darkness, breathing heavily, while she, like a fly that had fallen into the inkpot, was crawling painfully along the pavement and smirching Laevsky's side and arm with blackness.

If Kirilin should do anything horrid, she thought, not he but she would be to blame for it. There was a time when no man would have talked to her as Kirilin had done, and she had torn up her security like a thread and destroyed it irrevocably – who was to blame for it? Intoxicated by her passions she had smiled at a complete stranger, probably just because he was tall and a fine figure. After two meetings she was weary of him, had thrown him over, and did not that, she thought now, give him the right to treat her as he chose?

'Here I'll say good-bye to you, darling,' said Laevsky. 'Ilya Mihalitch will see you home.'

He nodded to Kirilin, and, quickly crossing the boulevard, walked along the street to Sheshkovsky's, where there were lights in the windows, and then they heard the gate bang as he went in.

'Allow me to have an explanation with you,' said Kirilin. 'I'm not a boy, not some Atchkasov or Latchkasov, Zatchkasov.... I demand serious attention.'

Nadyezhda Fyodorovna's heart began beating violently. She made no reply.

'The abrupt change in your behaviour to me I put down at first to coquetry,' Kirilin went on; 'now I see that you don't know how to behave with gentlemanly people. You simply wanted to play with me, as you are playing with that wretched Armenian boy; but

I'm a gentleman and I insist on being treated like a gentleman. And so I am at your service....'

'I'm miserable,' said Nadyezhda Fyodorovna beginning to cry, and to hide her tears she turned away.

'I'm miserable too,' said Kirilin, 'but what of that?'

Kirilin was silent for a space, then he said distinctly and emphatically:

'I repeat, madam, that if you do not give me an interview this evening, I'll make a scandal this very evening.'

'Let me off this evening,' said Nadyezhda Fyodorovna, and she did not recognize her own voice, it was so weak and pitiful.

'I must give you a lesson.... Excuse me for the roughness of my tone, but it's necessary to give you a lesson. Yes, I regret to say I must give you a lesson. I insist on two interviews – to-day and to-morrow. After to-morrow you are perfectly free and can go wherever you like with anyone you choose. To-day and to-morrow.'

Nadyezhda Fyodorovna went up to her gate and stopped.

'Let me go,' she murmured, trembling all over and seeing nothing before her in the darkness but his white tunic. 'You're right: I'm a horrible woman.... I'm to blame, but let me go... I beg you.' She touched his cold hand and shuddered. 'I beseech you....'

'Alas!' sighed Kirilin, 'alas! it's not part of my plan to let you go; I only mean to give you a lesson and make you realize. And what's more, madam, I've too little faith in women.'

'I'm miserable....'

Nadyezhda Fyodorovna listened to the even splash of the sea, looked at the sky studded with stars, and longed to make haste and end it all, and get away from the cursed sensation of life, with its sea, stars, men, fever.

'Only not in my home,' she said coldly. 'Take me somewhere else.'

'Come to Muridov's. That's better.'

'Where's that?'

'Near the old wall.'

She walked quickly along the street and then turned into the side-street that led towards the mountains. It was dark. There were pale streaks of light here and there on the pavement, from the lighted windows, and it seemed to her that, like a fly, she kept falling into the ink and crawling out into the light again. At one point he stumbled, almost fell down and burst out laughing.

'He's drunk,' thought Nadyezhda Fyodorovna. 'Never mind.... Never mind.... So be it.'

Atchmianov, too, soon took leave of the party and followed Nadyezhda Fyodorovna to ask her to go for a row. He went to her house and looked over the fence: the windows were wide open, there were no lights.

'Nadyezhda Fyodorovna!' he called.

A moment passed, he called again.

'Who's there?' he heard Olga's voice.

'Is Nadyezhda Fyodorovna at home?'

'No, she has not come in yet.'

'Strange... very strange,' thought Atchmianov, feeling very uneasy. 'She went home...'

He walked along the boulevard, then along the street, and glanced in at the windows of Sheshkovsky's. Laevsky was sitting at the table without his coat on, looking attentively at his cards.

'Strange, strange,' muttered Atchmianov, and remembering Laevsky's hysterics, he felt ashamed. 'If she is not at home, where is she?'

He went to Nadyezhda Fyodorovna's lodgings again, and looked at the dark windows.

'It's a cheat, a cheat...' he thought, remembering that, meeting him at midday at Marya Konstantinovna's, she had promised to go in a boat with him that evening.

The windows of the house where Kirilin lived were dark, and there was a policeman sitting asleep on a little bench at the gate. Everything was clear to Atchmianov when he looked at the windows and the policeman. He made up his mind to go home, and set off in that direction, but somehow found himself near Nadyezhda Fyodorovna's lodgings again. He sat down on the bench near the gate and took off his hat, feeling that his head was burning with jealousy and resentment.

The clock in the town church only struck twice in the twenty-four hours – at midday and midnight. Soon after it struck midnight he heard hurried footsteps.

'To-morrow evening, then, again at Muridov's,' Atchmianov heard, and he recognized Kirilin's voice. 'At eight o'clock; good-bye!'

Nadyezhda Fyodorovna made her appearance near the garden. Without noticing that Atchmianov was sitting on the bench, she passed beside him like a shadow, opened the gate, and leaving it open, went into the house. In her own room she lighted the candle and quickly undressed, but instead of getting into bed, she sank on her knees before a chair, flung her arms round it, and rested her head on it.

It was past two when Laevsky came home.

XV

HAVING made up his mind to lie, not all at once but piecemeal, Laevsky went soon after one o'clock next day to Samoylenko to ask for the money that he might be sure to get off on Saturday. After his hysterical attack, which had added an acute feeling of shame to his depressed state of mind, it was unthinkable to remain in the town. If Samoylenko should insist on his conditions, he thought it would be possible to agree to them and take the money, and next day, just as he was starting, to say that Nadyezhda Fyodorovna refused to go. He would be able to persuade her that evening that the whole arrangement would be for her benefit. If Samoylenko, who was obviously under the influence of Von Koren, should refuse the money altogether or make fresh conditions, then he, Laevsky, would go off that very evening in a cargo vessel, or even in a sailing-boat, to Novy Athon or Novorossiisk, would send from there an humiliating telegram, and would stay there till his mother sent him the money for the journey.

When he went into Samoylenko's, he found Von Koren in the drawing-room. The zoologist had just arrived for dinner, and, as usual, was turning over the album and scrutinizing the gentlemen in top-hats and the ladies in caps.

'How very unlucky!' thought Laevsky, seeing him. 'He may be in the way. Good-morning.'

'Good-morning,' answered Von Koren, without looking at him.

'Is Alexandr Daviditch at home?'

'Yes, in the kitchen.'

Laevsky went into the kitchen, but seeing from the door that Samoylenko was busy over the salad, he went back into the drawing-room and sat down. He always had a feeling of awkwardness in the zoologist's presence, and now he was afraid there would be talk about his attack of hysterics. There was more than a minute of silence. Von Koren suddenly raised his eyes to Laevsky and asked:

'How do you feel after yesterday?'

'Very well indeed,' said Laevsky, flushing. 'It really was nothing much....'

'Until yesterday I thought it was only ladies who had hysterics, and so at first I thought you had St. Vitus's dance.'

Laevsky smiled ingratiatingly, and thought:

'How indelicate on his part! He knows quite well how unpleasant it is for me....'

'Yes, it was a ridiculous performance,' he said, still smiling. 'I've been laughing over it the whole morning. What's so curious in an attack of hysterics is that you know it is absurd, and are laughing at it in your heart, and at the same time you sob. In our neurotic age we are the slaves of our nerves; they are our masters and do as they like with us. Civilization has done us a bad turn in that way....'

As Laevsky talked, he felt it disagreeable that Von Koren listened to him gravely, and looked at him steadily and attentively as though studying him; and he was vexed with himself that in spite of his dislike of Von Koren, he could not banish the ingratiating smile from his face.

'I must admit, though,' he added, 'that there were immediate causes for the attack, and quite sufficient ones too. My health has been terribly shaky of late. To which one must add boredom, constantly being hard up... the absence of people and general interests.... My position is worse than a governor's.'

'Yes, your position is a hopeless one,' answered Von Koren.

These calm, cold words, implying something between a jeer and an uninvited prediction, offended Laevsky. He recalled the zoologist's eyes the evening before, full of mockery and disgust. He was silent for a space and then asked, no longer smiling:

'How do you know anything of my position?'

'You were only just speaking of it yourself. Besides, your friends take such a warm interest in you, that I am hearing about you all day long.'

'What friends? Samoylenko, I suppose?'

'Yes, he too.'

'I would ask Alexandr Daviditch and my friends in general not to trouble so much about me.'

'Here is Samoylenko; you had better ask him not to trouble so much about you.'

'I don't understand your tone,' Laevsky muttered, suddenly feeling as though he had only just realized that the zoologist hated and despised him, and was jeering at him, and was his bitterest and most inveterate enemy.

'Keep that tone for someone else,' he said softly, unable to speak aloud for the hatred with which his chest and throat were choking, as they had been the night before with laughter.

Samoylenko came in in his shirt-sleeves, crimson and perspiring from the stifling kitchen.

'Ah, you here?' he said. 'Good-morning, my dear boy. Have you had dinner? Don't stand on ceremony. Have you had dinner?'

'Alexandr Daviditch,' said Laevsky, standing up, 'though I did appeal to you to help me in a private matter, it did not follow that I released you from the obligation of discretion and respect for other people's private affairs.'

'What's this?' asked Samoylenko, in astonishment.

'If you have no money,' Laevsky went on, raising his voice and shifting from one foot to the other in his excitement, 'don't give it; refuse it. But why spread abroad in every back street that my position is hopeless, and all the rest of it? I can't endure such benevolence and friend's assistance where there's a shilling's-worth of talk for a ha'p'orth of help! You can boast of your benevolence as much as you please, but no one has given you the right to gossip about my private affairs!'

'What private affairs?' asked Samoylenko, puzzled and beginning to be angry. 'If you've come here to be abusive, you had better clear out. You can come again afterwards!'

He remembered the rule that when one is angry with one's neighbour, one must begin to count a hundred, and one will grow calm again; and he began rapidly counting.

'I beg you not to trouble yourself about me,' Laevsky went on. 'Don't pay any attention to me, and whose business is it what I do and how I live? Yes, I want to go away. Yes, I get into debt, I drink, I am living with another man's wife, I'm hysterical, I'm ordinary. I am not so profound as some people, but whose business is that? Respect other people's privacy.'

'Excuse me, brother,' said Samoylenko, who had counted up to thirty-five, 'but . . . .'

'Respect other people's individuality!' interrupted Laevsky. 'This continual gossip about other people's affairs, this sighing and groaning and everlasting prying, this eavesdropping, this friendly sympathy . . . damn it all! They lend me money and make conditions as though I were a schoolboy! I am treated as the devil knows what! I don't want anything,' shouted Laevsky, staggering with excitement and afraid that it might end in another attack of hysterics. 'I shan't get away on Saturday, then,' flashed through his mind. 'I want nothing. All I ask of you is to spare me your protecting care. I'm not a boy, and I'm not mad, and I beg you to leave off looking after me.'

The deacon came in, and seeing Laevsky pale and gesticulating, addressing his strange speech to the portrait of Prince Vorontsov, stood still by the door as though petrified.

'This continual prying into my soul,' Laevsky went on, 'is insulting to my human dignity, and I beg these volunteer detectives to give up their spying! Enough!'

'What's that . . . what did you say?' said Samoylenko, who had counted up to a hundred. He turned crimson and went up to Laevsky.

'It's enough,' said Laevsky, breathing hard and snatching up his cap.

'I'm a Russian doctor, a nobleman by birth, and a civil councillor,' said Samoylenko emphatically. 'I've never been a spy, and I allow no one to insult me!' he shouted in a breaking voice, emphasizing the last word. 'Hold your tongue!'

The deacon, who had never seen the doctor so majestic, so swelling with dignity, so crimson and so ferocious, shut his mouth, ran out into the entry and there exploded with laughter.

As though through a fog, Laevsky saw Von Koren get up and, putting his hands in his trouser-pockets, stand still in an attitude of expectancy, as though waiting to see what would happen. This calm attitude struck Laevsky as insolent and insulting to the last degree.

'Kindly take back your words,' shouted Samoylenko.

Laevsky, who did not by now remember what his words were, answered:

'Leave me alone! I ask for nothing. All I ask is that you and German upstarts of Jewish origin should let me alone! Or I shall take steps to make you! I will fight you!'

'Now we understand,' said Von Koren, coming from behind the table. 'Mr. Laevsky wants to amuse himself with a duel before he goes away. I can give him that pleasure. Mr. Laevsky, I accept your challenge.'

'A challenge,' said Laevsky, in a low voice, going up to the zoologist and looking with hatred at his swarthy brow and curly hair. 'A challenge? By all means! I hate you! I hate you!'

'Delighted. To-morrow morning early near Kerbalay's. I leave all details to your taste. And now, clear out!'

'I hate you,' Laevsky said softly, breathing hard. 'I have hated you a long while! A duel! Yes!'

'Get rid of him, Alexandr Daviditch, or else I'm going,' said Von Koren. 'He'll bite me.'

Von Koren's cool tone calmed the doctor; he seemed suddenly to come to himself, to recover his reason; he put both arms round Laevsky's waist, and, leading him away from the zoologist, muttered in a friendly voice that shook with emotion:

'My friends... dear, good... you've lost your tempers and that's enough... and that's enough, my friends.'

Hearing his soft, friendly voice, Laevsky felt that something unheard of, monstrous, had just happened to him, as though he had been nearly run over by a train; he almost burst into tears, waved his hand, and ran out of the room.

'To feel that one is hated, to expose oneself before the man who hates one, in the most pitiful, contemptible, helpless state. My God, how hard it is!' he thought a little while afterwards as he sat in the pavilion, feeling as though his body were scarred by the hatred of which he had just been the object.

'How coarse it is, my God!'

Cold water with brandy in it revived him. He vividly pictured Von Koren's calm, haughty face; his eyes the day before, his shirt like a rug, his voice, his white hand; and heavy, passionate, hungry hatred rankled in his breast and clamoured for satisfaction. In his thoughts he felled Von Koren to the ground, and trampled him underfoot. He remembered to the minutest detail all that had happened, and wondered how he could have smiled ingratiatingly to that insignificant man, and how he could care for the opinion of wretched petty people whom nobody knew, living in a miserable little town which was not, it seemed, even on the map, and of which not one decent person in Petersburg had heard. If this wretched little town suddenly fell into ruins or caught fire, the telegram with the news would be read in Russia with no more interest than an advertisement of the sale of second-hand furniture. Whether he killed Von Koren next day or left him alive, it would be just the same, equally useless and uninteresting. Better to shoot him in the leg or hand, wound him, then laugh at him, and let him, like an insect with a broken leg lost in the grass – let him be lost with his obscure sufferings in the crowd of insignificant people like himself.

Laevsky went to Sheshkovsky, told him all about it, and asked him to be his second; then they both went to the superintendent of the postal telegraph department, and asked him, too to be a second, and stayed to dinner with him. At dinner there was a great deal of joking and laughing. Laevsky made jests at his own expense saying he hardly knew how to fire off a pistol, calling himself a royal archer and William Tell.

'We must give this gentleman a lesson . . .' he said.

After dinner they sat down to cards. Laevsky played, drank wine, and thought that duelling was stupid and senseless, as it did not decide the question but only complicated it, but that it was sometimes impossible to get on without it. In the given case, for instance, one could not, of course, bring an action against Von Koren. And this duel was so far good in that it made it impossible for Laevsky to remain in the town afterwards. He got a little drunk and interested in the game, and felt at ease.

But when the sun had set and it grew dark, he was possessed by a feeling of uneasiness. It was not fear at the thought of death, because while he was dining and playing cards, he had for some reason a confident belief that the duel would end in nothing; it was dread at the thought of something unknown which was to happen next morning for the first time in his life, and dread of the coming night.... He knew that the night would be long and sleepless, and that he would have to think not only of Von Koren and his hatred, but also of the mountain of lies which he had to get through, and which he had not strength or ability to dispense with. It was as though he had been taken suddenly ill; all at once he lost all interest in the cards and in people, grew restless, and began asking them to let him go home. He was eager to get into bed to lie without moving, and to prepare his thoughts for the night. Sheshkovsky and the postal superintendent saw him home and went on to Von Koren's to arrange about the duel.

Near his lodgings Laevsky met Atchmianov. The young man was breathless and excited.

'I am looking for you, Ivan Andreitch,' he said. 'I beg you to come quickly....'

'Where?'

'Someone wants to see you, someone you don't know, about very important business; he earnestly begs you to come for a minute. He wants to speak to you of something.... For him it's a question of life and death...'

In his excitement Atchmianov spoke in a strong Armenian accent.

'Who is it?' asked Laevsky.

'He asked me not to tell you his name.'

'Tell him I'm busy; to-morrow, if he likes....'

'How can you!' Atchmianov was aghast. 'He wants to tell you something very important for you... very important. If you don't come, something dreadful will happen.'

'Strange...' muttered Laevsky, unable to understand why Atchmianov was so excited and what mysteries there could be in this dull, useless little town.

'Strange,' he repeated in hesitation. 'Come along, though; I don't care.'

Atchmianov walked rapidly on ahead and Laevsky followed him. They walked down a street, then turned into an alley.

'What a bore this is!' said Laevsky.

'One minute, one minute... it's near.'

Near the old rampart they went down a narrow alley between two empty enclosures, then they came into a sort of large yard and went towards a small house.

'That's Muridov's, isn't it?' asked Laevsky.

'Yes.'

'But why we've come by the back yards I don't understand. We might have come by the street; it's nearer....'

'Never mind, never mind....'

It struck Laevsky as strange, too, that Atchmianov led him to a back entrance, and motioned to him as though bidding him go quietly and hold his tongue.

'This way, this way...' said Atchmianov, cautiously opening the door and going into the passage on tiptoe. 'Quietly, quietly, I beg you...they may hear.'

He listened, drew a deep breath and said in a whisper:

'Open that door, and go in...don't be afraid.'

Laevsky, puzzled, opened the door and went into a room with a low ceiling and curtained windows.

There was a candle on the table.

'What do you want?' asked someone in the next room. 'Is it you, Muridov?'

Laevsky turned into that room and saw Kirilin, and beside him Nadyezhda Fyodorovna.

He didn't hear what was said to him; he staggered back, and did not know how he found himself in the street. His hatred for Von Koren and his uneasiness – all had vanished from his soul. As he went home he waved his right arm awkwardly and looked carefully at the ground under his feet, trying to step where it was smooth. At home in his study he walked backwards and forwards, rubbing his hands, and awkwardly shrugging his shoulders and neck, as though his jacket and shirt were too tight; then he lighted a candle and sat down to the table....

XVI

'THE "humane studies" of which you speak will only satisfy human thought when, as they advance, they meet the exact sciences and progress side by side with them. Whether they will meet under a new microscope, or in the monologues of a new Hamlet, or in a new religion, I do not know, but I expect the earth will be covered with a crust of ice before it comes to pass. Of all humane learning the most durable and living is, of course, the teaching of Christ; but look how differently even that is interpreted! Some teach that we must love all our neighbours but make an exception of soldiers, criminals, and lunatics. They allow the first to be killed in war, the second to be isolated or executed, and the third they forbid to marry. Other interpreters teach that we must love all our neighbours without exception, with no distinction of *plus* or *minus*. According to their teaching, if a consumptive or a murderer or an epileptic asks your daughter in marriage, you must let him have her. If *crêtins* go to war against the physically and mentally healthy, don't defend yourselves. This advocacy of love for love's sake, like art for art's sake, if it could have power, would bring mankind in the long run to complete extinction, and so would become the vastest crime that has ever been committed upon earth. There are very many interpretations, and since there are many of them, serious thought is not satisfied by any one of them and hastens to add its own individual interpretation to the mass. For that reason you should never put a question on a philosophical or so-called Christian basis; by so doing you only remove the question further from solution.'

The deacon listened to the zoologist attentively, thought a little, and asked:

'Have the philosophers invented the moral law which is innate in every man, or did God create it together with the body?'

'I don't know. But that law is so universal among all peoples and all ages that I fancy we ought to recognize it as organically connected with man. It is not invented, but exists and will exist. I don't tell you that one day it will be seen under the microscope, but its organic connection is shown, indeed, by evidence: serious affections of the brain and all so-called mental diseases, to the best of my belief, show themselves first of all in the perversion of the moral law.'

'Good. So then, just as our stomach bids us eat, our moral sense bids us love our neighbours. Is that it? But our natural man through self-love opposes the voice of conscience and reason, and this gives rise to many brain-racking questions. To whom ought we to turn for the solution of those questions if you forbid us to put them on the philosophic basis?'

'Turn to what little exact science we have. Trust to evidence and the logic of facts. It is true it is but little, but, on the other hand, it is less fluid and shifting than philosophy. The moral law, let us suppose, demands that you love your neighbour. Well? Love ought to show itself in the removal of everything which in one way or another is injurious to men and threatens them with danger in the present or in the future. Our knowledge and the evidence tells us that the morally and physically abnormal are a menace to humanity. If so you must struggle against the abnormal; if you are not able to raise them to the normal standard, you must have strength and ability to render them harmless – that is, to destroy them.'

'So love consists in the strong overcoming the weak.'

'Undoubtedly.'

'But you know the strong crucified our Lord Jesus Christ,' said the deacon hotly.

'The fact is that those who crucified Him were not the strong but the weak. Human culture weakens and strives to nullify the struggle for existence and natural selection; hence the rapid advancement of the weak and their predominance over the strong. Imagine that you succeeded in instilling into bees humanitarian ideas in their crude and elementary form. What would come of it? The drones who ought to be killed would remain alive, would devour the honey, would corrupt and stifle the bees, resulting in the predominance of the weak over the strong and the degeneration of the latter. The same process is taking place now with humanity; the weak are oppressing the strong. Among savages untouched by civilization the strongest, cleverest, and most moral takes the lead; he is the chief and the master. But we civilized men have crucified Christ, and we go on crucifying Him, so there is something lacking in us. . . . And that something one ought to raise up in ourselves, or there will be no end to these errors.'

'But what criterion have you to distinguish the strong from the weak?'

'Knowledge and evidence. The tuberculous and the scrofulous are recognized by their diseases, and the insane and the immoral by their actions.'

'But mistakes may be made!'

'Yes, but it's no use to be afraid of getting your feet wet when you are threatened with the deluge!'

'That's philosophy,' laughed the deacon.

'Not a bit of it. You are so corrupted by your seminary philosophy that you want to see nothing but fog in everything. The abstract studies with which your youthful head is stuffed are called abstract just because they abstract your minds from what is obvious. Look the devil straight in the eye, and if he's the devil, tell him he's the devil, and don't go calling to Kant or Hegel for explanations.'

The zoologist paused and went on:

'Twice two's four, and a stone's a stone. Here tomorrow we have a duel. You and I will say it's stupid and absurd, that the duel is out of date, that there is no real difference between the aristocratic duel and the drunken brawl in the pot-house, and yet we shall not stop, we shall go there and fight. So there is some force stronger than our reasoning. We shout that war is plunder, robbery, atrocity, fratricide; we cannot look upon blood without fainting; but the French or the Germans have only to insult us for us to feel at once an exaltation of spirit; in the most genuine way we shout "Hurrah!" and rush to attack the foe. You will invoke the blessing of God on our weapons, and our valour will arouse universal and general enthusiasm. Again it follows that there is a force, if not higher, at any rate stronger, than us and our philosophy. We can no more stop it than that cloud which is moving upwards over the sea. Don't be hypocritical, don't make a long nose at it on the sly; and don't say, "Ah, old-fashioned, stupid! Ah, it's inconsistent with Scripture!" but look it straight in the face, recognize its rational lawfulness, and when, for instance, it wants to destroy a rotten, scrofulous, corrupt race, don't hinder it with your pilules and misunderstood quotations from the Gospel. Leskov has a story of a conscientious Danila who found a leper outside the town, and fed and warmed him in the name of love and of Christ. If that Danila had really loved humanity, he would have dragged the lover as far as possible from the town, and would have flung him in a pit, and would have gone to save the healthy. Christ, I hope, taught us a rational intelligent, practical love.

'What a fellow you are!' laughed the deacon. 'You don't believe in Christ. Why do you mention His name so often?'

'Yes, I do believe in Him. Only, of course, in my own way not in yours. Oh, deacon, deacon!' laughed the zoologist; he put his arm round the deacon's waist, and said gaily: 'Well? Are you coming with us to the duel to-morrow?'

'My orders don't allow it, or else I should come.'

'What do you mean by "orders"?'

'I have been consecrated. I am in a state of grace.'

'Oh, deacon, deacon,' repeated Von Koren, laughing, 'I love talking to you.'

'You say you have faith,' said the deacon. 'What sort of faith is it? Why, I have an uncle, a priest, and he believes so that when in time of drought he goes out into the fields to pray for rain, he takes his umbrella and leather overcoat for fear of getting wet through on his way home. That's faith! When he speaks of Christ, his face is full of radiance, and all the peasants, men and women, weep floods of tears. He would stop that cloud and put all those forces you talk about to flight. Yes . . . faith moves mountains.'

The deacon laughed and slapped the zoologist on the shoulder.

'Yes . . .' he went on; 'here you are teaching all the time, fathoming the depths of the ocean, dividing the weak and the strong, writing books and challenging to duels – and everything remains as it is; but, behold! some feeble old man will mutter just one word with a holy spirit, or a new Mahomet, with a sword, will gallop from Arabia, and everything will be topsy-turvy, and in Europe not one stone will be left standing upon another.'

'Well, deacon, that's on the knees of the gods.'

'Faith without works is dead, but works without faith are worse still – mere waste of time and nothing more.'

The doctor came into sight on the sea-front. He saw the deacon and the zoologist, and went up to them.

'I believe everything is ready,' he said, breathing hard. 'Govorovsky and Boyko will be the seconds. They will start at five o'clock in the morning. How it has clouded over,' he said, looking at the sky. 'One can see nothing; there will be rain directly.'

'I hope you are coming with us?' said the zoologist.

'No, God preserve me; I'm worried enough as it is. Ustimovitch is going instead of me. I've spoken to him already.'

Far over the sea was a flash of lightning, followed by a hollow roll of thunder.

'How stifling it is before a storm!' said Von Koren. 'I bet you've been to Laevsky already and have been weeping on his bosom.'

'Why should I go to him?' answered the doctor in confusion. 'What next?'

Before sunset he had walked several times along the boulevard and the street in the hope of meeting Laevsky. He was ashamed of his hastiness and the sudden outburst of friendliness which had followed it. He wanted to apologize to Laevsky in a joking tone, to give him a good talking to, to soothe him and to tell him that the duel was a survival of mediеval barbarism, but that Providence itself had brought them to the duel as a means of reconciliation; that the next day, both being splendid and highly intelligent people, they would, after exchanging shots, appreciate each other's noble qualities and would become friends. But he could not come across Laevsky.

'What should I go and see him for?' repeated Samoylenko. 'I did not insult him; he insulted me. Tell me, please, why he attacked me. What harm had I done him? I go into the drawing-room, and, all of a sudden, without the least provocation: "Spy!" There's a nice thing! Tell me, how did it begin? What did you say to him?'

'I told him his position was hopeless. And I was right. It is only honest men or scoundrels who can find an escape from any position, but one who wants to be at the same time an honest man and a scoundrel – it is a hopeless position. But it's eleven o'clock, gentlemen, and we have to be up early to-morrow.'

There was a sudden gust of wind; it blew up the dust on the sea-front, whirled it round in eddies, with a howl that drowned the roar of the sea.

'A squall,' said the deacon. 'We must go in, our eyes are getting full of dust.'

As they went, Samoylenko sighed and, holding his hat, said:

'I suppose I shan't sleep to-night.'

'Don't you agitate yourself,' laughed the zoologist. 'You can set your mind at rest; the duel will end in nothing. Laevsky will magnanimously fire into the air – he can do nothing else; and I dare say I shall not fire at all. To be arrested and lose my time on Laevsky's account – the game's not worth the candle. By the way, what is the punishment for duelling?'

'Arrest, and in the case of the death of your opponent a maximum of three years' imprisonment in the fortress.'

'The fortress of St. Peter and St. Paul?'

'No, in a military fortress, I believe.'

'Though this fine gentleman ought to have a lesson!'

Behind them on the sea, there was a flash of lightning, which for an instant lighted up the roofs of the houses and the mountains. The friends parted near the boulevard. When the doctor disappeared in the darkness and his steps had died away, Von Koren shouted to him:

'I only hope the weather won't interfere with us to-morrow!'

'Very likely it will! Please God it may!'

'Good-night!'

'What about the night? What do you say?'

In the roar of the wind and the sea and the crashes of thunder, it was difficult to hear.

'It's nothing,' shouted the zoologist, and hurried home.

XVII

'Upon my mind, weighed down with woe,
Crowd thoughts, a heavy multitude:
In silence memory unfolds
Her long, long scroll before my eyes.
Loathing and shuddering I curse
And bitterly lament in vain,
And bitter though the tears I weep
I do not wash those lines away.'

PUSHKIN.

WHETHER they killed him next morning, or mocked at him – that is, left him his life – he was ruined, anyway. Whether this disgraced woman killed herself in her shame and despair, or dragged on her pitiful existence, she was ruined, anyway.

So thought Laevsky as he sat at the table late in the evening, still rubbing his hands. The windows suddenly blew open with a bang; a violent gust of wind burst into the room, and the papers fluttered from the table. Laevsky closed the windows and bent down to pick up the papers. He was aware of something new in his body, a sort of awkwardness he had not felt before, and his movements were strange to him. He moved timidly, jerking with his elbows and shrugging his shoulders; and when he sat down to the table again, he again began rubbing his hands. His body had lost its suppleness.

On the eve of death one ought to write to one's nearest relation. Laevsky thought of this. He took a pen and wrote with a tremulous hand:

'Mother!'

He wanted to write to beg his mother, for the sake of the merciful God in whom she believed, that she would give shelter and bring a little warmth and kindness into the life of the unhappy woman who, by his doing, had been disgraced and was in solitude, poverty, and weakness, that she would forgive and forget everything, everything, everything, and by her sacrifice atone to some extent for her son's terrible sin. But he remembered how his mother, a stout, heavily-built old woman in a lace cap, used to go out into the garden in the morning, followed by her companion with the lap-dog; how she used to shout in a peremptory way to the gardener and the servants, and how proud and haughty her face was – he remembered all this and scratched out the word he had written.

There was a vivid flash of lightning at all three windows, and it was followed by a prolonged, deafening roll of thunder, beginning with a hollow rumble and ending with a crash so violent that all the window-panes rattled. Laevsky got up, went to the window, and pressed his forehead against the pane. There was a fierce, magnificent storm. On the horizon lightning-flashes were flung in white streams from the storm-clouds into the sea, lighting up the high, dark waves over the far-away expanse. And to right and to left, and, no doubt, over the house too, the lightning flashed.

'The storm!' whispered Laevsky; he had a longing to pray to someone or to something, if only to the lightning or the storm-clouds. 'Dear storm!'

He remembered how as a boy he used to run out into the garden without a hat on when there was a storm, and how two fair-haired girls with blue eyes used to run after him, and how they got wet through with the rain; they laughed with delight, but when there was a loud peal of thunder, the girls used to nestle up to the boy confidingly, while he crossed himself and made haste to repeat: 'Holy, holy, holy....' Oh, where had they vanished to! In what sea were they drowned, those dawning days of pure, fair life? He had no fear of the storm, no love of nature now; he had no God. All the confiding girls he had ever known had by now been ruined by him and those like him. All his life he had not planted one tree in his own garden, nor grown one blade of grass; and living among the living, he had not saved one fly; he had done nothing but destroy and ruin, and lie, lie....

'What in my past was not vice?' he asked himself, trying to clutch at some bright memory as a man falling down a precipice clutches at the bushes.

School? The university? But that was a sham. He had neglected his work and forgotten what he had learnt. The service of his country? That, too, was a sham, for he did nothing in the Service, took a salary for doing nothing, and it was an abominable swindling of the State for which one was not punished.

He had no craving for truth, and had not sought it; spellbound by vice and lying, his conscience had slept or been silent. Like a stranger, like an alien from another planet, he had taken no part in the common life of men, had been indifferent to their sufferings, their ideas, their religion, their sciences, their strivings, and their struggles. He had not said one good word, not written one line that was not useless and vulgar; he had not done his fellows one ha'p'orth of service, but had eaten their bread, drunk their wine, seduced their wives, lived on their thoughts, and to justify his contemptible, parasitic life in their eyes and in his own, he had always tried to assume an air of being higher and better than they. Lies, lies, lies. . . .

He vividly remembered what he had seen that evening at Muridov's, and he was in an insufferable anguish of loathing and misery. Kirilin and Atchmianov were loathsome, but they were only continuing what he had begun; they were his accomplices and his disciples. This young weak woman had trusted him more than a brother, and he had deprived her of her husband, of her friends and of her country, and had brought her here – to the heat, to fever, and to boredom; and from day to day she was bound to reflect, like a mirror, his idleness, his viciousness and falsity – and that was all she had had to fill her weak, listless, pitiable life. Then he had grown sick of her, had begun to hate her, but had not had the pluck to abandon her, and he had tried to entangle her more and more closely in a web of lies. . . . These men had done the rest.

Laevsky sat at the table, then got up and went to the window; at one minute he put out the candle and then he lighted it again. He cursed himself aloud, wept and wailed, and asked forgiveness; several times he ran to the table in despair, and wrote:

'Mother!'

Except his mother, he had no relations or near friends; but how could his mother help him? And where was she? He had an impulse to run to Nadyezhda Fyodorovna, to fall at her feet, to kiss her hands and feet, to beg her forgiveness; but she was his victim, and he was afraid of her as though she were dead.

'My life is ruined,' he repeated, rubbing his hands. 'Why am I still alive, my God!...'

He had cast out of heaven his dim star; it had fallen, and its track was lost in the darkness of night. It would never return to the sky again, because life was given only once and never came a second time. If he could have turned back the days and years of the past, he would have replaced the falsity with truth, the idleness with work, the boredom with happiness; he would have given back purity to those whom he had robbed of it. He would have found God and goodness, but that was as impossible as to put back the fallen star into the sky, and because it was impossible he was in despair.

When the storm was over, he sat by the open window and thought calmly of what was before him. Von Koren would most likely kill him. The man's clear, cold theory of life justified the destruction of the rotten and the useless; if it changed at the crucial moment, it would be the hatred and the repugnance that Laevsky inspired in him that would save him. If he missed his aim or, in mockery of his hated opponent, only wounded him, or fired in the air, what could he do then? Where could he go?

'Go to Petersburg?' Laevsky asked himself. But that would mean beginning over again the old life which he cursed. And the man who seeks salvation in change of place like a migrating bird would find nothing anywhere, for all the world is alike to him. Seek salvation in men? In whom and how? Samoylenko's kindness and generosity could no more save him than the deacon's laughter or Von Koren's hatred. He must look for salvation in himself alone, and if there were no finding it, why waste time? He must kill himself, that was all....

He heard the sound of a carriage. It was getting light. The carriage passed by, turned, and crunching on the wet sand, stopped near the house. There were two men in the carriage.

'Wait a minute; I'm coming directly,' Laevsky said to them out of the window. 'I'm not asleep. Surely it's not time yet?'

'Yes, it's four o'clock. By the time we get there....'

Laevsky put on his overcoat and cap, put some cigarettes in his pocket, and stood still hesitating. He felt as though there was something else he must do. In the street the seconds talked in low voices and the horses snorted, and this sound in the damp, early morning, when everybody was asleep and light was hardly dawning in the sky, filled Laevsky's soul with a disconsolate feeling which was like a presentiment of evil. He stood for a little, hesitating, and went into the bedroom.

Nadyezhda Fyodorovna was lying stretched out on the bed, wrapped from head to foot in a rug. She did not stir, and her whole appearance, especially her head, suggested an Egyptian mummy. Looking at her in silence, Laevsky mentally asked her forgiveness, and thought that if the heavens were not empty and there really were a God, then He would save her; if there were no God, then she had better perish – there was nothing for her to live for.

All at once she jumped up, and sat up in bed. Lifting her pale face and looking with horror at Laevsky, she asked:

'Is it you? Is the storm over?'

'Yes.'

She remembered; put both her hands to her head and shuddered all over.

'How miserable I am!' she said. 'If only you knew how miserable I am! I expected,' she went on, half closing her eyes, 'that you would kill me or turn me out of the house into the rain and storm, but you delay ... delay ....'

Warmly and impulsively he put his arms round her and covered her knees and hands with kisses. Then when she muttered something and shuddered with the thought of the past, he stroked her hair, and looking into her face, realized that this unhappy, sinful woman was the one creature near and dear to him, whom no one could replace.

When he went out of the house and got into the carriage he wanted to return home alive.

XVIII

THE deacon got up, dressed, took his thick gnarled stick and slipped quietly out of the house. It was dark, and for the first minute when he went into the street, he could not even see his white stick. There was not a single star in the sky, and it looked as though there would be rain again. There was a smell of wet sand and sea.

'It's to be hoped that the mountaineers won't attack us,' thought the deacon, hearing the tap of the stick on the pavement, and noticing how loud and lonely the taps sounded in the stillness of the night.

When he got out of town, he began to see both the road and his stick. Here and there in the black sky there were dark cloudy patches, and soon a star peeped out and timidly blinked its one eye. The deacon walked along the high rocky coast and did not see the sea; it was slumbering below, and its unseen waves broke languidly and heavily on the shore, as though sighing 'Ouf!' and how slowly! One wave broke – the deacon had time to count eight steps; then another broke, and six steps; later a third. As before, nothing could be seen, and in the darkness one could hear the languid, drowsy drone of the sea. One could hear the infinitely far-away, inconceivable time when God moved above chaos.

The deacon felt uncanny. He hoped God would not punish him for keeping company with infidels, and even going to look at their duels. The duel would be nonsensical, bloodless, absurd, but however that might be, it was a heathen spectacle, and it was altogether unseemly for an ecclesiastical person to be present at it. He stopped and wondered – should he go back? But an intense, restless curiosity triumphed over his doubts, and he went on.

'Though they are infidels, they are good people, and will be saved,' he assured himself. 'They are sure to be saved,' he said aloud, lighting a cigarette.

By what standard must one measure men's qualities, to judge rightly of them? The deacon remembered his enemy, the inspector of the clerical school, who believed in God, lived in chastity, and did not fight duels; but he used to feed the deacon on bread with sand in it, and on one occasion almost pulled off the deacon's ear. If human life was so artlessly constructed that everyone respected this cruel and dishonest inspector who stole the Government flour, and his health and salvation were prayed for in the schools, was it just to shun such men as Von Koren and Laevsky, simply because they were unbelievers? The deacon was weighing this question, but he recalled how absurd Samoylenko had looked yesterday, and that broke the thread of his ideas. What fun they would have next day! The deacon imagined how he would sit under a bush and look on, and when Von Koren began boasting next day at dinner, he, the deacon, would begin laughing and telling him all the details of the duel.

'How do you know all about it?' the zoologist would ask.

'Well, there you are! I stayed at home, but I know all about it.'

It would be nice to write a comic description of the duel. His father-in-law would read it and laugh. A good story, told or written, was more than meat and drink to his father-in-law.

The valley of the Yellow River opened before him. The stream was broader and fiercer for the rain, and instead of murmuring as before, it was raging. It began to get light. The grey, dingy morning, and the clouds racing towards the west to overtake the storm-clouds, the mountains girt with mist, and the wet trees, all struck the deacon as ugly and sinister. He washed at the brook, repeated his morning prayer, and felt a longing for tea and hot rolls, with sour cream, which were served every morning at his father-in-law's. He remembered his wife and the 'Days past Recall', which she played on the piano. What sort of woman was she? His wife had been introduced, betrothed, and married to him all in one week: he had lived with her less than a month when he was ordered here, so that he had not had time to find out what she was like. All the same, he rather missed her.

'I must write her a nice letter...' he thought.

The flag on the *duhan* hung limp, soaked by the rain, and the *duhan* itself with its wet roof seemed darker and lower than it had been before. Near the door was standing a cart; Kerbalay, with two mountaineers and a young Tatar woman in trousers – no doubt Kerbalay's wife or daughter – were bringing sacks of something out of the *duhan*, and putting them on maize straw in the cart.

Near the cart stood a pair of asses hanging their heads. When they had put in all the sacks, the mountaineers and the Tatar woman began covering them over with straw, while Kerbalay began hurriedly harnessing the asses.

'Smuggling, perhaps,' thought the deacon.

Here was the fallen tree with the dried pine-needles, here was the blackened patch from the fire. He remembered the picnic and all its incidents, the fire, the singing of the mountaineers, his sweet dreams of becoming a bishop, and of the Church procession.... The Black River had grown blacker and broader with the rain. The deacon walked cautiously over the narrow bridge, which by now was reached by the topmost crests of the dirty water, and went up through the little copse to the drying-shed.

'A splendid head,' he thought, stretching himself on the straw, and thinking of Von Koren. 'A fine head – God grant him health; only there is cruelty in him....'

Why did he hate Laevsky and Laevsky hate him? Why were they going to fight a duel? If from their childhood they had known poverty as the deacon had; if they had been brought up among ignorant, hard-hearted, grasping, coarse and ill-mannered people who grudged you a crust of bread, who spat on the floor and hiccoughed at dinner and at prayers; if they had not been spoilt from childhood by the pleasant surroundings and the select circle of friends they lived in – how they would have rushed at each other, how readily they would have overlooked each other's shortcomings and would have prized each other's strong points! Why, how few even outwardly decent people there were in the world! It was true that Laevsky was flighty, dissipated, queer, but he did not steal, did not spit loudly on the floor; he did not abuse his wife and say, 'You'll eat till you burst, but you don't want to work'; he would not beat a child with reins, or give his servants stinking meat to eat – surely this was reason enough to be indulgent to him? Besides, he was the chief sufferer from his failings, like a sick man from his sores. Instead of being led by boredom and some sort of misunderstanding to look for degeneracy, extinction, heredity, and other such incomprehensible things in each other, would they not do better to stoop a little lower and turn their hatred and anger where whole streets resounded with moanings from coarse ignorance, greed, scolding, impurity, swearing, the shrieks of women....

The sound of a carriage interrupted the deacon's thoughts. He glanced out of the door and saw a carriage and in it three persons: Laevsky, Sheshkovsky, and the superintendent of the post-office.

'Stop!' said Sheshkovsky.

All three got out of the carriage and looked at one another.

'They are not here yet,' said Sheshkovsky, shaking the mud off. 'Well? Till the show begins, let us go and find a suitable spot; there's not room to turn round here.'

They went further up the river and soon vanished from sight. The Tatar driver sat in the carriage with his head resting on his shoulder and fell asleep. After waiting ten minutes the deacon came out of the drying-shed, and taking off his black hat that he might not be noticed, he began threading his way among the bushes and strips of maize along the bank, crouching and looking about him. The grass and maize were wet, and big drops fell on his head from the trees and bushes. 'Disgraceful!' he muttered, picking up his wet and muddy skirt. 'Had I realized it, I would not have come.'

Soon he heard voices and caught sight of them. Laevsky was walking rapidly to and fro in the small glade with bowed back and hands thrust in his sleeves; his seconds were standing at the water's edge, rolling cigarettes.

'Strange,' thought the deacon, not recognizing Laevsky's walk; 'he looks like an old man....'

'How rude it is of them!' said the superintendent of the post-office, looking at his watch. 'It may be learned manners to be late, but to my thinking it's hoggish.'

Sheshkovsky, a stout man with a black beard, listened and said:

'They're coming!'

XIX

'IT'S the first time in my life I've seen it! How glorious!' said Von Koren, pointing to the glade and stretching out his hands to the east. 'Look: green rays!'

In the east behind the mountains rose two green streaks of light, and it really was beautiful. The sun was rising.

'Good-morning!' the zoologist went on, nodding to Laevsky's seconds. 'I'm not late, am I?'

He was followed by his seconds, Boyko and Govorovsky, two very young officers of the same height, wearing white tunics, and Ustimovitch, the thin, unsociable doctor; in one hand he had a bag of some sort, and in the other had, as usual, a cane which he held behind him. Laying the bag on the ground and greeting no one, he put the other hand, too, behind his back and began pacing up and down the glade.

Laevsky felt the exhaustion and awkwardness of a man who is soon perhaps to die, and is for that reason an object of general attention. He wanted to be killed as soon as possible or taken home. He saw the sunrise now for the first time in his life; the early morning, the green rays of light, the dampness, and the men in wet boots, seemed to him to have nothing to do with his life, to be superfluous and embarrassing. All this had no connection with the night he had been through, with his thoughts and his feeling of guilt, and so he would have gladly gone away without waiting for the duel.

Von Koren was noticeably excited and tried to conceal it, pretending that he was more interested in the green light than anything. The seconds were confused, and looked at one another as though wondering why they were here and what they were to do.

'I imagine, gentlemen, there is no need for us to go further,' said Sheshkovsky. 'This place will do.'

'Yes, of course,' Von Koren agreed.

A silence followed. Ustimovitch, pacing to and fro, suddenly turned sharply to Laevsky and said in a low voice, breathing into his face:

'They have very likely not told you my terms yet. Each side is to pay me fifteen roubles, and in the case of the death of one party, the survivor is to pay thirty.'

Laevsky was already acquainted with the man, but now for the first time he had a distinct view of his lustreless eyes, his stiff moustaches, and wasted, consumptive neck; he was a money-grubber, not a doctor; his breath had an unpleasant smell of beef.

'What people there are in the world!' thought Laevsky, and answered: 'Very good.'

The doctor nodded and began pacing to and fro again, and it was evident he did not need the money at all, but simply asked for it from hatred. Everyone felt it was time to begin, or to end what had been begun, but instead of beginning or ending, they stood about, moved to and fro and smoked. The young officers, who were present at a duel for the first time in their lives, and even now hardly believed in this civilian and to their thinking, unnecessary duel, looked critically at their tunics and stroked their sleeves. Sheshkovsky went up to them and said softly: 'Gentlemen, we must use every effort to prevent this duel; they ought to be reconciled.'

He flushed crimson and added:

'Kirilin was at my rooms last night complaining that Laevsky had found him with Nadyezhda Fyodorovna, and all that sort of thing.'

'Yes, we know that too,' said Boyko.

'Well, you see, then . . . Laevsky's hands are trembling and all that sort of thing . . . he can scarcely hold a pistol now. To fight with him is as inhuman as to fight a man who is drunk or who has typhoid. If a reconciliation cannot be arranged, we ought to put off the duel, gentlemen, or something. . . . It's such a sickening business, I can't bear to see it.'

'Talk to Von Koren.'

'I don't know the rules of duelling, damnation take them, and I don't want to either; perhaps he'll imagine Laevsky funks it and has sent me to him, but he can think what he likes – I'll speak to him.'

Sheshkovsky hesitatingly walked up to Von Koren with a slight limp, as though his leg had gone to sleep; and as he went towards him, clearing his throat, his whole figure was a picture of indolence.

'There's something I must say to you, sir,' he began, carefully scrutinizing the flowers on the zoologist's shirt. 'It's confidential. I don't know the rules of duelling, damnation take them, and I don't want to, and I look on the matter not as a second and that sort of thing, but as a man, and that's all about it.'

'Yes. Well?'

'When seconds suggest reconciliation they are usually not listened to; it is looked upon as a formality. *Amour propre* and all that. But I humbly beg you to look carefully at Ivan Andreitch. He's not in a normal state, so to speak, to-day – not in his right mind, and a pitiable object. He has had a misfortune. I can't endure gossip. . . .'

Sheshkovsky flushed crimson and looked round.

'But in view of the duel, I think it necessary to inform you, Laevsky found his madam last night at Muridov's with . . . another gentleman.'

'How disgusting!' muttered the zoologist; he turned pale, frowned, and spat loudly. 'Tfoo!'

His lower lip quivered, he walked away from Sheshkovsky, unwilling to hear more, and as though he had accidentally tasted something bitter, spat loudly again, and for the first time that morning looked with hatred at Laevsky. His excitement and awkwardness passed off; he tossed his head and said aloud:

'Gentlemen, what are we waiting for, I should like to know? Why don't we begin?'

Sheshkovsky glanced at the officers and shrugged his shoulders.

'Gentlemen,' he said aloud, addressing no one in particular. 'Gentlemen, we propose that you should be reconciled.'

'Let us make haste and get the formalities over,' said Von Koren. 'Reconciliation has been discussed already. What is the next formality? Make haste, gentlemen, time won't wait for us.'

'But we insist on reconciliation all the same,' said Sheshkovsky in a guilty voice, as a man compelled to interfere in another man's business; he flushed, laid his hand on his heart, and went on: 'Gentlemen, we see no grounds for associating the offence with the duel. There's nothing in common between duelling and offences against one another of which we are sometimes guilty through human weakness. You are university men and men of culture, and no doubt you see in the duel nothing but a foolish and out-of-date formality, and all that sort of thing. That's how we look at it ourselves, or we shouldn't have come, for we cannot allow that in our presence men should fire at one another, and all that.' Sheshkovsky wiped the perspiration off his face and went on: 'Make an end to your misunderstanding, gentlemen; shake hands, and let us go home and drink to peace. Upon my honour, gentlemen!'

Von Koren did not speak. Laevsky, seeing that they were looking at him, said:

'I have nothing against Nikolay Vassilitch; if he considers I'm to blame, I'm ready to apologize to him.'

Von Koren was offended.

'It is evident, gentlemen,' he said, 'you want Mr. Laevsky to return home a magnanimous and chivalrous figure, but I cannot give you and him that satisfaction. And there was no need to get up early and drive eight miles out of town simply to drink to peace, to have breakfast, and to explain to me that the duel is an out-of-date formality. A duel is a duel, and there is no need to make it more false and stupid than it is in reality. I want to fight!'

A silence followed. Boyko took a pair of pistols out of a box; one was given to Von Koren and one to

Laevsky, and then there followed a difficulty which afforded a brief amusement to the zoologist and the seconds. It appeared that of all the people present not one had ever in his life been at a duel, and no one knew precisely how they ought to stand, and what the seconds ought to say and do. But then Boyko remembered and began, with a smile, to explain.

'Gentlemen, who remembers the description in Lermontov?' asked Von Koren, laughing. 'In Turgenev, too, Bazarov had a duel with someone....'

'There's no need to remember,' said Ustimovitch impatiently. 'Measure the distance, that's all.'

And he took three steps as though to show how to measure it. Boyko counted out the steps while his companion drew his sabre and scratched the earth at the extreme points to mark the barrier. In complete silence the opponents took their places.

'Moles,' the deacon thought, sitting in the bushes.

Sheshkovsky said something, Boyko explained something again, but Laevsky did not hear – or rather heard, but did not understand. He cocked his pistol when the time came to do so, and raised the cold, heavy weapon with the barrel upwards. He forgot to unbutton his overcoat, and it felt very tight over his shoulder and under his arm, and his arm rose as awkwardly as though the sleeve had been cut out of tin. He remembered the hatred he had felt the night before for the swarthy brow and curly hair, and felt that even yesterday at the moment of intense hatred and anger he could not have shot a man. Fearing that the bullet might somehow hit Von Koren by accident, he raised the pistol higher and higher, and felt that this too obvious magnanimity was indelicate and anything but magnanimous, but he did not know how else to do and could do nothing else. Looking at the pale, ironically smiling face of Von Koren, who evidently had been convinced from the beginning that his opponent would fire in the air, Laevsky thought that, thank God, everything would be over directly, and all that he had to do was to press the trigger rather hard....

He felt a violent shock on the shoulder; there was the sound of a shot and an answering echo in the mountains: ping-ting!

Von Koren cocked his pistol and looked at Ustimovitch, who was pacing as before with his hands behind his back, taking no notice of anyone.

'Doctor,' said the zoologist, 'be so good as not to move to and fro like a pendulum. You take me dizzy.'

The doctor stood still. Von Koren began to take aim at Laevsky.

'It's all over!' thought Laevsky.

The barrel of the pistol aimed straight at his face, the expression of hatred and contempt in Von Koren's attitude and whole figure, and the murder just about to be committed by a decent man in broad daylight, in the presence of decent men, and the stillness and the unknown force that compelled Laevsky to stand still and not to run—how mysterious it all was, how incomprehensible and terrible!

The moment while Von Koren was taking aim seemed to Laevsky longer than a night; he glanced imploringly at the seconds; they were pale and did not stir.

'Make haste and fire,' thought Laevsky, and felt that his pale, quivering, and pitiful face must arouse even greater hatred in Von Koren.

'I'll kill him directly,' thought Von Koren, aiming at his forehead, with his finger already on the catch. 'Yes, of course, I'll kill him....'

'He'll kill him!' A despairing shout was suddenly heard somewhere very close at hand.

A shot rang out at once. Seeing that Laevsky remained standing where he was and did not fall, they all looked in the direction from which the shout had come, and saw the deacon. With pale face and wet hair sticking to his forehead and his cheeks, wet through and muddy, he was standing in the maize on the further bank, smiling rather queerly and waving his wet hat. Sheshkovsky laughed with joy, burst into tears, and moved away.

XX

A LITTLE while afterwards, Von Koren and the deacon met near the little bridge. The deacon was excited; he breathed hard, and avoided looking in people's faces. He felt ashamed both of his terror and his muddy, wet garments.

'I thought you meant to kill him...' he muttered. 'How contrary to human nature it is! How utterly contrary to human nature it is!'

'But how did you come here?' asked the zoologist.

'Don't ask,' said the deacon, waving his hand. 'The evil one tempted me, saying: "Go, go...." So I went and almost died of fright in the maize. But now, thank God, thank God.... I am awfully pleased with you,' muttered the deacon, 'Old Grandad Tarantula will be glad.... It's funny, it's too funny! Only I beg of you most earnestly don't tell anybody I was there, or I may get into hot water with the authorities. They will say: "The deacon was a second."'

'Gentlemen,' said Von Koren, 'the deacon asks you not to tell anyone you've seen him here. He might get into trouble.'

'How contrary to human nature it is!' sighed the deacon. 'Excuse my saying so, but your face was so dreadful that I thought you were going to kill him.'

'I was very much tempted to put an end to that scoundrel,' said Von Koren, 'but you shouted close by, and I missed my aim. The whole procedure is revolting to anyone who is not used to it, and it has exhausted me, deacon. I feel awfully tired. Come along....'

'No, you must let me walk back. I must get dry, for I am wet and cold.'

'Well, as you like,' said the zoologist, in a weary tone, feeling dispirited, and, getting into the carriage, he closed his eyes. 'As you like....'

While they were moving about the carriages and taking their seats, Kerbalay stood in the road, and, laying his hands on his stomach, he bowed low, showing his teeth; he imagined that the gentry had come to enjoy the beauties of nature and drink tea, and could not understand why they were getting into the carriages. The party set off in complete silence and only the deacon was left by the *duhan*.

'Come to the *duhan*, drink tea,' he said to Kerbalay. 'Me wants to eat.'

Kerbalay spoke good Russian, but the deacon imagined that the Tatar would understand him better if he talked to him in broken Russian. 'Cook omelette, give cheese....'

'Come, come, father,' said Kerbalay, bowing. 'I'll give you everything.... I've cheese and wine.... Eat what you like.'

'What is "God" in Tatar?' asked the deacon, going into the *duhan*.

'Your God and my God are the same,' said Kerbalay, not understanding him. 'God is the same for all men, only men are different. Some are Russian, some are Turks, some are English – there are many sorts of men, but God is one.'

'Very good. If all men worship the same God, why do you Mahomedans look upon Christians as your everlasting enemies?'

'Why are you angry?' said Kerbalay, laying both hands on his stomach. 'You are a priest; I am a Mussulman: you say, "I want to eat" – I give it you.... Only the rich man distinguishes your God from my God; for the poor man it is all the same. If you please, it is ready.'

While this theological conversation was taking place at the *duhan*, Laevsky was driving home thinking how dreadful it had been driving there at daybreak, when the roads, the rocks, and the mountains were wet and dark, and the uncertain future seemed like a terrible abyss, of which one could not see the bottom; while now the raindrops hanging on the grass and on the stones were sparkling in the sun like diamonds, nature was smiling joyfully, and the terrible future was left behind. He looked at Sheshkovsky's sullen, tear-stained face, and at the two carriages ahead of them in which Von Koren, his seconds, and the doctor were sitting, and it seemed to him as though they were all coming back from a graveyard in which a wearisome, insufferable man who was a burden to others had just been buried.

'Everything is over,' he thought of his past, cautiously touching his neck with his fingers.

On the right side of his neck was a small swelling, of the length and breadth of his little finger, and he felt a pain, as though someone had passed a hot iron over his neck. The bullet had bruised it.

Afterwards, when he got home, a strange, long, sweet day began for him, misty as forgetfulness. Like a man released from prison or from hospital, he stared at the long-familiar objects and wondered that the tables, the windows, the chairs, the light, and the sea stirred in him a keen, childish delight such as he had not known for long, long years. Nadyezhda Fyodorovna, pale and haggard, could not understand his gentle voice and strange movements; she made haste to tell him everything that had happened to her. ... It seemed to her that very likely he scarcely heard and did not understand her, and that if he did know everything he would curse her and kill her, but he listened to her, stroked her face and hair, looked into her eyes and said:

'I have nobody but you. . . .'

Then they sat a long while in the garden, huddled close together, saying nothing, or dreaming aloud of their happy life in the future, in brief, broken sentences, while it seemed to him that he had never spoken at such length or so eloquently.

XXI

MORE than three months had passed.

The day came that Von Koren had fixed on for his departure. A cold, heavy rain had been falling from early morning, a north-east wind was blowing, and the waves were high on the sea. It was said that the steamer would hardly be able to come into the harbour in such weather. By the time-table it should have arrived at ten o'clock in the morning, but Von Koren, who had gone on to the sea-front at midday and again after dinner, could see nothing through the field-glass but grey waves and rain covering the horizon.

Towards the end of the day the rain ceased and the wind began to drop perceptibly. Von Koren had already made up his mind that he would not be able to get off that day, and had settled down to play chess with Samoylenko; but after dark the orderly announced that there were lights on the sea and that a rocket had been seen.

Von Koren made haste. He put his satchel over his shoulder, and kissed Samoylenko and the deacon. Though there was not the slightest necessity, he went through the rooms again, said good-bye to the orderly and the cook, and went out into the street, feeling that he had left something behind, either at the doctor's or his lodging. In the street he walked beside Samoylenko, behind them came the deacon with a box, and last of all the orderly with two portmanteaus. Only Samoylenko and the orderly could distinguish the dim lights on the sea. The others gazed into the darkness and saw nothing. The steamer had stopped a long way from the coast.

'Make haste, make haste,' Von Koren hurried them. 'I am afraid it will set off.'

As they passed the little house with three windows, into which Laevsky had moved soon after the duel, Von Koren could not resist peeping in at the window. Laevsky was sitting, writing, bent over the table, with his back to the window.

'I wonder at him!' said the zoologist softly. 'What a screw he has put on himself!'

'Yes, one may well wonder,' said Samoylenko. 'He sits from morning till night, he's always at work. He works to pay off his debts. And he lives, brother, worse than a beggar!'

Half a minute of silence followed. The zoologist, the doctor, and the deacon stood at the window and went on looking at Laevsky.

'So he didn't get away from here, poor fellow,' said Samoylenko. 'Do you remember how hard he tried?'

'Yes, he has put a screw on himself,' Von Koren repeated. 'His marriage, the way he works all day long for his daily bread, a new expression in his face, and even in his walk – it's all so extraordinary that I don't know what to call it.'

The zoologist took Samoylenko's sleeve and went on with emotion in his voice:

'You tell him and his wife that when I went away I was full of admiration for them and wished them all happiness . . . and I beg him, if he can, not to remember evil against me. He knows me. He knows that if I could have foreseen this change, then I might have become his best friend.'

'Go in and say good-bye to him.'

'No, that wouldn't do.'

'Why? God knows, perhaps you'll never see him again.'

The zoologist reflected, and said:

'That's true.'

Samoylenko tapped softly at the window. Laevsky started and looked round.

'Vanya, Nikolay Vassilitch wants to say good-bye to you,' said Samoylenko. 'He is just going away.'

Laevsky got up from the table, and went into the passage to open the door. Samoylenko, the zoologist, and the deacon went into the house.

'I can only come for one minute,' began the zoologist, taking off his goloshes in the passage, and already wishing he had not given way to his feelings and come in, uninvited. 'It is as though I were forcing myself on him,' he thought, 'and that's stupid.'

'Forgive me for disturbing you,' he said as he went into the room with Laevsky, 'but I'm just going away, and I had an impulse to see you. God knows whether we shall ever meet again.'

'I am very glad to see you.... Please come in,' said Laevsky, and he awkwardly set chairs for his visitors as though he wanted to bar their way, and stood in the middle of the room, rubbing his hands.

'I should have done better to have left my audience in the street,' thought Von Koren, and he said firmly: 'Don't remember evil against me, Ivan Andreitch. To forget the past is, of course, impossible – it is too painful, and I've not come here to apologize or to declare that I was not to blame. I acted sincerely, and I have not changed my conviction since then.... It is true that I see, to my great delight, that I was mistaken in regard to you, but it's easy to make a false step even on a smooth road, and, in fact, it's the natural human lot: if one is not mistaken in the main, one is mistaken in the details. Nobody knows the real truth.'

'No, no one knows the truth,' said Laevsky.

'Well, good-bye. . . . God give you all happiness.'

Von Koren gave Laevsky his hand; the latter took it and bowed.

'Don't remember evil against me,' said Von Koren. 'Give my greetings to your wife, and say I am very sorry not to say good-bye to her.'

'She is at home.'

Laevsky went to the door of the next room, and said:

'Nadya, Nikolay Vassilitch wants to say good-bye to you.'

Nadyezhda Fyodorovna came in; she stopped near the doorway and looked shyly at the visitors. There was a look of guilt and dismay on her face, and she held her hands like a schoolgirl receiving a scolding.

'I'm just going away, Nadyezhda Fyodorovna,' said Von Koren, 'and have come to say good-bye.'

She held out her hand uncertainly while Laevsky bowed.

'What pitiful figures they are, though!' thought Von Koren. 'The life they are living does not come easy to them. I shall be in Moscow and Petersburg; can I send you anything?' he asked.

'Oh!' said Nadyezhda Fyodorovna, and she looked anxiously at her husband. 'I don't think there's anything. . . .'

'No, nothing . . .' said Laevsky, rubbing his hands. 'Our greetings.'

Von Koren did not know what he could or ought to say, though as he went in he thought he would say a very great deal that would be warm and good and important. He shook hands with Laevsky and his wife in silence, and left them with a depressed feeling.

'What people!' said the deacon in a low voice, as he walked behind them. 'My God, what people! Of a truth, the right hand of God has planted this vine! Lord! Lord! One man vanquishes thousands and another tens of thousands. Nikolay Vassilitch,' he said ecstatically, 'let me tell you that to-day you have conquered the greatest of man's enemies – pride.'

'Hush, deacon! Fine conquerors we are! Conquerors ought to look like eagles, while he's a pitiful figure, timid, crushed; he bows like a Chinese idol, and I, I am sad....'

They heard steps behind them. It was Laevsky, hurrying after them to see him off. The orderly was standing on the quay with the two portmanteaus, and at a little distance stood four boatmen.

'There is a wind, though....Brrr!' said Samoylenko. 'There must be a pretty stiff storm on the sea now! You are not going off at a nice time, Kolya.'

'I'm not afraid of sea-sickness.'

'That's not the point....I only hope these rascals won't upset you. You ought to have crossed in the agent's sloop. Where's the agent's sloop?' he shouted to the boatmen.

'It has gone, your Excellency.'

'And the Customs-house boat?'

'That's gone, too.'

'Why didn't you let us know?' said Samoylenko angrily. 'You dolts!'

'It's all the same, don't worry yourself...' said Von Koren. 'Well, good-bye. God keep you.'

Samoylenko embraced Von Koren and made the sign of the cross over him three times.

'Don't forget us, Kolya.... Write.... We shall look out for you next spring.'

'Good-bye, deacon,' said Von Koren, shaking hands with the deacon. 'Thank you for your company and for your pleasant conversation. Think about the expedition.'

'Oh Lord, yes! to the ends of the earth,' laughed the deacon. 'I've nothing against it.'

Von Koren recognized Laevsky in the darkness, and held out his hand without speaking. The boatmen were by now below, holding the boat, which was beating against the piles, though the breakwater screened it from the breakers. Von Koren went down the ladder, jumped into the boat, and sat at the helm.

'Write!' Samoylenko shouted to him. 'Take care of yourself.'

'No one knows the real truth,' thought Laevsky, turning up the collar of his coat and thrusting his hands into his sleeves.

The boat turned briskly out of the harbour into the open sea. It vanished in the waves, but at once from a deep hollow glided up on to a high breaker, so that they could distinguish the men and even the oars. The boat moved three yards forward and was sucked two yards back.

'Write!' shouted Samoylenko; 'it's devilish weather for you to go in.'

'Yes, no one knows the real truth...' thought Laevsky, looking wearily at the dark, restless sea.

'It flings the boat back,' he thought; 'she makes two steps forward and one step back; but the boatmen are stubborn, they work the oars unceasingly, and are not afraid of the high waves. The boat goes on and on. Now she is out of sight, but in half an hour the boatmen will see the steamer lights distinctly, and within an hour they will be by the steamer ladder. So it is in life. . . . In the search for truth man makes two steps forward and one step back. Suffering, mistakes, and weariness of life thrust them back, but the thirst for truth and stubborn will drive them on and on. And who knows? Perhaps they will reach the real truth at last.'

'Go – o – od-by – e,' shouted Samoylenko.

'There's no sight or sound of them,' said the deacon. 'Good luck on the journey!'

It began to spot with rain.

THE CHORUS GIRL

THE CHORUS GIRL

ONE day when she was younger and better-looking, and when her voice was stronger, Nikolay Petrovitch Kolpakov, her adorer, was sitting in the outer room in her summer villa. It was intolerably hot and stifling. Kolpakov, who had just dined and drunk a whole bottle of inferior port, felt ill-humoured and out of sorts. Both were bored and waiting for the heat of the day to be over in order to go for a walk.

All at once there was a sudden ring at the door. Kolpakov, who was sitting with his coat off, in his slippers, jumped up and looked inquiringly at Pasha.

'It must be the postman or one of the girls,' said the singer.

Kolpakov did not mind being found by the postman or Pasha's lady friends, but by way of precaution gathered up his clothes and went into the next room, while Pasha ran to open the door. To her great surprise in the doorway stood, not the postman and not a girl friend, but an unknown woman, young and beautiful, who was dressed like a lady, and from all outward signs was one.

The stranger was pale and was breathing heavily as though she had been running up a steep flight of stairs.

'What is it?' asked Pasha.

The lady did not at once answer. She took a step forward, slowly looked about the room, and sat down in a way that suggested that from fatigue, or perhaps illness, she could not stand; then for a long time her pale lips quivered as she tried in vain to speak.

'Is my husband here?' she asked at last, raising to Pasha her big eyes with their red tear-stained lids.

'Husband?' whispered Pasha, and was suddenly so frightened that her hands and feet turned cold. 'What husband?' she repeated, beginning to tremble.

'My husband . . . Nikolay Petrovitch Kolpakov.'

'N . . . no, madam. . . . I . . . I don't know any husband.'

A minute passed in silence. The stranger several times passed her handkerchief over her pale lips and held her breath to stop her inward trembling, while Pasha stood before her motionless, like a post, and looked at her with astonishment and terror.

'So you say he is not here?' the lady asked, this time speaking with a firm voice and smiling oddly.

'I . . . I don't know who it is you are asking about.'

'You are horrid, mean, vile . . .' the stranger muttered, scanning Pasha with hatred and repulsion. 'Yes, yes . . . you are horrid. I am very, very glad that at last I can tell you so!'

Pasha felt that on this lady in black with the angry eyes and white slender fingers she produced the impression of something horrid and unseemly, and she felt ashamed of her chubby red cheeks, the pock-mark on her nose, and the fringe on her forehead, which never could be combed back. And it seemed to her that if she had been thin, and had had no powder on her face and no fringe on her forehead, then she could have disguised the fact that she was not 're-spectable', and she would not have felt so frightened and ashamed to stand facing this unknown, mysterious lady.

'Where is my husband?' the lady went on. 'Though I don't care whether he is here or not, but I ought to tell you that the money has been missed, and they are looking for Nikolay Petrovitch.... They mean to arrest him. That's your doing!'

The lady got up and walked about the room in great excitement. Pasha looked at her and was so frightened that she could not understand.

'He'll be found and arrested to-day,' said the lady, and she gave a sob, and in that sound could be heard her resentment and vexation. 'I know who has brought him to this awful position! Low, horrid creature! Loathsome, mercenary hussy!' The lady's lips worked and her nose wrinkled up with disgust. 'I am helpless, do you hear, you low woman?... I am helpless; you are stronger than I am, but there is One to defend me and my children! God sees all! He is just! He will punish you for every tear I have shed, for all my sleepless nights! The time will come; you will think of me!...'

Silence followed again. The lady walked about the room and wrung her hands, while Pasha still gazed blankly at her in amazement, not understanding and expecting something terrible.

'I know nothing about it, madam,' she said, and suddenly burst into tears.

'You are lying!' cried the lady, and her eyes flashed angrily at her. 'I know all about it! I've known you a long time. I know that for the last month he has been spending every day with you!'

'Yes. What then? What of it? I have a great many visitors, but I don't force anyone to come. He is free to do as he likes.'

'I tell you they have discovered that money is missing! He has embezzled money at the office! For the sake of such a . . . creature as you, for your sake he has actually committed a crime. Listen,' said the lady in a resolute voice, stopping short, facing Pasha. 'You can have no principles; you live simply to do harm – that's your object; but one can't imagine you have fallen so low that you have no trace of human feeling left! He has a wife, children. . . . If he is condemned and sent into exile we shall starve, the children and I. . . . Understand that! And yet there is a chance of saving him and us from destitution and disgrace. If I take them nine hundred roubles to-day they will let him alone. Only nine hundred roubles!'

'What nine hundred roubles?' Pasha asked softly. 'I . . . I don't know. . . . I haven't taken it.'

'I am not asking you for nine hundred roubles. . . . You have no money, and I don't want your money. I ask you for something else. . . . Men usually give expensive things to women like you. Only give me back the things my husband has given you!'

'Madam, he has never made me a present of anything!' Pasha wailed, beginning to understand.

'Where is the money? He has squandered his own and mine and other people's. . . . What has become of it all? Listen, I beg you! I was carried away by indignation and have said a lot of nasty things to you, but I apologize. You must hate me, I know, but if you are capable of sympathy, put yourself in my position! I implore you to give me back the things!'

'H'm!' said Pasha, and she shrugged her shoulders. 'I would with pleasure, but, God is my witness, he never made me a present of anything. Believe me, on my conscience. However, you are right, though,' said the singer in confusion, 'he did bring me two little things. Certainly I will give them back, if you wish it.'

Pasha pulled out one of the drawers in the toilet-table and took out of it a hollow gold bracelet and a thin ring with a ruby in it.

'Here, madam!' she said, handing the visitor these articles.

The lady flushed and her face quivered. She was offended.

'What are you giving me?' she said. 'I am not asking for charity, but for what does not belong to you . . . what you have taken advantage of your position to squeeze out of my husband . . . that weak, unhappy man. . . . On Thursday, when I saw you with my husband at the harbour you were wearing expensive brooches and bracelets. So it's no use your playing the innocent lamb to me! I ask you for the last time: will you give me the things, or not?'

'You are a queer one, upon my word,' said Pasha, beginning to feel offended. 'I assure you that, except the bracelet and this little ring, I've never seen a thing from your Nikolay Petrovitch. He brings me nothing but sweet cakes.'

'Sweet cakes!' laughed the stranger. 'At home the children have nothing to eat, and here you have sweet cakes. You absolutely refuse to restore the presents?'

Receiving no answer, the lady sat down and stared into space, pondering.

'What's to be done now?' she said. 'If I don't get nine hundred roubles, he is ruined, and the children and I are ruined, too. Shall I kill this low woman or go down on my knees to her?'

The lady pressed her handkerchief to her face and broke into sobs.

'I beg you!' Pasha heard through the stranger's sobs. 'You see you have plundered and ruined my husband. Save him.... You have no feeling for him, but the children...the children....What have the children done?'

Pasha imagined little children standing in the street, crying with hunger, and she, too, sobbed.

'What can I do, madam?' she said. 'You say that I am a low woman and that I have ruined Nikolay Petrovitch, and I assure you...before God Almighty, I have had nothing from him whatever....There is only one girl in our chorus who has a rich admirer; all the rest of us live from hand to mouth on bread and kvass. Nikolay Petrovitch is a highly educated, refined gentleman, so I've made him welcome. We are bound to make gentlemen welcome.'

'I ask you for the things! Give me the things! I am crying....I am humiliating myself....If you like I will go down on my knees! If you wish it!'

Pasha shrieked with horror and waved her hands. She felt that this pale, beautiful lady who expressed herself so grandly, as though she were on the stage, really might go down on her knees to her, simply from pride, from grandeur, to exalt herself and humiliate the chorus girl.

'Very well, I will give you things!' said Pasha, wiping her eyes and bustling about. 'By all means. Only they are not from Nikolay Petrovitch.... I got these from other gentlemen. As you please....'

Pasha pulled out the upper drawer of the chest, took out a diamond brooch, a coral necklace, some rings and bracelets, and gave them all to the lady.

'Take them if you like, only I've never had anything from your husband. Take them and grow rich,' Pasha went on, offended at the threat to go down on her knees. 'And if you are a lady... his lawful wife, you should keep him to yourself. I should think so! I did not ask him to come; he came of himself.'

Through her tears the lady scrutinized the articles given her and said:

'This isn't everything.... There won't be five hundred roubles' worth here.'

Pasha impulsively flung out of the chest a gold watch, a cigar-case and studs, and said, flinging up her hands:

'I've nothing else left.... You can search!'

The visitor gave a sigh, with trembling hands twisted the things up in her handkerchief, and went out without uttering a word, without even nodding her head.

The door from the next room opened and Kolpakov walked in. He was pale and kept shaking his head nervously, as though he had swallowed something very bitter; tears were glistening in his eyes.

'What presents did you make me?' Pasha asked, pouncing upon him. 'When did you, allow me to ask you?'

'Presents . . . that's no matter!' said Kolpakov, and he tossed his head. 'My God! She cried before you, she humbled herself. . . .'

'I am asking you, what presents did you make me?' Pasha cried.

'My God! She, a lady, so proud, so pure. . . . She was ready to go down on her knees to . . . to this wench! And I've brought her to this! I've allowed it!'

He clutched his head in his hands and moaned.

'No, I shall never forgive myself for this! I shall never forgive myself! Get away from me . . . you low creature!' he cried with repulsion, backing away from Pasha, and thrusting her off with trembling hands. 'She would have gone down on her knees, and . . . and to you! Oh, my God!'

He rapidly dressed, and pushing Pasha aside contemptuously, made for the door and went out.

Pasha lay down and began wailing aloud. She was already regretting her things which she had given away so impulsively, and her feelings were hurt. She remembered how three years ago a merchant had beaten her for no sort of reason, and she wailed more loudly than ever.

WARD NO. 6

WARD NO. 6

I

IN the hospital yard there stands a small lodge surrounded by a perfect forest of burdocks, nettles, and wild hemp. Its roof is rusty, the chimney is tumbling down, the steps at the front-door are rotting away and overgrown with grass, and there are only traces left of the stucco. The front of the lodge faces the hospital; at the back it looks out into the open country, from which it is separated by the grey hospital fence with nails on it. These nails, with their points upwards, and the fence, and the lodge itself, have that peculiar, desolate, Godforsaken look which is only found in our hospital and prison buildings.

If you are not afraid of being stung by the nettles, come by the narrow footpath that leads to the lodge, and let us see what is going on inside. Opening the first door, we walk into the entry. Here along the walls and by the stove every sort of hospital rubbish lies littered about. Mattresses, old tattered dressing-gowns, trousers, blue striped shirts, boots and shoes no good for anything – all these remnants are piled up in heaps, mixed up and crumpled, mouldering and giving out a sickly smell.

The porter, Nikita, an old soldier wearing rusty good-conduct stripes, is always lying on the litter with a pipe between his teeth. He has a grim, surly, battered-looking face, overhanging eyebrows which give him the expression of a sheep-dog of the steppes, and a red nose; he is short and looks thin and scraggy, but he is of imposing deportment and his fists are vigorous. He belongs to the class of simple-hearted, practical, and dull-witted people, prompt in carrying out orders, who like discipline better than anything in the world, and so are convinced that it is their duty to beat people. He showers blows on the face, on the chest, on the back, on whatever comes first, and is convinced that there would be no order in the place if he did not.

Next you come into a big, spacious room which fills up the whole lodge except for the entry. Here the walls are painted a dirty blue, the ceiling is as sooty as in a hut without a chimney – it is evident that in the winter the stove smokes and the room is full of fumes. The windows are disfigured by iron gratings on the inside. The wooden floor is grey and full of splinters. There is a stench of sour cabbage, of smouldering wicks, of bugs, and of ammonia, and for the first minute this stench gives you the impression of having walked into a menagerie....

There are bedsteads screwed to the floor. Men in blue hospital dressing-gowns, and wearing nightcaps in the old style, are sitting and lying on them. These are the lunatics.

There are five of them in all here. Only one is of the upper class, the rest are all artisans. The one nearest the door – a tall, lean workman with shining red whiskers and tear-stained eyes – sits with his head propped on his hand, staring at the same point. Day and night he grieves, shaking his head, sighing and smiling bitterly. He rarely takes a part in conversation and usually makes no answer to questions; he eats and drinks mechanically when food is offered him. From his agonizing, throbbing cough, his thinness, and the flush on his cheeks, one may judge that he is in the first stage of consumption. Next him is a little, alert, very lively old man, with a pointed beard and curly black hair like a negro's. By day he walks up and down the ward from window to window, or sits on his bed, cross-legged like a Turk, and, ceaselessly as a bullfinch whistles, softly sings and titters. He shows his childish gaiety and lively character at night also when he gets up to say his prayers – that is, to beat himself on the chest with his fists, and to scratch with his fingers at the door. This is the Jew Moiseika, an imbecile, who went crazy twenty years ago when his hat factory was burnt down.

And of all the inhabitants of Ward No. 6, he is the only one who is allowed to go out of the lodge, and even out of the yard into the street. He has enjoyed this privilege for years, probably because he is an old inhabitant of the hospital – a quiet, harmless imbecile, the buffoon of the town, where people are used to seeing him surrounded by boys and dogs. In his wretched gown, in his absurd night-cap, and in slippers, sometimes with bare legs and even without trousers, he walks about the streets, stopping at the gates and little shops, and begging for a copper. In one place they will give him some kvass, in another some bread, in another a copper, so that he generally goes back to the ward feeling rich and well-fed. Everything that he brings back Nikita takes from him for his own benefit. The soldier does this roughly, angrily turning the Jew's pockets inside out, and calling God to witness that he will not let him go into the street again, and that breach of the regulations is worse to him than anything in the world.

Moiseika likes to make himself useful. He gives his companions water, and covers them up when they are asleep; he promises each of them to bring him back a kopeck, and to make him a new cap; he feeds with a spoon his neighbour on the left, who is paralysed. He acts in this way, not from compassion nor from any considerations of a humane kind, but through imitation, unconsciously dominated by Gromov, his neighbour on the right hand.

Ivan Dmitritch Gromov, a man of thirty-three, who is a gentleman by birth, and has been a court usher and provincial secretary, suffers from the mania of persecution. He either lies curled up in bed or walks from corner to corner as though for exercise; he very rarely sits down. He is always excited, agitated, and overwrought by a sort of vague, undefined expectation. The faintest rustle in the entry or shout in the yard is enough to make him raise his head and begin listening: whether they are coming for him, whether they are looking for him. And at such times his face expresses the utmost uneasiness and repulsion.

I like his broad face with its high cheek-bones, always pale and unhappy, and reflecting, as though in a mirror, a soul tormented by conflict and long-continued terror. His grimaces are strange and abnormal, but the delicate lines traced on his face by profound, genuine suffering show intelligence and sense, and there is a warm and healthy light in his eyes. I like the man himself courteous, anxious to be of use, and extraordinarily gentle to everyone except Nikita. When anyone drops a button or a spoon, he jumps up from his bed quickly and picks it up; every day he says good-morning to his companions, and when he goes to bed he wishes them good-night.

Besides his continually overwrought condition and his grimaces, his madness shows itself in the following way also. Sometimes in the evenings he wraps himself in his dressing-gown, and, trembling all over, with his teeth chattering, begins walking rapidly from corner to corner and between the bedsteads. It seems as though he is in a violent fever. From the way he suddenly stops and glances at his companions, it can be seen that he is longing to say something very important, but, apparently reflecting that they would not listen or would not understand him, he shakes his head impatiently and goes on pacing up and down. But soon the desire to speak gets the upper hand of every consideration, and he will let himself go and speak fervently and passionately. His talk is disordered and feverish like delirium, disconnected, and not always intelligible, but, on the other hand, something extremely fine may be felt in it, both in the words and the voice. When he talks you recognize in him the lunatic and the man. It is difficult to reproduce on paper his insane talk. He speaks of the baseness of mankind, of violence trampling on justice, of the glorious life which will one day be upon earth, of the window-gratings, which remind him every minute of the stupidity and cruelty of oppressors. It makes a disorderly, incoherent potpourri of themes old but not yet out of date.

II

SOME twelve or fifteen years ago an official called Gromov, a highly respectable and prosperous person, was living in his own house in the principal street of the town. He had two sons, Sergey and Ivan. When Sergey was a student in his fourth year he was taken ill with galloping consumption and died, and his death was, as it were, the first of a whole series of calamities which suddenly showered on the Gromov family. Within a week of Sergey's funeral the old father was put on his trial for fraud and misappropriation, and he died of typhoid in the prison hospital soon afterwards. The house, with all their belongings, was sold by auction, and Ivan Dmitritch and his mother were left entirely without means.

Hitherto, in his father's lifetime, Ivan Dmitritch, who was studying in the University of Petersburg, had received an allowance of sixty or seventy roubles a month, and had had no conception of poverty; now he had to make an abrupt change in his life. He had to spend his time from morning to night giving lessons for next to nothing, to work at copying, and with all that to go hungry, as all his earnings were sent to keep his mother. Ivan Dmitritch could not stand such a life; he lost heart and strength, and, giving up the university, went home.

Here, through interest, he obtained the post of teacher in the district school, but could not get on with his colleagues, was not liked by the boys, and soon gave up the post. His mother died. He was for six months without work, living on nothing but bread and water; then he became a court usher. He kept this post until he was dismissed owing to his illness.

He had never even in his young student days given the impression of being perfectly healthy. He had always been pale, thin, and given to catching cold; he ate little and slept badly. A single glass of wine went to his head and made him hysterical. He always had a craving for society, but, owing to his irritable temperament and suspiciousness, he never became very intimate with anyone, and had no friends. He always spoke with contempt of his fellow-townsmen, saying that their coarse ignorance and sleepy animal existence seemed to him loathsome and horrible. He spoke in a loud tenor, with heat, and invariably either with scorn and indignation, or with wonder and enthusiasm, and always with perfect sincerity. Whatever one talked to him about he always brought it round to the same subject: that life was dull and stifling in the town; that the townspeople had no lofty interests, but lived a dingy, meaningless life, diversified by violence, coarse profligacy, and hypocrisy; that scoundrels were well fed and clothed, while honest men lived from hand to mouth; that they needed schools, a progressive local paper, a theatre, public lectures, the co-ordination of the intellectual elements; that society must see its failings and be horrified. In his criticisms of people he laid on the colours thick, using only black and white, and no fine shades; mankind was divided for him into honest men and scoundrels: there was nothing in between. He always spoke with passion and enthusiasm of women and of love, but he had never been in love.

In spite of the severity of his judgments and his nervousness, he was liked, and behind his back was spoken of affectionately as Vanya. His innate refinement and readiness to be of service, his good breeding, his moral purity, and his shabby coat, his frail appearance and family misfortunes, aroused a kind, warm, sorrowful feeling. Moreover, he was well educated and well read; according to the townspeople's notions, he knew everything, and was in their eyes something like a walking encyclopædia.

He had read a great deal. He would sit at the club, nervously pulling at his beard and looking through the magazines and books; and from his face one could see that he was not reading, but devouring the pages without giving himself time to digest what he read. It must be supposed that reading was one of his morbid habits, as he fell upon anything that came into his hands with equal avidity, even last year's newspapers and calendars. At home he always read lying down.

III

ONE autumn morning Ivan Dmitritch, turning up the collar of his great-coat and splashing through the mud, made his way by side-streets and back lanes to see some artisan, and to collect some payment that was owing. He was in a gloomy mood, as he always was in the morning. In one of the side-streets he was met by two convicts in fetters and four soldiers with rifles in charge of them. Ivan Dmitritch had very often met convicts before, and they had always excited feelings of compassion and discomfort in him; but now this meeting made a peculiar, strange impression on him. It suddenly seemed to him for some reason that he, too, might be put into fetters and led through the mud to prison like that. After visiting the artisan, on the way home he met near the post-office a police superintendent of his acquaintance, who greeted him and walked a few paces along the street with him, and for some reason this seemed to him suspicious. At home he could not get the convicts or the soldiers with their rifles out of his head all day, and an unaccountable inward agitation prevented him from reading or concentrating his mind. In the evening he did not light his lamp, and at night he could not sleep, but kept thinking that he might be arrested, put into fetters, and thrown into prison. He did not know of any harm he had done, and could be certain that he would never be guilty of murder, arson, or theft in the future either; but was it not easy to commit a crime by accident, unconsciously, and was not false witness always possible, and, indeed, miscarriage of justice? It was not without good reason that the agelong experience of the simple people teaches that beggary and prison are ills none can be safe from. A judicial mistake is very possible as legal proceedings are conducted nowadays, and there is nothing to be wondered at in it. People who have an official, professional relation to other men's sufferings – for instance, judges, police officers, doctors – in course of time, through habit, grow so callous that they cannot, even if they wish it, take any but a formal attitude to their clients; in this respect they are not different from the peasant who slaughters sheep and calves in the back-yard, and does not notice the blood. With this formal, soulless attitude to human personality the judge needs but one thing – time – in order to deprive an innocent man of all rights of property, and to condemn him to penal servitude. Only the time spent on performing certain formalities for which the judge is paid his salary, and then – it is all over. Then you may look in vain for justice and protection in this dirty, wretched little town a hundred and fifty miles from a railway station! And, indeed, is it not absurd even to think of justice when every kind of violence is accepted by society as a rational and consistent necessity, and every act of mercy – for instance, a verdict of acquittal – calls forth a perfect outburst of dissatisfied and revengeful feeling?

In the morning Ivan Dmitritch got up from his bed in a state of horror, with cold perspiration on his forehead, completely convinced that he might be arrested any minute. Since his gloomy thoughts of yesterday had haunted him so long, he thought, it must be that there was some truth in them. They could not, indeed, have come into his mind without any grounds whatever.

A policeman walking slowly passed by the windows: that was not for nothing. Here were two men standing still and silent near the house. Why were they silent? And agonizing days and nights followed for Ivan Dmitritch. Everyone who passed by the windows or came into the yard seemed to him a spy or a detective. At midday the chief of the police usually drove down the street with a pair of horses; he was going from his estate near the town to the police department; but Ivan Dmitritch fancied every time that he was driving especially quickly, and that he had a peculiar expression: it was evident that he was in haste to announce that there was a very important criminal in the town. Ivan Dmitritch started at every ring at the bell and knock at the gate, and was agitated whenever he came upon anyone new at his landlady's; when he met police officers and gendarmes he smiled and began whistling so as to seem unconcerned. He could not sleep for whole nights in succession expecting to be arrested, but he snored loudly and sighed as though in deep sleep, that his landlady might think he was asleep; for if he could not sleep it meant that he was tormented by the stings of conscience – what a piece of evidence! Facts and common sense persuaded him that all these terrors were nonsense and morbidity, that if one looked at the matter more broadly there was nothing really terrible in arrest and imprisonment – so long as the conscience is at ease; but the more sensibly and logically he reasoned, the more acute and agonizing his mental distress became. It might be compared with the story of a hermit who tried to cut a dwelling-place for himself in a virgin forest: the more zealously he worked with his axe, the thicker the forest grew. In the end Ivan Dmitritch, seeing it was useless, gave up reasoning altogether, and abandoned himself entirely to despair and terror.

He began to avoid people and to seek solitude. His official work had been distasteful to him before: now it became unbearable to him. He was afraid they would somehow get him into trouble, would put a bribe in his pocket unnoticed and then denounce him, or that he would accidentally make a mistake in official papers that would appear to be fraudulent, or would lose other people's money. It is strange that his imagination had never at other times been so agile and inventive as now, when every day he thought of thousands of different reasons for being seriously anxious over his freedom and honour; but, on the other hand, his interest in the outer world, in books in particular, grew sensibly fainter, and his memory began to fail him.

In the spring when the snow melted there were found in the ravine near the cemetery two half-decomposed corpses – the bodies of an old woman and a boy bearing the traces of death by violence. Nothing was talked of but these bodies and their unknown murderers. That people might not think he had been guilty of the crime, Ivan Dmitritch walked about the streets, smiling, and when he met acquaintances he turned pale, flushed, and began declaring that there was no greater crime than the murder of the weak and defenceless. But this duplicity soon exhausted him, and after some reflection he decided that in his position the best thing to do was to hide in his landlady's cellar. He sat in the cellar all day and then all night, then another day, was fearfully cold, and, waiting till dusk, stole secretly like a thief back to his room. He stood in the middle of the room till daybreak, listening without stirring. Very early in the morning, before sunrise, some workmen came into the house. Ivan Dmitritch knew perfectly well that they had come to mend the stove in the kitchen, but terror told him that they were police officers disguised as workmen. He slipped stealthily out of the flat, and, overcome by terror, ran along the street without his cap and coat. Dogs raced after him barking, a peasant shouted somewhere behind him, the wind whistled in his ears, and it seemed to Ivan Dmitritch that the force and violence of the whole world was massed together behind his back and was chasing after him.

He was stopped and brought home, and his landlady sent for a doctor. Doctor Andrey Yefimitch, of whom we shall have more to say hereafter, prescribed cold compresses on his head and laurel drops, shook his head, and went away, telling the landlady he should not come again, as one should not interfere with people who are going out of their minds. As he had not the means to live at home and be nursed, Ivan Dmitritch was soon sent to the hospital, and was there put into the ward for venereal patients. He could not sleep at night, was full of whims and fancies, and disturbed the patients, and was soon afterwards, by Andrey Yefimitch's orders, transferred to Ward No. 6.

Within a year Ivan Dmitritch was completely forgotten in the town, and his books, heaped up by his landlady in a sledge in the shed, were pulled to pieces by boys.

IV

IVAN DMITRITCH'S neighbour on the left hand is, as I have said already, the Jew Moiseika; his neighbour on the right hand is a peasant so rolling in fat that he is almost spherical, with a blankly stupid face, utterly devoid of thought. This is a motionless, gluttonous, unclean animal who has long ago lost all powers of thought or feeling. An acrid, stifling stench always comes from him.

Nikita, who has to clean up after him, beats him terribly with all his might, not sparing his fists; and what is dreadful is not his being beaten – that one can get used to – but the fact that this stupefied creature does not respond to the blows with a sound or a movement, nor by a look in the eyes, but only sways a little like a heavy barrel.

The fifth and last inhabitant of Ward No. 6 is a man of the artisan class who has once been a sorter in the post-office, a thinnish, fair little man with a good-natured but rather sly face. To judge from the clear, cheerful look in his calm and intelligent eyes, he has some pleasant idea in his mind, and has some very important and agreeable secret. He has under his pillow and under his mattress something that he never shows anyone, not from fear of its being taken from him and stolen, but from modesty. Sometimes he goes to the window, and turning his back to his companions, puts something on his breast, and bending his head, looks at it; if you go up to him at such a moment, he is overcome with confusion and snatches something off his breast. But it is not difficult to guess his secret.

'Congratulate me,' he often says to Ivan Dmitritch; 'I have been presented with the Stanislav Order of the second degree with the star. The second degree with the star is only given to foreigners, but for some reason they want to make an exception for me,' he says with a smile, shrugging his shoulders in perplexity. 'That I must confess I did not expect.'

'I don't understand anything about that,' Ivan Dmitritch replies morosely.

'But do you know what I shall attain to sooner or later?' the former sorter persists, screwing up his eyes slily. 'I shall certainly get the Swedish "Polar Star." That's an order it is worth working for, a white cross with a black ribbon. It's very beautiful.'

Probably in no other place is life so monotonous as in this ward. In the morning the patients, except the paralytic and the fat peasant, wash in the entry at a big tub and wipe themselves with the skirts of their dressing-gowns; after that they drink tea out of tin mugs which Nikita brings them out of the main building. Everyone is allowed one mugful. At midday they have soup made out of sour cabbage and boiled grain, in the evening their supper consists of grain left from dinner. In the intervals they lie down, sleep, look out of the window, and walk from one corner to the other. And so every day. Even the former sorter always talks of the same orders.

Fresh faces are rarely seen in Ward No. 6. The doctor has not taken in any new mental cases for a long time, and the people who are fond of visiting lunatic asylums are few in this world. Once every two months Semyon Lazaritch, the barber, appears in the ward. How he cuts the patients' hair, and how Nikita helps him to do it, and what a trepidation the lunatics are always thrown into by the arrival of the drunken, smiling barber, we will not describe.

No one even looks into the ward except the barber. The patients are condemned to see day after day no one but Nikita.

A rather strange rumour has, however, been circulating in the hospital of late.

It is rumoured that the doctor has begun to visit Ward No. 6.

V

A STRANGE rumour!

Doctor Andrey Yefimitch Ragin is a strange man in his way. They say that when he was young he was very religious, and prepared himself for a clerical career, and that when he had finished his studies at the high school in 1863 he intended to enter a theological academy, but that his father, a surgeon and doctor of medicine, jeered at him and declared point-blank that he would disown him if he became a priest. How far this is true I don't know, but Andrey Yefimitch himself has more than once confessed that he has never had a natural bent for medicine or science in general.

However that may have been, when he finished his studies in the medical faculty he did not enter the priesthood. He showed no special devoutness, and was no more like a priest at the beginning of his medical career than he is now.

His exterior is heavy, coarse like a peasant's, his face, his beard, his flat hair, and his coarse, clumsy figure, suggest an overfed, intemperate, and harsh innkeeper on the highroad. His face is surly-looking and covered with blue veins, his eyes are little and his nose is red. With his height and broad shoulders he has huge hands and feet; one would think that a blow from his fist would knock the life out of anyone, but his step is soft, and his walk is cautious and insinuating; when he meets anyone in a narrow passage he is always the first to stop and make way, and to say, not in a bass, as one would expect, but in a high, soft tenor: 'I beg your pardon!' He has a little swelling on his neck which prevents him from wearing stiff starched collars, and so he always goes about in soft linen or cotton shirts. Altogether he does not dress like a doctor. He wears the same suit for ten years, and the new clothes, which he usually buys at a Jewish shop, look as shabby and crumpled on him as his old ones; he sees patients and dines and pays visits all in the same coat; but this is not due to niggardliness, but to complete carelessness about his appearance.

When Andrey Yefimitch came to the town to take up his duties the 'institution founded to the glory of God' was in a terrible condition. One could hardly breathe for the stench in the wards, in the passages, and in the courtyards of the hospital. The hospital servants, the nurses, and their children slept in the wards together with the patients. They complained that there was no living for beetles, bugs, and mice. The surgical wards were never free from erysipelas. There were only two scalpels and not one thermometer in the whole hospital; potatoes were kept in the baths. The superintendent, the housekeeper, and the medical assistant robbed the patients, and of the old doctor, Andrey Yefimitch's predecessor, people declared that he secretly sold the hospital alcohol, and that he kept a regular harem consisting of nurses and female patients. These disorderly proceedings were perfectly well known in the town, and were even exaggerated, but people took them calmly; some justified them on the ground that there were only peasants and working men in the hospital, who could not be dissatisfied, since they were much worse off at home than in the hospital – they couldn't be fed on woodcocks! Others said in excuse that the town alone, without help from the Zemstvo, was not equal to maintaining a good hospital; thank God for having one at all, even a poor one. And the newly formed Zemstvo did not open infirmaries either in the town or the neighbourhood, relying on the fact that the town already had its hospital.

After looking over the hospital Andrey Yefimitch came to the conclusion that it was an immoral institution and extremely prejudicial to the health of the townspeople. In his opinion the most sensible thing that could be done was to let out the patients and close the hospital. But he reflected that his will alone was not enough to do this, and that it would be useless; if physical and moral impurity were driven out of one place, they would only move to another; one must wait for it to wither away of itself. Besides, if people open a hospital and put up with having it, it must be because they need it; superstition and all the nastiness and abominations of daily life were necessary, since in process of time they worked out to something sensible, just as manure turns into black earth. There was nothing on earth so good that it had not something nasty about its first origin.

When Andrey Yefimitch undertook his duties he was apparently not greatly concerned about the irregularities at the hospital. He only asked the attendants and nurses not to sleep in the wards, and had two cupboards of instruments put up; the superintendent, the housekeeper, the medical assistant, and the erysipelas remained unchanged.

Andrey Yefimitch loved intelligence and honesty intensely, but he had no strength of will nor belief in his right to organize an intelligent and honest life about him. He was absolutely unable to give orders, to forbid things, and to insist. It seemed as though he had taken a vow never to raise his voice and never to make use of the imperative. It was difficult for him to say 'Fetch' or 'Bring'; when he wanted his meals he would cough hesitatingly and say to the cook: 'How about tea? . . .' or 'How about dinner? . . .' To dismiss the superintendent or to tell him to leave off stealing, or to abolish the unnecessary parasitic post altogether, was absolutely beyond his powers. When Andrey Yefimitch was deceived or flattered, or accounts he knew to be cooked were brought him to sign, he would turn as red as a crab and feel guilty, but yet he would sign the accounts. When the patients complained to him of being hungry or of the roughness of the nurses, he would be confused and mutter guiltily: 'Very well, very well, I will go into it later. . . . Most likely there is some misunderstanding. . . .'

At first Andrey Yefimitch worked very zealously. He saw patients every day from morning till dinner-time, performed operations, and even attended confinements. The ladies said of him that he was attentive and clever at diagnosing diseases, especially those of women and children. But in process of time the work unmistakably wearied him by its monotony and obvious uselessness. To-day one sees thirty patients, and to-morrow they have increased to thirty-five, the next day forty, and so on from day to day, from year to year, while the mortality in the town did not decrease and the patients did not leave off coming. To be any real help to forty patients between morning and dinner was not physically possible, so it could but lead to deception. If twelve thousand patients were seen in a year it meant, if one looked at it simply, that twelve thousand men were deceived. To put those who were seriously ill into wards, and to treat them according to the principles of science, was impossible, too, because though there were principles there was no science; if he were to put aside philosophy and pedantically follow the rules as other doctors did, the things above all necessary were cleanliness and ventilation instead of dirt, wholesome nourishment instead of broth made of stinking, sour cabbage, and good assistants instead of thieves; and, indeed, why hinder people dying if death is the normal and legitimate end of everyone? What is gained if some shopkeeper or clerk lives an extra five or ten years? If the aim of medicine is by drugs to alleviate suffering, the question forces itself on one: why alleviate it? In the first place, they say that suffering leads man to perfection; and in the second, if mankind really learns to alleviate its sufferings with pills and drops, it will completely abandon religion and philosophy, in which it has hitherto found not merely protection from all sorts of trouble, but even happiness. Pushkin suffered terrible agonies before his death, poor Heine lay paralysed for several years; why, then, should not some Andrey Yefimitch or Matryona Savishna be ill, since their lives had nothing of importance in them, and would have been entirely empty and like the life of an amœba except for suffering?

Oppressed by such reflections, Andrey Yefimitch relaxed his efforts and gave up visiting the hospital every day.

VI

HIS life was passed like this. As a rule he got up at eight o'clock in the morning, dressed, and drank his tea. Then he sat down in his study to read, or went to the hospital. At the hospital the out-patients were sitting in the dark, narrow little corridor waiting to be seen by the doctor. The nurses and the attendants, tramping with their boots over the brick floors, ran by them; gaunt-looking patients in dressing-gowns passed; dead bodies and vessels full of filth were carried by; the children were crying, and there was a cold draught. Andrey Yefimitch knew that such surroundings were torture to feverish, consumptive, and impressionable patients; but what could be done? In the consulting-room he was met by his assistant, Sergey Sergeyitch – a fat little man with a plump, well-washed, shaven face, with soft, smooth manners, wearing a new loosely cut suit, and looking more like a senator than a medical assistant. He had an immense practice in the town, wore a white tie, and considered himself more proficient than the doctor, who had no practice. In the corner of the consulting-room there stood a huge ikon in a shrine with a heavy lamp in front of it, and near it a candle-stand with a white cover on it. On the walls hung portraits of bishops, a view of the Svyatogorsky Monastery, and wreaths of dried cornflowers. Sergey Sergeyitch was religious, and liked solemnity and decorum. The ikon had been put up at his expense; at his instructions some one of the patients read the hymns of praise in the consulting-room on Sundays, and after the reading Sergey Sergeyitch himself went through the ward with a censer and burned incense.

There were a great many patients, but the time was short, and so the work was confined to the asking of a few brief questions and the administration of some drugs, such as castor-oil or volatile ointment. Andrey Yefimitch would sit with his cheek resting in his hand, lost in thought and asking questions mechanically. Sergey Sergeyitch sat down too, rubbing his hands, and from time to time putting in his word.

'We suffer pain and poverty,' he would say, 'because we do not pray to the merciful God as we should. Yes!'

Andrey Yefimitch never performed any operations when he was seeing patients; he had long ago given up doing so, and the sight of blood upset him. When he had to open a child's mouth in order to look at its throat, and the child cried and tried to defend itself with its little hands, the noise in his ears made his head go round and brought tears into his eyes. He would make haste to prescribe a drug, and motion to the woman to take the child away.

He was soon wearied by the timidity of the patients and their incoherence, by the proximity of the pious Sergey Sergeyitch, by the portraits on the walls, and by his own questions which he had asked over and over again for twenty years. And he would go away after seeing five or six patients. The rest would be seen by his assistant in his absence.

With the agreeable thought that, thank God, he had no private practice now, and that no one would interrupt him, Andrey Yefimitch sat down to the table immediately on reaching home and took up a book. He read a great deal and always with enjoyment. Half his salary went on buying books, and of the six rooms that made up his abode three were heaped up with books and old magazines. He liked best of all works on history and philosophy; the only medical publication to which he subscribed was *The Doctor*, of which he always read the last pages first. He would always go on reading for several hours without a break and without being weary. He did not read as rapidly and impulsively as Ivan Dmitritch had done in the past, but slowly and with concentration, often pausing over a passage which he liked or did not find intelligible. Near the books there always stood a decanter of vodka, and a salted cucumber or a pickled apple lay beside it, not on a plate, but on the baize tablecloth. Every half-hour he would pour himself out a glass of vodka and drink it without taking his eyes off the book. Then without looking at it he would feel for the cucumber and bite off a bit.

At three o'clock he would go cautiously to the kitchen door, cough, and say: 'Daryushka, what about dinner?...'

After his dinner – a rather poor and untidily served one – Andrey Yefimitch would walk up and down his rooms with his arms folded, thinking. The clock would strike four, then five, and still he would be walking up and down thinking. Occasionally the kitchen door would creak, and the red and sleepy face of Daryushka would appear.

'Andrey Yefimitch, isn't it time for you to have your beer?' she would ask anxiously.

'No, it is not time yet...' he would answer. 'I'll wait a little.... I'll wait a little....'

Towards the evening the postmaster, Mihail Averyanitch, the only man in the town whose society did not bore Andrey Yefimitch, would come in. Mihail Averyanitch had once been a very rich landowner, and had served in the cavalry, but had come to ruin, and was forced by poverty to take a job in the post-office late in life. He had a hale and hearty appearance, luxuriant grey whiskers, the manners of a well-bred man, and a loud, pleasant voice. He was good-natured and emotional, but hot-tempered. When anyone in the post-office made a protest, expressed disagreement, or even began to argue, Mihail Averyanitch would turn crimson, shake all over, and shout in a voice of thunder, 'Hold your tongue!' so that the post-office had long enjoyed the reputation of an institution which it was terrible to visit. Mihail Averyanitch liked and respected Andrey Yefimitch for his culture and the loftiness of his soul; he treated the other inhabitants of the town superciliously, as though they were his subordinates.

'Here I am,' he would say, going in to Andrey Yefimitch. 'Good-evening, my dear fellow! I'll be bound, you are getting sick of me, aren't you?'

'On the contrary, I am delighted,' said the doctor. 'I am always glad to see you.'

The friends would sit down on the sofa in the study and for some time would smoke in silence.

'Daryushka, what about the beer?' Andrey Yefimitch would say.

They would drink their first bottle still in silence, the doctor brooding and Mihail Averyanitch with a gay and animated face, like a man who has something very interesting to tell. The doctor was always the one to begin the conversation.

'What a pity,' he would say quietly and slowly, not looking his friend in the face (he never looked anyone in the face) – 'what a great pity it is that there are no people in our town who are capable of carrying on intelligent and interesting conversation, or care to do so. It is an immense privation for us. Even the educated class do not rise above vulgarity; the level of their development, I assure you, is not a bit higher than that of the lower orders.'

'Perfectly true. I agree.'

'You know, of course,' the doctor went on quietly and deliberately, 'that everything in this world is insignificant and uninteresting except the higher spiritual manifestations of the human mind. Intellect draws a sharp line between the animals and man, suggests the divinity of the latter, and to some extent even takes the place of the immortality which does not exist. Consequently the intellect is the only possible source of enjoyment. We see and hear of no trace of intellect about us, so we are deprived of enjoyment. We have books, it is true, but that is not at all the same as living talk and converse. If you will allow me to make a not quite apt comparison: books are the printed score, while talk is the singing.'

'Perfectly true.'

A silence would follow. Daryushka would come out of the kitchen and with an expression of blank dejection would stand in the doorway to listen, with her face propped on her fist.

'Eh!' Mihail Averyanitch would sigh. 'To expect intelligence of this generation!'

And he would describe how wholesome, entertaining, and interesting life had been in the past. How intelligent the educated class in Russia used to be, and what lofty ideas it had of honour and friendship; how they used to lend money without an IOU, and it was thought a disgrace not to give a helping hand to a comrade in need; and what campaigns, what adventures, what skirmishes, what comrades, what women! And the Caucasus, what a marvellous country! The wife of a battalion commander, a queer woman, used to put on an officer's uniform and drive off into the mountains in the evening, alone, without a guide. It was said that she had a love affair with some princeling in the native village.

'Queen of Heaven, Holy Mother...' Daryushka would sigh.

'And how we drank! And how we ate! And what desperate liberals we were!'

Andrey Yefimitch would listen without hearing; he was musing as he sipped his beer.

'I often dream of intellectual people and conversation with them,' he said suddenly, interrupting Mihail Averyanitch. 'My father gave me an excellent education, but under the influence of the ideas of the sixties made me become a doctor. I believe if I had not obeyed him then, by now I should have been in the very centre of the intellectual movement. Most likely I should have become a member of some university. Of course, intellect, too, is transient and not eternal, but you know why I cherish a partiality for it. Life is a vexatious trap; when a thinking man reaches maturity and attains to full consciousness he cannot help feeling that he is in a trap from which there is no escape. Indeed, he is summoned without his choice by fortuitous circumstances from non-existence into life... what for? He tries to find out the meaning and object of his existence; he is told nothing, or he is told absurdities; he knocks and it is not opened to him; death comes to him – also without his choice. And so, just as in prison men held together by common misfortune feel more at ease when they are together, so one does not notice the trap in life when people with a bent for analysis and generalization meet together and pass their time in the interchange of proud and free ideas. In that sense the intellect is the source of an enjoyment nothing can replace.'

'Perfectly true.'

Not looking his friend in the face, Andrey Yefimitch would go on, quietly and with pauses, talking about intellectual people and conversation with them, and Mihail Averyanitch would listen attentively and agree: 'Perfectly true.'

'And you do not believe in the immortality of the soul?' he would ask suddenly.

'No, honoured Mihail Averyanitch; I do not believe it, and have no grounds for believing it.'

'I must own I doubt it too. And yet I have a feeling as though I should never die. Oh, I think to myself: "Old fogey, it is time you were dead!" But there is a little voice in my soul says: "Don't believe it; you won't die."'

Soon after nine o'clock Mihail Averyanitch would go away. As he put on his fur coat in the entry he would say with a sigh:

'What a wilderness fate has carried us to, though, really! What's most vexatious of all is to have to die here. Ech!...'

VII

AFTER seeing his friend out Andrey Yefimitch would sit down at the table and begin reading again. The stillness of the evening, and afterwards of the night, was not broken by a single sound, and it seemed as though time were standing still and brooding with the doctor over the book, and as though there were nothing in existence but the books and the lamp with the green shade. The doctor's coarse peasant-like face was gradually lighted up by a smile of delight and enthusiasm over the progress of the human intellect. Oh, why is not man immortal? he thought. What is the good of the brain centres and convolutions, what is the good of sight, speech, self-consciousness, genius, if it is all destined to depart into the soil, and in the end to grow cold together with the earth's crust, and then for millions of years to fly with the earth round the sun with no meaning and no object? To do that there was no need at all to draw man with his lofty, almost godlike intellect out of non-existence, and then, as though in mockery, to turn him into clay. The transmutation of substances! But what cowardice to comfort oneself with that cheap substitute for immortality! The unconscious processes that take place in nature are lower even than the stupidity of man, since in stupidity there is, anyway, consciousness and will, while in those processes there is absolutely nothing. Only the coward who has more fear of death than dignity can comfort himself with the fact that his body will in time live again in the grass, in the stones, in the toad. To find one's immortality in the transmutation of substances is as strange as to prophesy a brilliant future for the case after a precious violin has been broken and become useless.

When the clock struck, Andrey Yefimitch would sink back into his chair and close his eyes to think a little. And under the influence of the fine ideas of which he had been reading he would, unawares, recall his past and his present. The past was hateful – better not to think of it. And it was the same in the present as in the past. He knew that at the very time when his thoughts were floating together with the cooling earth round the sun, in the main building beside his abode people were suffering in sickness and physical impurity: someone perhaps could not sleep and was making war upon the insects, someone was being infected by erysipelas, or moaning over too tight a bandage; perhaps the patients were playing cards with the nurses and drinking vodka. According to the yearly return, twelve thousand people had been deceived; the whole hospital rested as it had done twenty years ago on thieving, filth, scandals, gossip, on gross quackery, and, as before, it was an immoral institution extremely injurious to the health of the inhabitants. He knew that Nikita knocked the patients about behind the barred windows of Ward

No. 6, and that Moiseika went about the town every day begging alms.

On the other hand, he knew very well that a magical change had taken place in medicine during the last twenty-five years. When he was studying at the university he had fancied that medicine would soon be overtaken by the fate of alchemy and metaphysics; but now when he was reading at night the science of medicine touched him and excited his wonder, and even enthusiasm. What unexpected brilliance, what a revolution! Thanks to the antiseptic system operations were performed such as the great Pirogov had considered impossible even *in spe*. Ordinary Zemstvo doctors were venturing to perform the resection of the kneecap; of abdominal operations only one per cent. was fatal; while stone was considered such a trifle that they did not even write about it. A radical cure for syphilis had been discovered. And the theory of heredity, hypnotism, the discoveries of Pasteur and of Koch, hygiene based on statistics, and the work of our Zemstvo doctors!

Psychiatry with its modern classification of mental diseases, methods of diagnosis, and treatment, was a perfect Elborus in comparison with what had been in the past. They no longer poured cold water on the heads of lunatics nor put strait-waistcoats upon them; they treated them with humanity, and even, so it was stated in the papers, got up balls and entertainments for them. Andrey Yefimitch knew that with modern tastes and views such an abomination as Ward No. 6 was possible only a hundred and fifty miles from a railway in a little town where the mayor and all the town council were half-illiterate tradesmen who looked upon the doctor as an oracle who must be believed without any criticism even if he had poured molten lead into their mouths; in any other place the public and the newspapers would long ago have torn this little Bastille to pieces.

'But, after all, what of it?' Andrey Yefimitch would ask himself, opening his eyes. 'There is the antiseptic system, there is Koch, there is Pasteur, but the essential reality is not altered a bit; ill-health and mortality are still the same. They get up balls and entertainments for the mad, but still they don't let them go free; so it's all nonsense and vanity, and there is no difference in reality between the best Vienna clinic and my hospital.' But depression and a feeling akin to envy prevented him from feeling indifferent; it must have been owing to exhaustion. His heavy head sank on to the book, he put his hands under his face to make it softer, and thought: 'I serve in a pernicious institution and receive a salary from people whom I am deceiving. I am not honest, but then, I of myself am nothing, I am only part of an inevitable social evil: all local officials are pernicious and receive their salary for doing nothing.... And so for my dishonesty it is not I who am to blame, but the times.... If I had been born two hundred years later I should have been different....'

When it struck three he would put out his lamp and go into his bedroom; he was not sleepy.

VIII

TWO years before, the Zemstvo in a liberal mood had decided to allow three hundred roubles a year to pay for additional medical service in the town till the Zemstvo hospital should be opened, and the district doctor, Yevgeny Fyodoritch Hobotov, was invited to the town to assist Andrey Yefimitch. He was a very young man – not yet thirty – tall and dark, with broad cheek-bones and little eyes; his forefathers had probably come from one of the many alien races of Russia. He arrived in the town without a farthing, with a small portmanteau, and a plain young woman whom he called his cook. This woman had a baby at the breast. Yevgeny Fyodoritch used to go about in a cap with a peak, and in high boots, and in the winter wore a sheepskin. He made great friends with Sergey Sergeyitch, the medical assistant, and with the treasurer, but held aloof from the other officials, and for some reason called them aristocrats. He had only one book in his lodgings, 'The Latest Prescriptions of the Vienna Clinic for 1881.' When he went to a patient he always took this book with him. He played billiards in the evening at the club: he did not like cards. He was very fond of using in conversation such expressions as 'endless bobbery', 'canting soft soap', 'shut up with your finicking. . .'.

He visited the hospital twice a week, made the round of the wards, and saw out-patients. The complete absence of antiseptic treatment and the cupping roused his indignation, but he did not introduce any new system, being afraid of offending Andrey Yefimitch. He regarded his colleague as a sly old rascal, suspected him of being a man of large means, and secretly envied him. He would have been very glad to have his post.

IX

ON a spring evening towards the end of March, when there was no snow left on the ground and the starlings were singing in the hospital garden, the doctor went out to see his friend the postmaster as far as the gate. At that very moment the Jew Moiseika, returning with his booty, came into the yard. He had no cap on, and his bare feet were thrust into goloshes; in his hand he had a little bag of coppers.

'Give me a kopeck!' he said to the doctor, smiling, and shivering with cold. Andrey Yefimitch, who could never refuse anyone anything, gave him a ten-kopeck piece.

'How bad that is!' he thought, looking at the Jew's bare feet with their thin red ankles. 'Why, it's wet.'

And stirred by a feeling akin both to pity and disgust, he went into the lodge behind the Jew, looking now at his bald head, now at his ankles. As the doctor went in, Nikita jumped up from his heap of litter and stood at attention.

'Good-day, Nikita,' Andrey Yefimitch said mildly. 'That Jew should be provided with boots or something, he will catch cold.'

'Certainly, your Honour. I'll inform the superintendent.'

'Please do; ask him in my name. Tell him that I asked.'

The door into the ward was open. Ivan Dmitritch, lying propped on his elbow on the bed, listened in alarm to the unfamiliar voice, and suddenly recognized the doctor. He trembled all over with anger, jumped up, and with a red and wrathful face, with his eyes starting out of his head, ran out into the middle of the road.

'The doctor has come!' he shouted, and broke into a laugh. 'At last! Gentlemen, I congratulate you. The doctor is honouring us with a visit! Cursed reptile!' he shrieked, and stamped in a frenzy such as had never been seen in the ward before. 'Kill the reptile! No, killing's too good. Drown him in the midden-pit!'

Andrey Yefimitch, hearing this, looked into the ward from the entry and asked gently: 'What for?'

'What for?' shouted Ivan Dmitritch, going up to him with a menacing air and convulsively wrapping himself in his dressing-gown. 'What for? Thief!' he said with a look of repulsion, moving his lips as though he would spit at him. 'Quack! hangman!'

'Calm yourself,' said Andrey Yefimitch, smiling guiltily. 'I assure you I have never stolen anything; and as to the rest, most likely you greatly exaggerate. I see you are angry with me. Calm yourself, I beg, if you can, and tell me coolly what are you angry for?'

'What are you keeping me here for?'

'Because you are ill.'

'Yes, I am ill. But you know dozens, hundreds of madmen are walking about in freedom because your ignorance is incapable of distinguishing them from the sane. Why am I and these poor wretches to be shut up here like scapegoats for all the rest? You, your assistant, the superintendent, and all your hospital rabble, are immeasurably inferior to every one of us morally; why then are we shut up and you not? Where's the logic of it?'

'Morality and logic don't come in, it all depends on chance. If anyone is shut up he has to stay, and if anyone is not shut up he can walk about, that's all. There is neither morality nor logic in my being a doctor and your being a mental patient, there is nothing but idle chance.'

'That twaddle I don't understand...' Ivan Dmitritch brought out in a hollow voice, and he sat down on his bed.

Moiseika, whom Nikita did not venture to search in the presence of the doctor, laid out on his bed pieces of bread, bits of paper, and little bones, and, still shivering with cold, began rapidly in a sing-song voice saying something in Yiddish. He most likely imagined that he had opened a shop.

'Let me out,' said Ivan Dmitritch, and his voice quivered.

'I cannot.'

'But why, why?'

'Because it is not in my power. Think, what use will it be to you if I do let you out? Go. The townspeople or the police will detain you or bring you back.'

'Yes, yes, that's true,' said Ivan Dmitritch, and he rubbed his forehead. 'It's awful! But what am I to do, what?'

Andrey Yefimitch liked Ivan Dmitritch's voice and his intelligent young face with its grimaces. He longed to be kind to the young man and soothe him; he sat down on the bed beside him, thought, and said:

'You ask me what to do. The very best thing in your position would be to run away. But, unhappily, that is useless. You would be taken up. When society protects itself from the criminal, mentally deranged, or otherwise inconvenient people, it is invincible.

There is only one thing left for you: to resign yourself to the thought that your presence here is inevitable.'

'It is no use to anyone.'

'So long as prisons and madhouses exist someone must be shut up in them. If not you, I. If not I, some third person. Wait till in the distant future prisons and madhouses no longer exist, and there will be neither bars on the windows nor hospital gowns. Of course, that time will come sooner or later.'

Ivan Dmitritch smiled ironically.

'You are jesting,' he said, screwing up his eyes. 'Such gentlemen as you and your assistant Nikita have nothing to do with the future, but you may be sure, sir, better days will come! I may express myself cheaply, you may laugh, but the dawn of a new life is at hand; truth and justice will triumph, and – our turn will come! I shall not live to see it, I shall perish, but some people's great-grandsons will see it. I greet them with all my heart and rejoice, rejoice with them! Onward! God be your help, friends!'

With shining eyes Ivan Dmitritch got up, and stretching his hands towards the window, went on with emotion in his voice:

'From behind these bars I bless you! Hurrah for truth and justice! I rejoice!'

'I see no particular reason to rejoice,' said Andrey Yefimitch, who thought Ivan Dmitritch's movement theatrical, though he was delighted by it. 'Prisons and madhouses there will not be, and truth, as you have just expressed it, will triumph; but the reality of things, you know, will not change, the laws of nature will still remain the same. People will suffer pain, grow old, and die just as they do now. However magnificent a dawn lighted up your life, you would yet in the end be nailed up in a coffin and thrown into a hole.'

'And immortality?'

'Oh, come, now!'

'You don't believe in it, but I do. Somebody in Dostoevsky or Voltaire said that if there had not been a God men would have invented him. And I firmly believe that if there is no immortality the great intellect of man will sooner or later invent it.'

'Well said,' observed Andrey Yefimitch, smiling with pleasure; 'it's a good thing you have faith. With such a belief one may live happily even shut up within walls. You have studied somewhere, I presume?'

'Yes, I have been at the university, but did not complete my studies.'

'You are a reflecting and a thoughtful man. In any surroundings you can find tranquillity in yourself. Free and deep thinking which strives for the comprehension of life, and complete contempt for the foolish bustle of the world – those are two blessings beyond any that man has ever known. And you can possess them even though you lived behind threefold bars. Diogenes lived in a tub, yet he was happier than all the kings of the earth.'

'Your Diogenes was a blockhead,' said Ivan Dmitritch morosely. 'Why do you talk to me about Diogenes and some foolish comprehension of life?' he cried, growing suddenly angry and leaping up. 'I love life; I love it passionately. I have the mania of persecution, a continual agonizing terror; but I have moments when I am overwhelmed by the thirst for life, and then I am afraid of going mad. I want dreadfully to live, dreadfully!'

He walked up and down the ward in agitation, and said, dropping his voice:

'When I dream, I am haunted by phantoms. People come to me, I hear voices and music, and I fancy I am walking through woods or by the sea-shore, and I long so passionately for movement, for interests.... Come, tell me, what news is there?' asked Ivan Dmitritch; 'what's happening?'

'Do you wish to know about the town or in general?'

'Well, tell me first about the town, and then in general.'

'Well, in the town it is appallingly dull.... There's no one to say a word to, no one to listen to. There are no new people. A young doctor called Hobotov has come here recently.'

'He had come in my time. Well, he is a low cad, isn't he?'

'Yes, he is a man of no culture. It's strange, you know.... Judging by every sign, there is no intellectual stagnation in our capital cities; there is a movement – so there must be real people there too; but for some reason they always send us such men as I would rather not see. It's an unlucky town!'

'Yes, it is an unlucky town,' sighed Ivan Dmitritch, and he laughed. 'And how are things in general? What are they writing in the papers and reviews?'

It was by now dark in the ward. The doctor got up, and, standing, began to describe what was being written abroad and in Russia, and the tendency of thought that could be noticed now. Ivan Dmitritch listened attentively and put questions, but suddenly, as though recalling something terrible, clutched at his head and lay down on the bed with his back to the doctor.

'What's the matter?' asked Andrey Yefimitch.

'You will not hear another word from me,' said Ivan Dmitritch rudely. 'Leave me alone.'

'Why so?'

'I tell you, leave me alone. Why the devil do you persist?'

Andrey Yefimitch shrugged his shoulders, heaved a sigh, and went out. As he crossed the entry he said: 'You might clear up here, Nikita . . . there's an awfully stuffy smell.'

'Certainly, your Honour.'

'What an agreeable young man!' thought Andrey Yefimitch, going back to his flat. 'In all the years I have been living here I do believe he is the first I have met with whom one can talk. He is capable of reasoning and is interested in just the right things.'

While he was reading, and afterwards, while he was going to bed, he kept thinking about Ivan Dmitritch, and when he woke next morning he remembered that he had the day before made the acquaintance of an intelligent and interesting man, and determined to visit him again as soon as possible.

X

IVAN DMITRITCH was lying in the same position as on the previous day, with his head clutched in both hands and his legs drawn up. His face was not visible.

'Good-day, my friend,' said Andrey Yefimitch. 'You are not asleep, are you?'

'In the first place, I am not your friend,' Ivan Dmitritch articulated into the pillow; 'and in the second, your efforts are useless; you will not get one word out of me.'

'Strange,' muttered Andrey Yefimitch in confusion. 'Yesterday we talked peacefully, but suddenly for some reason you took offence and broke off all at once.... Probably I expressed myself awkwardly, or perhaps gave utterance to some idea which did not fit in with your convictions....'

'Yes, a likely idea!' said Ivan Dmitritch, sitting up and looking at the doctor with irony and uneasiness. His eyes were red. 'You can go and spy and probe somewhere else, it's no use your doing it here. I knew yesterday what you had come for.'

'A strange fancy,' laughed the doctor. 'So you suppose me to be a spy?'

'Yes, I do.... A spy or a doctor who has been charged to test me – it's all the same –'

'Oh, excuse me, what a queer fellow you are really!'

The doctor sat down on the stool near the bed and shook his head reproachfully.

'But let us suppose you are right,' he said, 'let us suppose that I am treacherously trying to trap you into saying something so as to betray you to the police. You would be arrested and then tried. But would you be any worse off being tried and in prison than you are here? If you are banished to a settlement, or even sent to penal servitude, would it be worse than being shut up in this ward? I imagine it would be no worse.... What, then, are you afraid of?'

These words evidently had an effect on Ivan Dmitritch. He sat down quietly.

It was between four and five in the afternoon – the time when Andrey Yefimitch usually walked up and down his rooms, and Daryushka asked whether it was not time for his beer. It was a still, bright day.

'I came out for a walk after dinner, and here I have come, as you see,' said the doctor. 'It is quite spring.'

'What month is it? March?' asked Ivan Dmitritch.

'Yes, the end of March.'

'Is it very muddy?'

'No, not very. There are already paths in the garden.'

'It would be nice now to drive in an open carriage somewhere into the country,' said Ivan Dmitritch, rubbing his red eyes as though he were just awake, 'then to come home to a warm, snug study, and... and to have a decent doctor to cure one's headache.... It's so long since I have lived like a human being. It's disgusting here! Insufferably disgusting!'

After his excitement of the previous day he was exhausted and listless, and spoke unwillingly. His fingers twitched, and from his face it could be seen that he had a splitting headache.

'There is no real difference between a warm, snug study and this ward,' said Andrey Yefimitch. 'A man's peace and contentment do not lie outside a man, but in himself.'

'What do you mean?'

'The ordinary man looks for good and evil in external things – that is, in carriages, in studies – but a thinking man looks for it in himself.'

'You should go and preach that philosophy in Greece, where it's warm and fragrant with the scent of pomegranates, but here it is not suited to the climate. With whom was it I was talking of Diogenes? Was it with you?'

'Yes, with me yesterday.'

'Diogenes did not need a study or a warm habitation; it's hot there without. You can lie in your tub and eat oranges and olives. But bring him to Russia to live: he'd be begging to be let indoors in May, let alone December. He'd be doubled up with the cold.'

'No. One can be insensible to cold as to every other pain. Marcus Aurelius says: "A pain is a vivid idea of pain; make an effort of will to change that idea, dismiss it, cease to complain, and the pain will disappear." That is true. The wise man, or simply the reflecting, thoughtful man, is distinguished precisely by his contempt for suffering; he is always contented and surprised at nothing.'

'Then I am an idiot, since I suffer and am discontented and surprised at the baseness of mankind.'

'You are wrong in that; if you will reflect more on the subject you will understand how insignificant is all that external world that agitates us. One must strive for the comprehension of life, and in that is true happiness.'

'Comprehension ...' repeated Ivan Dmitritch, frowning. 'External, internal.... Excuse me, but I don't understand it. I only know,' he said, getting up and looking angrily at the doctor – 'I only know that God has created me of warm blood and nerves, yes, indeed! If organic tissue is capable of life it must react to every stimulus. And I do! To pain I respond with tears and outcries, to baseness with indignation, to filth with loathing. To my mind, that is just what is called life. The lower the organism, the less sensitive it is, and the more feebly it reacts to stimulus; and the higher it is, the more responsively and vigorously it reacts to reality. How is it you don't know that? A doctor, and not know such trifles! To despise suffering, to be always contented, and to be surprised at nothing, one must reach this condition' – and Ivan Dmitritch pointed to the peasant who was a mass of fat – 'or to harden oneself by suffering to such a point that one loses all sensibility to it – that is, in other words, to cease to live. You must excuse me, I am not a sage or a philosopher,' Ivan Dmitritch continued with irritation, 'and I don't understand anything about it. I am not capable of reasoning.'

'On the contrary, your reasoning is excellent.'

'The Stoics, whom you are parodying, were remarkable people, but their doctrine crystallized two thousand years ago and has not advanced, and will not advance, an inch forward, since it is not practical or living. It had a success only with the minority which spends its life in savouring all sorts of theories and ruminating over them; the majority did not understand it. A doctrine which advocates indifference to wealth and to the comforts of life, and a contempt for suffering and death, is quite unintelligible to the vast majority of men, since that majority has never known wealth or the comforts of life; and to despise suffering would mean to it despising life itself, since the whole existence of man is made up of the sensations of hunger, cold, injury, loss, and a Hamlet-like dread of death. The whole of life lies in these sensations; one may be oppressed by it, one may hate it, but one cannot despise it. Yes, so, I repeat, the doctrine of the Stoics can never have a future; from the beginning of time up to to-day you see continually increasing the struggle, the sensibility to pain, the capacity of responding to stimulus.'

Ivan Dmitritch suddenly lost the thread of his thoughts, stopped, and rubbed his forehead with vexation.

'I meant to say something important, but I have lost it,' he said. 'What was I saying? Oh yes! This is what I mean: one of the Stoics sold himself into slavery to redeem his neighbour, so, you see, even a Stoic did react to stimulus, since, for such a generous act as the destruction of oneself for the sake of one's neighbour, he must have had a soul capable of pity and indignation. Here in prison I have forgotten everything I have learned, or else I could have recalled something else. Take Christ, for instance: Christ responded to reality by weeping, smiling, being sorrowful and moved to wrath, even overcome by misery. He did not go to meet His sufferings with a smile, He did not despise death, but prayed in the Garden of Gethsemane that this cup might pass Him by.'

Ivan Dmitritch laughed and sat down.

'Granted that a man's peace and contentment lie not outside but in himself,' he said, 'granted that one must despise suffering and not be surprised at anything, yet on what ground do you preach the theory? Are you a sage? A philosopher?'

'No, I am not a philosopher, but everyone ought to preach it because it is reasonable.'

'No, I want to know how it is that you consider yourself competent to judge of "comprehension", contempt for suffering, and so on. Have you ever suffered? Have you any idea of suffering? Allow me to ask you, were you ever thrashed in your childhood?'

'No, my parents had an aversion for corporal punishment.'

'My father used to flog me cruelly; my father was a harsh, sickly Government clerk with a long nose and a yellow neck. But let us talk of you. No one has laid a finger on you all your life, no one has scared you nor beaten you; you are as strong as a bull. You grew up under your father's wing and studied at his expense, and then you dropped at once into a sinecure. For more than twenty years you have lived rent free with heating, lighting, and service all provided, and had the right to work how you pleased and as much as you pleased, even to do nothing. You were naturally a flabby, lazy man, and so you have tried to arrange your life so that nothing should disturb you or make you move. You have handed over your work to the assistant and the rest of the rabble while you sit in peace and warmth, save money, read, amuse yourself with reflections, with all sorts of lofty nonsense, and' (Ivan Dmitritch looked at the doctor's red nose) 'with boozing; in fact, you have seen nothing of life, you know absolutely nothing of it, and are only theoretically acquainted with reality; you despise suffering and are surprised at nothing for a very simple reason: vanity of vanities, the external and the internal, contempt for life, for suffering and for death, comprehension, true happiness – that's the philosophy that suits the Russian sluggard best. You see a peasant beating his wife, for instance. Why interfere? Let him beat her, they will both die sooner or later, anyway; and, besides, he who beats injures by his blows, not the person he is beating, but himself. To get drunk is stupid and unseemly, but if you drink you die, and if you don't drink you die. A peasant woman comes with toothache...well, what of it? Pain is the idea of pain, and besides "there is no living in this world without illness; we shall all die, and so, go away, woman, don't hinder me from thinking and drinking vodka". A young man asks advice, what he is to do, how he is to live; anyone else would think before answering, but you have got the answer ready: strive for "comprehension" or for true happiness. And what is that fantastic "true happiness"? There's no answer, of course. We are kept here behind barred windows, tortured, left to rot; but that is very good and reasonable, because there is no difference at all between this ward and a warm, snug study. A convenient philosophy. You can do nothing, and your conscience is clear, and you feel you are wise....No, sir, it is not philosophy, it's not thinking, it's not breadth of vision, but laziness, fakirism, drowsy stupefaction. Yes,' cried Ivan Dmitritch, getting angry again, 'you despise suffering, but I'll be bound if you pinch your finger in the door you will howl at the top of your voice.'

'And perhaps I shouldn't howl,' said Andrey Yefimitch, with a gentle smile.

'Oh, I dare say! Well, if you had a stroke of paralysis, or supposing some fool or bully took advantage of his position and rank to insult you in public, and if you knew he could do it with impunity, then you would understand what it means to put people off with comprehension and true happiness.'

'That's original,' said Andrey Yefimitch, laughing with pleasure and rubbing his hands. 'I am agreeably struck by your inclination for drawing generalizations, and the sketch of my character you have just drawn is simply brilliant. I must confess that talking to you gives me great pleasure. Well, I've listened to you, and now you must graciously listen to me.'

XI

THE conversation went on for about an hour longer, and apparently made a deep impression on Andrey Yefimitch. He began going to the ward every day. He went there in the mornings and after dinner, and often the dusk of evening found him in conversation with Ivan Dmitritch. At first Ivan Dmitritch held aloof from him, suspected him of evil designs, and openly expressed his hostility. But afterwards he got used to him, and his abrupt manner changed to one of condescending irony.

Soon it was all over the hospital that the doctor, Andrey Yefimitch, had taken to visiting Ward No. 6. No one – neither Sergey Sergeyitch, nor Nikita, nor the nurses – could conceive why he went there, why he stayed there for hours together, what he was talking about, and why he did not write prescriptions. His actions seemed strange. Often Mihail Averyanitch did not find him at home, which had never happened in the past, and Daryushka was greatly perturbed, for the doctor drank his beer now at no definite time, and sometimes was even late for dinner.

One day – it was at the end of June – Dr. Hobotov went to see Andrey Yefimitch about something. Not finding him at home, he proceeded to look for him in the yard; there he was told that the old doctor had gone to see the mental patients. Going into the lodge and stopping in the entry, Hobotov heard the following conversation:

'We shall never agree, and you will not succeed in converting me to your faith,' Ivan Dmitritch was saying irritably; 'you are utterly ignorant of reality, and you have never known suffering, but have only like a leech fed beside the sufferings of others, while I have been in continual suffering from the day of my birth till to-day. For that reason, I tell you frankly, I consider myself superior to you and more competent in every respect. It's not for you to teach me.'

'I have absolutely no ambition to convert you to my faith,' said Andrey Yefimitch gently, and with regret that the other refused to understand him. 'And that is not what matters, my friend; what matters is not that you have suffered and I have not. Joy and suffering are passing; let us leave them, never mind them. What matters is that you and I think; we see in each other people who are capable of thinking and reasoning, and that is a common bond between us however different our views. If you knew, my friend, how sick I am of the universal senselessness, ineptitude, stupidity, and with what delight I always talk with you! You are an intelligent man, and I enjoy your company.'

Hobotov opened the door an inch and glanced into the ward; Ivan Dmitritch in his night-cap and the doctor Andrey Yefimitch were sitting side by side on the bed. The madman was grimacing, twitching, and convulsively wrapping himself in his gown, while the doctor sat motionless with bowed head, and his face was red and looked helpless and sorrowful. Hobotov shrugged his shoulders, grinned, and glanced at Nikita. Nikita shrugged his shoulders too.

Next day Hobotov went to the lodge, accompanied by the assistant. Both stood in the entry and listened.

'I fancy our old man has gone clean off his chump!' said Hobotov as he came out of the lodge.

'Lord have mercy upon us sinners!' sighed the decorous Sergey Sergeyitch, scrupulously avoiding the puddles that he might not muddy his polished boots. 'I must own, honoured Yevgeny Fyodoritch, I have been expecting it for a long time.'

XII

AFTER this Andrey Yefimitch began to notice a mysterious air in all around him. The attendants, the nurses, and the patients looked at him inquisitively when they met him, and then whispered together. The superintendent's little daughter Masha, whom he liked to meet in the hospital garden, for some reason ran away from him now when he went up with a smile to stroke her on the head. The postmaster no longer said, 'Perfectly true', as he listened to him, but in unaccountable confusion muttered, 'Yes, yes, yes...' and looked at him with a grieved and thoughtful expression; for some reason he took to advising his friend to give up vodka and beer, but as a man of delicate feeling he did not say this directly, but hinted it, telling him first about the commanding officer of his battalion, an excellent man, and then about the priest of the regiment, a capital fellow, both of whom drank and fell ill, but on giving up drinking completely regained their health. On two or three occasions Andrey Yefimitch was visited by his colleague Hobotov, who also advised him to give up spirituous liquors, and for no apparent reason recommended him to take bromide.

In August Andrey Yefimitch got a letter from the mayor of the town asking him to come on very important business. On arriving at the town hall at the time fixed, Andrey Yefimitch found there the military commander, the superintendent of the district school, a member of the town council, Hobotov, and a plump, fair gentleman who was introduced to him as a doctor. This doctor, with a Polish surname difficult to pronounce, lived at a pedigree stud-farm twenty miles away, and was now on a visit to the town.

'There's something that concerns you,' said the member of the town council, addressing Andrey Yefimitch after they had all greeted one another and sat down to the table. 'Here Yevgeny Fyodoritch says that there is not room for the dispensary in the main building, and that it ought to be transferred to one of the lodges. That's of no consequence – of course it can be transferred, but the point is that the lodge wants doing up.'

'Yes, it would have to be done up,' said Andrey Yefimitch after a moment's thought. 'If the corner lodge, for instance, were fitted up as a dispensary, I imagine it would cost at least five hundred roubles. An unproductive expenditure!'

Everyone was silent for a space.

'I had the honour of submitting to you ten years ago,' Andrey Yefimitch went on in a low voice, 'that the hospital in its present form is a luxury for the town beyond its means. It was built in the forties, but things were different then. The town spends too much on unnecessary buildings and superfluous staff. I believe with a different system two model hospitals might be maintained for the same money.'

'Well, let us have a different system, then!' the member of the town council said briskly.

'I have already had the honour of submitting to you that the medical department should be transferred to the supervision of the Zemstvo.'

'Yes, transfer the money to the Zemstvo and they will steal it,' laughed the fair-haired doctor.

'That's what it always comes to,' the member of the council assented, and he also laughed.

Andrey Yefimitch looked with apathetic, lustreless eyes at the fair-haired doctor and said: 'One should be just.'

Again there was silence. Tea was brought in. The military commander, for some reason much embarrassed, touched Andrey Yefimitch's hand across the table and said: 'You have quite forgotten us, doctor. But of course you are a hermit: you don't play cards and don't like women. You would be dull with fellows like us.'

They all began saying how boring it was for a decent person to live in such a town. No theatre, no music, and at the last dance at the club there had been about twenty ladies and only two gentlemen. The young men did not dance, but spent all the time crowding round the refreshment bar or playing cards.

Not looking at anyone and speaking slowly in a low voice, Andrey Yefimitch began saying what a pity, what a terrible pity it was that the towns-people should waste their vital energy, their hearts, and their minds on cards and gossip, and should have neither the power nor the inclination to spend their time in interesting conversation and reading, and should refuse to take advantage of the enjoyments of the mind. The mind alone was interesting and worthy of attention, all the rest was low and petty. Hobotov listened to his colleague attentively and suddenly asked:

'Andrey Yefimitch, what day of the month is it?'

Having received an answer, the fair-haired doctor and he, in the tone of examiners conscious of their lack of skill, began asking Andrey Yefimitch what was the day of the week, how many days there were in the year, and whether it was true that there was a remarkable prophet living in Ward No. 6.

In response to the last question Andrey Yefimitch turned rather red and said: 'Yes, he is mentally deranged, but he is an interesting young man.'

They asked him no other questions.

When he was putting on his overcoat in the entry, the military commander laid a hand on his shoulder and said with a sigh:

'It's time for us old fellows to rest!'

As he came out of the hall, Andrey Yefimitch understood that it had been a committee appointed to enquire into his mental condition. He recalled the questions that had been asked him, flushed crimson, and for some reason, for the first time in his life, felt bitterly grieved for medical science.

'My God...' he thought, remembering how these doctors had just examined him; 'why, they have only lately been hearing lectures on mental pathology; they have passed an examination – what's the explanation of this crass ignorance? They have not a conception of mental pathology!'

And for the first time in his life he felt insulted and moved to anger.

In the evening of the same day Mihail Averyanitch came to see him. The postmaster went up to him without waiting to greet him, took him by both hands, and said in an agitated voice:

'My dear fellow, my dear friend, show me that you believe in my genuine affection and look on me as your friend!' And preventing Andrey Yefimitch from speaking, he went on, growing excited: 'I love you for your culture and nobility of soul. Listen to me, my dear fellow. The rules of their profession compel the doctors to conceal the truth from you, but I blurt out the plain truth like a soldier. You are not well! Excuse me, my dear fellow, but it is the truth; everyone about you has been noticing it for a long time. Doctor Yevgeny Fyodoritch has just told me that it is essential for you to rest and distract your mind for the sake of your health. Perfectly true! Excellent! In a day or two I am taking a holiday and am going away for a sniff of a different atmosphere. Show that you are a friend to me, let us go together! Let us go for a jaunt as in the good old days.'

'I feel perfectly well,' said Andrey Yefimitch after a moment's thought. 'I can't go away. Allow me to show you my friendship in some other way.'

To go off with no object, without his books, without his Daryushka, without his beer, to break abruptly through the routine of life, established for twenty years – the idea for the first minute struck him as wild and fantastic, but he remembered the conversation at the Zemstvo committee and the depressing feelings with which he had returned home, and the thought of a brief absence from the town in which stupid people looked on him as a madman was pleasant to him.

'And where precisely do you intend to go?' he asked.

'To Moscow, to Petersburg, to Warsaw.... I spent the five happiest years of my life in Warsaw. What a marvellous town! Let us go, my dear fellow!'

XIII

A WEEK later it was suggested to Andrey Yefimitch that he should have a rest – that is, send in his resignation – a suggestion he received with indifference, and a week later still, Mihail Averyanitch and he were sitting in a posting carriage driving to the nearest railway station. The days were cool and bright, with a blue sky and a transparent distance. They were two days driving the hundred and fifty miles to the railway station, and stayed two nights on the way. When at the posting station the glasses given them for their tea had not been properly washed, or the drivers were slow in harnessing the horses, Mihail Averyanitch would turn crimson, and quivering all over would shout:

'Hold your tongue! Don't argue!'

And in the carriage he talked without ceasing for a moment, describing his campaigns in the Caucasus and in Poland. What adventures he had had, what meetings! He talked loudly and opened his eyes so wide with wonder that he might well be thought to be lying. Moreover, as he talked he breathed in Andrey Yefimitch's face and laughed into his ear. This bothered the doctor and prevented him from thinking or concentrating his mind.

In the train they travelled, from motives of economy, third-class in a non-smoking compartment. Half the passengers were decent people. Mihail Averyanitch soon made friends with everyone, and moving from one seat to another, kept saying loudly that they ought not to travel by these appalling lines. It was a regular swindle! A very different thing riding on a good horse: one could do over seventy miles a day and feel fresh and well after it. And our bad harvests were due to the draining of the Pinsk marshes; altogether, the way things were done was dreadful. He got excited, talked loudly, and would not let others speak. This endless chatter to the accompaniment of loud laughter and expressive gestures wearied Andrey Yefimitch.

'Which of us is the madman?' he thought with vexation. 'I, who try not to disturb my fellow-passengers in any way, or this egoist who thinks that he is cleverer and more interesting than anyone here, and so will leave no one in peace?'

In Moscow Mihail Averyanitch put on a military coat without epaulettes and trousers with red braid on them. He wore a military cap and overcoat in the street, and soldiers saluted him. It seemed to Andrey

Yefimitch, now, that his companion was a man who had flung away all that was good and kept only what was bad of all the characteristics of a country gentleman that he had once possessed. He liked to be waited on even when it was quite unnecessary. The matches would be lying before him on the table, and he would see them and shout to the waiter to give him the matches; he did not hesitate to appear before a maidservant in nothing but his underclothes; he used the familiar mode of address to all footmen indiscriminately, even old men, and when he was angry called them fools and blockheads. This, Andrey Yefimitch thought, was like a gentleman, but disgusting.

First of all Mihail Averyanitch led his friend to the Iversky Madonna. He prayed fervently, shedding tears and bowing down to the earth, and when he had finished, heaved a deep sigh and said:

'Even though one does not believe it makes one somehow easier when one prays a little. Kiss the ikon, my dear fellow.'

Andrey Yefimitch was embarrassed and he kissed the image, while Mihail Averyanitch pursed up his lips and prayed in a whisper, and again tears came into his eyes. Then they went to the Kremlin and looked there at the Tsar-cannon and the Tsar-bell, and even touched them with their fingers, admired the view over the river, visited St. Saviour's and the Rumyantsev museum.

They dined at Tyestov's. Mihail Averyanitch looked a long time at the menu, stroking his whiskers, and said in the tone of a gourmand accustomed to dine in restaurants:

'We shall see what you give us to eat to-day, angel!'

XIV

THE doctor walked about, looked at things, ate and drank, but he had all the while one feeling: annoyance with Mihail Averyanitch. He longed to have a rest from his friend, to get away from him, to hide himself, while the friend thought it his duty not to let the doctor move a step away from him, and to provide him with as many distractions as possible. When there was nothing to look at he entertained him with conversation. For two days Andrey Yefimitch endured it, but on the third he announced to his friend that he was ill and wanted to stay at home for the whole day; his friend replied that in that case he would stay too – that really he needed rest, for he was run off his legs already. Andrey Yefimitch lay on the sofa, with his face to the back, and clenching his teeth, listened to his friend, who assured him with heat that sooner or later France would certainly thrash Germany, that there were a great many scoundrels in Moscow, and that it was impossible to judge of a horse's quality by its outward appearance. The doctor began to have a buzzing in his ears and palpitations of the heart, but out of delicacy could not bring himself to beg his friend to go away or hold his tongue. Fortunately Mihail Averyanitch grew weary of sitting in the hotel room, and after dinner he went out for a walk.

As soon as he was alone Andrey Yefimitch abandoned himself to a feeling of relief. How pleasant to lie motionless on the sofa and to know that one is alone in the room! Real happiness is impossible without solitude. The fallen angel betrayed God probably because he longed for solitude, of which the angels know nothing. Andrey Yefimitch wanted to think about what he had seen and heard during the last few days, but he could not get Mihail Averyanitch out of his head.

'Why, he has taken a holiday and come with me out of friendship, out of generosity,' thought the doctor with vexation; 'nothing could be worse than this friendly supervision. I suppose he is good-natured and generous and a lively fellow, but he is a bore. An insufferable bore. In the same way there are people who never say anything but what is clever and good, yet one feels that they are dull-witted people.'

For the following days Andrey Yefimitch declared himself ill and would not leave the hotel room; he lay with his face to the back of the sofa, and suffered agonies of weariness when his friend entertained him with conversation, or rested when his friend was absent. He was vexed with himself for having come, and with his friend, who grew every day more talkative and more free-and-easy; he could not succeed in attuning his thoughts to a serious and lofty level.

'This is what I get from the real life Ivan Dmitritch talked about,' he thought, angry at his own pettiness. 'It's of no consequence, though.... I shall go home, and everything will go on as before....'

It was the same thing in Petersburg too; for whole days together he did not leave the hotel room, but lay on the sofa and only got up to drink beer.

Mihail Averyanitch was all haste to get to Warsaw.

'My dear man, what should I go there for?' said Andrey Yefimitch in an imploring voice. 'You go alone and let me get home! I entreat you!'

'On no account,' protested Mihail Averyanitch. 'It's a marvellous town.'

Andrey Yefimitch had not the strength of will to insist on his own way, and much against his inclination went to Warsaw. There he did not leave the hotel room, but lay on the sofa, furious with himself, with his friend, and with the waiters, who obstinately refused to understand Russian; while Mihail Averyanitch, healthy, hearty, and full of spirits as usual, went about the town from morning to night, looking for his old acquaintances. Several times he did not return home at night. After one night spent in some unknown haunt he returned home early in the morning, in a violently excited condition, with a red face and tousled hair. For a long time he walked up and down the rooms muttering something to himself, then stopped and said:

'Honour before everything.'

After walking up and down a little longer he clutched his head in both hands and pronounced in a tragic voice: 'Yes, honour before everything! Accursed be the moment when the idea first entered my head to visit this Babylon! My dear friend,' he added, addressing the doctor, 'you may despise me, I have played and lost; lend me five hundred roubles!'

Andrey Yefimitch counted out five hundred roubles and gave them to his friend without a word. The latter, still crimson with shame and anger, incoherently articulated some useless vow, put on his cap, and went out. Returning two hours later he flopped into an easy-chair, heaved a loud sigh, and said:

'My honour is saved. Let us go, my friend; I do not care to remain another hour in this accursed town. Scoundrels! Austrian spies!'

By the time the friends were back in their own town it was November, and deep snow was lying in the streets. Dr. Hobotov had Andrey Yefimitch's post; he was still living in his old lodgings, waiting for Andrey Yefimitch to arrive and clear out of the hospital apartments. The plain woman whom he called his cook was already established in one of the lodges.

Fresh scandals about the hospital were going the round of the town. It was said that the plain woman had quarrelled with the superintendent, and that the latter had crawled on his knees before her begging forgiveness. On the very first day he arrived Andrey Yefimitch had to look out for lodgings.

'My friend,' the postmaster said to him timidly, 'excuse an indiscreet question: what means have you at your disposal?'

Andrey Yefimitch, without a word, counted out his money and said: 'Eighty-six roubles.'

'I don't mean that,' Mihail Averyanitch brought out in confusion, misunderstanding him; 'I mean, what have you to live on?'

'I tell you, eighty-six roubles... I have nothing else.'

Mihail Averyanitch looked upon the doctor as an honourable man, yet he suspected that he had accumulated a fortune of at least twenty thousand. Now learning that Andrey Yefimitch was a beggar, that he had nothing to live on, he was for some reason suddenly moved to tears and embraced his friend.

XV

ANDREY YEFIMITCH now lodged in a little house with three windows. There were only three rooms besides the kitchen in the little house. The doctor lived in two of them which looked into the street, while Daryushka and the landlady with her three children lived in the third room and the kitchen. Sometimes the landlady's lover, a drunken peasant who was rowdy and reduced the children and Daryushka to terror, would come for the night. When he arrived and established himself in the kitchen and demanded vodka, they all felt very uncomfortable, and the doctor would be moved by pity to take the crying children into his room and let them lie on his floor, and this gave him great satisfaction.

He got up as before at eight o'clock, and after his morning tea sat down to read his old books and magazines: he had no money for new ones. Either because the books were old, or perhaps because of the change in his surroundings, reading exhausted him, and did not grip his attention as before. That he might not spend his time in idleness he made a detailed catalogue of his books and gummed little labels on their backs, and this mechanical, tedious work seemed to him more interesting than reading. The monotonous, tedious work lulled his thoughts to sleep in some unaccountable way, and the time passed quickly while he thought of nothing. Even sitting in the kitchen, peeling potatoes with Daryushka or picking over the buckwheat grain, seemed to him interesting. On Saturdays and Sundays he went to church. Standing near the wall and half closing his eyes, he listened to the singing and thought of his father, of his mother, of the university, of the religions of the world; he felt calm and melancholy, and as he went out of the church afterwards he regretted that the service was so soon over. He went twice to the hospital to talk to Ivan Dmitritch. But on both occasions Ivan Dmitritch was unusually excited and ill-humoured; he bade the doctor leave him in peace, as he had long been sick of empty chatter, and declared, to make up for all his sufferings, he asked from the damned scoundrels only one favour – solitary confinement. Surely they would not refuse him even that? On both occasions when Andrey Yefimitch was taking leave of him and wishing him good-night, he answered rudely and said:

'Go to hell!'

And Andrey Yefimitch did not know now whether to go to him for the third time or not. He longed to go.

In old days Andrey Yefimitch used to walk about his rooms and think in the interval after dinner, but now from dinner-time till evening tea he lay on the sofa with his face to the back and gave himself up to trivial thoughts which he could not struggle against. He was mortified that after more than twenty years of service he had been given neither a pension nor any assistance. It is true that he had not done his work honestly, but, then, all who are in the Service get a pension without distinction whether they are honest or not. Contemporary justice lies precisely in the bestowal of grades, orders, and pensions, not for moral qualities or capacities, but for service whatever it may have been like. Why was he alone to be an exception? He had no money at all. He was ashamed to pass by the shop and look at the woman who owned it. He owed thirty-two roubles for beer already. There was money owing to the landlady also. Daryushka sold old clothes and books on the sly, and told lies to the landlady, saying that the doctor was just going to receive a large sum of money.

He was angry with himself for having wasted on travelling the thousand roubles he had saved up. How useful that thousand roubles would have been now! He was vexed that people would not leave him in peace. Hobotov thought it his duty to look in on his sick colleague from time to time. Everything about him was revolting to Andrey Yefimitch – his well-fed face and vulgar, condescending tone, and his use of the word 'colleague', and his high top-boots; the most revolting thing was that he thought it was his duty to treat Andrey Yefimitch, and thought that he really was treating him. On every visit he brought a bottle of bromide and rhubarb pills.

Mihail Averyanitch, too, thought it his duty to visit his friend and entertain him. Every time he went in to Andrey Yefimitch with an affectation of ease, laughed constrainedly, and began assuring him that he was looking very well to-day, and that, thank God, he was on the highroad to recovery, and from this it might be concluded that he looked on his friend's condition as hopeless. He had not yet repaid his Warsaw debt, and was overwhelmed by shame; he was constrained, and so tried to laugh louder and talk more amusingly. His anecdotes and descriptions seemed endless now, and were an agony both to Andrey Yefimitch and himself.

In his presence Andrey Yefimitch usually lay on the sofa with his face to the wall, and listened with his teeth clenched; his soul was oppressed with rankling disgust, and after every visit from his friend he felt as though this disgust had risen higher, and was mounting into his throat.

To stifle petty thoughts he made haste to reflect that he himself, and Hobotov, and Mihail Averyanitch, would all sooner or later perish without leaving any trace on the world. If one imagined some spirit flying by the earthly globe in space in a million years he would see nothing but clay and bare rocks. Everything – culture and the moral law – would pass away and not even a burdock would grow out of them. Of what consequence was shame in the presence of a shopkeeper, of what consequence was the insignificant Hobotov or the wearisome friendship of Mihail Averyanitch? It was all trivial and nonsensical.

But such reflections did not help him now. Scarcely had he imagined the earthly globe in a million years, when Hobotov in his high top-boots or Mihail Averyanitch with his forced laugh would appear from behind a bare rock, and he even heard the shamefaced whisper: 'The Warsaw debt.... I will repay it in a day or two, my dear fellow, without fail....'

XVI

ONE day Mihail Averyanitch came after dinner when Andrey Yefimitch was lying on the sofa. It so happened that Hobotov arrived at the same time with his bromide. Andrey Yefimitch got up heavily and sat down, leaning both arms on the sofa.

'You have a much better colour to-day than you had yesterday, my dear man,' began Mihail Averyanitch. 'Yes, you look jolly. Upon my soul, you do!'

'It's high time you were well, colleague,' said Hobotov, yawning. 'I'll be bound, you are sick of this bobbery.'

'And we shall recover,' said Mihail Averyanitch cheerfully. 'We shall live another hundred years! To be sure!'

'Not a hundred years, but another twenty,' Hobotov said reassuringly. 'It's all right, all right, colleague; don't lose heart.... Don't go piling it on!'

'We'll show what we can do,' laughed Mihail Averyanitch, and he slapped his friend on the knee. 'We'll show them yet! Next summer, please God, we shall be off to the Caucasus, and we will ride all over it on horseback – trot, trot, trot! And when we are back from the Caucasus I shouldn't wonder if we will all dance at the wedding.' Mihail Averyanitch gave a sly wink. 'We'll marry you, my dear boy, we'll marry you....'

Andrey Yefimitch felt suddenly that the rising disgust had mounted to his throat, his heart began beating violently.

'That's vulgar,' he said, getting up quickly and walking away to the window. 'Don't you understand that you are talking vulgar nonsense?'

He meant to go on softly and politely, but against his will he suddenly clenched his fists and raised them above his head.

'Leave me alone,' he shouted in a voice unlike his own, flushing crimson and shaking all over. 'Go away, both of you!'

Mihail Averyanitch and Hobotov got up and stared at him first with amazement and then with alarm.

'Go away, both!' Andrey Yefimitch went on shouting. 'Stupid people! Foolish people! I don't want either your friendship or your medicines, stupid man! Vulgar! Nasty!'

Hobotov and Mihail Averyanitch, looking at each other in bewilderment, staggered to the door and went out. Andrey Yefimitch snatched up the bottle of bromide and flung it after them; the bottle broke with a crash on the door-frame.

'Go to the devil!' he shouted in a tearful voice, running out into the passage. 'To the devil!'

When his guests were gone Andrey Yefimitch lay down on the sofa, trembling as though in a fever, and went on for a long while repeating: 'Stupid people! Foolish people!'

When he was calmer, what occurred to him first of all was the thought that poor Mihail Averyanitch must be feeling fearfully ashamed and depressed now, and that it was all dreadful. Nothing like this had ever happened to him before. Where was his intelligence and his tact? Where was his comprehension of things and his philosophical indifference?

The doctor could not sleep all night for shame and vexation with himself, and at ten o'clock next morning he went to the post-office and apologized to the postmaster.

'We won't think again of what has happened,' Mihail Averyanitch, greatly touched, said with a sigh, warmly pressing his hand. 'Let bygones be bygones. Lyubavkin,' he suddenly shouted so loud that all the postmen and other persons present started, 'hand a chair; and you wait,' he shouted to a peasant woman who was stretching out a registered letter to him through the grating. 'Don't you see that I am busy? We will not remember the past,' he went on, affectionately addressing Andrey Yefimitch; 'sit down, I beg you, my dear fellow.'

For a minute he stroked his knees in silence, and then said:

'I have never had a thought of taking offence. Illness is no joke, I understand. Your attack frightened the doctor and me yesterday, and we had a long talk about you afterwards. My dear friend, why won't you treat your illness seriously? You can't go on like this. ... Excuse me speaking openly as a friend,' whispered Mihail Averyanitch. 'You live in the most unfavourable surroundings, in a crowd, in uncleanliness, no one to look after you, no money for proper treatment. ... My dear friend, the doctor and I implore you with all our hearts, listen to our advice: go into the hospital! There you will have wholesome food and attendance and treatment. Though, between ourselves, Yevgeny Fyodoritch is *mauvais ton*, yet he does understand his work, you can fully rely upon him. He has promised me he will look after you.'

Andrey Yefimitch was touched by the postmaster's genuine sympathy and the tears which suddenly glittered on his cheeks.

'My honoured friend, don't believe it!' he whispered, laying his hand on his heart; 'don't believe them. It's all a sham. My illness is only that in twenty years I have only found one intelligent man in the whole town, and he is mad. I am not ill at all, it's simply that I have got into an enchanted circle which there is no getting out of. I don't care; I am ready for anything.'

'Go into the hospital, my dear fellow.'

'I don't care if it were into the pit.'

'Give me your word, my dear man, that you will obey Yevgeny Fyodoritch in everything.'

'Certainly I will give you my word. But I repeat, my honoured friend, I have got into an enchanted circle. Now everything, even the genuine sympathy of my friends, leads to the same thing – to my ruin. I am going to my ruin, and I have the manliness to recognize it.'

'My dear fellow, you will recover.'

'What's the use of saying that?' said Andrey Yefimitch, with irritation. 'There are few men who at the end of their lives do not experience what I am experiencing now. When you are told that you have something such as diseased kidneys or enlarged heart, and you begin being treated for it, or are told you are mad or a criminal – that is, in fact, when people suddenly turn their attention to you – you may be sure you have got into an enchanted circle from which you will not escape. You will try to escape and make things worse. You had better give in, for no human efforts can save you. So it seems to me.'

Meanwhile the public was crowding at the grating. That he might not be in their way, Andrey Yefimitch got up and began to take leave. Mihail Averyanitch made him promise on his honour once more, and escorted him to the outer door.

Towards evening on the same day Hobotov, in his sheepskin and his high top-boots, suddenly made his appearance, and said to Andrey Yefimitch in a tone as though nothing had happened the day before:

'I have come on business, colleague. I have come to ask you whether you would not join me in a consultation. Eh?'

Thinking that Hobotov wanted to distract his mind with an outing, or perhaps really to enable him to earn something, Andrey Yefimitch put on his coat and hat, and went out with him into the street. He was glad of the opportunity to smooth over his fault of the previous day and to be reconciled, and in his heart thanked Hobotov, who did not even allude to yesterday's scene and was evidently sparing him. One would never have expected such delicacy from this uncultured man.

'Where is your invalid?' asked Andrey Yefimitch.

'In the hospital. . . . I have long wanted to show him to you. A very interesting case.'

They went into the hospital yard, and going round the main building, turned towards the lodge where the mental cases were kept, and all this, for some reason, in silence. When they went into the lodge Nikita as usual jumped up and stood at attention.

'One of the patients here has a lung complication,' Hobotov said in an undertone, going into the ward with Andrey Yefimitch. 'You wait here, I'll be back directly. I am going for a stethoscope.'

And he went away.

XVII

It was getting dusk. Ivan Dmitritch was lying on his bed with his face thrust into his pillow; the paralytic was sitting motionless, crying quietly and moving his lips. The fat peasant and the former sorter were asleep. It was quiet.

Andrey Yefimitch sat down on Ivan Dmitritch's bed and waited. But half an hour passed, and instead of Hobotov, Nikita came into the ward with a dressing-gown, some underlinen, and a pair of slippers in a heap on his arm.

'Please change your things, your Honour,' he said softly. 'Here is your bed; come this way,' he added, pointing to an empty bedstead which had obviously been recently brought into the ward. 'It's all right; please God, you will recover.'

Andrey Yefimitch understood it all. Without saying a word he crossed to the bed to which Nikita pointed and sat down; seeing that Nikita was standing waiting, he undressed entirely and he felt ashamed. Then he put on the hospital clothes; the drawers were very short, the shirt was long, and the dressing-gown smelt of smoked fish.

'Please God, you will recover,' repeated Nikita, and he gathered up Andrey Yefimitch's clothes into his arms, went out, and shut the door after him.

'No matter...' thought Andrey Yefimitch, wrapping himself in his dressing-gown in a shamefaced way and feeling that he looked like a convict in his new costume. 'It's no matter.... It does not matter whether it's a dress-coat or a uniform or this dressing-gown....'

But how about his watch? And the notebook that was in the side-pocket? And his cigarettes? Where had Nikita taken his clothes? Now perhaps to the day of his death he would not put on trousers, a waistcoat, and high boots. It was all somehow strange and even incomprehensible at first. Andrey Yefimitch was even now convinced that there was no difference between his landlady's house and Ward No. 6, that everything in this world was nonsense and vanity of vanities. And yet his hands were trembling, his feet were cold, and he was filled with dread at the thought that soon Ivan Dmitritch would get up and see that he was in a dressing-gown. He got up and walked across the room and sat down again.

Here he had been sitting already half an hour, an hour, and he was miserably sick of it: was it really possible to live here a day, a week, and even years like these people? Why, he had been sitting here, had walked about and sat down again; he could get up and look out of window and walk from corner to corner again, and then what? Sit so all the time, like a post, and think? No, that was scarcely possible.

Andrey Yefimitch lay down, but at once got up, wiped the cold sweat from his brow with his sleeve, and felt that his whole face smelt of smoked fish. He walked about again.

'It's some misunderstanding...' he said, turning out the palms of his hands in perplexity. 'It must be cleared up. There is a misunderstanding....'

Meanwhile Ivan Dmitritch woke up; he sat up and propped his cheeks on his fists. He spat. Then he glanced lazily at the doctor, and apparently for the first minute did not understand; but soon his sleepy face grew malicious and mocking.

'Aha! so they have put you in here, too, old fellow?' he said in a voice husky from sleepiness, screwing up one eye. 'Very glad to see you. You sucked the blood of others, and now they will suck yours. Excellent!'

'It's a misunderstanding...' Andrey Yefimitch brought out, frightened by Ivan Dmitritch's words; he shrugged his shoulders and repeated: 'It's some misunderstanding....'

Ivan Dmitritch spat again and lay down.

'Cursed life,' he grumbled, 'and what's bitter and insulting, this life will not end in compensation for our sufferings, it will not end with apotheosis as it would in an opera, but with death; peasants will come and drag one's dead body by the arms and the legs to the cellar. Ugh! Well, it does not matter.... We shall have our good time in the other world.... I shall come here as a ghost from the other world and frighten these reptiles. I'll turn their hair grey.'

Moiseika returned, and, seeing the doctor, held out his hand.

'Give me one little kopeck,' he said.

XVIII

ANDREY YEFIMITCH walked away to the window and looked out into the open country. It was getting dark, and on the horizon to the right a cold crimson moon was mounting upwards. Not far from the hospital fence, not much more than two hundred yards away, stood a tall white house shut in by a stone wall. This was the prison.

'So this is real life,' thought Andrey Yefimitch, and he felt frightened.

The moon and the prison, and the nails on the fence, and the far-away flames at the bone-charring factory were all terrible. Behind him there was the sound of a sigh. Andrey Yefimitch looked round and saw a man with glittering stars and orders on his breast, who was smiling and slyly winking. And this, too, seemed terrible.

Andrey Yefimitch assured himself that there was nothing special about the moon or the prison, that even sane persons wear orders, and that everything in time will decay and turn to earth, but he was suddenly overcome with despair; he clutched at the grating with both hands and shook it with all his might. The strong grating did not yield.

Then, that it might not be so dreadful, he went to Ivan Dmitritch's bed and sat down.

'I have lost heart, my dear fellow,' he muttered, trembling and wiping away the cold sweat, 'I have lost heart.'

'You should be philosophical,' said Ivan Dmitritch ironically.

'My God, my God.... Yes, yes.... You were pleased to say once that there was no philosophy in Russia, but that all people, even the paltriest, talk philosophy. But you know the philosophizing of the paltriest does not harm anyone,' said Andrey Yefimitch in a tone as if he wanted to cry and complain. 'Why, then, that malignant laugh, my friend, and how can these paltry creatures help philosophizing if they are not satisfied? For an intelligent, educated man, made in God's image, proud and loving freedom, to have no alternative but to be a doctor in a filthy, stupid, wretched little town, and to spend his whole life among bottles, leeches, mustard plasters! Quackery, narrowness, vulgarity! Oh, my God!'

'You are talking nonsense. If you don't like being a doctor you should have gone in for being a statesman.'

'I could not, I could not do anything. We are weak, my dear friend. . . . I used to be indifferent. I reasoned boldly and soundly, but at the first coarse touch of life upon me I have lost heart. . . . Prostration. . . . We are weak, we are poor creatures . . . and you, too, my dear friend, you are intelligent, generous, you drew in good impulses with your mother's milk, but you had hardly entered upon life when you were exhausted and fell ill. . . . Weak, weak!'

Andrey Yefimitch was all the while at the approach of evening tormented by another persistent sensation besides terror and the feeling of resentment. At last he realized that he was longing for a smoke and for beer.

'I am going out, my friend,' he said. 'I will tell them to bring a light; I can't put up with this. . . . I am not equal to it. . . .'

Andrey Yefimitch went to the door and opened it, but at once Nikita jumped up and barred his way.

'Where are you going? You can't, you can't!' he said. 'It's bedtime.'

'But I'm only going out for a minute to walk about the yard,' said Andrey Yefimitch.

'You can't, you can't; it's forbidden. You know that yourself.'

'But what difference will it make to anyone if I do

go out?' asked Andrey Yefimitch, shrugging his shoulders. 'I don't understand. Nikita, I must go out!' he said in a trembling voice. 'I must.'

'Don't be disorderly, it's not right,' Nikita said peremptorily.

'This is beyond everything,' Ivan Dmitritch cried suddenly, and he jumped up. 'What right has he not to let you out? How dare they keep us here? I believe it is clearly laid down in the law that no one can be deprived of freedom without trial! It's an outrage! It's tyranny!'

'Of course it's tyranny,' said Andrey Yefimitch, encouraged by Ivan Dmitritch's outburst. 'I must go out, I want to. He has no right! Open, I tell you.'

'Do you hear, you dull-witted brute?' cried Ivan Dmitritch, and he banged on the door with his fist. 'Open the door, or I will break it open! Torturer!'

'Open the door,' cried Andrey Yefimitch, trembling all over; 'I insist!'

'Talk away!' Nikita answered through the door, 'talk away....'

'Anyhow, go and call Yevgeny Fyodoritch! Say that I beg him to come for a minute!'

'His Honour will come of himself to-morrow.'

'They will never let us out,' Ivan Dmitritch was going on meanwhile. 'They will leave us to rot here! Oh, Lord, can there really be no hell in the next world, and will these wretches be forgiven? Where is justice? Open the door, you wretch! I am choking!' he cried in a hoarse voice, and flung himself upon the door. 'I'll dash out my brains, murderers!'

Nikita opened the door quickly, and roughly with both his hands and his knee shoved Andrey Yefimitch back, then swung his arm and punched him in the face with his fist. It seemed to Andrey Yefimitch as though a huge salt wave enveloped him from his head downwards and dragged him to the bed; there really was a salt taste in his mouth: most likely the blood was running from his teeth. He waved his arms as though he were trying to swim out and clutched at a bedstead, and at the same moment felt Nikita hit him twice on the back.

Ivan Dmitritch gave a loud scream. He must have been beaten too.

Then all was still, the faint moonlight came through the grating, and a shadow like a net lay on the floor. It was terrible. Andrey Yefimitch lay and held his breath: he was expecting with horror to be struck again. He felt as though someone had taken a sickle, thrust it into him, and turned it round several times in his breast and bowels. He bit the pillow from pain and clenched his teeth, and all at once through the chaos in his brain there flashed the terrible unbearable thought that these people, who seemed now like black shadows in the moonlight, had to endure such pain day by day for years. How could it have happened that for more than twenty years he had not known it and had refused to know it? He knew nothing of pain, had no conception of it, so he was not to blame, but his conscience, as inexorable and as rough as Nikita, made him turn cold from the crown of his head to his heels. He leaped up, tried to cry out with all his might, and to run in haste to kill Nikita, and then Hobotov, the superintendent and the assistant, and then himself; but no sound came from his chest, and his legs would not obey him. Gasping for breath, he tore at the dressing-gown and the shirt on his breast, rent them, and fell senseless on the bed.

XIX

NEXT morning his head ached, there was a droning in his ears and a feeling of utter weakness all over. He was not ashamed at recalling his weakness the day before. He had been cowardly, had even been afraid of the moon, had openly expressed thoughts and feelings such as he had not expected in himself before; for instance, the thought that the paltry people who philosophized were really dissatisfied. But now nothing mattered to him.

He ate nothing, he drank nothing. He lay motionless and silent.

'It is all the same to me,' he thought when they asked him questions. 'I am not going to answer.... It's all the same to me.'

After dinner Mihail Averyanitch brought him a quarter of a pound of tea and a pound of fruit pastilles. Daryushka came too and stood for a whole hour by the bed with an expression of dull grief on her face. Dr. Hobotov visited him. He brought a bottle of bromide and told Nikita to fumigate the ward with something.

Towards evening Andrey Yefimitch died of an apoplectic stroke. At first he had a violent shivering fit and a feeling of sickness; something revolting, as it seemed, penetrating through his whole body, even to his finger-tips, strained from his stomach to his head and flooded his eyes and ears. There was a greenness before his eyes. Andrey Yefimitch understood that his end had come, and remembered that Ivan Dmitritch, Mihail Averyanitch, and millions of people believed in immortality. And what if it really existed? But he did not want immortality, and he thought of it only for one instant. A herd of deer, extraordinarily beautiful and graceful, of which he had been reading the day before, ran by him; then a peasant woman stretched out her hand to him with a registered letter.... Mihail Averyanitch said something, then it all vanished, and Andrey Yefimitch sank into oblivion for ever.

The hospital porters came, took him by his arms and his legs, and carried him away to the chapel.

There he lay on the table, with open eyes, and the moon shed its light upon him at night. In the morning Sergey Sergeyitch came, prayed piously before the crucifix, and closed his former chief's eyes.

Next day Andrey Yefimitch was buried. Mihail Averyanitch and Daryushka were the only people at the funeral.

THE TEACHER OF LITERATURE

THE TEACHER OF LITERATURE

I

THERE was the thud of horses' hoofs on the wooden floor; they brought out of the stable the black horse, Count Nulin; then the white, Giant; then his sister Maika. They were all magnificent, expensive horses. Old Shelestov saddled Giant and said, addressing his daughter Masha:

'Well, Marie Godefroi, come, get on! Hopla!'

Masha Shelestov was the youngest of the family; she was eighteen, but her family could not get used to thinking that she was not a little girl, and so they still called her Manya and Manyusa; and after there had been a circus in the town which she had eagerly visited, everyone began to call her Marie Godefroi.

'Hop-la!' she cried, mounting Giant. Her sister Varya got on Maika, Nikitin on Count Nulin, the officers on their horses, and the long picturesque cavalcade, with the officers in white tunics and the ladies in their riding habits, moved at a walking pace out of the yard.

Nikitin noticed that when they were mounting the horses and afterwards riding out into the street, Masha for some reason paid attention to no one but himself. She looked anxiously at him and at Count Nulin and said:

'You must hold him all the time on the curb, Sergey Vassilitch. Don't let him shy. He's pretending.'

And either because her Giant was very friendly with Count Nulin, or perhaps by chance, she rode all the time beside Nikitin, as she had done the day before, and the day before that. And he looked at her graceful little figure sitting on the proud white beast, at her delicate profile, at the chimney-pot hat, which did not suit her at all and made her look older than her age – looked at her with joy, with tenderness, with rapture; listened to her, taking in little of what she said, and thought:

'I promise on my honour, I swear to God, I won't be afraid and I'll speak to her to-day.'

It was seven o'clock in the evening – the time when the scent of white acacia and lilac is so strong that the air and the very trees seem heavy with the fragrance. The band was already playing in the town gardens. The horses made a resounding thud on the pavement, on all sides there were sounds of laughter, talk, and the banging of gates. The soldiers they met saluted the officers, the schoolboys bowed to Nikitin, and all the people who were hurrying to the gardens to hear the band were pleased at the sight of the party. And how warm it was! How soft-looking were the clouds scattered carelessly about the sky, how kindly and comforting the shadows of the poplars and the acacias, which stretched across the street and reached as far as the balconies and second storeys of the houses on the other side.

They rode on out of the town and set off at a trot

along the highroad. Here there was no scent of lilac and acacia, no music of the band, but there was the fragrance of the fields, there was the green of young rye and wheat, the marmots were squeaking, the rooks were cawing. Wherever one looked it was green, with only here and there black patches of bare ground, and far away to the left in the cemetery a white streak of apple-blossom.

They passed the slaughter-houses, then the brewery, and overtook a military band hastening to the suburban gardens.

'Polyansky has a very fine horse, I don't deny that,' Masha said to Nikitin, with a glance towards the officer who was riding beside Varya. 'But it has blemishes. That white patch on its left leg ought not to be there, and, look, it tosses its head. You can't train it not to now; it will toss its head till the end of its days.'

Masha was as passionate a lover of horses as her father. She felt a pang when she saw other people with fine horses, and was pleased when she saw defects in them. Nikitin knew nothing about horses; it made absolutely no difference to him whether he held his horse on the bridle or on the curb, whether he trotted or galloped; he only felt that his position was strained and unnatural, and that consequently the officers who knew how to sit in their saddles must please Masha more than he could. And he was jealous of the officers.

As they rode by the suburban gardens someone suggested their going in and getting some seltzer-water. They went in. There were no trees but oaks in the gardens; they had only just come into leaf, so that through the young foliage the whole garden could still be seen with its platform, little tables, and swings, and the crows' nests were visible, looking like big hats. The party dismounted near a table and asked for seltzer-water. People they knew, walking about the garden, came up to them. Among them the army doctor in high boots, and the conductor of the band, waiting for the musicians. The doctor must have taken Nikitin for a student, for he asked:

'Have you come for the summer holidays?'

'No, I am here permanently,' answered Nikitin. 'I am a teacher at the school.'

'You don't say so?' said the doctor, with surprise. 'So young and already a teacher?'

'Young, indeed! My goodness, I'm twenty-six!'

'You have a beard and moustache, but yet one would never guess you were more than twenty-two or twenty-three. How young-looking you are!'

'What a beast!' thought Nikitin. 'He, too, takes me for a whipper-snapper!'

He disliked it extremely when people referred to his youth, especially in the presence of women or the schoolboys. Ever since he had come to the town as a master in the school he had detested his own youthful appearance. The schoolboys were not afraid of him, old people called him 'young man', ladies preferred dancing with him to listening to his long arguments, and he would have given a great deal to be ten years older.

From the garden they went on to the Shelestovs' farm. There they stopped at the gate and asked the bailiff's wife, Praskovya, to bring some new milk. Nobody drank the milk; they all looked at one another, laughed, and galloped back. As they rode back the band was playing in the suburban garden; the sun was setting behind the cemetery, and half the sky was crimson from the sunset.

Masha again rode beside Nikitin. He wanted to tell her how passionately he loved her, but he was afraid he would be overheard by the officers and Varya, and he was silent. Masha was silent, too, and he felt why she was silent and why she was riding beside him, and was so happy that the earth, the sky, the lights of the town, the black outline of the brewery – all blended for him into something very pleasant and comforting, and it seemed to him as though Count Nulin were stepping on air and would climb up into the crimson sky.

They arrived home. The samovar was already boiling on the table, old Shelestov was sitting with his friends, officials in the Circuit Court, and as usual he was criticizing something.

'It's loutishness!' he said. 'Loutishness and nothing more. Yes!'

Since Nikitin had been in love with Masha, everything at the Shelestovs' pleased him: the house, the garden, and the evening tea, and the wickerwork chairs, and the old nurse, and even the word 'loutishness', which the old man was fond of using. The only thing he did not like was the number of cats and dogs and the Egyptian pigeons, who moaned disconsolately in a big cage in the verandah. There were so many house-dogs and yard-dogs that he had only learnt to recognize two of them in the course of his acquaintance with the Shelestovs: Mushka and Som.

Mushka was a little mangy dog with a shaggy face, spiteful and spoiled. She hated Nikitin: when she saw him she put her head on one side, showed her teeth, and began: 'Rrr . . . nga-nga-nga . . . rrr . . . !' Then she would get under his chair, and when he would try to drive her away she would go off into piercing yaps, and the family would say: 'Don't be frightened. She doesn't bite. She is a good dog.'

Som was a tall black dog with long legs and a tail as hard as a stick. At dinner and tea he usually moved about under the table, and thumped on people's boots and on the legs of the table with his tail. He was a good-natured, stupid dog, but Nikitin could not endure him because he had the habit of putting his head on people's knees at dinner and messing their trousers with saliva. Nikitin had more than once tried to hit him on his head with a knife-handle, to flip him on the nose, had abused him, had complained of him, but nothing saved his trousers.

After their ride the tea, jam, rusks, and butter seemed very nice. They all drank their first glass in silence and with great relish; over the second they began an argument. It was always Varya who started the arguments at tea; she was good-looking, handsomer than Masha, and was considered the cleverest and most cultured person in the house, and she behaved with dignity and severity, as an eldest daughter should who has taken the place of her dead mother in the house. As the mistress of the house, she felt herself entitled to wear a dressing-gown in the presence of her guests, and to call the officers by their surnames; she looked on Masha as a little girl, and talked to her as though she were a schoolmistress. She used to speak of herself as an old maid – so she was certain she would marry.

Every conversation, even about the weather, she invariably turned into an argument. She had a passion for catching at words, pouncing on contradictions, quibbling over phrases. You would begin talking to her, and she would stare at you and suddenly interrupt: 'Excuse me, excuse me, Petrov, the other day you said the very opposite!'

Or she would smile ironically and say: 'I notice, though, you begin to advocate the principles of the secret police. I congratulate you.'

If you jested or made a pun, you would hear her voice at once: 'That's stale', 'That's pointless.' If an officer ventured on a joke, she would make a contemptuous grimace and say, 'An army joke!'

And she rolled the *r* so impressively that Mushka invariably answered from under a chair, 'Rrr . . . nga-nga-nga . . . !'

On this occasion at tea the argument began with Nikitin's mentioning the school examinations.

'Excuse me, Sergey Vassilitch,' Varya interrupted him. 'You say it's difficult for the boys. And whose fault is that, let me ask you? For instance, you set the boys in the eighth class an essay on "Pushkin as a Psychologist." To begin with, you shouldn't set such a difficult subject; and, secondly, Pushkin was not a psychologist. Shtchedrin now, or Dostoevsky let us say, is a different matter, but Pushkin is a great poet and nothing more.'

'Shtchedrin is one thing, and Pushkin is another,' Nikitin answered sulkily.

'I know you don't think much of Shtchedrin at the

high school, but that's not the point. Tell me, in what sense is Pushkin a psychologist?'

'Why, do you mean to say he was not a psychologist? If you like, I'll give you examples.'

And Nikitin recited several passages from 'Onyegin' and then from 'Boris Godunov.'

'I see no psychology in that.' Varya sighed. 'The psychologist is the man who describes the recesses of the human soul, and that's fine poetry and nothing more.'

'I know the sort of psychology you want,' said Nikitin, offended. 'You want someone to saw my finger with a blunt saw while I howl at the top of my voice – that's what you mean by psychology.'

'That's poor! But still you haven't shown me in what sense Pushkin is a psychologist?'

When Nikitin had to argue against anything that seemed to him narrow, conventional, or something of that kind, he usually leaped up from his seat, clutched at his head with both hands, and began with a moan, running from one end of the room to another. And it was the same now: he jumped up, clutched his head in his hands, and with a moan walked round the table, then he sat down a little way off.

The officers took his part. Captain Polyansky began assuring Varya that Pushkin really was a psychologist, and to prove it quoted two lines from Lermontov; Lieutenant Gernet said that if Pushkin had not been a psychologist they would not have erected a monument to him in Moscow.

'That's loutishness!' was heard from the other end of the table. 'I said as much to the governor: "It's loutishness, your Excellency," I said.'

'I won't argue any more,' cried Nikitin. 'It's unending. . . . Enough! Ach, get away, you nasty dog!' he cried to Som, who laid his head and paw on his knee.

'Rrr . . . nga-nga-nga!' came from under the table.

'Admit that you are wrong!' cried Varya. 'Own up!'

But some young ladies came in, and the argument dropped of itself. They all went into the drawing-room. Varya sat down at the piano and began playing dances. They danced first a waltz, then a polka, then a quadrille with a grand chain which Captain Polyansky led through all the rooms, then a waltz again.

During the dancing the old men sat in the drawing-room, smoking and looking at the young people. Among them was Shebaldin, the director of the municipal bank, who was famed for his love of literature and dramatic art. He had founded the local Musical and Dramatic Society, and took part in the performances himself, confining himself, for some reason, to playing comic footmen or to reading in a sing-song voice 'The Woman who was a Sinner.' His nickname in the town was 'the Mummy', as he was tall, very lean and scraggy, and always had a solemn air and a fixed, lustreless eye. He was so devoted to the dramatic art that he even shaved his moustache and beard, and this made him still more like a mummy.

After the grand chain, he shuffled up to Nikitin sideways, coughed, and said:

'I had the pleasure of being present during the argument at tea. I fully share your opinion. We are of one mind, and it would be a great pleasure to me to talk to you. Have you read Lessing on the dramatic art of Hamburg?'

'No, I haven't.'

Shebaldin was horrified, and waved his hands as though he had burnt his fingers, and saying nothing more, staggered back from Nikitin. Shebaldin's appearance, his question, and his surprise, struck Nikitin as funny, but he thought none the less:

'It really is awkward. I am a teacher of literature, and to this day I've not read Lessing. I must read him.'

Before supper the whole company, old and young, sat down to play 'fate'. They took two packs of cards: one pack was dealt round to the company, the other was laid on the table face downwards.

'The one who has this card in his hand,' old Shelestov began solemnly, lifting the top card of the second pack, 'is fated to go into the nursery and kiss nurse.'

The pleasure of kissing the nurse fell to the lot of Shebaldin. They all crowded round him, took him to the nursery, and laughing and clapping their hands, made him kiss the nurse. There was a great uproar and shouting.

'Not so ardently!' cried Shelestov with tears of laughter. 'Not so ardently!'

It was Nikitin's 'fate' to hear the confessions of all. He sat on a chair in the middle of the drawing-room. A shawl was brought and put over his head. The first who came to confess to him was Varya.

'I know your sins,' Nikitin began, looking in the darkness at her stern profile. 'Tell me, madam, how do you explain your walking with Polyansky every day? Oh, it's not for nothing she walks with an hussar!'

'That's poor,' said Varya, and walked away.

Then under the shawl he saw the shine of big motionless eyes, caught the lines of a dear profile in the dark, together with a familiar, precious fragrance which reminded Nikitin of Masha's room.

'Marie Godefroi,' he said, and did not know his own voice, it was so soft and tender, 'what are your sins?'

Masha screwed up her eyes and put out the tip of her tongue at him, then she laughed and went away. And a minute later she was standing in the middle of the room, clapping her hands and crying:

'Supper, supper, supper!'

And they all streamed into the dining-room. At supper Varya had another argument, and this time with her father. Polyansky ate stolidly, drank red wine, and described to Nikitin how once in a winter campaign he had stood all night up to his knees in a bog; the enemy was so near that they were not allowed to speak or smoke, the night was cold and dark, a piercing wind was blowing. Nikitin listened and stole side-glances at Masha. She was gazing at him immovably, without blinking, as though she was pondering something or was lost in a reverie.... It was pleasure and agony to him both at once.

'Why does she look at me like that?' was the question that fretted him. 'It's awkward. People may notice it. Oh, how young, how naïve she is!'

The party broke up at midnight. When Nikitin went out at the gate, a window opened on the first floor, and Masha showed herself at it.

'Sergey Vassilitch!' she called.

'What is it?'

'I tell you what...' said Masha, evidently thinking of something to say. 'I tell you what.... Polyansky said he would come in a day or two with his camera and take us all. We must meet here.'

'Very well.'

Masha vanished, the window was slammed, and someone immediately began playing the piano in the house.

'Well, it is a house!' thought Nikitin while he crossed the street. 'A house in which there is no moaning except from Egyptian pigeons, and they only do it because they have no other means of expressing their joy!'

But the Shelestovs were not the only festive household. Nikitin had not gone two hundred paces before he heard the strains of a piano from another house. A little further he met a peasant playing the balalaika at the gate. In the gardens the band struck up a pot-pourri of Russian songs.

Nikitin lived nearly half a mile from the Shelestovs' in a flat of eight rooms at the rent of three hundred roubles a year, which he shared with his colleague Ippolit Ippolititch, a teacher of geography and history. When Nikitin went in, this Ippolit Ippolititch, a snub-nosed, middle-aged man with a reddish beard, with a coarse, good-natured, unintellectual face like a workman's, was sitting at the table correcting his pupils' maps. He considered that the most important and necessary part of the study of geography was the drawing of maps, and of the study of history the learning of dates: he would sit for nights together correcting in blue pencil the maps drawn by the boys and girls he taught, or making chronological tables.

'What a lovely day it has been!' said Nikitin, going in to him. 'I wonder at you – how can you sit indoors?'

Ippolit Ippolititch was not a talkative person; he either remained silent or talked of things which everybody knew already. Now what he answered was:

'Yes, very fine weather. It's May now; we soon shall have real summer. And summer's a very different thing from winter. In the winter you have to heat the stoves, but in summer you can keep warm without. In summer you have your window open at night and still are warm, and in winter you are cold even with the double frames in.'

Nikitin had not sat at the table for more than one minute before he was bored.

'Good-night!' he said, getting up and yawning. 'I wanted to tell you something romantic concerning myself, but you are – geography! If one talks to you of love, you will ask one at once, "What was the date of the Battle of Kalka?" Confound you, with your battles and your capes in Siberia!'

'What are you cross about?'

'Why, it is vexatious!'

And vexed that he had not spoken to Masha, and that he had no one to talk to of his love, he went to his study and lay down upon the sofa. It was dark and still in the study. Lying gazing into the darkness, Nikitin for some reason began thinking how in two or three years he would go to Petersburg, how Masha would see him off at the station and would cry; in Petersburg he would get a long letter from her in which she would entreat him to come home as quickly as possible. And he would write to her.... He would begin his letter like that: 'My dear little rat!'

'Yes, my dear little rat!' he said, and he laughed.

He was lying in an uncomfortable position. He put his arms under his head and put his left leg over the back of the sofa. He felt more comfortable. Meanwhile a pale light was more and more perceptible at the windows, sleepy cocks crowed in the yard. Nikitin went on thinking how he would come back from Petersburg, how Masha would meet him at the station, and with a shriek of delight would fling herself on his neck; or, better still, he would cheat her and come home by stealth late at night: the cook would open the door, then he would go on tiptoe to the bedroom, undress noiselessly, and jump into bed! And she would wake up and be overjoyed.

It was beginning to get quite light. By now there were no windows, no study. On the steps of the brewery by which they had ridden that day Masha was sitting, saying something. Then she took Nikitin by the arm and went with him to the suburban garden. There he saw the oaks and the crows' nests like hats. One of the nests rocked; out of it peeped Shebaldin, shouting loudly: 'You have not read Lessing!'

Nikitin shuddered all over and opened his eyes. Ippolit Ippolititch was standing before the sofa, and, throwing back his head, was putting on his cravat.

'Get up; it's time for school,' he said. 'You shouldn't sleep in your clothes; it spoils your clothes. You should sleep in your bed, undressed.'

And as usual he began slowly and emphatically saying what everybody knew.

Nikitin's first lesson was on Russian language in the second class. When at nine o'clock punctually he went into the class-room, he saw written on the blackboard two large letters – *M. S.* That, no doubt, meant Masha Shelestov.

'They've scented it out already, the rascals...' thought Nikitin. 'How is it they know everything?'

The second lesson was in the fifth class. And there two letters, *M. S.*, were written on the blackboard; and when he went out of the class-room at the end of the lesson, he heard the shout behind him as though from a theatre gallery:

'Hurrah for Masha Shelestov!'

His head was heavy from sleeping in his clothes, his limbs were weighed down with inertia. The boys, who were expecting every day to break up before the examinations, did nothing, were restless, and so bored that they got into mischief. Nikitin, too, was restless, did not notice their pranks, and was continually going to the window. He could see the street brilliantly lighted up with the sun; above the houses the blue limpid sky, the birds, and far, far away, beyond the gardens and the houses, vast indefinite distance, the forests in the blue haze, the smoke from a passing train....

Here two officers in white tunics, playing with their whips, passed in the street in the shade of the acacias. Here a lot of Jews, with grey beards, and caps on, drove past in a waggonette.... The governess walked by with the director's granddaughter. Som ran by in the company of two other dogs.... And then Varya, wearing a simple grey dress and red stockings, carrying the 'Vyestnik Evropi' in her hand, passed by. She must have been to the town library....

And it would be a long time before lessons were over at three o'clock! And after school he could not go home nor to the Shelestovs', but must go to give a lesson at Wolf's. This Wolf, a wealthy Jew who had turned Lutheran, did not send his children to the high school, but had them taught at home by the high-school masters, and paid five roubles a lesson.

He was bored, bored, bored.

At three o'clock he went to Wolf's and spent there, as it seemed to him, an eternity. He left there at five o'clock, and before seven he had to be at the high school again to a meeting of the masters – to draw up the plan for the *viva voce* examination of the fourth and sixth classes.

When late in the evening he left the high school and went to the Shelestovs', his heart was beating and his face was flushed. A month before, even a week before, he had, every time that he made up his mind to speak to her, prepared a whole speech, with an introduction and a conclusion. Now he had not one word ready; everything was in a muddle in his head, and all he knew was that to-day he would *certainly* declare himself, and that it was utterly impossible to wait any longer.

'I will ask her to come to the garden,' he thought; 'we'll walk about a little and I'll speak.'

There was not a soul in the hall; he went into the dining-room and then into the drawing-room.... There was no one there either. He could hear Varya arguing with someone upstairs and the clink of the dressmaker's scissors in the nursery.

There was a little room in the house which had three names: the little room, the passage room, and the dark room. There was a big cupboard in it where they kept medicines, gunpowder, and their hunting gear. Leading from this room to the first floor was a narrow wooden staircase where cats were always asleep. There were two doors in it – one leading to the nursery, one to the drawing-room. When Nikitin went into this room to go upstairs, the door from the nursery opened and shut with such a bang that it made the stairs and the cupboard tremble; Masha, in a dark dress, ran in with a piece of blue material in her hand, and, not noticing Nikitin, darted towards the stairs.

'Stay...' said Nikitin, stopping her. 'Good-evening, Godefroi.... Allow me....'

He gasped, he did not know what to say; with one hand he held her hand and with the other the blue material. And she was half frightened, half surprised, and looked at him with big eyes.

'Allow me...' Nikitin went on, afraid she would go away. 'There's something I must say to you.... Only ... it's inconvenient here. I cannot, I am incapable.... Understand, Godefroi, I can't – that's all....'

The blue material slipped on to the floor, and Nikitin took Masha by the other hand. She turned pale, moved her lips, then stepped back from Nikitin and found herself in the corner between the wall and the cupboard.

'On my honour, I assure you...' he said softly. 'Masha, on my honour....'

She threw back her head and he kissed her lips, and that the kiss might last longer he put his fingers to her cheeks; and it somehow happened that he found himself in the corner between the cupboard and the wall, and she put her arms round his neck and pressed her head against his chin.

Then they both ran into the garden. The Shelestovs had a garden of nine acres. There were about twenty old maples and lime-trees in it; there was one fir-tree, and all the rest were fruit-trees: cherries, apples, pears, horse-chestnuts, silvery olive-trees.... There were heaps of flowers, too.

Nikitin and Masha ran along the avenues in silence, laughed, asked each other from time to time disconnected questions which they did not answer. A crescent moon was shining over the garden, and drowsy tulips and irises were stretching up from the dark grass in its faint light, as though entreating for words of love for them, too.

When Nikitin and Masha went back to the house, the officers and the young ladies were already assembled and dancing the mazurka. Again Polyansky led the grand chain through all the rooms, again after dancing they played 'fate'. Before supper, when the visitors had gone into the dining-room, Masha, left alone with Nikitin, pressed close to him and said:

'You must speak to papa and Varya yourself; I am ashamed.'

After supper he talked to the old father. After listening to him, Shelestov thought a little and said:

'I am very grateful for the honour you do me and my daughter, but let me speak to you as a friend. I will speak to you, not as a father, but as one gentleman to another. Tell me, why do you want to be married so young? Only peasants are married so young, and that, of course, is loutishness. But why should you? Where's the satisfaction of putting on the fetters at your age?'

'I am not young!' said Nikitin, offended. 'I am in my twenty-seventh year.'

'Papa, the farrier has come!' cried Varya from the other room.

And the conversation broke off. Varya, Masha, and Polyansky saw Nikitin home. When they reached his gate, Varya said:

'Why is it your mysterious Metropolit Metropolititch never shows himself anywhere? He might come and see us.'

The mysterious Ippolit Ippolititch was sitting on his bed, taking off his trousers, when Nikitin went in to him.

'Don't go to bed, my dear fellow,' said Nikitin breathlessly. 'Stop a minute; don't go to bed!'

Ippolit Ippolititch put on his trousers hurriedly and asked in a flutter:

'What is it?'

'I am going to be married.'

Nikitin sat down beside his companion, and looking at him wonderingly, as though surprised at himself, said:

'Only fancy, I am going to be married! To Masha Shelestov! I made an offer to-day.'

'Well? She seems a good sort of girl. Only she is very young.'

'Yes, she is young,' sighed Nikitin, and shrugged his shoulders with a careworn air. 'Very, very young!'

'She was my pupil at the high school. I know her. She wasn't bad at geography, but she was no good at history. And she was inattentive in class, too.'

Nikitin for some reason felt suddenly sorry for his companion, and longed to say something kind and comforting to him.

'My dear fellow, why don't you get married?' he asked. 'Why don't you marry Varya, for instance? She is a splendid, first-rate girl! It's true she is very fond of arguing, but a heart . . . what a heart! She was just asking about you. Marry her, my dear boy! Eh?'

He knew perfectly well that Varya would not marry this dull, snub-nosed man, but still persuaded him to marry her – why?

'Marriage is a serious step,' said Ippolit Ippolititch after a moment's thought. 'One has to look at it all round and weigh things thoroughly; it's not to be done rashly. Prudence is always a good thing, and especially in marriage, when a man, ceasing to be a bachelor, begins a new life.'

And he talked of what everyone has known for ages. Nikitin did not stay to listen, said goodnight, and went to his own room. He undressed quickly and quickly got into bed, in order to be able to think the sooner of his happiness, of Masha, of the future; he smiled, then suddenly recalled that he had not read Lessing.

'I must read him,' he thought. 'Though, after all, why should I? Bother him!'

And exhausted by his happiness, he fell asleep at once and went on smiling till the morning.

He dreamed of the thud of horses' hoofs on a wooden floor; he dreamed of the black horse Count

Nulin, then of the white Giant and its sister Maika, being led out of the stable.

II

'It was very crowded and noisy in the church, and once someone cried out, and the head priest, who was marrying Masha and me, looked through his spectacles at the crowd, and said severely: "Don't move about the church, and don't make a noise, but stand quietly and pray. You should have the fear of God in your hearts."

'My best men were two of my colleagues, and Masha's best men were Captain Polyansky and Lieutenant Gernet. The bishop's choir sang superbly. The sputtering of the candles, the brilliant light, the gorgeous dresses, the officers, the numbers of gay, happy faces, and a special ethereal look in Masha, everything together – the surroundings and the words of the wedding prayers – moved me to tears and filled me with triumph. I thought how my life had blossomed, how poetically it was shaping itself! Two years ago I was still a student, I was living in cheap furnished rooms, without money, without relations, and, as I fancied then, with nothing to look forward to. Now I am a teacher in the high school in one of the best provincial towns, with a secure income, loved, spoiled. It is for my sake, I thought, this crowd is collected, for my sake three candelabra have been lighted, the deacon is booming, the choir is doing its best; and it's for my sake that this young creature, whom I soon shall call my wife, is so young, so elegant, and so joyful. I recalled our first meetings, our rides into the country, my declaration of love and the weather, which, as though expressly, was so exquisitely fine all the summer; and the happiness which at one time in my old rooms seemed to me possible only in novels and stories, I was now experiencing in reality – I was now, as it were, holding it in my hands.

'After the ceremony they all crowded in disorder round Masha and me, expressed their genuine pleasure, congratulated us and wished us joy. The brigadier-general, an old man of seventy, confined himself to congratulating Masha, and said to her in a squeaky, aged voice, so loud that it could be heard all over the church:

' "I hope that even after you are married you may remain the rose you are now, my dear."

'The officers, the director, and all the teachers smiled from politeness, and I was conscious of an agreeable artificial smile on my face, too. Dear Ippolit Ippolititch, the teacher of history and geography, who always says what everyone has heard before, pressed my hand warmly and said with feeling:

' "Hitherto you have been unmarried and have lived alone, and now you are married and no longer single.'

'From the church we went to a two-storeyed house which I am receiving as part of the dowry. Besides that house Masha is bringing me twenty thousand roubles, as well as a piece of waste land with a shanty on it, where I am told there are numbers of hens and ducks which are not looked after and are turning wild. When I got home from the church, I stretched myself at full length on the low sofa in my new study and began to smoke; I felt snug, cosy, and comfortable, as I never had in my life before. And meanwhile the wedding party were shouting "Hurrah!" while a wretched band in the hall played flourishes and all sorts of trash. Varya, Masha's sister, ran into the study with a wineglass in her hand, and with a queer, strained expression, as though her mouth were full of water; apparently she had meant to go on further, but she suddenly burst out laughing and sobbing, and the wineglass crashed on the floor. We took her by the arms and led her away.

'"Nobody can understand!" she muttered afterwards, lying on the old nurse's bed in a back room. "Nobody, nobody! My God, nobody can understand!"

'But everyone understood very well that she was four years older than her sister Masha, and still unmarried, and that she was crying, not from envy, but from the melancholy consciousness that her time was passing, and perhaps had passed. When they danced the quadrille, she was back in the drawing-room with a tear-stained and heavily powdered face, and I saw Captain Polyansky holding a plate of ice before her while she ate it with a spoon.

'It is past five o'clock in the morning. I took up my diary to describe my complete and perfect happiness, and thought I would write a good six pages, and read it to-morrow to Masha; but, strange to say, everything is muddled in my head and as misty as a dream, and I can remember vividly nothing but that episode with Varya, and I want to write, "Poor Varya!" I could go on sitting here and writing "Poor Varya!" By the way, the trees have begun rustling; it will rain. The crows are cawing, and my Masha, who has just gone to sleep, has for some reason a sorrowful face.'

For a long while afterwards Nikitin did not write his diary. At the beginning of August he had the school examinations, and after the fifteenth the classes began. As a rule he set off for school before nine in the morning, and before ten o'clock he was looking at his watch and pining for his Masha and his new house. In the lower forms he would set some boy to dictate, and while the boys were writing, would sit in the window with his eyes shut, dreaming; whether he dreamed of the future or recalled the past, everything seemed to him equally delightful, like a fairy tale. In the senior classes they were reading aloud Gogol or Pushkin's prose works, and that made him sleepy; people, trees, fields, horses, rose before his imagination, and he would say with a sigh, as though fascinated by the author:

'How lovely!'

At the midday recess Masha used to send him lunch in a snow-white napkin, and he would eat it slowly, with pauses, to prolong the enjoyment of it; and Ippolit Ippolititch, whose lunch as a rule consisted of nothing but bread, looked at him with respect and envy, and gave expression to some familiar fact, such as:

'Men cannot live without food.'

After school Nikitin went straight to give his private lessons, and when at last by six o'clock he got home, he felt excited and anxious, as though he had been away for a year. He would run upstairs breathless, find Masha, throw his arms round her, and kiss her and swear that he loved her, that he could not live without her, declare that he had missed her fearfully, and ask her in trepidation how she was and why she looked so depressed. Then they would dine together. After dinner he would lie on the sofa in his study and smoke, while she sat beside him and talked in a low voice.

His happiest days now were Sundays and holidays, when he was at home from morning till evening. On those days he took part in the naïve but extraordinarily pleasant life which reminded him of a pastoral idyl. He was never weary of watching how his sensible and practical Masha was arranging her nest, and anxious to show that he was of some use in the house, he would do something useless – for instance, bring the chaise out of the stable and look at it from every side. Masha had installed a regular dairy with three cows, and in her cellar she had many jugs of milk and pots of sour cream, and she kept it all for butter. Sometimes, by way of a joke, Nikitin would ask her for a glass of milk, and she would be quite upset because it was against her rules; but he would laugh and throw his arms round her, saying:

'There, there; I was joking, my darling! I was joking!'

Or he would laugh at her strictness when, finding in the cupboard some stale bit of cheese or sausage as hard as a stone, she would say seriously:

'They will eat that in the kitchen.'

He would observe that such a scrap was only fit for a mousetrap, and she would reply warmly that men knew nothing about housekeeping, and that it was just the same to the servants if you were to send down a hundredweight of savouries to the kitchen.

He would agree, and embrace her enthusiastically. Everything that was just in what she said seemed to him extraordinary and amazing; and what did not fit in with his convictions seemed to him naïve and touching.

Sometimes he was in a philosophical mood, and he would begin to discuss some abstract subject while she listened and looked at his face with curiosity.

'I am immensely happy with you, my joy,' he used to say, playing with her fingers or plaiting and unplaiting her hair. 'But I don't look upon this happiness of mine as something that has come to me by chance, as though it had dropped from heaven. This happiness is a perfectly natural, consistent, logical consequence. I believe that man is the creator of his own happiness, and now I am enjoying just what I have myself created. Yes, I speak without false modesty: I have created this happiness myself and I have a right to it. You know my past. My unhappy childhood, without father or mother; my depressing youth, poverty – all this was a struggle, all this was the path by which I made my way to happiness. . . .'

In October the school sustained a heavy loss: Ippolit Ippolititch was taken ill with erysipelas on the head and died. For two days before his death he was unconscious and delirious, but even in his delirium he said nothing that was not perfectly well known to everyone.

'The Volga flows into the Caspian Sea. . . . Horses eat oats and hay. . . .'

There were no lessons at the high school on the day of his funeral. His colleagues and pupils were the coffin-bearers, and the school choir sang all the way to the grave the anthem 'Holy God.' Three priests, two deacons, all his pupils and the staff of the boys' high school, and the bishop's choir in their best kaftans, took part in the procession. And passers-by who met the solemn procession crossed themselves and said:

'God grant us all such a death.'

Returning home from the cemetery much moved, Nikitin got out his diary from the table and wrote:

'We have just consigned to the tomb Ippolit Ippolititch Ryzhitsky. Peace to your ashes, modest worker! Masha, Varya, and all the women at the funeral, wept from genuine feeling, perhaps because they knew this uninteresting, humble man had never been loved by a woman. I wanted to say a warm word at my colleague's grave, but I was warned that this might displease the director, as he did not like our poor friend. I believe that this is the first day since my marriage that my heart has been heavy.'

There was no other event of note in the scholastic year.

The winter was mild, with wet snow and no frost; on Epiphany Eve, for instance, the wind howled all night as though it were autumn, and water trickled off the roofs; and in the morning, at the ceremony of the blessing of the water, the police allowed no one to go on the river, because they said the ice was swelling up and looked dark. But in spite of bad weather Nikitin's life was as happy as in summer. And, indeed, he acquired another source of pleasure; he learned to play *vint*. Only one thing troubled him, moved him to anger, and seemed to prevent him from being perfectly happy: the cats and dogs which formed part of his wife's dowry. The rooms, especially in the morning, always smelt like a menagerie, and nothing could destroy the odour; the cats frequently fought with the dogs. The spiteful beast Mushka was fed a dozen times a day; she still refused to recognize Nikitin and growled at him: 'Rrr . . . nga-nga-nga!'

One night in Lent he was returning home from the club where he had been playing cards. It was dark, raining, and muddy. Nikitin had an unpleasant feeling at the bottom of his heart and could not account for it. He did not know whether it was because he had lost twelve roubles at cards, or whether because one of the players, when they were settling up, had said that of course Nikitin had pots of money, with obvious reference to his wife's portion. He did not regret the twelve roubles, and there was nothing offensive in what had been said; but, still, there was the unpleasant feeling. He did not even feel a desire to go home.

'Foo, how horrid!' he said, standing still at a lamp-post.

It occurred to him that he did not regret the twelve roubles because he got them for nothing. If he had been a working man he would have known the value of every farthing, and would not have been so careless whether he lost or won. And his good-fortune had all, he reflected, come to him by chance, for nothing, and really was as superfluous for him as medicine for the healthy. If, like the vast majority of people, he had been harassed by anxiety for his daily bread, had been struggling for existence, if his back and chest had ached from work, then supper, a warm snug home, and domestic happiness, would have been the necessity, the compensation, the crown of his life; as it was, all this had a strange, indefinite significance for him.

'Foo, how horrid!' he repeated, knowing perfectly well that these reflections were in themselves a bad sign.

When he got home Masha was in bed: she was breathing evenly and smiling, and was evidently sleeping with great enjoyment. Near her the white cat lay curled up, purring. While Nikitin lit the candle and lighted his cigarette, Masha woke up and greedily drank a glass of water.

'I ate too many sweets,' she said, and laughed. 'Have you been home?' she asked after a pause.

'No.'

Nikitin knew already that Captain Polyansky, on whom Varya had been building great hopes of late, was being transferred to one of the western provinces, and was already making his farewell visits in the town, and so it was depressing at his father-in-law's.

'Varya looked in this evening,' said Masha, sitting up. 'She did not say anything, but one could see from her face how wretched she is, poor darling! I can't bear Polyansky. He is fat and bloated, and when he walks or dances his cheeks shake.... He is not a man I would choose. But, still, I did think he was a decent person.'

'I think he is a decent person now,' said Nikitin.

'Then why has he treated Varya so badly?'

'Why badly?' asked Nikitin, beginning to feel irritation against the white cat, who was stretching and arching its back. 'As far as I know, he has made no proposal and has given her no promises.'

'Then why was he so often at the house? If he didn't mean to marry her, he oughtn't to have come.'

Nikitin put out the candle and got into bed. But he felt disinclined to lie down and to sleep. He felt as though his head were immense and empty as a barn, and that new, peculiar thoughts were wandering about in it like tall shadows. He thought that, apart from the soft light of the ikon lamp, that beamed upon their quiet domestic happiness, that apart from this little world in which he and this cat lived so peacefully and happily, there was another world.... And he had a passionate, poignant longing to be in that other world, to work himself at some factory or big workshop, to address big audiences, to write, to publish, to raise a stir, to exhaust himself, to suffer.... He wanted something that would engross him till he forgot himself, ceased to care for the personal happiness which yielded him only sensations so monotonous. And suddenly there rose vividly before his imagination the figure of Shebaldin with his clean-shaven face, saying to him with horror: 'You haven't even read Lessing! You are quite behind the times! How you have gone to seed!'

Masha woke up and again drank some water. He glanced at her neck, at her plump shoulders and throat, and remembered the word the brigadier-general had used in church – 'rose'.

'Rose,' he muttered, and laughed.

His laugh was answered by a sleepy growl from Mushka under the bed: 'Rrr... nga-nga-nga...!'

A heavy anger sank like a cold weight on his heart, and he felt tempted to say something rude to Masha, and even to jump up and hit her; his heart began throbbing.

'So then,' he asked, restraining himself, 'since I went to your house, I was bound in duty to marry you?'

'Of course. You know that very well.'

'That's nice.' And a minute later he repeated: 'That's nice.'

To relieve the throbbing of his heart, and to avoid saying too much, Nikitin went to his study and lay down on the sofa, without a pillow; then he lay on the floor on the carpet.

'What nonsense it is!' he said to reassure himself. 'You are a teacher, you are working in the noblest of callings.... What need have you of any other world? What rubbish!'

But almost immediately he told himself with conviction that he was not a real teacher, but simply a government employee, as commonplace and mediocre as the Czech who taught Greek. He had never had a vocation for teaching, he knew nothing of the theory of teaching, and never had been interested in the subject; he did not know how to treat children; he did not understand the significance of what he taught, and perhaps did not teach the right things. Poor Ippolit Ippolititch had been frankly stupid, and all the boys, as well as his colleagues, knew what he was and what to expect from him; but he, Nikitin, like the Czech, knew how to conceal his stupidity and cleverly deceived everyone by pretending that, thank God, his teaching was a success. These new ideas frightened

Nikitin; he rejected them, called them stupid, and believed that all this was due to his nerves, that he would laugh at himself.

And he did, in fact, by the morning laugh at himself and call himself an old woman; but it was clear to him that his peace of mind was lost, perhaps, for ever, and that in that little two-storey house happiness was henceforth impossible for him. He realized that the illusion had evaporated, and that a new life of unrest and clear sight was beginning which was incompatible with peace and personal happiness.

Next day, which was Sunday, he was at the school chapel, and there met his colleagues and the director. It seemed to him that they were entirely preoccupied with concealing their ignorance and discontent with life, and he, too, to conceal his uneasiness, smiled affably and talked of trivialities. Then he went to the station and saw the mail train come in and go out, and it was agreeable to him to be alone and not to have to talk to anyone.

At home he found Varya and his father-in-law, who had come to dinner. Varya's eyes were red with crying, and she complained of a headache, while Shelestov ate a great deal, saying that young men nowadays were unreliable, and that there was very little gentlemanly feeling among them.

'It's loutishness!' he said. 'I shall tell him so to his face: "It's loutishness, sir," I shall say.'

Nikitin smiled affably and helped Masha to look after their guests, but after dinner he went to his study and shut the door.

The March sun was shining brightly in at the windows and shedding its warm rays on the table. It was only the twentieth of the month, but already the cabmen were driving with wheels, and the starlings were noisy in the garden. It was just the weather in which Masha would come in, put one arm round his neck, tell him the horses were saddled or the chaise was at the door, and ask him what she should put on to keep warm. Spring was beginning as exquisitely as last spring, and it promised the same joys.... But Nikitin was thinking that it would be nice to take a holiday and go to Moscow, and stay at his old lodgings there. In the next room they were drinking coffee and talking of Captain Polyansky, while he tried not to listen and wrote in his diary: 'Where am I, my God? I am surrounded by vulgarity and vulgarity. Wearisome, insignificant people, pots of sour cream, jugs of milk, cockroaches, stupid women.... There is nothing more terrible, mortifying, and distressing than vulgarity. I must escape from here, I must escape to-day, or I shall go out of my mind!'

AN ARTIST'S STORY

AN ARTIST'S STORY

I

It was six or seven years ago when I was living in one of the districts of the province of T —, on the estate of a young landowner called Byelokurov, who used to get up very early, wear a peasant tunic, drink beer in the evenings, and continually complain to me that he never met with sympathy from anyone. He lived in the lodge in the garden, and I in the old seigniorial house, in a big room with columns, where there was no furniture except a wide sofa on which I used to sleep, and a table on which I used to lay out patience. There was always, even in still weather, a droning noise in the old Amos stoves, and in thunderstorms the whole house shook and seemed to be cracking into pieces; and it was rather terrifying, especially at night, when all the ten big windows were suddenly lit up by lightning.

Condemned by destiny to perpetual idleness, I did absolutely nothing. For hours together I gazed out of the window at the sky, at the birds, at the avenue, read everything that was brought me by post, slept. Sometimes I went out of the house and wandered about till late in the evening.

One day as I was returning home, I accidentally strayed into a place I did not know. The sun was already sinking, and the shades of evening lay across the flowering rye. Two rows of old, closely planted, very tall fir-trees stood like two dense walls forming a picturesque, gloomy avenue. I easily climbed over the fence and walked along the avenue, slipping over the fir-needles which lay two inches deep on the ground. It was still and dark, and only here and there on the high tree-tops the vivid golden light quivered and made rainbows in the spiders' webs. There was a strong, almost stifling smell of resin. Then I turned into a long avenue of limes. Here, too, all was desolation and age; last year's leaves rustled mournfully under my feet and in the twilight shadows lurked between the trees. From the old orchard on the right came the faint, reluctant note of the golden oriole, who must have been old too. But at last the limes ended. I walked by an old white house of two storeys with a terrace, and there suddenly opened before me a view of a courtyard, a large pond with a bathing-house, a group of green willows, and a village on the further bank, with a high, narrow belfry on which there glittered a cross reflecting the setting sun.

For a moment it breathed upon me the fascination of something near and very familiar, as though I had seen that landscape at some time in my childhood.

At the white stone gates which led from the yard to the fields, old-fashioned solid gates with lions on them, were standing two girls. One of them, the elder, a slim, pale, very handsome girl with a perfect haystack of chestnut hair and a little obstinate mouth, had a severe expression and scarcely took notice of me, while the other, who was still very young, not more than seventeen or eighteen, and was also slim and pale, with a large mouth and large eyes, looked at me with astonishment as I passed by, said something in English, and was overcome with embarrassment. And it seemed to me that these two charming faces, too, had long been familiar to me. And I returned home feeling as though I had had a delightful dream.

One morning soon afterwards, as Byelokurov and I were walking near the house, a carriage drove unexpectedly into the yard, rustling over the grass, and in it was sitting one of those girls. It was the elder one. She had come to ask for subscriptions for some villagers whose cottages had been burnt down. Speaking with great earnestness and precision, and not looking at us, she told us how many houses in the village of Siyanovo had been burnt, how many men, women, and children were left homeless, and what steps were proposed, to begin with, by the Relief Committee, of which she was now a member. After handing us the subscription list for our signatures, she put it away and immediately began to take leave of us.

'You have quite forgotten us, Pyotr Petrovitch,' she said to Byelokurov as she shook hands with him. 'Do come, and if Monsieur N. (she mentioned my name) cares to make the acquaintance of admirers of his work, and will come and see us, mother and I will be delighted.'

I bowed.

When she had gone Pyotr Petrovitch began to tell me about her. The girl was, he said, of good family, and her name was Lidia Voltchaninov, and the estate on which she lived with her mother and sister, like the village on the other side of the pond, was called Shelkovka. Her father had once held an important position in Moscow, and had died with the rank of a privy councillor. Although they had ample means, the Voltchaninovs lived on their estate summer and winter without going away. Lidia was a teacher in the Zemstvo school in her own village, and received a salary of twenty-five roubles a month. She spent nothing on herself but her salary, and was proud of earning her own living.

'An interesting family,' said Byelokurov. 'Let us go over one day. They will be delighted to see you.'

One afternoon on a holiday we thought of the Voltchaninovs, and went to Shelkovka to see them. They – the mother and two daughters – were at home. The mother, Ekaterina Pavlovna, who at one time had been handsome, but now, asthmatic, depressed, vague, and over-feeble for her years, tried to entertain me with conversation about painting. Having heard from her daughter that I might come to Shelkovka, she had hurriedly recalled two or three of my landscapes which she had seen in exhibitions in Moscow, and now asked what I meant to express by them. Lidia, or as they all called her, Lida, talked more to Byelokurov than to me. Earnest and unsmiling, she asked him why he was not on the Zemstvo, and why he had not attended any of its meetings.

'It's not right, Pyotr Petrovitch,' she said reproachfully. 'It's not right. It's too bad.'

'That's true, Lida – that's true,' the mother assented. 'It isn't right.'

'Our whole district is in the hands of Balagin,' Lida went on, addressing me. 'He is the chairman of the

Zemstvo Board, and he has distributed all the posts in the district among his nephews and sons-in-law; and he does as he likes. He ought to be opposed. The young men ought to make a strong party, but you see what the young men among us are like. It's a shame, Pyotr Petrovitch!'

The younger sister, Genya, was silent while they were talking of the Zemstvo. She took no part in serious conversation. She was not looked upon as quite grown up by her family, and, like a child, was always called by the nickname of Misuce, because that was what she had called her English governess when she was a child. She was all the time looking at me with curiosity, and when I glanced at the photographs in the album, she explained to me: 'That's uncle... that's godfather', moving her finger across the photograph. As she did so she touched me with her shoulder like a child, and I had a close view of her delicate, undeveloped chest, her slender shoulders, her plait, and her thin little body tightly drawn in by her sash.

We played croquet and lawn tennis, we walked about the garden, drank tea, and then sat a long time over supper. After the huge empty room with columns, I felt, as it were, at home in this small snug house where there were no oleographs on the walls and where the servants were spoken to with civility. And everything seemed to me young and pure, thanks to the presence of Lida and Misuce, and there was an atmosphere of refinement over everything. At supper Lida talked to Byelokurov again of the Zemstvo, of Balagin, and of school libraries. She was an energetic, genuine girl, with convictions, and it was interesting to listen to her, though she talked a great deal and in a loud voice – perhaps because she was accustomed to talking at school. On the other hand, Pyotr Petrovitch, who had retained from his student days the habit of turning every conversation into an argument, was tedious, flat, long-winded, and unmistakably anxious to appear clever and advanced. Gesticulating, he upset a sauce-boat with his sleeve, making a huge pool on the tablecloth, but no one except me appeared to notice it.

It was dark and still as we went home.

'Good breeding is shown, not by not upsetting the sauce, but by not noticing it when somebody else does,' said Byelokurov, with a sigh. 'Yes, a splendid, intellectual family! I've dropped out of all decent society; it's dreadful how I've dropped out of it! It's all through work, work, work!'

He talked of how hard one had to work if one wanted to be a model farmer. And I thought what a heavy, sluggish fellow he was! Whenever he talked of anything serious he articulated 'Er-er' with intense effort, and worked just as he talked – slowly, always late and behind-hand. I had little faith in his business capacity if only from the fact that when I gave him letters to post he carried them about in his pocket for weeks together.

'The hardest thing of all,' he muttered as he walked beside me – 'the hardest thing of all is that, work as one may, one meets with no sympathy from anyone. No sympathy!'

II

I TOOK to going to see the Voltchaninovs. As a rule I sat on the lower step of the terrace; I was fretted by dissatisfaction with myself; I was sorry at the thought of my life passing so rapidly and uninterestingly, and felt as though I would like to tear out of my breast the heart which had grown so heavy. And meanwhile I heard talk on the terrace, the rustling of dresses, the pages of a book being turned. I soon grew accustomed to the idea that during the day Lida received patients, gave out books, and often went into the village with a parasol and no hat, and in the evening talked aloud of the Zemstvo and schools. This slim, handsome, invariably austere girl, with her small well-cut mouth, always said dryly when the conversation turned on serious subjects:

'That's of no interest to you.'

She did not like me. She disliked me because I was a landscape painter and did not in my pictures portray the privations of the peasants, and that, as she fancied, I was indifferent to what she put such faith in. I remember when I was travelling on the banks of Lake Baikal, I met a Buriat girl on horseback, wearing a shirt and trousers of blue Chinese canvas; I asked her if she would sell me her pipe. While we talked she looked contemptuously at my European face and hat, and in a moment she was bored with talking to me; she shouted to her horse and galloped on. And in just the same way Lida despised me as an alien. She never outwardly expressed her dislike for me, but I felt it, and sitting on the lower step of the terrace, I felt irritated, and said that doctoring peasants when one was not a doctor was deceiving them, and that it was easy to be benevolent when one had six thousand acres.

Meanwhile her sister Misuce had no cares, and spent her life in complete idleness just as I did. When she got up in the morning she immediately took up a book and sat down to read on the terrace in a deep arm-chair, with her feet hardly touching the ground, or hid herself with her book in the lime avenue, or walked out into the fields. She spent the whole day reading, poring greedily over her book, and only from the tired, dazed look in her eyes and the extreme paleness of her face one could divine how this continual reading exhausted her brain. When I arrived she would flush a little, leave her book, and looking into my face with her big eyes, would tell me eagerly of anything that had happened – for instance, that the chimney had been on fire in the servants' hall, or that one of the men had caught a huge fish in the pond. On ordinary days she usually went about in a light blouse and a dark blue skirt. We went for walks together, picked cherries for making jam, went out in the boat. When she jumped up to reach a cherry or sculled in the boat, her thin, weak arms showed through her transparent sleeves. Or I painted a sketch, and she stood beside me watching rapturously.

One Sunday at the end of July I came to the Voltchaninovs about nine o'clock in the morning. I walked about the park, keeping a good distance from the house, looking for white mushrooms, of which there was a great number that summer, and noting their position so as to come and pick them afterwards with Genya. There was a warm breeze. I saw Genya and her mother both in light holiday dresses coming home from church, Genya holding her hat in the wind. Afterwards I heard them having tea on the terrace.

For a careless person like me, trying to find justification for my perpetual idleness, these holiday mornings in our country-houses in the summer have always had a particular charm. When the green garden, still wet with dew, is all sparkling in the sun and looks radiant with happiness, when there is a scent of mignonette and oleander near the house, when the young people have just come back from church and are having breakfast in the garden, all so charmingly dressed and gay, and one knows that all these healthy, well-fed, handsome people are going to do nothing the whole long day, one wishes that all life were like that. Now, too, I had the same thought, and walked about the garden prepared to walk about like that, aimless and unoccupied, the whole day, the whole summer.

Genya came out with a basket; she had a look in her face as though she knew she would find me in the garden, or had a presentiment of it. We gathered mushrooms and talked, and when she asked a question she walked a little ahead so as to see my face.

'A miracle happened in the village yesterday,' she said. 'The lame woman Pelagea has been ill the whole year. No doctors or medicines did her any good; but yesterday an old woman came and whispered something over her, and her illness passed away.'

'That's nothing much,' I said. 'You mustn't look for miracles only among sick people and old women.

Isn't health a miracle? And life itself? Whatever is beyond understanding is a miracle.'

'And aren't you afraid of what is beyond understanding?'

'No. Phenomena I don't understand I face boldly, and am not overwhelmed by them. I am above them. Man ought to recognize himself as superior to lions, tigers, stars, superior to everything in nature, even what seems miraculous and is beyond his understanding, or else he is not a man, but a mouse afraid of everything.'

Genya believed that as an artist I knew a very great deal, and could guess correctly what I did not know. She longed for me to initiate her into the domain of the Eternal and the Beautiful – into that higher world in which, as she imagined, I was quite at home. And she talked to me of God, of the eternal life, of the miraculous. And I, who could never admit that my self and my imagination would be lost for ever after death, answered: 'Yes, men are immortal'; 'Yes, there is eternal life in store for us.' And she listened, believed, and did not ask for proofs.

As we were going home she stopped suddenly and said:

'Our Lida is a remarkable person – isn't she? I love her very dearly, and would be ready to give my life for her any minute. But tell me' – Genya touched my sleeve with her finger – 'tell me, why do you always argue with her? Why are you irritated?'

'Because she is wrong.'

Genya shook her head and tears came into her eyes.

'How incomprehensible that is!' she said.

At that minute Lida had just returned from somewhere, and standing with a whip in her hand, a slim, beautiful figure in the sunlight, at the steps, she was giving some orders to one of the men. Talking loudly, she hurriedly received two or three sick villagers; then with a busy and anxious face she walked about the rooms, opening one cupboard after another, and went upstairs. It was a long time before they could find her and call her to dinner, and she came in when we had finished our soup. All these tiny details I remember with tenderness, and that whole day I remember vividly, though nothing special happened. After dinner Genya lay in a long arm-chair reading, while I sat upon the bottom step of the terrace. We were silent. The whole sky was overcast with clouds, and it began to spot with fine rain. It was hot; the wind had dropped, and it seemed as though the day would never end. Ekaterina Pavlovna came out on the terrace, looking drowsy and carrying a fan.

'Oh, mother,' said Genya, kissing her hand, 'it's not good for you to sleep in the day.'

They adored each other. When one went into the garden, the other would stand on the terrace, and, looking towards the trees, call 'Aa – oo, Genya!' or 'Mother, where are you?' They always said their prayers together, and had the same faith; and they understood each other perfectly even when they did not speak. And their attitude to people was the same. Ekaterina Pavlovna, too, grew quickly used to me and fond of me, and when I did not come for two or three days, sent to ask if I were well. She, too, gazed at my sketches with enthusiasm, and with the same openness and readiness to chatter as Misuce, she told me what had happened, and confided to me her domestic secrets.

She had a perfect reverence for her elder daughter. Lida did not care for endearments, she talked only of serious matters; she lived her life apart, and to her mother and sister was as sacred and enigmatic a person as the admiral, always sitting in his cabin, is to the sailors.

'Our Lida is a remarkable person,' the mother would often say. 'Isn't she?'

Now, too, while it was drizzling with rain, we talked of Lida.

'She is a remarkable girl,' said her mother, and added in an undertone, like a conspirator, looking about her timidly: 'You wouldn't easily find another like her; only, do you know, I am beginning to be a little uneasy. The school, the dispensary, books – all that's very good, but why go to extremes? She is three-and-twenty, you know; it's time for her to think seriously of herself. With her books and her dispensary she will find life has slipped by without having noticed it.... She must be married.'

Genya, pale from reading, with her hair disarranged, raised her head and said as it were to herself, looking at her mother:

'Mother, everything is in God's hands.'

And again she buried herself in her book.

Byelokurov came in his tunic and embroidered shirt. We played croquet and tennis, then when it got dark, sat a long time over supper and talked again about schools, and about Balagin, who had the whole district under his thumb. As I went away from the Voltchaninovs that evening, I carried away the impression of a long, long idle day, with a melancholy consciousness that everything ends in this world, however long it may be.

Genya saw us out to the gate, and perhaps because she had been with me all day, from morning till night, I felt dull without her, and that all that charming family were near and dear to me, and for the first time that summer I had a yearning to paint.

'Tell me, why do you lead such a dreary, colourless life?' I asked Byelokurov as I went home. 'My life is dreary, difficult, and monotonous because I am an artist, a strange person. From my earliest days I've been wrung by envy, self-dissatisfaction, distrust in my work. I'm always poor, I'm a wanderer, but you – you're a healthy, normal man, a landowner, and a gentleman. Why do you live in such an uninteresting way? Why do you get so little out of life? Why haven't you, for instance, fallen in love with Lida or Genya?'

'You forget that I love another woman,' answered Byelokurov.

He was referring to Liubov Ivanovna, the lady who shared the lodge with him. Every day I saw this lady, very plump, rotund, and dignified, not unlike a fat goose, walking about the garden, in the Russian national dress and beads, always carrying a parasol; and the servant was continually calling her in to dinner or to tea. Three years before she had taken one of the lodges for a summer holiday, and had settled down at Byelokurov's apparently for ever. She was ten years older than he was, and kept a sharp hand over him, so much so that he had to ask her permission when he went out of the house. She often sobbed in a deep masculine note, and then I used to send word to her that if she did not leave off, I should give up my rooms there; and she left off.

When we got home Byelokurov sat down on the sofa and frowned thoughtfully, and I began walking up and down the room, conscious of a soft emotion as though I were in love. I wanted to talk about the Voltchaninovs.

'Lida could only fall in love with a member of the Zemstvo, as devoted to schools and hospitals as she is,' I said. 'Oh, for the sake of a girl like that one might not only go into the Zemstvo, but even wear out iron shoes, like the girl in the fairy tale. And Misuce? What a sweet creature she is, that Misuce!'

Byelokurov, drawling out 'Er–er', began a long-winded disquisition on the malady of the age – pessimism. He talked confidently, in a tone that suggested that I was opposing him. Hundreds of miles of desolate, monotonous, burnt-up steppe cannot induce such deep depression as one man when he sits and talks, and one does not know when he will go.

'It's not a question of pessimism or optimism,' I said irritably; 'it's simply that ninety-nine people out of a hundred have no sense.'

Byelokurov took this as aimed at himself, was offended, and went away.

III

'THE prince is staying at Malozyomovo, and he asks to be remembered to you,' said Lida to her mother. She had just come in, and was taking off her gloves. 'He gave me a great deal of interesting news… He promised to raise the question of a medical relief centre at Malozyomovo again at the provincial assembly, but he says there is very little hope of it.' And turning to me, she said: 'Excuse me, I always forget that this cannot be interesting to you.'

I felt irritated.

'Why not interesting to me?' I said, shrugging my shoulders. 'You do not care to know my opinion, but I assure you the question has great interest for me.'

'Yes?'

'Yes. In my opinion a medical relief centre at Malozyomovo is quite unnecessary.'

My irritation infected her; she looked at me, screwing up her eyes, and asked:

'What is necessary? Landscapes?'

'Landscapes are not, either. Nothing is.'

She finished taking off her gloves, and opened the newspaper, which had just been brought from the post. A minute later she said quietly, evidently restraining herself:

'Last week Anna died in childbirth, and if there had been a medical relief centre near, she would have lived. And I think even landscape painters ought to have some opinions on the subject.'

'I have a very definite opinion on that subject, I assure you,' I answered; and she screened herself with the newspaper, as though unwilling to listen to me. 'To my mind, all these schools, dispensaries, libraries, medical relief centres, under present conditions, only serve to aggravate the bondage of the people. The peasants are fettered by a great chain, and you do not break the chain, but only add fresh links to it – that's my view of it.'

She raised her eyes to me and smiled ironically, and I went on trying to formulate my leading idea.

'What matters is not that Anna died in childbirth, but that all these Annas, Mavras, Pelageas, toil from early morning till dark, fall ill from working beyond their strength, all their lives tremble for their sick and hungry children, all their lives are being doctored, and in dread of death and disease, fade and grow old early, and die in filth and stench. Their children begin the same story over again as soon as they grow up, and so it goes on for hundreds of years and milliards of men live worse than beasts – in continual terror, for a mere crust of bread. The whole horror of their position lies in their never having time to think of their souls, of their image and semblance. Cold, hunger, animal terror, a burden of toil, like avalanches of snow, block for them every way to spiritual activity – that is, to what distinguishes man from the brutes and what is the only thing which makes life worth living. You go to their help with hospitals and schools, but you don't free them from their fetters by that; on the contrary, you bind them in closer bonds, as, by introducing new prejudices, you increase the number of their wants, to say nothing of the fact that they've got to pay the Zemstvo for blisters and books, and so toil harder than ever.'

'I am not going to argue with you,' said Lida, putting down the paper. 'I've heard all that before. I will only say one thing: one cannot sit with one's hands in one's lap. It's true that we are not saving humanity, and perhaps we make a great many mistakes; but we do what we can, and we are right. The highest and holiest task for a civilized being is to serve his neighbours, and we try to serve them as best we can. You don't like it, but one can't please everyone.'

'That's true, Lida,' said her mother – 'that's true.'

In Lida's presence she was always a little timid, and looked at her nervously as she talked, afraid of saying something superfluous or inopportune. And she never contradicted her, but always assented: 'That's true, Lida – that's true.'

'Teaching the peasants to read and write, books of wretched precepts and rhymes, and medical relief centres, cannot diminish either ignorance or the death-rate, just as the light from your windows cannot light up this huge garden,' said I. 'You give nothing. By meddling in these people's lives you only create new wants in them, and new demands on their labour.'

'Ach! Good heavens! But one must do something!' said Lida with vexation, and from her tone one could see that she thought my arguments worthless and despised them.

'The people must be freed from hard physical labour,' said I. 'We must lighten their yoke, let them have time to breathe, that they may not spend all their lives at the stove, at the wash-tub, and in the fields, but may also have time to think of their souls, of God – may have time to develop their spiritual capacities. The highest vocation of man is spiritual activity – the perpetual search for truth and the meaning of life. Make coarse animal labour unnecessary for them, let them feel themselves free, and then you will see what a mockery these dispensaries and books are. Once a man recognizes his true vocation, he can only be satisfied by religion, science, and art, and not by these trifles.'

'Free them from labour?' laughed Lida. 'But is that possible?'

'Yes. Take upon yourself a share of their labour. If all of us, townspeople and country people, all without exception, would agree to divide between us the labour which mankind spends on the satisfaction of their physical needs, each of us would perhaps need to work only for two or three hours a day. Imagine that we all, rich and poor, work only for three hours a day, and the rest of our time is free. Imagine further that in order to depend even less upon our bodies and to labour less, we invent machines to replace our work, we try to cut down our needs to the minimum. We would harden ourselves and our children that they should not be afraid of hunger and cold, and that we shouldn't be continually trembling for their health like Anna, Mavra, and Pelagea. Imagine that we don't doctor ourselves, don't keep dispensaries, tobacco factories, distilleries – what a lot of free time would be left us after all! All of us together would devote our leisure to science and art. Just as the peasants sometimes work, the whole community together mending the roads, so all of us, as a community, would search for truth and the meaning of life, and I am convinced that the truth would be discovered very quickly; man would escape from this continual, agonizing, oppressive dread of death, and even from death itself.'

'You contradict yourself, though,' said Lida. 'You talk about science, and are yourself opposed to elementary education.'

'Elementary education when a man has nothing to read but the signs on public-houses and sometimes books which he cannot understand – such education has existed among us since the times of Rurik; Gogol's Petrushka has been reading for ever so long, yet as the village was in the days of Rurik so it has remained. What is needed is not elementary education, but freedom for a wide development of spiritual capacities. What are wanted are not schools, but universities.'

'You are opposed to medicine, too.'

'Yes. It would be necessary only for the study of diseases as natural phenomena, and not for the cure of them. If one must cure, it should not be diseases, but the causes of them. Remove the principal cause – physical labour, and then there will be no disease. I don't believe in a science that cures disease,' I went on excitedly. 'When science and art are real, they aim not at temporary, private ends, but at eternal and universal – they seek for truth and the meaning of life, they seek for God, for the soul, and when they are tied down to the needs and evils of the day, to dispensaries and libraries, they only complicate and hamper life. We have plenty of doctors, chemists, lawyers, plenty of people can read and write, but we are quite without biologists, mathematicians, philosophers, poets. The whole of our intelligence, the whole of our spiritual energy, is spent on satisfying temporary, passing needs. Scientific men, writers, artists, are hard at work; thanks to them, the conveniences of life are multiplied from day to day. Our physical demands increase, yet truth is still a long way off, and man still remains the most rapacious and dirty animal; everything is tending to the degeneration of the majority of mankind, and the loss for ever of all fitness for life. In such conditions an artist's work has no meaning, and the more talented he is, the stranger and the more unintelligible is his position, as when one looks into it, it is evident that he is working for the amusement of a rapacious and unclean animal, and is supporting the existing order. And I don't care to work and I won't work.... Nothing is any use; let the earth sink to perdition!'

'Misuce, go out of the room!' said Lida to her sister, apparently thinking my words pernicious to the young girl.

Genya looked mournfully at her mother and sister, and went out of the room.

'These are the charming things people say when they want to justify their indifference,' said Lida. 'It is easier to disapprove of schools and hospitals, than to teach or heal.'

'That's true, Lida – that's true,' the mother assented.

'You threaten to give up working,' said Lida. 'You evidently set a high value on your work. Let us give up arguing; we shall never agree, since I put the most imperfect dispensary or library of which you have just spoken so contemptuously on a higher level than any landscape.' And turning at once to her mother, she began speaking in quite a different tone: 'The prince is very much changed, and much thinner than when he was with us last. He is being sent to Vichy.'

She told her mother about the prince in order to avoid talking to me. Her face glowed, and to hide her feeling she bent low over the table as though she were short-sighted, and made a show of reading the newspaper. My presence was disagreeable to her. I said good-bye and went home.

IV

It was quite still out of doors; the village on the further side of the pond was already asleep; there was not a light to be seen, and only the stars were faintly reflected in the pond. At the gate with the lions on it Genya was standing motionless, waiting to escort me.

'Everyone is asleep in the village,' I said to her, trying to make out her face in the darkness, and I saw her mournful dark eyes fixed upon me. 'The publican and the horse-stealers are asleep, while we, well-bred people, argue and irritate each other.'

It was a melancholy August night – melancholy because there was already a feeling of autumn; the moon was rising behind a purple cloud, and it shed a faint light upon the road and on the dark fields of winter corn by the sides. From time to time a star fell. Genya walked beside me along the road, and tried not to look at the sky, that she might not see the falling stars, which for some reason frightened her.

'I believe you are right,' she said, shivering with the damp night air. 'If people, all together, could devote themselves to spiritual ends, they would soon know everything.'

'Of course. We are higher beings, and if we were really to recognize the whole force of human genius and lived only for higher ends, we should in the end become like gods. But that will never be – mankind will degenerate till no traces of genius remain.'

When the gates were out of sight, Genya stopped and shook hands with me.

'Good-night,' she said, shivering; she had nothing but her blouse over her shoulders and was shrinking with cold. 'Come to-morrow.'

I felt wretched at the thought of being left alone, irritated and dissatisfied with myself and other people; and I, too, tried not to look at the falling stars.

'Stay another minute,' I said to her, 'I entreat you.'

I loved Genya. I must have loved her because she met me when I came and saw me off when I went away; because she looked at me tenderly and enthusiastically. How touchingly beautiful were her pale face, slender neck, slender arms, her weakness, her idleness, her reading. And intelligence? I suspected in her intelligence above the average. I was fascinated by the breadth of her views, perhaps because they were different from those of the stern, handsome Lida, who disliked me. Genya liked me, because I was an artist. I had conquered her heart by my talent, and had a passionate desire to paint for her sake alone; and I dreamed of her as of my little queen who with me would possess those trees, those fields, the mists, the dawn, the exquisite and beautiful scenery in the midst of which I had felt myself hopelessly solitary and useless.

'Stay another minute,' I begged her. 'I beseech you.'

I took off my overcoat and put it over her chilly shoulders; afraid of looking ugly and absurd in a man's overcoat, she laughed, threw it off, and at that instant I put my arms round her and covered her face, shoulders, and hands with kisses.

'Till to-morrow,' she whispered, and softly, as though afraid of breaking upon the silence of the night, she embraced me. 'We have no secrets from one another. I must tell my mother and my sister at once.... It's so dreadful! Mother is all right; mother likes you – but Lida!'

She ran to the gates.

'Good-bye!' she called.

And then for two minutes I heard her running. I did not want to go home, and I had nothing to go for. I stood still for a little time hesitating, and made my way slowly back, to look once more at the house in which she lived, the sweet, simple old house, which seemed to be watching me from the windows of its upper storey, and understanding all about it. I walked by the terrace, sat on the seat by the tennis ground, in the dark under the old elm-tree, and looked from there at the house. In the windows of the top storey where Misuce slept there appeared a bright light, which changed to a soft green – they had covered the lamp with the shade. Shadows began to move.... I was full of tenderness, peace, and satisfaction with myself – satisfaction at having been able to be carried away by my feelings and having fallen in love, and at the same time I felt uncomfortable at the thought that only a few steps away from me, in one of the rooms of that house there was Lida, who disliked and perhaps hated me. I went on sitting there wondering whether Genya would come out; I listened and fancied I heard voices talking upstairs.

About an hour passed. The green light went out, and the shadows were no longer visible. The moon was standing high above the house, and lighting up the sleeping garden and the paths; the dahlias and the roses in front of the house could be seen distinctly, and looked all the same colour. It began to grow very cold. I went out of the garden, picked up my coat on the road, and slowly sauntered home.

When next day after dinner I went to the Voltchaninovs, the glass door into the garden was wide open. I sat down on the terrace, expecting Genya every minute, to appear from behind the flower-beds on the lawn, or from one of the avenues, or that I should hear her voice from the house. Then I walked into the drawing-room, the dining-room. There was not a soul to be seen. From the dining-room I walked along the long corridor to the hall and back. In this corridor there were several doors, and through one of them I heard the voice of Lida:

'"God... sent... a crow,"' she said in a loud, emphatic voice, probably dictating – '"God sent a crow a piece of cheese.... A crow.... A piece of cheese...." Who's there?' she called suddenly, hearing my steps.

'It's I.'

'Ah! Excuse me, I cannot come out to you this minute; I'm giving Dasha her lesson.'

'Is Ekaterina Pavlovna in the garden?'

'No, she went away with my sister this morning to our aunt in the province of Penza. And in the winter they will probably go abroad,' she added after a pause. '"God sent... the crow... a piece... of cheese...." Have you written it?'

I went into the hall, and stared vacantly at the pond and the village, and the sound reached me of 'A piece of cheese... God sent the crow a piece of cheese.'

And I went back by the way I had come here for the first time – first from the yard into the garden past the house, then into the avenue of lime-trees.... At this point I was overtaken by a small boy who gave me a note:

'I told my sister everything and she insists on my parting from you,' I read. 'I could not wound her by disobeying. God will give you happiness. Forgive me. If only you knew how bitterly my mother and I are crying!'

Then there was the dark fir avenue, the broken-down fence.... On the field where then the rye was in flower and the corncrakes were calling, now there were cows and hobbled horses. On the slopes there were bright green patches of winter corn. A sober workaday feeling came over me and I felt ashamed of all I had said at the Voltchaninovs', and felt bored with life as I had been before. When I got home, I packed and set off that evening for Petersburg.

* * * * *

I NEVER saw the Voltchaninovs again. Not long ago, on my way to the Crimea, I met Byelokurov in the train. As before, he was wearing a jerkin and an embroidered shirt, and when I asked how he was, he replied that, God be praised, he was well. We began talking. He had sold his old estate and bought another smaller one, in the name of Liubov Ivanovna. He could tell me little about the Voltchaninovs. Lida, he said, was still living in Shelkovka and teaching in the school; she had by degrees succeeded in gathering round her a circle of people sympathetic to her who made a strong party, and at the last election had turned out Balagin, who had till then had the whole district under his thumb. About Genya he only told me that she did not live at home, and that he did not know where she was.

I am beginning to forget the old house, and only sometimes when I am painting or reading I suddenly, apropos of nothing, remember the green light in the window, the sound of my footsteps as I walked home through the fields in the night, with my heart full of love, rubbing my hands in the cold. And still more rarely, at moments when I am sad and depressed by loneliness, I have dim memories, and little by little I begin to feel that she is thinking of me, too – that she is waiting for me, and that we shall meet....

Misuce, where are you?

MY LIFE

MY LIFE

THE STORY OF A PROVINCIAL

I

THE Superintendent said to me: 'I only keep you out of regard for your worthy father; but for that you would have been sent flying long ago.' I replied to him: 'You flatter me too much, your Excellency, in assuming that I am capable of flying.' And then I heard him say: 'Take that gentleman away; he gets upon my nerves.'

Two days later I was dismissed. And in this way I have, during the years I have been regarded as grown up, lost nine situations, to the great mortification of my father, the architect of our town. I have served in various departments, but all these nine jobs have been as alike as one drop of water is to another: I had to sit, write, listen to rude or stupid observations, and go on doing so till I was dismissed.

When I came in to my father he was sitting buried in a low arm-chair with his eyes closed. His dry, emaciated face, with a shade of dark blue where it was shaved (he looked like an old Catholic organist), expressed meekness and resignation. Without responding to my greeting or opening his eyes, he said:

'If my dear wife and your mother were living, your life would have been a source of continual distress to her. I see the Divine Providence in her premature death. I beg you, unhappy boy,' he continued, opening his eyes, 'tell me: what am I to do with you?'

In the past when I was younger my friends and relations had known what to do with me: some of them used to advise me to volunteer for the army, others to get a job in a pharmacy, and others in the telegraph department; now that I am over twenty-five, that grey hairs are beginning to show on my temples, and that I have been already in the army, and in a pharmacy, and in the telegraph department, it would seem that all earthly possibilities have been exhausted, and people have given up advising me, and merely sigh or shake their heads.

'What do you think about yourself?' my father went on. 'By the time they are your age, young men have a secure social position, while look at you: you are a proletarian, a beggar, a burden on your father!'

And as usual he proceeded to declare that the young people of to-day were on the road to perdition through infidelity, materialism, and self-conceit, and that amateur theatricals ought to be prohibited, because they seduced young people from religion and their duties.

'To-morrow we shall go together, and you shall apologize to the superintendent, and promise him to work conscientiously,' he said in conclusion. 'You ought not to remain one single day with no regular position in society.'

'I beg you to listen to me,' I said sullenly, expecting nothing good from this conversation. 'What you call a position in society is the privilege of capital and education. Those who have neither wealth nor education earn their daily bread by manual labour, and I see no grounds for my being an exception.'

'When you begin talking about manual labour it is always stupid and vulgar!' said my father with irritation. 'Understand, you dense fellow – understand, you addle-pate, that besides coarse physical strength you have the divine spirit, a spark of the holy fire, which distinguishes you in the most striking way from the ass or the reptile, and brings you nearer to the Deity! This fire is the fruit of the efforts of the best of mankind during thousands of years. Your great-grandfather Poloznev, the general, fought at Borodino; your grandfather was a poet, an orator, and a Marshal of Nobility; your uncle is a schoolmaster; and lastly, I, your father, am an architect! All the Poloznevs have guarded the sacred fire for you to put it out!'

'One must be just,' I said. 'Millions of people put up with manual labour.'

'And let them put up with it! They don't know how to do anything else! Anybody, even the most abject fool or criminal, is capable of manual labour; such labour is the distinguishing mark of the slave and the barbarian, while the holy fire is vouchsafed only to a few!'

To continue this conversation was unprofitable. My father worshipped himself, and nothing was convincing to him but what he said himself. Besides, I knew perfectly well that the disdain with which he talked of physical toil was founded not so much on reverence for the sacred fire as on a secret dread that I should become a workman, and should set the whole town talking about me; what was worse, all my contemporaries had long ago taken their degrees and were getting on well, and the son of the manager of the State Bank was already a collegiate assessor, while I, his only son, was nothing! To continue the conversation was unprofitable and unpleasant, but I still sat on and feebly retorted, hoping that I might at last be understood. The whole question, of course, was clear and simple, and only concerned with the means of my earning my living; but the simplicity of it was not seen, and I was talked to in mawkishly rounded phrases of Borodino, of the sacred fire, of my uncle a forgotten poet, who had once written poor and artificial verses; I was rudely called an addle-pate and a dense fellow. And how I longed to be understood! In spite of everything, I loved my father and my sister and it had been my habit from childhood to consult them – a habit so deeply rooted that I doubt whether I could ever have got rid of it; whether I were in the right or the wrong, I was in constant dread of wounding them, constantly afraid that my father's thin neck would turn crimson and that he would have a stroke.

'To sit in a stuffy room,' I began, 'to copy, to compete with a typewriter, is shameful and humiliating for a man of my age. What can the sacred fire have to do with it?'

'It's intellectual work, anyway,' said my father. 'But that's enough; let us cut short this conversation, and in any case I warn you: if you don't go back to your work again, but follow your contemptible propensities, then my daughter and I will banish you from our hearts. I shall strike you out of my will, I swear by the living God!'

With perfect sincerity to prove the purity of the motives by which I wanted to be guided in all my doings, I said:

'The question of inheritance does not seem very important to me. I shall renounce it all beforehand.'

For some reason or other, quite to my surprise, these words were deeply resented by my father. He turned crimson.

'Don't dare to talk to me like that, stupid!' he shouted in a thin, shrill voice. 'Wastrel!' and with a rapid, skilful, and habitual movement he slapped me twice in the face. 'You are forgetting yourself.'

When my father beat me as a child I had to stand up straight, with my hands held stiffly to my trouser seams, and look him straight in the face. And now when he hit me I was utterly overwhelmed, and, as though I were still a child, drew myself up and tried to look him in the face. My father was old and very thin, but his delicate muscles must have been as strong as leather, for his blows hurt a good deal.

I staggered back into the passage, and there he snatched up his umbrella, and with it hit me several times on the head and shoulders; at that moment my sister opened the drawing-room door to find out what the noise was, but at once turned away with a look of horror and pity without uttering a word in my defence.

My determination not to return to the Government office, but to begin a new life of toil, was not to be shaken. All that was left for me to do was to fix upon the special employment, and there was no particular difficulty about that, as it seemed to me that I was very strong and fitted for the very heaviest labour. I was faced with a monotonous life of toil in the midst of hunger, coarseness, and stench, continually preoccupied with earning my daily bread. And – who knows? – as I returned from my work along Great Dvoryansky Street, I might very likely envy Dolzhikov the engineer, who lived by intellectual work, but, at the moment, thinking over all my future hardships made me lighthearted. At times I had dreamed of spiritual activity, imagining myself a teacher, a doctor, or a writer, but these dreams remained dreams. The taste for intellectual pleasures – for the theatre, for instance, and for reading – was a passion with me, but whether I had any ability for intellectual work I don't know. At school I had had an unconquerable aversion for Greek, so that I was only in the fourth class when they had to take me from school. For a long while I had coaches preparing me for the fifth class. Then I served in various Government offices, spending the greater part of the day in complete idleness, and I was told that was intellectual work. My activity in the scholastic and official sphere had required neither mental application nor talent, nor special qualifications, nor creative impulse; it was mechanical. Such intellectual work I put on a lower level than physical toil; I despise it, and I don't think that for one moment it could serve as a justification for an idle, careless life, as it is indeed nothing but a sham, one of the forms of that same idleness. Real intellectual work I have in all probability never known.

Evening came on. We lived in Great Dvoryansky Street; it was the principal street in the town, and in the absence of decent public gardens our *beau monde* used to use it as a promenade in the evenings. This charming street did to some extent take the place of a public garden, as on each side of it there was a row of poplars which smelt sweet, particularly after rain, and acacias, tall bushes of lilac, wild-cherries and apple-trees hung over the fences and palings. The May twilight, the tender young greenery with its shifting shades, the scent of the lilac, the buzzing of the insects, the stillness, the warmth – how fresh and marvellous it all is, though spring is repeated every year! I stood at the garden gate and watched the passers-by. With most of them I had grown up and at one time played pranks; now they might have been disconcerted by my being near them, for I was poorly and unfashionably dressed, and they used to say of my very narrow trousers and huge, clumsy boots that they were like sticks of macaroni stuck in boats. Besides, I had a bad reputation in the town because I had no decent social position, and used often to play billiards in cheap taverns, and also, perhaps, because I had on two occasions been hauled up before an officer of the police, though I had done nothing whatever to account for this.

In the big house opposite someone was playing the piano at Dolzhikov's. It was beginning to get dark, and stars were twinkling in the sky. Here my father, in an old top-hat with wide upturned brim, walked slowly by with my sister on his arm, bowing in response to greetings.

'Look up,' he said to my sister, pointing to the sky with the same umbrella with which he had beaten me that afternoon. 'Look up at the sky! Even the tiniest stars are all worlds! How insignificant is man in comparison with the universe!'

And he said this in a tone that suggested that it was particularly agreeable and flattering to him that he was so insignificant. How absolutely devoid of talent and imagination he was! Sad to say, he was the only architect in the town, and in the fifteen to twenty years that I could remember not one single decent house had been built in it. When anyone asked him to plan a house, he usually drew first the reception hall and drawing-room; just as in old days the boarding-school misses always started from the stove when they danced, so his artistic ideas could only begin and develop from the hall and drawing-room. To them he tacked on a dining-room, a nursery, a study, linking the rooms together with doors, and so they all inevitably turned into passages, and every one of them had two or even three unnecessary doors. His imagination must have been lacking in clearness, extremely muddled, curtailed. As though feeling that something was lacking, he invariably had recourse to all sorts of outbuildings, planting one beside another; and I can see now the narrow entries, the poky little passages, the crooked staircases leading to half-landings where one could not stand upright, and where, instead of a floor, there were three huge steps like the shelves of a bath-house; and the kitchen was invariably in the basement with a brick floor and vaulted ceilings. The front of the house had a harsh, stubborn expression; the lines of it were stiff and timid; the roof was low-pitched and, as it were, squashed down; and the fat, well-fed-looking chimneys were invariably crowned by wire caps with squeaking black cowls. And for some reason all these houses, built by my father exactly like one another, vaguely reminded me of his top-hat and the back of his head, stiff and stubborn-looking. In the course of years they have grown used in the town to the poverty of my father's imagination. It has taken root and become our local style.

This same style my father had brought into my sister's life also, beginning with christening her Kleopatra (just as he had named me Misail). When she was a little girl he scared her by references to the stars, to the sages of ancient times, to our ancestors, and discoursed at length on the nature of life and duty; and now, when she was twenty-six, he kept up the same habits, allowing her to walk arm in arm with no one but himself, and imagining for some reason that sooner or later a suitable young man would be sure to appear, and to desire to enter into matrimony with her from respect for his personal qualities. She adored my father, feared him, and believed in his exceptional intelligence.

It was quite dark, and gradually the street grew empty. The music had ceased in the house opposite; the gate was thrown wide open, and a team with three horses trotted frolicking along our street with a soft tinkle of little bells. That was the engineer going for a drive with his daughter. It was bedtime.

I had my own room in the house, but I lived in a shed in the yard, under the same roof as a brick barn which had been built some time or other, probably to keep harness in; great hooks were driven into the wall. Now it was not wanted, and for the last thirty years my father had stowed away in it his newspapers, which for some reason he had bound in half-yearly volumes and allowed nobody to touch. Living here, I was less liable to be seen by my father and his visitors, and I fancied that if I did not live in a real room, and did not go into the house every day to dinner, my father's words that I was a burden upon him did not sound so offensive.

My sister was waiting for me. Unseen by my father, she had brought me some supper: not a very large slice of cold veal and a piece of bread. In our house such sayings as: 'A penny saved is a penny gained', and 'Take care of the pence and the pounds will take care of themselves', and so on, were frequently repeated, and my sister, weighed down by these vulgar maxims, did her utmost to cut down the expenses, and so we fared badly. Putting the plate on the table, she sat down on my bed and began to cry.

'Misail,' she said, 'what a way to treat us!'

She did not cover her face; her tears dropped on her bosom and hands, and there was a look of distress on her face. She fell back on the pillow, and abandoned herself to her tears, sobbing and quivering all over.

'You have left the service again...' she articulated. 'Oh, how awful it is!'

'But do understand, sister, do understand...' I said, and I was overcome with despair because she was crying.

As ill-luck would have it, the kerosene in my little lamp was exhausted; it began to smoke, and was on the point of going out, and the old hooks on the walls looked down sullenly, and their shadows flickered.

'Have mercy on us,' said my sister, sitting up. 'Father is in terrible distress and I am ill; I shall go out of my mind. What will become of you?' she said, sobbing and stretching out her arms to me. 'I beg you, I implore you, for our dear mother's sake, I beg you to go back to the office!'

'I can't, Kleopatra!' I said, feeling that a little more and I should give way. 'I cannot!'

'Why not?' my sister went on. 'Why not? Well, if you can't get on with the Head, look out for another post. Why shouldn't you get a situation on the railway, for instance? I have just been talking to Anyuta Blagovo; she declares they would take you on the railway-line, and even promised to try and get a post for you. For God's sake, Misail, think a little! Think a little, I implore you.'

We talked a little longer and I gave way. I said that the thought of a job on the railway that was being constructed had never occurred to me, and that if she liked I was ready to try it.

She smiled joyfully through her tears and squeezed my hand, and then went on crying because she could not stop, while I went to the kitchen for some kerosene.

II

AMONG the devoted supporters of amateur theatricals, concerts, and *tableaux vivants* for charitable objects, the Azhogins, who lived in their own house in Great Dvoryansky Street, took a foremost place; they always provided the room, and took upon themselves all the troublesome arrangements and the expenses. They were a family of wealthy landowners who had an estate of some nine thousand acres in the district and a capital house, but they did not care for the country, and lived winter and summer alike in the town. The family consisted of the mother, a tall, spare, refined lady, with short hair, a short jacket, and a flat-looking skirt in the English fashion, and three daughters who, when they were spoken of, were called not by their names but simply: the eldest, the middle, and the youngest. They all had ugly sharp chins, and were short-sighted and round-shouldered. They were dressed like their mother, they lisped disagreeably, and yet, in spite of that, infallibly took part in every performance and were continually doing something with a charitable object – acting, reciting, singing. They were very serious and never smiled, and even in a musical comedy they played without the faintest trace of gaiety, with a businesslike air, as though they were engaged in bookkeeping.

I loved our theatricals, especially the numerous, noisy, and rather incoherent rehearsals, after which they always gave a supper. In the choice of the plays and the distribution of the parts I had no hand at all. The post assigned to me lay behind the scenes. I painted the scenes, copied out the parts, prompted, made up the actors' faces; and I was entrusted, too, with various stage effects such as thunder, the singing of nightingales, and so on. Since I had no proper social position and no decent clothes, at the rehearsals I held aloof from the rest in the shadows of the wings and maintained a shy silence.

I painted the scenes at the Azhogins' either in the barn or in the yard. I was assisted by Andrey Ivanov, a house painter, or, as he called himself, a contractor for all kinds of house decoration, a tall, very thin, pale man of fifty, with a hollow chest, with sunken temples, with blue rings round his eyes, rather terrible to look at in fact. He was afflicted with some internal malady, and every autumn and spring people said that he wouldn't recover, but after being laid up for a while he would get up and say afterwards with surprise: 'I have escaped dying again.'

In the town he was called Radish, and they declared that this was his real name. He was as fond of the theatre as I was, and as soon as rumours reached him that a performance was being got up he threw aside all his work and went to the Azhogins' to paint scenes.

The day after my talk with my sister, I was working at the Azhogins' from morning till night. The rehearsal was fixed for seven o'clock in the evening, and an hour before it began all the amateurs were gathered together in the hall, and the eldest, the middle, and the youngest Azhogins were pacing about the stage, reading from manuscript books. Radish, in a long rusty-red overcoat and a scarf muffled round his neck, already stood leaning with his head against the wall, gazing with a devout expression at the stage. Madame Azhogin went up first to one and then to another guest, saying something agreeable to each. She had a way of gazing into one's face, and speaking softly as though telling a secret.

'It must be difficult to paint scenery,' she said softly, coming up to me. 'I was just talking to Madame Mufke about superstitions when I saw you come in. My goodness, my whole life I have been waging war against superstitions! To convince the servants what nonsense all their terrors are, I always light three candles, and begin all my important undertakings on the thirteenth of the month.'

Dolzhikov's daughter came in, a plump, fair beauty, dressed, as people said, in everything from Paris. She did not act, but a chair was set for her on the stage at the rehearsals, and the performances never began till she had appeared in the front row, dazzling and astounding everyone with her fine clothes. As a product of the capital she was allowed to make remarks during the rehearsals; and she did so with a sweet indulgent smile, and one could see that she looked upon our performance as a childish amusement. It was said she had studied singing at the Petersburg Conservatoire, and even sang for a whole winter in a private opera. I thought her very charming, and I usually watched her through the rehearsals and performances without taking my eyes off her.

I had just picked up the manuscript book to begin prompting when my sister suddenly made her appearance. Without taking off her cloak or hat, she came up to me and said:

'Come along, I beg you.'

I went with her. Anyuta Blagovo, also in her hat and wearing a dark veil, was standing behind the scenes at the door. She was daughter of the Assistant President of the Court, who had held that office in our town almost ever since the establishment of the circuit court. Since she was tall and had a good figure, her assistance was considered indispensable for *tableaux vivants*, and when she represented a fairy or something like Glory her face burned with shame; but she took no part in dramatic performances, and came to the rehearsals only for a moment on some special errand, and did not go into the hall. Now, too, it was evident that she had only looked in for a minute.

'My father was speaking about you,' she said drily, blushing and not looking at me. 'Dolzhikov has promised you a post on the railway-line. Apply to him to-morrow; he will be at home.'

I bowed and thanked her for the trouble she had taken.

'And you can give up this,' she said, indicating the exercise book.

My sister and she went up to Madame Azhogin and for two minutes they were whispering with her looking towards me; they were consulting about something.

'Yes, indeed,' said Madame Azhogin, softly coming up to me and looking intently into my face. 'Yes, indeed, if this distracts you from serious pursuits' – she took the manuscript book from my hands – 'you can hand it over to someone else; don't distress yourself, my friend, go home, and good luck to you.'

I said good-bye to her, and went away overcome with confusion. As I went down the stairs I saw my sister and Anyuta Blagovo going away; they were hastening along, talking eagerly about something, probably about my going into the railway service. My sister had never been at a rehearsal before, and now she was most likely conscience-stricken, and afraid her father might find out that, without his permission, she had been to the Azhogins'!

I went to Dolzhikov's next day between twelve and one. The footman conducted me into a very beautiful room, which was the engineer's drawing-room and, at the same time, his working study. Everything here was soft and elegant, and, for a man so unaccustomed to luxury as I was, it seemed strange. There were costly rugs, huge arm-chairs, bronzes, pictures, gold and plush frames; among the photographs scattered about the walls there were very beautiful women, clever, lovely faces, easy attitudes; from the drawing-room there was a door leading straight into the garden on to a verandah: one could see lilac-trees; one could see a table laid for lunch, a number of bottles, a bouquet of roses; there was a fragrance of spring and expensive cigars, a fragrance of happiness – and everything seemed as though it would say: 'Here is a man who has lived and laboured, and has attained at last the happiness possible on earth.' The engineer's daughter was sitting at the writing-table, reading a newspaper.

'You have come to see my father?' she asked. 'He is having a shower bath; he will be here directly. Please sit down and wait.'

I sat down.

'I believe you live opposite?' she questioned me, after a brief silence.

'Yes.'

'I am so bored that I watch you every day out of the window; you must excuse me,' she went on, looking at the newspaper, 'and I often see your sister; she always has such a look of kindness and concentration.'

Dolzhikov came in. He was rubbing his neck with a towel.

'Papa, Monsieur Poloznev,' said his daughter.

'Yes, yes, Blagovo was telling me,' he turned briskly to me without giving me his hand. 'But listen, what can I give you? What sort of posts have I got? You are a queer set of people!' he went on aloud in a tone as though he were giving me a lecture. 'A score of you keep coming to me every day; you imagine I am the head of a department! I am constructing a railway-line, my friends; I have employment for heavy labour: I need mechanics, smiths, navvies, carpenters, well-sinkers, and none of you can do anything but sit and write! You are all clerks.'

And he seemed to me to have the same air of happiness as his rugs and easy chairs. He was stout and healthy, ruddy-cheeked and broad-chested, in a print cotton shirt and full trousers like a toy china sledge-driver. He had a curly, round beard – and not a single grey hair – a hooked nose, and clear, dark, guileless eyes.

'What can you do?' he went on. 'There is nothing you can do: I am an engineer. I am a man of an assured position, but before they gave me a railway-line I was for years in harness; I have been a practical mechanic. For two years I worked in Belgium as an oiler. You can judge for yourself, my dear fellow, what kind of work can I offer you?'

'Of course that is so . . .' I muttered in extreme confusion, unable to face his clear, guileless eyes.

'Can you work the telegraph, anyway?' he asked, after a moment's thought.

'Yes, I have been a telegraph clerk.'

'H'm! Well, we will see then. Meanwhile, go to Dubetchnya. I have got a fellow there, but he is a wretched creature.'

'And what will my duties consist of?' I asked.

'We shall see. Go there; meanwhile I will make arrangements. Only please don't get drunk, and don't worry me with requests of any sort, or I shall send you packing.'

He turned away from me without even a nod.

I bowed to him and his daughter who was reading a newspaper, and went away. My heart felt so heavy, that when my sister began asking me how the engineer had received me, I could not utter a single word.

I got up early in the morning, at sunrise, to go to Dubetchnya. There was not a soul in our Great Dvoryansky Street; everyone was asleep, and my footsteps rang out with a solitary, hollow sound. The poplars, covered with dew, filled the air with soft fragrance. I was sad, and did not want to go away from the town. I was fond of my native town. It seemed to be so beautiful and so snug! I loved the fresh greenery, the still, sunny morning, the chiming of our bells; but the people with whom I lived in this town were boring, alien to me, sometimes even repulsive. I did not like them nor understand them.

I did not understand what these sixty-five thousand people lived for and by. I knew that Kimry lived by boots, that Túa made samovars and guns, that Odessa was a sea-port, but what our town was, and what it did, I did not know. Great Dvoryansky Street and the two other smartest streets lived on the interest of capital, or on salaries received by officials from the public treasury; but what the other eight streets, which ran parallel for over two miles and vanished beyond the hills, lived upon, was always an insoluble riddle to me. And the way these people lived one is ashamed to describe! No garden, no theatre, no decent band; the public library and the club library were only visited by Jewish youths, so that the magazines and new books lay for months uncut; rich and well-educated people slept in close, stuffy bedrooms, on wooden bedsteads infested with bugs; their children were kept in revoltingly dirty rooms called nurseries, and the servants, even the old and respected ones, slept on the floor in the kitchen, covered with rags. On ordinary days the houses smelt of beetroot soup, and on fast days of sturgeon cooked in sunflower oil. The food was not good, and the drinking water was unwholesome. In the town council, at the governor's at the head priest's, on all sides in private houses, people had been saying for years and years that our town had not a good and cheap water-supply, and that it was necessary to obtain a loan of two hundred thousand from the Treasury for laying on water; very rich people, of whom three dozen could have been counted up in our town, and who at times lost whole estates at cards, drank the polluted water too, and talked all their lives with great excitement of a loan for the water-supply – and I did not understand that; it seemed to me it would have been simpler to take the two hundred thousand out of their own pockets and lay it out on that object.

I did not know one honest man in the town. My father took bribes, and imagined that they were given him out of respect for his moral qualities; at the high school, in order to be moved up rapidly from class to class, the boys went to board with their teachers, who charged them exorbitant sums; the wife of the military commander took bribes from the recruits when they were called up before the board and even deigned to accept refreshments from them, and on one occasion could not get up from her knees in church because she was drunk; the doctors took bribes, too, when the recruits came up for examination, and the town doctor and the veterinary surgeon levied a regular tax on the butchers' shops and the restaurants; at the district school they did a trade in certificates, qualifying for partial exemption from military service; the higher clergy took bribes from the humbler priests and from the church elders; at the Municipal, the Artisans', and all the other Boards every petitioner was pursued by a shout: 'Don't forget your thanks!' and the petitioner would turn back to give sixpence or a shilling. And those who did not take bribes, such as the higher officials of the Department of Justice, were haughty, offered two fingers instead of shaking hands, were distinguished by the frigidity and narrowness of their judgments, spent a great deal of time over cards, drank to excess, married heiresses, and undoubtedly had a pernicious corrupting influence on those around them. It was only the girls who had still the fresh fragrance of moral purity; most of them had higher impulses, pure and honest hearts; but they had no understanding of life, and believed that bribes were given out of respect for moral qualities, and after they were married grew old quickly, let themselves go completely, and sank hopelessly in the mire of vulgar, petty, bourgeois existence.

III

A RAILWAY-LINE was being constructed in our neighbourhood. On the eve of feast days the streets were thronged with ragged fellows whom the townspeople called 'navvies', and of whom they were afraid. And more than once I had seen one of these tatterdemalions with a bloodstained countenance being led to the police station, while a samovar or some linen, wet from the wash, was carried behind by way of material evidence. The navvies usually congregated about the taverns and the market-place; they drank, ate, and used bad language, and pursued with shrill whistles every woman of light behaviour who passed by. To entertain this hungry rabble our shopkeepers made cats and dogs drunk with vodka, or tied an old kerosene can to a dog's tail; a hue and cry was raised, and the dog dashed along the street, jingling the can, squealing with terror; it fancied some monster was close upon its heels; it would run far out of the town into the open country and there sink exhausted. There were in the town several dogs who went about trembling, with their tails between their legs; and people said this diversion had been too much for them, and had driven them mad.

A station was being built four miles from the town. It was said that the engineers asked for a bribe of fifty thousand roubles for bringing the line right up to the town, but the town council would only consent to give forty thousand; they could not come to an agreement over the difference, and now the townspeople regretted it, as they had to make a road to the station and that, it was reckoned, would cost more. The sleepers and rails had been laid throughout the whole length of the line, and trains ran up and down it, bringing building materials and labourers, and further progress was only delayed on account of the bridges which Dolzhikov was building, and some of the stations were not yet finished.

Dubetchnya, as our first station was called, was a little under twelve miles from the town. I walked. The cornfields, bathed in the morning sunshine, were bright green. It was a flat, cheerful country, and in the distance there were the distinct outlines of the station, of ancient barrows, and far-away homesteads. ... How nice it was out there in the open! And how I longed to be filled with the sense of freedom, if only for that one morning, that I might not think of what was being done in the town, not think of my needs, not feel hungry! Nothing has so marred my existence as an acute feeling of hunger, which made images of buckwheat porridge, rissoles, and baked fish mingle strangely with my best thoughts. Here I was standing alone in the open country, gazing upward at a lark which hovered in the air at the same spot, trilling as though in hysterics, and meanwhile I was thinking: 'How nice it would be to eat a piece of bread and butter!' Or I would sit down by the roadside to rest, and shut my eyes to listen to the delicious sounds of May, and what haunted me was the smell of hot potatoes. Though I was tall and strongly built, I had as a rule to eat little, and so the predominant sensation throughout the day was hunger, and perhaps that was why I knew so well how it is that such multitudes of people toil merely for their daily bread, and can talk of nothing but things to eat.

At Dubetchnya they were plastering the inside of the station, and building a wooden upper storey to the pumping shed. It was hot; there was a smell of lime, and the workmen sauntered listlessly between the heaps of shavings and mortar rubble. The pointsman lay asleep near his sentry box, and the sun was blazing full on his face. There was not a single tree. The telegraph wire hummed faintly and hawks were perching on it here and there. I, wandering, too, among the heaps of rubbish, and not knowing what to do, recalled how the engineer, in answer to my question what my duties would consist in, had said: 'We shall see when you are there'; but what could one see in that wilderness?

The plasterers spoke of the foreman, and of a certain Fyodot Vasilyev. I did not understand, and gradually I was overcome by depression – the physical depression in which one is conscious of one's arms and legs and huge body, and does not know what to do with them or where to put them.

After I had been walking about for at least a couple of hours, I noticed that there were telegraph poles running off to the right from the station, and that they ended a mile or a mile and a half away at a white stone wall. The workmen told me the office was there, and at last I reflected that that was where I ought to go.

It was a very old manor house, deserted long ago. The wall round it, of porous white stone, was mouldering and had fallen away in places, and the lodge, the blank wall of which looked out on the open country, had a rusty roof with patches of tin-plate gleaming here and there on it. Within the gates could be seen a spacious courtyard overgrown with rough weeds, and an old manor house with sunblinds on the windows, and a high roof red with rust. Two lodges, exactly alike, stood one on each side of the house to right and to left: one had its windows nailed up with boards; near the other, of which the windows were open, there was washing on the line, and there were calves moving about. The last of the telegraph poles stood in the courtyard, and the wire from it ran to the window of the lodge, of which the blank wall looked out into the open country. The door stood open; I went in. By the telegraph apparatus a gentleman with a curly dark head, wearing a reefer coat made of sailcloth, was sitting at a table; he glanced at me morosely from under his brows, but immediately smiled and said:

'Hullo, Better-than-nothing!'

It was Ivan Tcheprakov, an old schoolfellow of mine, who had been expelled from the second class for smoking. We used at one time, during autumn, to catch goldfinches, finches, and linnets together, and to sell them in the market early in the morning, while our parents were still in their beds. We watched for flocks of migrating starlings and shot at them with small shot, then we picked up those that were wounded, and some of them died in our hands in terrible agonies (I remember to this day how they moaned in the cage at night); those that recovered we sold, and swore with the utmost effrontery that they were all cocks. On one occasion at the market I had only one starling left, which I had offered to purchasers in vain, till at last I sold it for a farthing. 'Anyway, it's better than nothing,' I said to comfort myself, as I put the farthing in my pocket, and from that day the street urchins and the schoolboys called after me: 'Better-than-nothing'; and to this day the street boys and the shopkeepers mock at me with the nickname, though no one remembers how it arose.

Tchéprakov was not of robust constitution: he was narrow-chested, round-shouldered, and long-legged. He wore a silk cord for a tie, had no trace of a waistcoat, and his boots were worse than mine, with the heels trodden down on one side. He stared, hardly even blinking, with a strained expression, as though he were just going to catch something, and he was always in a fuss.

'You wait a minute,' he would say fussily. 'You listen.... Whatever was I talking about?'

We got into conversation. I learned that the estate on which I now was had until recently been the property of the Tcheprakovs, and had only the autumn before passed into the possession of Dolzhikov, who considered it more profitable to put his money into land than to keep it in notes, and had already bought up three good-sized mortgaged estates in our neighbourhood. At the sale Tcheprakov's mother had reserved for herself the right to live for the next two years in one of the lodges at the side, and had obtained a post for her son in the office.

'I should think he could buy!' Tcheprakov said of the engineer. 'See what he fleeces out of the contractors alone! He fleeces everyone!'

Then he took me to dinner, deciding fussily that I should live with him in the lodge, and have my meals from his mother.

'She is a bit stingy,' he said, 'but she won't charge you much.'

It was very cramped in the little rooms in which his mother lived; they were all, even the passage and the entry, piled up with furniture which had been brought from the big house after the sale; and the furniture was all old-fashioned mahogany. Madame Tcheprakov, a very stout middle-aged lady with slanting Chinese eyes, was sitting in a big arm-chair by the window, knitting a stocking. She received me ceremoniously.

'This is Poloznev, mamma,' Tcheprakov introduced me. 'He is going to serve here.'

'Are you a nobleman?' she asked in a strange, disagreeable voice: it seemed to me to sound as though fat were bubbling in her throat.

'Yes,' I answered.

'Sit down.'

The dinner was a poor one. Nothing was served but pies filled with bitter curd, and milk soup. Elena Nikiforovna, who presided, kept blinking in a queer way, first with one eye and then with the other. She talked, she ate, but yet there was something deathly about her whole figure, and one almost fancied the faint smell of a corpse. There was only a glimmer of life in her, a glimmer of consciousness that she had been a lady who had once had her own serfs, that she was the widow of a general whom the servants had to address as 'your Excellency'; and when these feeble relics of life flickered up in her for an instant she would say to her son:

'Jean, you are not holding your knife properly!'

Or she would say to me, drawing a deep breath, with the mincing air of a hostess trying to entertain a visitor:

'You know we have sold our estate. Of course, it is a pity, we are used to the place, but Dolzhikov has promised to make Jean stationmaster of Dubetchnya, so we shall not have to go away; we shall live here at the station, and that is just the same as being on our own property! The engineer is so nice! Don't you think he is very handsome?'

Until recently the Tcheprakovs had lived in a wealthy style, but since the death of the general everything had been changed. Elena Nikiforovna had taken to quarrelling with the neighbours, to going to law, and to not paying her bailiffs or her labourers; she was in constant terror of being robbed, and in some ten years Dubetchnya had become unrecognizable.

Behind the great house was an old garden which had already run wild, and was overgrown with rough weeds and bushes. I walked up and down the verandah, which was still solid and beautiful; through the glass doors one could see a room with parqueted floor, probably the drawing-room; an old-fashioned piano and pictures in deep mahogany frames – there was nothing else. In the old flower-beds all that remained were peonies and poppies, which lifted their white and bright red heads above the grass. Young maples and elms, already nibbled by the cows, grew beside the paths, drawn up and hindering each other's growth. The garden was thickly overgrown and seemed impassable, but this was only near the house where there stood poplars, fir-trees, and old lime-trees, all of the same age, relics of the former avenues. Further on, beyond them the garden had been cleared for the sake of hay, and here it was not moist and stuffy, and there were no spiders' webs in one's mouth and eyes. A light breeze was blowing. The further one went the more open it was, and here in the open space were cherries, plums, and spreading apple-trees, disfigured by props and by canker; and pear-trees so tall that one could not believe they were pear-trees. This part of the garden was let to some shopkeepers of the town, and it was protected from thieves and starlings by a feeble-minded peasant who lived in a shanty in it.

The garden, growing more and more open, till it became definitely a meadow, sloped down to the river, which was overgrown with green weeds and osiers. Near the milldam was the millpond, deep and full of fish; a little mill with a thatched roof was working away with a wrathful sound, and frogs croaked furiously. Circles passed from time to time over the smooth, mirror-like water, and the water-lilies trembled, stirred by the lively fish. On the further side of the river was the little village Dubetchnya. The still, blue millpond was alluring with its promise of coolness and peace. And now all this – the millpond and the mill and the snug-looking banks – belonged to the engineer!

And so my new work began. I received and forwarded telegrams, wrote various reports, and made fair copies of the notes of requirements, the complaints, and the reports sent to the office by the illiterate foremen and workmen. But for the greater part of the day I did nothing but walk about the room waiting for telegrams, or made a boy sit in the lodge while I went for a walk in the garden, until the boy ran to tell me that there was a tapping at the operating machine. I had dinner at Madame Tcheprakov's. Meat we had very rarely: our dishes were all made of milk, and Wednesdays and Fridays were fast days, and on those days we had pink plates which were called Lenten plates. Madame Tcheprakov was continually blinking – it was her invariable habit, and I always felt ill at ease in her presence.

As there was not enough work in the lodge for one, Tcheprakov did nothing, but simply dozed, or went with his gun to shoot ducks on the millpond. In the evenings he drank too much in the village or the station, and before going to bed stared in the looking-glass and said: 'Hullo, Ivan Tcheprakov.'

When he was drunk he was very pale, and kept rubbing his hands and laughing with a sound like a neigh: 'hee-hee-hee!' By way of bravado he used to strip and run about the country naked. He used to eat flies and say they were rather sour.

IV

ONE day, after dinner, he ran breathless into the lodge and said: 'Go along, your sister has come.'

I went out, and there I found a hired brake from the town standing before the entrance of the great house. My sister had come in it with Anyuta Blagovo and a gentleman in a military tunic. Going up closer I recognized the latter: it was the brother of Anyuta Blagovo, the army doctor.

'We have come to you for a picnic,' he said; 'is that all right?'

My sister and Anyuta wanted to ask how I was getting on here, but both were silent, and simply gazed at me. I was silent too. They saw that I did not like the place, and tears came into my sister's eyes, while Anyuta Blagovo turned crimson.

We went into the garden. The doctor walked ahead of us all and said enthusiastically:

'What air! Holy Mother, what air!'

In appearance he was still a student. And he walked and talked like a student, and the expression of his grey eyes was as keen, honest, and frank as a nice student's. Beside his tall and handsome sister he looked frail and thin; and his beard was thin too, and his voice, too, was a thin but rather agreeable tenor. He was serving in a regiment somewhere, and had come home to his people for a holiday, and said he was going in the autumn to Petersburg for his examination as a doctor of medicine. He was already a family man, with a wife and three children; he had married very young, in his second year at the University, and now people in the town said he was unhappy in his family life and was not living with his wife.

'What time is it?' my sister asked uneasily. 'We must get back in good time. Papa let me come to see my brother on condition I was back at six.'

'Oh, bother your papa!' sighed the doctor.

I set the samovar. We put down a carpet before the verandah of the great house and had our tea there, and the doctor knelt down, drank out of his saucer, and declared that he now knew what bliss was. Then Tchepraköv came with the key and opened the glass door, and we all went into the house. There it was half dark and mysterious, and smelt of mushrooms, and our footsteps had a hollow sound as though there were cellars under the floor. The doctor stopped and touched the keys of the piano, and it responded faintly with a husky, quivering, but melodious chord; he tried his voice and sang a song, frowning and tapping impatiently with his foot when some note was mute. My sister did not talk about going home, but walked about the rooms and kept saying:

'How happy I am! How happy I am!'

There was a note of astonishment in her voice, as though it seemed to her incredible that she, too, could feel light-hearted. It was the first time in my life I had seen her so happy. She actually looked prettier. In profile she did not look nice; her nose and mouth seemed to stick out and had an expression as though she were pouting, but she had beautiful dark eyes, a pale, very delicate complexion, and a touching expression of goodness and melancholy, and when she talked she seemed charming and even beautiful. We both, she and I, took after our mother, were broad shouldered, strongly built, and capable of endurance, but her pallor was a sign of ill-health; she often had a cough, and I sometimes caught in her face that look one sees in people who are seriously ill, but for some reason conceal the fact. There was something naïve and childish in her gaiety now, as though the joy that had been suppressed and smothered in our childhood by harsh education had now suddenly awakened in her soul and had found a free outlet.

But when evening came on and the horses were brought round, my sister sank into silence and looked thin and shrunken, and she got into the brake as though she were going to the scaffold.

When they had all gone, and the sound had died away... I remembered that Anyuta Blagovo had not said a word to me all day.

'She is a wonderful girl!' I thought. 'Wonderful girl!'

St. Peter's fast came, and we had nothing but Lenten dishes every day. I was weighed down by physical depression due to idleness and my unsettled position, and dissatisfied with myself. Listless and hungry, I lounged about the garden and only waited for a suitable mood to go away.

Towards evening one day, when Radish was sitting in the lodge, Dolzhikov, very sunburnt and grey with dust, walked in unexpectedly. He had been spending three days on his land, and had come now to Dubetchnya by the steamer, and walked to us from the station. While waiting for the carriage, which was to come for him from the town, he walked round the grounds with his bailiff, giving orders in a loud voice, then sat for a whole hour in our lodge, writing letters. While he was there telegrams came for him, and he himself tapped off the answers. We three stood in silence at attention.

'What a muddle!' he said, glancing contemptuously at a record book. 'In a fortnight I am transferring the office to the station, and I don't know what I am to do with you, my friends.'

'I do my best, your honour,' said Tcheprakov.

'To be sure, I see how you do your best. The only thing you can do is to take your salary,' the engineer went on, looking at me; 'you keep relying on patronage to *faire la carrière* as quickly and as easily as possible. Well, I don't care for patronage. No one took any trouble on my behalf. Before they gave me a railway contract I went about as a mechanic and worked in Belgium as an oiler. And you, Panteley, what are you doing here?' he asked, turning to Radish. 'Drinking with them?'

He, for some reason, always called humble people Panteley, and such as me and TchepRakov he despised, and called them drunkards, beasts, and rabble to their face. Altogether he was cruel to humble subordinates, and used to fine them and turn them off coldly without explanations.

At last the horses came for him. As he said goodbye he promised to turn us all off in a fortnight; he called his bailiff a blockhead; and then, lolling at ease in his carriage, drove back to the town.

'Andrey Ivanitch,' I said to Radish, 'take me on as a workman.'

'Oh, all right!'

And we set off together in the direction of the town. When the station and the big house with its buildings were left behind I asked: 'Andrey Ivanitch, why did you come to Dubetchnya this evening?'

'In the first place my fellows are working on the line, and in the second place I came to pay the general's lady my interest. Last year I borrowed fifty roubles from her, and I pay her now a rouble a month interest.'

The painter stopped and took me by the button.

'Misail Alexeyitch, our angel,' he went on. 'The way I look at it is that if any man, gentle or simple, takes even the smallest interest, he is doing evil. There cannot be truth and justice in such a man.'

Radish, lean, pale, dreadful-looking, shut his eyes, shook his head, and, in the tone of a philosopher, pronounced:

'Lice consume the grass, rust consumes the iron, and lying the soul. Lord, have mercy upon us sinners.'

V

RADISH was not practical, and was not at all good at forming an estimate; he took more work than he could get through, and when calculating he was agitated, lost his head, and so was almost always out of pocket over his jobs. He undertook painting, glazing, paperhanging, and even tiling roofs, and I can remember his running about for three days to find tilers for the sake of a paltry job. He was a first-rate workman; he sometimes earned as much as ten roubles a day; and if it had not been for the desire at all costs to be a master, and to be called a contractor, he would probably have had plenty of money.

He was paid by the job, but he paid me and the other workmen by the day, from one and twopence to two shillings a day. When it was fine and dry we did all kinds of outside work, chiefly painting roofs. When I was new to the work it made my feet burn as though I were walking on hot bricks, and when I put on felt boots they were hotter than ever. But this was only at first; later on I got used to it, and everything went swimmingly. I was living now among people to whom labour was obligatory, inevitable, and who worked like cart-horses, often with no idea of the moral significance of labour, and, indeed, never using the word 'labour' in conversation at all. Beside them I, too, felt like a cart-horse, growing more and more imbued with the feeling of the obligatory and inevitable character of what I was doing, and this made my life easier, setting me free from all doubt and uncertainty.

At first everything interested me, everything was new, as though I had been born again. I could sleep on the ground and go about barefoot, and that was extremely pleasant; I could stand in a crowd of the common people and be no constraint to anyone, and when a cab horse fell down in the street I ran to help it up without being afraid of soiling my clothes. And the best of it all was, I was living on my own account and no burden to anyone!

Painting roofs, especially with our own oil and colours, was regarded as a particularly profitable job, and so this rough, dull work was not disdained, even by such good workmen as Radish. In short breeches, and wasted, purple-looking legs, he used to go about the roofs, looking like a stork, and I used to hear him, as he plied his brush, breathing heavily and saying: 'Woe, woe to us sinners!'

He walked about the roofs as freely as though he were upon the ground. In spite of his being ill and pale as a corpse, his agility was extraordinary: he used to paint the domes and cupolas of the churches without scaffolding, like a young man, with only the help of a ladder and a rope, and it was rather horrible when standing on a height far from the earth; he would draw himself up erect, and for some unknown reason pronounce:

'Lice consume grass, rust consumes iron, and lying the soul!'

Or, thinking about something, would answer his thoughts aloud:

'Anything may happen! Anything may happen!'

When I went home from my work, all the people who were sitting on benches by the gates, all the shopmen and boys and their employers, made sneering and spiteful remarks after me, and this upset me at first and seemed to be simply monstrous.

'Better-than-nothing!' I heard on all sides. 'House painter! Yellow ochre!'

And none behaved so ungraciously to me as those who had only lately been humble people themselves, and had earned their bread by hard manual labour. In the streets full of shops I was once passing an iron-monger's when water was thrown over me as though by accident, and on one occasion someone darted out with a stick at me, while a fishmonger, a grey-headed old man, barred my way and said, looking at me angrily:

'I am not sorry for you, you fool! It's your father I am sorry for.'

And my acquaintances were for some reason over-come with embarrassment when they met me. Some of them looked upon me as a queer fish and a comic fool; others were sorry for me; others did not know what attitude to take up to me, and it was difficult to make them out. One day I met Anyuta Blagovo in a side street near Great Dvoryansky Street. I was going to work, and was carrying two long brushes and a pail of paint. Recognizing me Anyuta flushed crimson.

'Please do not bow to me in the street,' she said nervously, harshly, and in a shaking voice, without offering me her hand, and tears suddenly gleamed in her eyes. 'If to your mind all this is necessary, so be it . . . so be it, but I beg you not to meet me!'

I no longer lived in Great Dvoryansky Street, but in the suburb with my old nurse Karpovna, a good-natured but gloomy old woman, who always foreboded some harm, was afraid of all dreams, and even in the bees and wasps that flew into her room saw omens of evil, and the fact that I had become a workman, to her thinking, boded nothing good.

'Your life is ruined,' she would say, mournfully shaking her head, 'ruined.'

Her adopted son Prokofy, a huge, uncouth, red-headed fellow of thirty, with bristling moustaches, a butcher by trade, lived in the little house with her. When he met me in the passage he would make way for me in respectful silence, and if he was drunk he would salute me with all five fingers at once. He used to have supper in the evening, and through the partition wall of boards I could hear him clear his throat and sigh as he drank off glass after glass.

'Mamma,' he would call in an undertone.

'Well,' Karpovna, who was passionately devoted to her adopted son, would respond: 'What is it, sonny?'

'I can show you a testimony of my affection, mamma. All this earthly life I will cherish you in your declining years in this vale of tears, and when you die I will bury you at my expense; I have said it, and you can believe it.'

I got up every morning before sunrise, and went to bed early. We house painters ate a great deal and slept soundly; the only thing amiss was that my heart used to beat violently at night. I did not quarrel with my mates. Violent abuse, desperate oaths, and wishes such as, 'Blast your eyes', or 'Cholera take you', never ceased all day, but, nevertheless, we lived on very friendly terms. The other fellows suspected me of being some sort of religious sectary, and made good-natured jokes at my expense, saying that even my own father had disowned me, and thereupon would add that they rarely went into the temple of God themselves, and that many of them had not been to confession for ten years. They justified this laxity on their part by saying that a painter among men was like a jackdaw among birds.

The men had a good opinion of me, and treated me with respect; it was evident that my not drinking, not smoking, but leading a quiet, steady life pleased them very much. It was only an unpleasant shock to them that I took no hand in stealing oil, and did not go with them to ask for tips from people on whose property we were working. Stealing oil and paints from those who employed them was a house painter's custom, and was not regarded as theft, and it was remarkable that even so upright a man as Radish would always carry away a little white lead and oil as he went home from work. And even the most respectable old fellows, who owned the houses in which they lived in the suburb, were not ashamed to ask for a tip, and it made me feel vexed and ashamed to see the men go in a body to congratulate some nonentity on the commencement or the completion of the job, and thank him with degrading servility when they had received a few coppers.

With people on whose work they were engaged they behaved like wily courtiers, and almost every day I was reminded of Shakespeare's Polonius.

'I fancy it is going to rain,' the man whose house was being painted would say, looking at the sky.

'It is, there is not a doubt it is,' the painters would agree.

'I don't think it is a rain-cloud, though. Perhaps it won't rain after all.'

'No, it won't your honour! I am sure it won't.'

But their attitude to their patrons behind their backs was usually one of irony, and when they saw, for instance, a gentleman sitting in the verandah reading a newspaper, they would observe:

'He reads the paper, but I daresay he has nothing to eat.'

I never went home to see my own people. When I came back from work I often found waiting for me little notes, brief and anxious, in which my sister wrote to me about my father; that he had been particularly preoccupied at dinner and had eaten nothing, or that he had been giddy and staggering, or that he had locked himself in his room and had not come out for a long time. Such items of news troubled me; I could not sleep, and at times even walked up and down Great Dvoryansky Street at night by our house, looking in at the dark windows and trying to guess whether everything was well at home. On Sundays my sister came to see me, but came in secret, as though it were not to see me but our nurse. And if she came in to see me she was very pale, with tear-stained eyes, and she began crying at once.

'Our father will never live through this,' she would say. 'If anything should happen to him – God grant it may not – your conscience will torment you all your life. It's awful, Misail; for our mother's sake I beseech you: reform your ways.'

'My darling sister,' I would say, 'how can I reform my ways if I am convinced that I am acting in accordance with my conscience? Do understand!'

'I know you are acting on your conscience, but perhaps it could be done differently, somehow, so as not to wound anybody.'

'Ah, holy Saints!' the old woman sighed through the door. 'Your life is ruined! There will be trouble, my dears, there will be trouble!'

VI

ONE Sunday Dr. Blagovo turned up unexpectedly. He was wearing a military tunic over a silk shirt and high boots of patent leather.

'I have come to see you,' he began, shaking my hand heartily like a student. 'I am hearing about you every day, and I have been meaning to come and have a heart-to-heart talk, as they say. The boredom in the town is awful, there is not a living soul, no one to say a word to. It's hot, Holy Mother,' he went on, taking off his tunic and sitting in his silk shirt. 'My dear fellow, let me talk to you.'

I was dull myself, and had for a long time been craving for the society of someone not a house painter. I was genuinely glad to see him.

'I'll begin by saying,' he said, sitting down on my bed, 'that I sympathize with you from the bottom of my heart, and deeply respect the life you are leading. They don't understand you here in the town, and, indeed, there is no one to understand, seeing that, as you know, they are all, with very few exceptions, regular Gogolesque pig faces here. But I saw what you were at once that time at the picnic. You are a noble soul, an honest, high-minded man! I respect you, and feel it a great honour to shake hands with you!' he went on enthusiastically. 'To have made such a complete and violent change of life as you have done, you must have passed through a complicated spiritual crisis, and to continue this manner of life now, and to keep up to the high standard of your convictions continually, must be a strain on your mind and heart from day to day. Now to begin our talk, tell me, don't you consider that if you had spent your strength of will, this strained activity, all these powers on something else, for instance, on gradually becoming a great scientist, or artist, your life would have been broader and deeper and would have been more productive?'

We talked, and when we got upon manual labour I expressed this idea: that what is wanted is that the strong should not enslave the weak, that the minority should not be a parasite on the majority, nor a vampire forever sucking its vital sap; that is, all, without exception, strong and weak, rich and poor, should take part equally in the struggle for existence, each one on his own account, and that there was no better means for equalizing things in that way than manual labour, in the form of universal service, compulsory for all.

'Then do you think everyone without exception ought to engage in manual labour?' asked the doctor.

'Yes.'

'And don't you think that if everyone, including the best men, the thinkers and great scientists, taking part in the struggle for existence, each on his own account, are going to waste their time breaking stones and painting roofs, may not that threaten a grave danger to progress?'

'Where is the danger?' I asked. 'Why, progress is in deeds of love, in fulfilling the moral law; if you don't enslave anyone, if you don't oppress anyone, what further progress do you want?'

'But, excuse me,' Blagovo suddenly fired up, rising to his feet. 'But, excuse me! If a snail in its shell busies itself over perfecting its own personality and muddles about with the moral law, do you call that progress?'

'Why muddles?' I said, offended. 'If you don't force your neighbour to feed and clothe you, to transport you from place to place and defend you from your enemies, surely in the midst of a life entirely resting on slavery, that is progress, isn't it? To my mind it is the most important progress, and perhaps the only one possible and necessary for man.'

'The limits of universal world progress are in infinity, and to talk of some "possible" progress limited by our needs and temporary theories is, excuse my saying so, positively strange.'

'If the limits of progress are in infinity as you say, it follows that its aims are not definite,' I said. 'To live without knowing definitely what you are living for!'

'So be it! But that "not knowing" is not so dull as your "knowing". I am going up a ladder which is called progress, civilization, culture; I go on and up without knowing definitely where I am going, but really it is worth living for the sake of that delightful ladder; while you know what you are living for, you live for the sake of some people's not enslaving others, that the artist and the man who rubs his paints may dine equally well. But you know that's the petty, bourgeois, kitchen, grey side of life, and surely it is revolting to live for that alone? If some insects do enslave others, bother them, let them devour each other! We need not think about them. You know they will die and decay just the same, however zealously you rescue them from slavery. We must think of that great millennium which awaits humanity in the remote future.'

Blagovo argued warmly with me, but at the same time one could see he was troubled by some irrelevant idea.

'I suppose your sister is not coming?' he said, looking at his watch. 'She was at our house yesterday, and said she would be seeing you to-day. You keep saying slavery, slavery...' he went on. 'But you know that is a special question, and all such questions are solved by humanity gradually.'

We began talking of doing things gradually. I said that 'the question of doing good or evil everyone settles for himself, without waiting till humanity settles it by the way of gradual development. Moreover, this gradual process has more than one aspect. Side by side with the gradual development of human ideas the gradual growth of ideas of another order is observed. Serfdom is no more, but the capitalist system is growing. And in the very heyday of emancipating ideas, just as in the days of Baty, the majority feeds, clothes, and defends the minority while remaining hungry, inadequately clad, and defenceless. Such an order of things can be made to fit in finely with any tendencies and currents of thought you like, because the art of enslaving is also gradually being cultivated. We no longer flog our servants in the stable, but we give to slavery refined forms, at least, we succeed in finding a justification for it in each particular case. Ideas are ideas with us, but if now, at the end of the nineteenth century, it were possible to lay the burden of the most unpleasant of our physiological functions upon the working class, we should certainly do so, and afterwards, of course, justify ourselves by saying that if the best people, the thinkers and great scientists, were to waste their precious time on these functions, progress might be menaced with great danger.'

But at this point my sister arrived. Seeing the doctor she was flustered and troubled, and began saying immediately that it was time for her to go home to her father.

'Kleopatra Alexyevna,' said Blagovo earnestly, pressing both hands to his heart, 'what will happen to your father if you spend half an hour or so with your brother and me?'

He was frank, and knew how to communicate his liveliness to others. After a moment's thought, my sister laughed, and all at once became suddenly gay as she had been at the picnic. We went out into the country, and lying in the grass went on with our talk, and looked towards the town where all the windows facing west were like glittering gold because the sun was setting.

After that, whenever my sister was coming to see me Blagovo turned up too, and they always greeted each other as though their meeting in my room was accidental. My sister listened while the doctor and I argued, and at such times her expression was joyfully enthusiastic, full of tenderness and curiosity, and it seemed to me that a new world she had never dreamed of before, and which she was now striving to fathom, was gradually opening before her eyes. When the doctor was not there she was quiet and sad, and now if she sometimes shed tears as she sat on my bed it was for reasons of which she did not speak.

In August Radish ordered us to be ready to go to the railway-line. Two days before we were 'banished' from the town my father came to see me. He sat down and in a leisurely way, without looking at me, wiped his red face, then took out of his pocket our town *Messenger*, and deliberately, with emphasis on each word, read out the news that the son of the branch manager of the State Bank, a young man of my age, had been appointed head of a Department in the Exchequer.

'And now look at you,' he said, folding up the newspaper, 'a beggar, in rags, good for nothing! Even working-class people and peasants obtain education in order to become men, while you, a Poloznev, with ancestors of rank and distinction, aspire to the gutter! But I have not come here to talk to you; I have washed my hands of you –' he added in a stifled voice, getting up. 'I have come to find out where your sister is, you worthless fellow. She left home after dinner, and here it is nearly eight and she is not back. She has taken to going out frequently, without telling me; she is less dutiful – and I see in it your evil and degrading influence. Where is she?'

In his hand he had the umbrella I knew so well, and I was already flustered and drew myself up like a schoolboy, expecting my father to begin hitting me with it, but he noticed my glance at the umbrella and most likely that restrained him.

'Live as you please!' he said. 'I shall not give you my blessing!'

'Holy Saints!' my nurse muttered behind the door. 'You poor, unlucky child! Ah, my heart bodes ill!'

I worked on the railway-line. It rained without stopping all August; it was damp and cold; they had not carried the corn in the fields, and on big farms where the wheat had been cut by machines it lay not in sheaves but in heaps, and I remember how those luckless heaps of wheat turned blacker every day and the grain was sprouting in them. It was hard to work; the pouring rain spoiled everything we managed to do. We were not allowed to live or to sleep in the railway buildings, and we took refuge in the damp and filthy mud huts in which the navvies had lived during the summer, and I could not sleep at night for the cold and the woodlice crawling on my face and hands. And when we worked near the bridges the navvies used to come in the evenings in a gang, simply in order to beat the painters – it was a form of sport to them. They used to beat us, to steal our brushes. And to annoy us and rouse us to fight they used to spoil our work; they would, for instance, smear over the signal boxes with green paint. To complete our troubles, Radish took to paying us very irregularly. All the painting work on the line was given out to a contractor; he gave it out to another; and this subcontractor gave it to Radish after subtracting twenty per cent. for himself. The job was not a profitable one in itself, and the rain made it worse; time was wasted; we could not work while Radish was obliged to pay the fellows by the day. The hungry painters almost came to beating him, called him a cheat, a blood-sucker, a Judas, while he, poor fellow, sighed, lifted up his hand to Heaven in despair, and was continually going to Madame Tcheprakov for money.

VII

AUTUMN came on, rainy, dark, and muddy. The season of unemployment set in, and I used to sit at home out of work for three days at a stretch, or did various little jobs, not in the painting line. For instance, I wheeled earth, earning about fourpence a day by it. Dr. Blagovo had gone away to Petersburg. My sister had given up coming to see me. Radish was laid up at home ill, expecting death from day to day.

And my mood was autumnal too. Perhaps because, having become a workman, I saw our town life only from the seamy side, it was my lot almost every day to make discoveries which reduced me almost to despair. Those of my fellow-citizens, about whom I had no opinion before, or who had externally appeared perfectly decent, turned out now to be base, cruel people, capable of any dirty action. We common people were deceived, cheated, and kept waiting for hours together in the cold entry or the kitchen; we were insulted and treated with the utmost rudeness. In the autumn I papered the reading-room and two other rooms at the club; I was paid a penny three-farthings the piece, but had to sign a receipt at the rate of twopence halfpenny, and when I refused to do so, a gentleman of benevolent appearance in gold-rimmed spectacles, who must have been one of the club committee, said to me:

'If you say much more, you blackguard, I'll pound your face into a jelly!'

And when the flunkey whispered to him what I was, the son of Poloznev the architect, he became embarrassed, turned crimson, but immediately recovered himself and said: 'Devil take him.'

In the shops they palmed off on us workmen putrid meat, musty flour, and tea that had been used and dried again; the police hustled us in church, the assistants and nurses in the hospital plundered us, and if we were too poor to give them a bribe they revenged themselves by bringing us food in dirty vessels. In the post-office the pettiest official considered he had a right to treat us like animals, and to shout with coarse insolence: 'You wait!' 'Where are you shoving to?' Even the housedogs were unfriendly to us, and fell upon us with peculiar viciousness. But the thing that struck me most of all in my new position was the complete lack of justice, what is defined by the peasants in the words: 'They have forgotten God.' Rarely did a day pass without swindling. We were swindled by the merchants who sold us oil, by the contractors and the workmen and the people who employed us. I need not say that there could never be a question of our rights, and we always had to ask for the money we earned as though it were a charity, and to stand waiting for it at the back door, cap in hand.

I was papering a room at the club next to the reading-room; in the evening, when I was just getting ready to go, the daughter of Dolzhikov, the engineer, walked into the room with a bundle of books under her arm.

I bowed to her.

'Oh, how do you do!' she said, recognizing me at once, and holding out her hand. 'I'm very glad to see you.'

She smiled and looked with curiosity and wonder at my smock, my pail of paste, the paper stretched on the floor; I was embarrassed, and she, too, felt awkward.

'You must excuse my looking at you like this,' she said. 'I have been told so much about you. Especially by Dr. Blagovo; he is simply in love with you. And I have made the acquaintance of your sister too; a sweet, dear girl, but I can never persuade her that there is nothing awful about your adopting the simple life. On the contrary, you have become the most interesting man in the town.'

She looked again at the pail of paste and the wall-paper, and went on:

'I asked Dr. Blagovo to make me better acquainted with you, but apparently he forgot, or had not time. Anyway, we are acquainted all the same, and if you would come and see me quite simply I should be extremely indebted to you. I so long to have a talk. I am a simple person,' she added, holding out her hand to me, 'and I hope that you will feel no constraint with me. My father is not here, he is in Petersburg.'

She went off into the reading-room, rustling her skirts, while I went home, and for a long time could not get to sleep.

That cheerless autumn some kind soul, evidently wishing to alleviate my existence, sent me from time to time tea and lemons, or biscuits, or roast game. Karpovna told me that they were always brought by a soldier, and from whom they came she did not know; and the soldier used to enquire whether I was well, and whether I dined every day, and whether I had warm clothing. When the frosts began I was presented in the same way in my absence with a soft knitted scarf brought by the soldier. There was a faint elusive smell of scent about it, and I guessed who my good fairy was. The scarf smelt of lilies-of-the-valley, the favourite scent of Anyuta Blagovo.

Towards winter there was more work and it was more cheerful. Radish recovered, and we worked together in the cemetery church, where we were putting the ground-work on the ikon-stand before gilding. It was a clean, quiet job, and, as our fellows used to say, profitable. One could get through a lot of work in a day, and the time passed quickly, imperceptibly. There was no swearing, no laughter, no loud talk. The place itself compelled one to quietness and decent behaviour, and disposed one to quiet, serious thoughts. Absorbed in our work we stood or sat motionless like statues; there was a deathly silence in keeping with the cemetery, so that if a tool fell, or a flame spluttered in the lamp, the noise of such sounds rang out abrupt and resonant, and made us look round. After a long silence we would hear a buzzing like the swarming of bees: it was the requiem of a baby being chanted slowly in subdued voices in the porch; or an artist, painting a dove with stars round it on a cupola would begin softly whistling, and recollecting himself with a start would at once relapse into silence; or Radish, answering his thoughts, would say with a sigh: 'Anything is possible! Anything is possible!' or a slow disconsolate bell would begin ringing over our heads, and the painters would observe that it must be for the funeral of some wealthy person....

My days I spent in this stillness in the twilight of the church, and in the long evenings I played billiards or went to the theatre in the gallery wearing the new trousers I had bought out of my own earnings. Concerts and performances had already begun at the Azhogins'; Radish used to paint the scenes alone now. He used to tell me the plot of the plays and describe the *tableaux vivants* which he witnessed. I listened to him with envy. I felt greatly drawn to the rehearsals, but I could not bring myself to go to the Azhogins'.

A week before Christmas Dr. Blagovo arrived. And again we argued and played billiards in the evenings. When he played he used to take off his coat and unbutton his shirt over his chest, and for some reason tried altogether to assume the air of a desperate rake. He did not drink much, but made a great uproar about it, and had a special faculty for getting through twenty roubles in an evening at such a poor cheap tavern as the *Volga*.

My sister began coming to see me again; they both expressed surprise every time on seeing each other, but from her joyful, guilty face it was evident that these meetings were not accidental. One evening, when we were playing billiards, the doctor said to me:

'I say, why don't you go and see Miss Dolzhikov? You don't know Mariya Viktorovna; she is a clever creature, a charmer, a simple, good-natured soul.'

I described how her father had received me in the spring.

'Nonsense!' laughed the doctor, 'the engineer's one thing and she's another. Really, my dear fellow, you mustn't be nasty to her; go and see her sometimes. For instance, let's go and see her to-morrow evening. What do you say?'

He persuaded me. The next evening I put on my new serge trousers, and in some agitation I set off to Miss Dolzhikov's. The footman did not seem so haughty and terrible, nor the furniture so gorgeous, as on that morning when I had come to ask a favour. Mariya Viktorovna was expecting me, and she received me like an old acquaintance, shaking hands with me in a friendly way. She was wearing a grey cloth dress with full sleeves, and had her hair done in the style which we used to call 'dogs' ears', when it came into fashion in the town a year before. The hair was combed down over the ears, and this made Mariya Viktorovna's face look broader, and she seemed to me this time very much like her father, whose face was broad and red, with something in its expression like a sledge-driver. She was handsome and elegant, but not youthful looking; she looked thirty, though in reality she was not more than twenty-five.

'Dear Doctor, how grateful I am to him,' she said, making me sit down. 'If it hadn't been for him you wouldn't have come to see me. I am bored to death! My father has gone away and left me alone, and I don't know what to do with myself in this town.'

Then she began asking me where I was working now, how much I earned, where I lived.

'Do you spend on yourself nothing but what you earn?' she asked.

'No.'

'Happy man!' she sighed. 'All the evil in life, it seems to me, comes from idleness, boredom, and spiritual emptiness, and all that is inevitable when one is accustomed to living at other people's expense. Don't think I am showing off, I tell you truthfully: it is not interesting or pleasant to be rich. "Make to yourselves friends of the mammon of unrighteousness" is said, because there is not and cannot be a mammon that's righteous.'

She looked round at the furniture with a grave, cold expression, as though she wanted to count it over, and went on:

'Comfort and luxury have a magical power; little by little they draw into their clutches even strong-willed people. At one time father and I lived simply, not in a rich style, but now you see how! It is something monstrous,' she said, shrugging her shoulders; 'we spend up to twenty thousand a year! In the provinces!'

'One comes to look at comfort and luxury as the invariable privilege of capital and education,' I said, 'and it seems to me that the comforts of life may be combined with any sort of labour, even the hardest and dirtiest. Your father is rich, and yet he says himself that it has been his lot to be a mechanic and an oiler.'

She smiled and shook her head doubtfully: 'My father sometimes eats bread dipped in kvass,' she said. 'It's a fancy, a whim!'

At that moment there was a ring and she got up.

'The rich and well-educated ought to work like everyone else,' she said, 'and if there is comfort it ought to be equal for all. There ought not to be any privileges. But that's enough philosophizing. Tell me something amusing. Tell me about the painters. What are they like? Funny?'

The doctor came in; I began telling them about the painters, but, being unaccustomed to talking, I was constrained, and described them like an ethnologist, gravely and tediously. The doctor, too, told us some anecdotes of working men: he staggered about, shed tears, dropped on his knees, and, even, mimicking a drunkard, lay on the floor; it was as good as a play, and Mariya Viktorovna laughed till she cried as she looked at him. Then he played on the piano and sang in his thin, pleasant tenor, while Mariya Viktorovna stood by and picked out what he was to sing, and corrected him when he made a mistake.

'I've heard that you sing, too?' I enquired.

'Sing, too!' cried the doctor in horror. 'She sings exquisitely, a perfect artist, and you talk of her "singing too"! What an idea!'

'I did study in earnest at one time,' she said, answering my question, 'but now I have given it up.'

Sitting on a low stool she told us of her life in Petersburg, and mimicked some celebrated singers, imitating their voice and manner of singing. She made a sketch of the doctor in her album, then of me; she did not draw well, but both the portraits were like us. She laughed, and was full of mischief and charming grimaces, and this suited her better than talking about the mammon of unrighteousness, and it seemed to me that she had been talking just before about wealth and luxury, not in earnest, but in imitation of someone. She was a superb comic actress. I mentally compared her with our young ladies, and even the handsome, dignified Anyuta Blagovo could not stand comparison with her; the difference was immense, like the difference between a beautiful, cultivated rose and a wild briar.

We had supper together, the three of us. The doctor and Mariya Viktorovna drank red wine, champagne, and coffee with brandy in it; they clinked glasses and drank to friendship, to enlightenment, to progress, to liberty, and they did not get drunk but only flushed, and were continually, for no reason, laughing till they cried. So as not to be tiresome I drank claret too.

'Talented, richly endowed natures,' said Miss Dolzhikov, 'know how to live, and go their own way; mediocre people, like myself for instance, know nothing and can do nothing of themselves; there is nothing left for them but to discern some deep social movement, and to float where they are carried by it.'

'How can one discern what doesn't exist?' asked the doctor.

'We think so because we don't see it.'

'Is that so? The social movements are the invention of the new literature. There are none among us.'

An argument began.

'There are no deep social movements among us and never have been,' the doctor declared loudly. 'There is no end to what the new literature has invented! It has invented intellectual workers in the country, and you may search through all our villages and find at the most some lout in a reefer jacket or a black frock-coat who will make four mistakes in spelling a word of three letters. Cultured life has not yet begun among us. There's the same savagery, the same uniform boorishness, the same triviality, as five hundred years ago. Movements, currents there have been, but it has all been petty, paltry, bent upon vulgar and mercenary interests – and one cannot see anything important in them. If you think you have discerned a deep social movement, and in following it you devote yourself to tasks in the modern taste, such as the emancipation of insects from slavery or abstinence from beef rissoles, I congratulate you, Madam. We must study, and study, and study, and we must wait a bit with our deep, social movements; we are not mature enough for them yet; and to tell the truth, we don't know anything about them.'

'You don't know anything about them, but I do,' said Mariya Viktorovna. 'Goodness, how tiresome you are to-day!'

'Our duty is to study and to study, to try to accumulate as much knowledge as possible, for genuine social movements arise where there is knowledge; and the happiness of mankind in the future lies only in knowledge. I drink to science!'

'There is no doubt about one thing: one must organize one's life somehow differently,' said Mariya Viktorovna, after a moment's silence and thought. 'Life, such as it has been hitherto, is not worth having. Don't let us talk about it.'

As we came away from her the cathedral clock struck two.

'Did you like her?' asked the doctor; 'she's nice, isn't she?'

On Christmas day we dined with Mariya Viktorovna, and all through the holidays we went to see her almost every day. There was never anyone there but ourselves, and she was right when she said that she had no friends in the town but the doctor and me. We spent our time for the most part in conversation; sometimes the doctor brought some book or magazine and read aloud to us. In reality he was the first well-educated man I had met in my life: I cannot judge whether he knew a great deal, but he always displayed his knowledge as though he wanted other people to share it. When he talked about anything relating to medicine he was not like any one of the doctors in our town, but made a fresh, peculiar impression upon me, and I fancied that if he liked he might have become a real man of science. And he was perhaps the only person who had a real influence upon me at that time. Seeing him, and reading the books he gave me, I began little by little to feel a thirst for the knowledge which would have given significance to my cheerless labour. It seemed strange to me, for instance, that I had not known till then that the whole world was made up of sixty elements, I had not known what oil was, what paints were, and that I could have got on without knowing these things. My acquaintance with the doctor elevated me morally too. I was continually arguing with him and, though I usually remained of my own opinion, yet, thanks to him, I began to perceive that everything was not clear to me, and I began trying to work out as far as I could definite convictions in myself, that the dictates of conscience might be definite, and that there might be nothing vague in my mind. Yet, though he was the most cultivated and best man in the town, he was nevertheless far from perfection. In his manners, in his habit of turning every conversation into an argument, in his pleasant tenor, even in his friendliness, there was something coarse, like a divinity student, and when he took off his coat and sat in his silk shirt, or flung a tip to a waiter in the restaurant, I always fancied that culture might be all very well, but the Tatar was fermenting in him still.

At Epiphany he went back to Petersburg. He went off in the morning, and after dinner my sister came in. Without taking off her fur coat and her cap she sat down in silence, very pale, and kept her eyes fixed on the same spot. She was chilled by the frost and one could see that she was upset by it.

'You must have caught cold,' I said.

Her eyes filled with tears; she got up and went out to Karpovna without saying a word to me, as though I had hurt her feelings. And a little later I heard her saying, in a tone of bitter reproach:

'Nurse, what have I been living for till now? What? Tell me, haven't I wasted my youth? All the best years of my life to know nothing but keeping accounts, pouring out tea, counting the halfpence, entertaining visitors, and thinking there was nothing better in the world! Nurse, do understand, I have the cravings of a human being, and I want to live, and they have turned me into something like a housekeeper. It's horrible, horrible!'

She flung her keys towards the door, and they fell with a jingle into my room. They were the keys of the sideboard, of the kitchen cupboard, of the cellar, and of the tea-caddy, the keys which my mother used to carry.

'Oh, merciful heavens!' cried the old woman in horror. 'Holy Saints above!'

Before going home my sister came into my room to pick up the keys, and said:

'You must forgive me. Something queer has happened to me lately.'

VIII

ON returning home late one evening from Mariya Viktorovna's I found waiting in my room a young police inspector in a new uniform; he was sitting at my table, looking through my books.

'At last,' he said, getting up and stretching himself. 'This is the third time I have been to you. The Governor commands you to present yourself before him at nine o'clock in the morning. Without fail.'

He took from me a signed statement that I would act upon his Excellency's command, and went away. This late visit of the police inspector and unexpected invitation to the Governor's had an overwhelmingly oppressive effect upon me. From my earliest childhood I have felt terror-stricken in the presence of gendarmes, policemen, and law court officials, and now I was tormented by uneasiness, as though I were really guilty in some way. And I could not get to sleep. My nurse and Prokofy were also upset and could not sleep. My nurse had earache too; she moaned, and several times began crying with pain. Hearing that I was awake, Prokofy came into my room with a lamp and sat down at the table.

'You ought to have a drink of pepper cordial,' he said, after a moment's thought. 'If one does have a drink in this vale of tears it does no harm. And if mamma were to pour a little pepper cordial in her ear it would do her a lot of good.'

Between two and three he was going to the slaughter-house for the meat. I knew I should not sleep till morning now, and to get through the time till nine o'clock I went with him. We walked with a lantern, while his boy Nikolka, aged thirteen, with blue patches on his cheeks from frostbites, a regular young brigand to judge by his expression, drove after us in the sledge, urging on the horse in a husky voice.

'I suppose they will punish you at the Governor's,' Prokofy said to me on the way. 'There are rules of the trade for governors, and rules for the higher clergy, and rules for the officers, and rules for the doctors, and every class has its rules. But you haven't kept to your rules, and you can't be allowed.'

The slaughter-house was behind the cemetery, and till then I had only seen it in the distance. It consisted of three gloomy barns, surrounded by a grey fence, and when the wind blew from that quarter on hot days in summer, it brought a stifling stench from them. Now going into the yard in the dark I did not see the barns; I kept coming across horses and sledges, some empty, some loaded up with meat. Men were walking about with lanterns, swearing in a disgusting way. Prokofy and Nikolka swore just as revoltingly, and the air was in a continual uproar with swearing, coughing, and the neighing of horses.

There was a smell of dead bodies and of dung. It was thawing, the snow was changing into mud; and in the darkness it seemed to me that I was walking through pools of blood.

Having piled up the sledges full of meat we set off to the butcher's shop in the market. It began to get light. Cooks with baskets and elderly ladies in mantles came along one after another. Prokofy, with a chopper in his hand, in a white apron spattered with blood, swore fearful oaths, crossed himself at the church, shouted aloud for the whole market to hear, that he was giving away the meat at cost price and even at a loss to himself. He gave short weight and short change, the cooks saw that, but, deafened by his shouts, did not protest, and only called him a hangman. Brandishing and bringing down his terrible chopper he threw himself into picturesque attitudes, and each time uttered the sound 'Geck' with a ferocious expression, and I was afraid he really would chop off somebody's head or hand.

I spent all the morning in the butcher's shop, and when at last I went to the Governor's, my overcoat smelt of meat and blood. My state of mind was as though I were being sent spear in hand to meet a bear. I remember the tall staircase with a striped carpet on it, and the young official, with shiny buttons, who mutely motioned me to the door with both hands, and ran to announce me. I went into a hall luxuriously but frigidly and tastelessly furnished, and the high, narrow mirrors in the spaces between the walls, and the bright yellow window curtains, struck the eye particularly unpleasantly. One could see that the governors were changed, but the furniture remained the same. Again the young official motioned me with both hands to the door, and I went up to a big green table at which a military general, with the Order of Vladimir on his breast, was standing.

'Mr. Poloznev, I have asked you to come,' he began, holding a letter in his hand, and opening his mouth wide like a round 'o', 'I have asked you to come here to inform you of this. Your highly respected father has appealed by letter and by word of mouth to the Marshal of the Nobility begging him to summon you, and to lay before you the inconsistency of your behaviour with the rank of the nobility to which you have the honour to belong. His Excellency Alexandr Pavlovitch, justly supposing that your conduct might serve as a bad example, and considering that mere persuasion on his part would not be sufficient, but that official intervention in earnest was essential, presents me here in this letter with his views in regard to you, which I share.'

He said this, quietly, respectfully, standing erect, as though I were his superior officer and looking at me with no trace of severity. His face looked worn and wizened, and was all wrinkles; there were bags under his eyes; his hair was dyed; and it was impossible to tell from his appearance how old he was – forty or sixty.

'I trust,' he went on, 'that you appreciate the delicacy of our honoured Alexandr Pavlovitch, who has addressed himself to me not officially, but privately. I, too, have asked you to come here unofficially, and I am speaking to you, not as a Governor, but from a sincere regard for your father. And so I beg you either to alter your line of conduct and return to duties in keeping with your rank, or to avoid setting a bad example, remove to another district where you are not known, and where you can follow any occupation you please. In the other case, I shall be forced to take extreme measures.'

He stood for half a minute in silence, looking at me with his mouth open.

'Are you a vegetarian?' he asked.

'No, your Excellency, I eat meat.'

He sat down and drew some papers towards him. I bowed and went out.

It was not worth while now to go to work before dinner. I went home to sleep, but could not sleep from an unpleasant, sickly feeling, induced by the slaughter-house and my conversation with the Governor, and when the evening came I went, gloomy and out of sorts, to Mariya Viktorovna. I told her how I had been at the Governor's, while she stared at me in perplexity as though she did not believe it, then suddenly began laughing gaily, loudly, irrepressibly, as only good-natured, laughter-loving people can.

'If only one could tell that in Petersburg!' she brought out, almost falling over with laughter, and propping herself against the table. 'If one could tell that in Petersburg!'

IX

NOW we used to see each other often, sometimes twice a day. She used to come to the cemetery almost every day after dinner, and read the epitaphs on the crosses and tombstones while she waited for me. Sometimes she would come into the church, and, standing by me, would look on while I worked. The stillness, the naïve work of the painters and gilders, Radish's sage reflections, and the fact that I did not differ externally from the other workmen, and worked just as they did in my waistcoat with no socks on, and that I was addressed familiarly by them – all this was new to her and touched her. One day a workman, who was painting a dove on the ceiling, called out to me in her presence:

'Misail, hand me up the white paint.'

I took him the white paint, and afterwards, when I let myself down by the frail scaffolding, she looked at me, touched to tears and smiling.

'What a dear you are!' she said.

I remembered from my childhood how a green parrot, belonging to one of the rich men of the town, had escaped from its cage, and how for quite a month afterwards the beautiful bird had haunted the town, flying from garden to garden, homeless and solitary. Mariya Viktorovna reminded me of that bird.

'There is positively nowhere for me to go now but the cemetery,' she said to me with a laugh. 'The town has become disgustingly dull. At the Azhogins' they are still reciting, singing, lisping. I have grown to detest them of late; your sister is an unsociable creature; Mademoiselle Blagovo hates me for some reason. I don't care for the theatre. Tell me where am I to go?'

When I went to see her I smelt of paint and turpentine, and my hands were stained – and she liked that; she wanted me to come to her in my ordinary working clothes; but in her drawing-room those clothes made me feel awkward. I felt embarrassed, as though I were in uniform, so I always put on my new serge trousers when I went to her. And she did not like that.

'You must own you are not quite at home in your new character,' she said to me one day. 'Your workman's dress does not feel natural to you; you are awkward in it. Tell me, isn't that because you haven't a firm conviction, and are not satisfied? The very kind of work you have chosen – your painting – surely it does not satisfy you, does it?' she asked, laughing. 'I know paint makes things look nicer and last longer, but those things belong to rich people who live in towns, and after all they are luxuries. Besides, you have often said yourself that everybody ought to get his bread by the work of his own hands, yet you get money and not bread. Why shouldn't you keep to the literal sense of your words? You ought to be getting bread, that is, you ought to be ploughing, sowing, reaping, threshing, or doing something which has a direct connection with agriculture, for instance, looking after cows, digging, building huts of logs. . . .'

She opened a pretty cupboard that stood near her writing-table, and said:

'I am saying all this to you because I want to let you into my secret. *Voilà!* This is my agricultural library. Here I have fields, kitchen garden and orchard, and cattleyard and beehives. I read them greedily, and have already learnt all the theory to the tiniest detail. My dream, my darling wish, is to go to our Dubetchnya as soon as March is here. It's marvellous there, exquisite, isn't it? The first year I shall have a look round and get into things, and the year after I shall begin to work properly myself, putting my back into it as they say. My father has promised to give me Dubetchnya, and I shall do exactly what I like with it.'

Flushed, excited to tears, and laughing, she dreamed aloud how she would live at Dubetchnya, and what an interesting life it would be! I envied her. March was near, the days were growing longer and longer, and on bright sunny days water dripped from the roofs at midday, and there was a fragrance of spring; I, too, longed for the country.

And when she said that she should move to Dubetchnya, I realized vividly that I should remain in the town alone, and I felt that I envied her with her cupboard of books and her agriculture. I knew nothing of work on the land, and did not like it, and I should have liked to have told her that work on the land was slavish toil, but I remembered that something similar had been said more than once by my father, and I held my tongue.

Lent began. Viktor Ivanitch, whose existence I had begun to forget, arrived from Petersburg. He arrived unexpectedly, without even a telegram to say he was coming. When I went in, as usual, in the evening, he was walking about the drawing-room, telling some story, with his face freshly washed and shaven, looking ten years younger: his daughter was kneeling on the floor, taking out of his trunks boxes, bottles, and books, and handing them to Pavel the footman. I involuntarily drew back a step when I saw the engineer, but he held out both hands to me and said, smiling, showing his strong white teeth that looked like a sledge-driver's:

'Here he is, here he is! Very glad to see you, Mr. House-painter! Masha has told me all about it; she has been singing your praises. I quite understand and approve,' he went on, taking my arm. 'To be a good workman is ever so much more honest and more sensible than wasting government paper and wearing a cockade on your head. I myself worked in Belgium with these very hands and then spent two years as a mechanic....'

He was wearing a short reefer jacket and indoor slippers; he walked like a man with the gout, rolling slightly from side to side and rubbing his hands. Humming something he softly purred and hugged himself with satisfaction at being at home again at last, and able to have his beloved shower bath.

'There is no disputing,' he said to me at supper, 'there is no disputing; you are all nice and charming people, but for some reason, as soon as you take to manual labour, or go in for saving the peasants, in the long run it all comes to no more than being a dissenter. Aren't you a dissenter? Here you don't take vodka. What's the meaning of that if it is not being a dissenter?'

To satisfy him I drank some vodka and I drank some wine, too. We tasted the cheese, the sausage, the pâtés, the pickles, and the savouries of all sorts that the engineer had brought with him, and the wine that had come in his absence from abroad. The wine was first-rate. For some reason the engineer got wine and cigars from abroad without paying duty; the caviare and the dried sturgeon someone sent him for nothing; he did not pay rent for his flat as the owner of the house provided the kerosene for the line; and altogether he and his daughter produced on me the impression that all the best in the world was at their service, and provided for them for nothing.

I went on going to see them, but not with the same eagerness. The engineer made me feel constrained, and in his presence I did not feel free. I could not face his clear, guileless eyes, his reflections wearied and sickened me; I was sickened, too, by the memory that so lately I had been in the employment of this red-faced, well-fed man, and that he had been brutally rude to me. It is true that he put his arm round my waist, slapped me on the shoulder in a friendly way, approved my manner of life, but I felt that, as before, he despised my insignificance, and only put up with me to please his daughter, and I couldn't now laugh and talk as I liked, and I behaved unsociably and kept expecting that in another minute he would address me as Panteley as he did his footman Pavel. How my pride as a provincial and a working man was revolted. I, a proletarian, a house painter, went every day to rich people who were alien to me, and whom the whole town regarded as though they were foreigners, and every day I drank costly wines with them and ate unusual dainties – my conscience refused to be reconciled to it! On my way to the house I sullenly avoided meeting people, and looked at them from under my brows as though I really were a dissenter, and when I was going home from the engineer's I was ashamed of my well-fed condition.

Above all I was afraid of being carried away. Whether I was walking along the street, or working, or talking to the other fellows, I was all the time thinking of one thing only, of going in the evening to see Mariya Viktorovna and was picturing her voice, her laugh, her movements. When I was getting ready to go to her I always spent a long time before my nurse's warped looking-glass, as I fastened my tie; my serge trousers were detestable in my eyes, and I suffered torments, and at the same time despised myself for being so trivial. When she called to me out of the other room that she was not dressed and asked me to wait, I listened to her dressing; it agitated me, I felt as though the ground were giving way under my feet. And when I saw a woman's figure in the street, even at a distance, I invariably compared it. It seemed to me that all our girls and women were vulgar, that they were absurdly dressed, and did not know how to hold themselves; and these comparisons aroused a feeling of pride in me: Mariya Viktorovna was the best of them all! And I dreamed of her and myself at night.

One evening at supper with the engineer we ate a whole lobster. As I was going home afterwards I remembered that the engineer twice called me 'My dear fellow' at supper, and I reflected that they treated me very kindly in that house, as they might an unfortunate big dog who had been kicked out by its owners, that they were amusing themselves with me, and that when they were tired of me they would turn me out like a dog. I felt ashamed and wounded, wounded to the point of tears as though I had been insulted, and looking up at the sky I took a vow to put an end to all this.

The next day I did not go to the Dolzhikovs'. Late in the evening, when it was quite dark and raining, I walked along Great Dvoryansky Street, looking up at the windows. Everyone was asleep at the Azhogins', and the only light was in one of the furthest windows. It was Madame Azhogin in her own room, sewing by the light of three candles, imagining that she was combating superstition. Our house was in darkness, but at the Dolzhikovs', on the contrary, the windows were lighted up, but one could distinguish nothing through the flowers and the curtains. I kept walking up and down the street; the cold March rain drenched me through. I heard my father come home from the club; he stood knocking at the gate. A minute later a light appeared at the window, and I saw my sister, who was hastening down with a lamp, while with the other hand she was twisting her thick hair together as she went. Then my father walked about the drawing-room, talking and rubbing his hands, while my sister sat in a low chair, thinking and not listening to what he said.

But then they went away; the light went out.... I glanced round at the engineer's, and there, too, all was darkness now. In the dark and the rain I felt hopelessly alone, abandoned to the whims of destiny; I felt that all my doings, my desires, and everything I had thought and said till then were trivial in comparison with my loneliness, in comparison with my present suffering, and the suffering that lay before me in the future. Alas, the thoughts and doings of living creatures are not nearly so significant as their sufferings! And without clearly realizing what I was doing, I pulled at the bell of the Dolzhikovs' gate, broke it, and ran along the street like some naughty boy, with a feeling of terror in my heart, expecting every moment that they would come out and recognize me. When I stopped at the end of the street to take breath

I could hear nothing but the sound of the rain, and somewhere in the distance a watchman striking on a sheet of iron.

For a whole week I did not go to the Dolzhikovs'. My serge trousers were sold. There was nothing doing in the painting trade. I knew the pangs of hunger again, and earned from twopence to fourpence a day, where I could, by heavy and unpleasant work. Struggling up to my knees in the cold mud, straining my chest, I tried to stifle my memories, and, as it were, to punish myself for the cheeses and preserves with which I had been regaled at the engineer's. But all the same, as soon as I lay in bed, wet and hungry, my sinful imagination immediately began to paint exquisite, seductive pictures, and with amazement I acknowledged to myself that I was in love, passionately in love, and I fell into a sound, heavy sleep, feeling that hard labour only made my body stronger and younger.

One evening snow began falling most inappropriately, and the wind blew from the north as though winter had come back again. When I returned from work that evening I found Mariya Viktorovna in my room. She was sitting in her fur coat, and had both hands in her muff.

'Why don't you come to see me?' she asked, raising her clear, clever eyes, and I was utterly confused with delight and stood stiffly upright before her, as I used to stand facing my father when he was going to beat me; she looked into my face and I could see from her eyes that she understood why I was confused.

'Why don't you come to see me?' she repeated. 'If you don't want to come, you see, I have come to you.'

She got up and came close to me.

'Don't desert me,' she said, and her eyes filled with tears. 'I am alone, utterly alone.'

She began crying; and, hiding her face in her muff, articulated:

'Alone! My life is hard, very hard, and in all the world I have no one but you. Don't desert me!'

Looking for a handkerchief to wipe her tears she smiled; we were silent for some time, then I put my arms round her and kissed her, scratching my cheek till it bled with her hatpin as I did it.

And we began talking to each other as though we had been on the closest terms for ages and ages.

X

TWO days later she sent me to Dubetchnya and I was unutterably delighted to go. As I walked towards the station and afterwards, as I was sitting in the train, I kept laughing from no apparent cause, and people looked at me as though I were drunk. Snow was falling, and there were still frosts in the mornings, but the roads were already dark-coloured and rooks hovered over them, cawing.

At first I had intended to fit up an abode for us two, Masha and me, in the lodge at the side opposite Madame Tcheprakov's lodge, but it appeared that the doves and the ducks had been living there for a long time, and it was impossible to clean it without destroying a great number of nests. There was nothing for it but to live in the comfortless rooms of the big house with the sunblinds. The peasants called the house the palace; there were more than twenty rooms in it, and the only furniture was a piano and a child's arm-chair lying in the attic. And if Masha had brought all her furniture from the town we should even then have been unable to get rid of the impression of immense emptiness and cold. I picked out three small rooms with windows looking into the garden, and worked from early morning till night, setting them to rights, putting in new panes, papering the walls, filling up the holes and chinks in the floors. It was easy, pleasant work. I was continually running to the river to see whether the ice were not going; I kept fancying that starlings were flying. And at night, thinking of Masha, I listened with an unutterably sweet feeling, with clutching delight to the noise of the rats and the wind droning and knocking above the ceiling. It seemed as though some old house spirit were coughing in the attic.

The snow was deep; a great deal had fallen even at the end of March, but it melted quickly, as though by magic, and the spring floods passed in a tumultuous rush, so that by the beginning of April the starlings were already noisy, and yellow butterflies were flying in the garden. It was exquisite weather. Every day, towards evening, I used to walk to the town to meet Masha, and what a delight it was to walk with bare feet along the gradually drying, still soft road. Halfway I used to sit down and look towards the town, not venturing to go near it. The sight of it troubled me. I kept wondering how the people I knew would behave to me when they heard of my love. What would my father say? What troubled me particularly was the thought that my life was more complicated, and that I had completely lost all power to set it right, and that, like a balloon, it was bearing me away, God knows whither. I no longer considered the problem how to earn my daily bread, how to live, but thought about – I really don't know what.

Masha used to come in a carriage; I used to get in with her, and we drove to Dubetchnya, feeling light-hearted and free. Or, after waiting till the sun had set, I would go back dissatisfied and dreary, wondering why Masha had not come; at the gate or in the garden I would be met by a sweet, unexpected apparition – it was she! It would turn out that she had come by rail, and had walked from the station. What a festival it was! In a simple woollen dress with a kerchief on her head, with a modest sunshade, but laced in, slender, in expensive foreign boots – it was a talented actress playing the part of a little workgirl. We looked round our domain and decided which should be her room, and which mine, where we would have our avenue, our kitchen garden, our beehives.

We already had hens, ducks, and geese, which we loved because they were ours. We had, all ready for sowing, oats, clover, timothy grass, buckwheat, and vegetable seeds, and we always looked at all these stores and discussed at length the crop we might get; and everything Masha said to me seemed extraordinarily clever, and fine. This was the happiest time of my life.

Soon after St. Thomas's week we were married at our parish church in the village of Kurilovka, two miles from Dubetchnya. Masha wanted everything to be done quietly; at her wish our 'best men' were peasant lads, the sacristan sang alone, and we came back from the church in a small, jolting chaise which she drove herself. Our only guest from the town was my sister Kleopatra, to whom Masha sent a note three days before the wedding. My sister came in a white dress and wore gloves. During the wedding she cried quietly from joy and tenderness. Her expression was motherly and infinitely kind. She was intoxicated with our happiness, and smiled as though she were absorbing a sweet delirium, and, looking at her during our wedding, I realized that for her there was nothing in the world higher than love, earthly love, and that she was dreaming of it secretly, timidly, but continually and passionately. She embraced and kissed Masha, and, not knowing how to express her rapture, said to her of me: 'He is good! He is very good!'

Before she went away she changed into her ordinary dress, and drew me into the garden to talk to me alone.

'Father is very much hurt,' she said, 'that you have written nothing to him. You ought to have asked for his blessing. But in reality he is very much pleased. He says that this marriage will raise you in the eyes of all society, and that under the influence of Mariya Viktorovna you will begin to take a more serious view of life. We talk of nothing but you in the evenings now, and yesterday he actually used the expression: "Our Misail." That pleased me. It seems as though he had some plan in his mind, and I fancy he wants to set you an example of magnanimity and be the first to speak of reconciliation. It is very possible he may come here to see you in a day or two.'

She hurriedly made the sign of the cross over me several times and said:

'Well, God be with you. Be happy. Anyuta Blagovo is a very clever girl; she says about your marriage that God is sending you a fresh ordeal. To be sure – married life does not bring only joy but suffering too. That's bound to be so.'

Masha and I walked a couple of miles to see her on her way; we walked back slowly and in silence, as though we were resting. Masha held my hand, my heart felt light, and I had no inclination to talk about love; we had become closer and more akin now that we were married, and we felt that nothing now could separate us.

'Your sister is a nice creature,' said Masha, 'but it seems as though she had been tormented for years. Your father must be a terrible man.'

I began telling her how my sister and I had been brought up, and what a senseless torture our childhood had really been. When she heard how my father had so lately beaten me, she shuddered and drew closer to me.

'Don't tell me any more,' she said. 'It's horrible!'

Now she never left me. We lived together in the three rooms in the big house, and in the evenings we bolted the door which led to the empty part of the house, as though someone were living there whom we did not know, and were afraid of. I got up early, at dawn, and immediately set to work of some sort. I mended the carts, made paths in the garden, dug the flower beds, painted the roof of the house. When the time came to sow the oats I tried to plough the ground over again, to harrow and to sow, and I did it all conscientiously, keeping up with our labourer; I was worn out, the rain and the cold wind made my face and feet burn for hours afterwards. I dreamed of ploughed land at night. But field labour did not attract me. I did not understand farming, and I did not care for it; it was perhaps because my forefathers had not been tillers of the soil, and the very blood that flowed in my veins was purely of the city. I loved nature tenderly; I loved the fields and meadows and kitchen gardens, but the peasant who turned up the soil with his plough and urged on his pitiful horse, wet and tattered, with his craning neck, was to me the expression of coarse, savage, ugly force, and every time I looked at his uncouth movements I involuntarily began thinking of the legendary life of the remote past, before men knew the use of fire. The fierce bull that ran with the peasants' herd, and the horses, when they dashed about the village, stamping their hoofs, moved me to fear, and everything rather big, strong, and angry, whether it was the ram with its horns, the gander, or the yard-dog, seemed to me the expression of the same coarse, savage force. This mood was particularly strong in me in bad weather, when heavy clouds were hanging over the black ploughed land. Above all, when I was ploughing or sowing, and two or three people stood looking how I was doing it, I had not the feeling that this work was inevitable and obligatory, and it seemed to me that I was amusing myself. I preferred doing something in the yard, and there was nothing I liked so much as painting the roof.

I used to walk through the garden and the meadow to our mill. It was let to a peasant of Kurilovka called Stepan, a handsome, dark fellow with a thick black beard, who looked very strong. He did not like the miller's work, and looked upon it as dreary and unprofitable, and only lived at the mill in order not to live at home. He was a leather-worker, and was always surrounded by a pleasant smell of tar and leather. He was not fond of talking, he was listless and sluggish, and was always sitting in the doorway or on the river bank, humming 'oo-loo-loo'. His wife and mother-in-law, both white-faced, languid, and meek, used sometimes to come from Kurilovka to see him; they made low bows to him and addressed him formally, 'Stepan Petrovitch', while he went on sitting on the river bank, softly humming 'oo-loo-loo', without responding by word or movement to their bows. One hour and then a second would pass in silence. His mother-in-law and wife, after whispering together, would get up and gaze at him for some time, expecting him to look round; then they would make a low bow, and in sugary, chanting voices, say:

'Good-bye, Stepan Petrovitch!'

And they would go away. After that Stepan, picking up the parcel they had left, containing cracknels or a shirt, would have a sigh and say, winking in their direction:

'The female sex!'

The mill with two sets of millstones worked day and night. I used to help Stepan; I liked the work, and when he went off I was glad to stay and take his place.

XI

AFTER bright warm weather came a spell of wet; all May it rained and was cold. The sound of the millwheels and of the rain disposed one to indolence and slumber. The floor trembled, there was a smell of flour, and that, too, induced drowsiness. My wife in a short fur-lined jacket, and in men's high golosh boots, would make her appearance twice a day, and she always said the same thing:

'And this is called summer! Worse than it was in October!'

We used to have tea and make the porridge together, or we would sit for hours at a stretch without speaking, waiting for the rain to stop. Once, when Stepan had gone off to the fair, Masha stayed all night at the mill. When we got up we could not tell what time it was, as the rainclouds covered the whole sky; but sleepy cocks were crowing at Dubetchnya, and landrails were calling in the meadows; it was still very, very early.... My wife and I went down to the millpond and drew out the net which Stepan had thrown in overnight in our presence. A big pike was struggling in it, and a cray-fish was twisting about, clawing upwards with its pincers.

'Let them go,' said Masha. 'Let them be happy too.'

Because we got up so early and afterwards did nothing, that day seemed very long, the longest day in my life. Towards evening Stepan came back and I went home.

'Your father came to-day,' said Masha.

'Where is he?' I asked.

'He has gone away. I would not see him.'

Seeing that I remained standing and silent, that I was sorry for my father, she said:

'One must be consistent. I would not see him, and sent word to him not to trouble to come and see us again.'

A minute later I was out at the gate and walking to the town to explain things to my father. It was muddy, slippery, cold. For the first time since my marriage I felt suddenly sad, and in my brain, exhausted by that long grey day, there was stirring the thought that perhaps I was not living as I ought. I was worn out; little by little I was overcome by despondency and indolence, I did not want to move or think, and after going on a little I gave it up with a wave of my hand and turned back.

The engineer in a leather overcoat with a hood was standing in the middle of the yard.

'Where's the furniture? There used to be lovely furniture in the Empire style: there used to be pictures, there used to be vases, while now you could play ball in it! I bought the place with the furniture. The devil take her!'

Moisey, a thin pock-marked fellow of twenty-five, with insolent little eyes, who was in the service of the general's widow, stood near him crumpling up his cap in his hands; one of his cheeks was bigger than the other, as though he had lain too long on it.

'Your honour was graciously pleased to buy the place without the furniture,' he brought out irresolutely, 'I remember.'

'Hold your tongue!' shouted the engineer; he turned crimson and shook with anger . . . and the echo in the garden loudly repeated his shout.

XII

WHEN I was doing anything in the garden or the yard, Moisey would stand beside me, and folding his arms behind his back he would stand lazily and impudently staring at me with his little eyes. And this irritated me to such a degree that I threw up my work and went away.

From Stepan we heard that Moisey was Madame Tcheprakov's lover. I noticed that when people came to her to borrow money they addressed themselves first to Moisey, and once I saw a peasant, black from head to foot – he must have been a coalheaver – bow down at Moisey's feet. Sometimes, after a little whispering, he gave out money himself, without consulting his mistress, from which I concluded that he did a little business on his own account.

He used to shoot in our garden under our windows, carried off victuals from our cellar, borrowed our horses without asking permission, and we were indignant and began to feel as though Dubetchnya were not ours, and Masha would say, turning pale:

'Can we really have to go on living with these reptiles another eighteen months?'

Madame Tcheprakov's son, Ivan, was serving as a guard on our railway-line. He had grown much thinner and feebler during the winter, so that a single glass was enough to make him drunk, and he shivered out of the sunshine. He wore the guard's uniform with aversion and was ashamed of it, but considered his post a good one, as he could steal the candles and sell them. My new position excited in him a mixed feeling of wonder, envy, and a vague hope that something of the same sort might happen to him. He used to watch Masha with ecstatic eyes, ask me what I had for dinner now, and his lean and ugly face wore a sad and sweetish expression, and he moved his fingers as though he were feeling my happiness with them.

'Listen, Better-than-nothing,' he said fussily, re-lighting his cigarette at every instant; there was always a litter where he stood, for he wasted dozens of matches, lighting one cigarette. 'Listen, my life now is the nastiest possible. The worst of it is any subaltern can shout: "Hi, there, guard!" I have overheard all sorts of things in the train, my boy, and do you know, I have learned that life's a beastly thing! My mother has been the ruin of me! A doctor in the train told me that if parents are immoral, their children are drunkards or criminals. Think of that!'

Once he came into the yard, staggering; his eyes gazed about blankly, his breathing was laboured; he laughed and cried and babbled as though in a high fever, and the only words I could catch in his muddled talk were, 'My mother! Where's my mother?' which he uttered with a wail like a child who has lost his mother in a crowd. I led him into our garden and laid him down under a tree, and Masha and I took turns to sit by him all that day and all night. He was very sick, and Masha looked with aversion at his pale, wet face, and said:

'Is it possible these reptiles will go on living another year and a half in our yard? It's awful! It's awful!'

And how many mortifications the peasants caused us! How many bitter disappointments in those early days in the spring months, when we so longed to be happy. My wife built a school. I drew a plan of a school for sixty boys, and the Zemstvo Board approved of it, but advised us to build the school at

Kurilovka the big village which was only two miles from us. Moreover, the school at Kurilovka in which children – from four villages, our Dubetchnya being one of the number – were taught, was old and too small, and the floor was scarcely safe to walk upon. At the end of March, at Masha's wish, she was appointed guardian of the Kurilovka school, and at the beginning of April we three times summoned the village assembly, and tried to persuade the peasants that their school was old and overcrowded, and that it was essential to build a new one. A member of the Zemstvo Board and the Inspector of Peasant Schools came, and they, too, tried to persuade them. After each meeting the peasants surrounded us, begging for a bucket of vodka; we were hot in the crowd; we were soon exhausted, and returned home dissatisfied and a little ill at ease. In the end the peasants set apart a plot of ground for the school, and were obliged to bring all the building material from the town with their own horses. And the very first Sunday after the spring corn was sown carts set off from Kurilovka and Dubetchnya to fetch bricks for the foundations. They set off as soon as it was light, and came back late in the evening; the peasants were drunk, and said that they were worn out.

As ill-luck would have it, the rain and the cold persisted all through May. The road was in an awful state: it was deep in mud. The carts usually drove into our yard when they came back from the town – and what a horrible ordeal it was. A pot-bellied horse would appear at the gate, setting its front legs wide apart; it would stumble forward before coming into the yard; a beam, nine yards long, wet and slimy-looking, crept in on a waggon. Beside it, muffled up against the rain, strode a peasant with the skirts of his coat tucked up in his belt, not looking where he was going, but stepping through the puddles. Another cart would appear with boards, then a third with a beam, a fourth... and the space before our house was gradually crowded up with horses, beams, and planks. Men and women, with their heads muffled and their skirts tucked up, would stare angrily at our windows, make an uproar, and clamour for the mistress to come out to them; coarse oaths were audible. Meanwhile Moisey stood at one side, and we fancied he was enjoying our discomfiture.

'We are not going to cart any more,' the peasants would shout. 'We are worn out! Let her go and get the stuff herself.'

Masha, pale and flustered, expecting every minute that they would break into the house, would send them out a half-pail of vodka; after that the noise would subside and the long beams, one after another, would crawl slowly out of the yard.

When I was setting off to see the building my wife was worried and said:

'The peasants are spiteful; I only hope they won't do you a mischief. Wait a minute, I'll come with you.'

We drove to Kurilovka together, and there the carpenters asked us for a drink. The framework of the house was ready. It was time to lay the foundation, but the masons had not come; this caused delay, and the carpenters complained. And when at last the masons did come, it appeared that there was no sand; it had been somehow overlooked that it would be needed. Taking advantage of our helpless position, the peasants demanded thirty kopecks for each cartload, though the distance from the building to the river where they got the sand was less than a quarter of a mile, and more than five hundred cartloads were found to be necessary. There was no end to the misunderstandings, swearing, and importunity; my wife was indignant, and the foreman of the masons, Tit Petrov, an old man of seventy, took her by the arm, and said:

'You look here! You look here! You only bring me the sand; I set ten men on at once, and in two days it will be done! You look here!'

But they brought the sand and two days passed, and four, and a week, and instead of the promised foundations there was still a yawning hole.

'It's enough to drive one out of one's senses,' said my wife, in distress. 'What people! What people!'

In the midst of these disorderly doings the engineer arrived; he brought with him parcels of wine and savouries, and after a prolonged meal lay down for a nap on the verandah and snored so loudly that the labourers shook their heads and said: 'Well!'

Masha was not pleased at his coming, she did not trust him, though at the same time she asked his advice. When, after sleeping too long after dinner, he got up in a bad humour and said unpleasant things about our management of the place, or expressed regret that he had bought Dubetchnya, which had already been a loss to him, poor Masha's face wore an expression of misery. She would complain to him, and he would yawn and say that the peasants ought to be flogged.

He called our marriage and our life a farce, and said it was a caprice, a whim.

'She has done something of the sort before,' he said about Masha. 'She once fancied herself a great opera singer and left me; I was looking for her for two months, and, my dear soul, I spent a thousand roubles on telegrams alone.'

He no longer called me a dissenter or Mr. Painter, and did not as in the past express approval of my living like a workman, but said:

'You are a strange person! You are not a normal person! I won't venture to prophesy, but you will come to a bad end!'

And Masha slept badly at night, and was always sitting at our bedroom window thinking. There was no laughter at supper now, no charming grimaces. I was wretched and, when it rained, every drop that fell seemed to pierce my heart, like small shot, and I felt ready to fall on my knees before Masha and apologize for the weather. When the peasants made a noise in the yard I felt guilty also. For hours at a time I sat still in one place, thinking of nothing but what a splendid person Masha was, what a wonderful person. I loved her passionately, and I was fascinated by everything she did, everything she said. She had a bent for quiet studious pursuits; she was fond of reading for hours together, of studying. Although her knowledge of farming was only from books she surprised us all by what she knew; and every piece of advice she gave was of value; not one was ever thrown away; and, with all that, what nobility, what taste, what graciousness, that graciousness which is only found in well-educated people.

To this woman, with her sound, practical intelligence, the disorderly surroundings with petty cares and sordid anxieties in which we were living now were an agony: I saw that and could not sleep at night; my brain worked feverishly and I had a lump in my throat. I rushed about not knowing what to do.

I galloped to the town and brought Masha books, newspapers, sweets, flowers; with Stepan I caught fish, wading for hours up to my neck in the cold water in the rain to catch eel-pout to vary our fare; I demeaned myself to beg the peasants not to make a noise; I plied them with vodka, bought them off, made all sorts of promises. And how many other foolish things I did!

At last the rain ceased, the earth dried. One would get up at four o'clock in the morning; one would go out into the garden – where there was dew sparkling on the flowers, the twitter of birds, the hum of insects, not one cloud in the sky; and the garden, the meadows, and the river were so lovely, yet there were memories of the peasants, of their carts, of the engineer. Masha and I drove out together in the racing droshky to the fields to look at the oats. She used to drive, I sat behind; her shoulders were raised and the wind played with her hair.

'Keep to the right!' she shouted to those she met.

'You are like a sledge-driver,' I said to her one day.

'Maybe! Why, my grandfather, the engineer's father, was a sledge-driver. Didn't you know that?' she asked, turning to me, and at once she mimicked the way sledge-drivers shout and sing.

'And thank God for that,' I thought as I listened to her. 'Thank God.'

And again memories of the peasants, of the carts, of the engineer....

XIII

DR. BLAGOVO arrived on his bicycle. My sister began coming often. Again there were conversations about manual labour, about progress, about a mysterious millennium awaiting mankind in the remote future. The doctor did not like our farmwork, because it interfered with arguments, and said that ploughing, reaping, grazing calves were unworthy of a free man, and all these coarse forms of the struggle for existence men would in time relegate to animals and machines, while they would devote themselves exclusively to scientific investigation. My sister kept begging them to let her go home earlier, and if she stayed on till late in the evening, or spent the night with us, there would be no end to the agitation.

'Good Heavens, what a baby you are still!' said Masha reproachfully. 'It is positively absurd.'

'Yes, it is absurd,' my sister agreed, 'I know it's absurd; but what is to be done if I haven't the strength to get over it? I keep feeling as though I were doing wrong.'

At haymaking I ached all over from the unaccustomed labour; in the evening, sitting on the verandah and talking with the others, I suddenly dropped asleep, and they laughed aloud at me. They waked me up and made me sit down to supper; I was overpowered with drowsiness, and I saw the lights, the faces, and the plates as it were in a dream, heard the voices, but did not understand them. And getting up early in the morning, I took up the scythe at once, or went to the building and worked hard all day.

When I remained at home on holidays I noticed that my sister and Masha were concealing something from me, and even seemed to be avoiding me. My wife was tender to me as before, but she had thoughts of her own apart, which she did not share with me. There was no doubt that her exasperation with the peasants was growing, the life was becoming more and more distasteful to her, and yet she did not complain to me. She talked to the doctor now more readily than she did to me, and I did not understand why it was so.

It was the custom in our province at haymaking and harvest time for the labourers to come to the manor house in the evening and be regaled with vodka; even young girls drank a glass. We did not keep up this practice; the mowers and the peasant women stood about in our yard till late in the evening expecting vodka, and then departed abusing us. And all the time Masha frowned grimly and said nothing, or murmured to the doctor with exasperation: 'Savages! Petchenyegs!'

In the country newcomers are met ungraciously, almost with hostility, as they are at school. And we were received in this way. At first we were looked upon as stupid, silly people, who had bought an estate simply because we did not know what to do with our money. We were laughed at. The peasants grazed their cattle in our wood and even in our garden; they drove away our cows and horses to the village, and then demanded money for the damage done by them. They came in whole companies into our yard, and loudly clamoured that at the mowing we had cut some piece of land that did not belong to us; and as we did not yet know the boundaries of our estate very accurately, we took their word for it and paid damages. Afterwards it turned out that there had been no mistake at the mowing. They barked the lime-trees in our wood. One of the Dubetchnya peasants, a regular shark, who did a trade in vodka without a licence, bribed our labourers, and in collaboration with them cheated us in a most treacherous way. They took the new wheels off our cart and replaced them with old ones, stole our ploughing harness and actually sold them to us, and so on. But what was most mortifying of all was what happened at the building; the peasant women stole by night boards, bricks, tiles, pieces of iron. The village elder with witnesses made a search in their huts; the village meeting fined them two roubles each, and afterwards this money was spent on drink by the whole commune.

When Masha heard about this, she would say to the doctor or my sister, indignantly:

'What beasts! It's awful! awful!'

And I heard her more than once express regret that she had ever taken it into her head to build the school.

'You must understand,' the doctor tried to persuade her, 'that if you build this school and do good in general, it's not for the sake of the peasants, but in the name of culture, in the name of the future; and the worse the peasants are the more reason for building the school. Understand that!'

But there was a lack of conviction in his voice, and it seemed to me that both he and Masha hated the peasants.

Masha often went to the mill, taking my sister with her, and they both said, laughing, that they went to have a look at Stepan, he was so handsome. Stepan, it appeared, was torpid and taciturn only with men; in feminine society his manners were free and easy, and he talked incessantly. One day, going down to the river to bathe, I accidentally overheard a conversation. Masha and Kleopatra, both in white dresses, were sitting on the bank in the spreading shade of a willow, and Stepan was standing by them with his hands behind his back, and was saying:

'Are peasants men? They are not men, but, asking your pardon, wild beasts, impostors. What life has a peasant? Nothing but eating and drinking; all he cares for is victuals to be cheaper and swilling liquor at the tavern like a fool; and there's no conversation, no manners, no formality, nothing but ignorance! He lives in filth, his wife lives in filth, and his children live in filth. What he stands up in, he lies down to sleep in; he picks the potatoes out of the soup with his fingers; he drinks kvass with a cockroach in it, and doesn't bother to blow it away!'

'It's their poverty, of course,' my sister put in.

'Poverty? There is want to be sure, there's different sorts of want, Madam. If a man is in prison, or let us say blind or crippled, that really is trouble I wouldn't wish anyone, but if a man's free and has all his senses, if he has his eyes and his hands and his strength and God, what more does he want? It's cockering themselves, and it's ignorance, Madam, it's not poverty. If you, let us suppose, good gentlefolk, by your education, wish out of kindness to help him he will drink away your money in his low way; or, what's worse, he will open a drinkshop, and with your money start robbing the people. You say poverty, but does the rich peasant live better? He, too, asking your pardon, lives like a swine: coarse, loud-mouthed, cudgel-headed, broader than he is long, fat, red-faced mug, I'd like to swing my fist and send him flying, the scoundrel. There's Larion, another rich one at Dubetchnya, and I bet he strips the bark off your trees as much as any poor one; and he is a foul-mouthed fellow; his children are the same, and when he has had a drop too much he'll topple with his nose in a puddle and sleep there. They are all a worthless lot, Madam. If you live in a village with them it is like hell. It has stuck in my teeth, that village has, and thank the Lord, the King of Heaven, I've plenty to eat and clothes to wear, I served out my time in the dragoons, I was village elder for three years, and now I am a free Cossack, I live where I like. I don't want to live in the village, and no one has the right to force me. They say – my wife. They say you are bound to live in your cottage with your wife. But why so? I am not her hired man.'

'Tell me, Stepan, did you marry for love?' asked Masha.

'Love among us in the village!' answered Stepan, and he gave a laugh. 'Properly speaking, Madam, if you care to know, this is my second marriage. I am not a Kurilovka man, I am from Zalegoshtcho, but afterwards I was taken into Kurilovka when I married. You see my father did not want to divide the land among us. There were five of us brothers. I took my leave and went to another village to live with my wife's family, but my first wife died when she was young.'

'What did she die of?'

'Of foolishness. She used to cry and cry and cry for no reason, and so she pined away. She was always drinking some sort of herbs to make her better looking, and I suppose she damaged her inside. And my second wife is a Kurilovka woman too, there is nothing in her. She's a village woman, a peasant woman, and nothing more. I was taken in when they plighted me to her. I thought she was young and fair-skinned, and that they lived in a clean way. Her mother was just like a Flagellant and she drank coffee, and the chief thing, to be sure, they were clean in their ways. So I married her, and next day we sat down to dinner; I bade my mother-in-law give me a spoon, and she gives me a spoon, and I see her wipe it out with her finger. So much for you, thought I; nice sort of cleanliness yours is. I lived a year with them and then I went away. I might have married a girl from the town,' he went on after a pause. 'They say a wife is a helpmate to her husband. What do I want with a helpmate? I help myself; I'd rather she talked to me, and not clack, clack, clack, but circumstantially, feelingly. What is life without good conversation?'

Stepan suddenly paused, and at once there was the sound of his dreary, monotonous 'oo-loo-loo-loo'. This meant that he had seen me.

Masha used often to go to the mill, and evidently found pleasure in her conversations with Stepan. Stepan abused the peasants with such sincerity and conviction, and she was attracted to him. Every time she came back from the mill the feeble-minded peasant, who looked after the garden, shouted at her:

'Wench Palashka! Hullo, wench Palashka!' and he would bark like a dog: 'Ga! Ga!'

And she would stop and look at him attentively, as though in that idiot's barking she found an answer to her thoughts, and probably he attracted her in the same way as Stepan's abuse. At home some piece of news would await her, such, for instance, as that the geese from the village had ruined our cabbage in the garden, or that Larion had stolen the reins; and, shrugging her shoulders, she would say with a laugh:

'What do you expect of these people?'

She was indignant, and there was rancour in her heart, and meanwhile I was growing used to the peasants, and I felt more and more drawn to them. For the most part they were nervous, irritable, downtrodden people; they were people whose imagination had been stifled, ignorant, with a poor, dingy outlook on life, whose thoughts were ever the same – of the grey earth, of grey days, of black bread, people who cheated, but like birds hiding nothing but their head behind the tree – people who could not count. They would not come to mow for us for twenty roubles, but they came for half a pail of vodka, though for twenty roubles they could have bought four pails. There really was filth and drunkenness and foolishness and deceit, but with all that one yet felt that the life of the peasants rested on a firm, sound foundation. However uncouth a wild animal the peasant following the plough seemed, and however he might stupefy himself with vodka, still, looking at him more closely, one felt that there was in him what was needed, something very important, which was lacking in Masha and in the doctor, for instance, and that was that he believed the chief thing on earth was truth and justice, and that his salvation, and that of the whole people, was only to be found in truth and justice, and so more than anything in the world he loved just dealing. I told my wife she saw the spots on the glass, but not the glass itself; she said nothing in reply, or hummed like Stepan 'oo-loo-loo-loo'. When this good-hearted and clever woman turned pale with indignation, and with a quiver in her voice spoke to the doctor of the drunkenness and dishonesty, it perplexed me, and I was struck by the shortness of her memory. How could she forget that her father the engineer drank too, and drank heavily, and that the money with which Dubetchnya had been bought had been acquired by a whole series of shameless, impudent dishonesties? How could she forget it?

XIV

MY sister, too, was leading a life of her own which she carefully hid from me. She was often whispering with Masha. When I went up to her she seemed to shrink into herself, and there was a guilty, imploring look in her eyes; evidently there was something going on in her heart of which she was afraid or ashamed. So as to avoid meeting me in the garden, or being left alone with me, she always kept close to Masha, and I rarely had an opportunity of talking to her except at dinner.

One evening I was walking quietly through the garden on my way back from the building. It was beginning to get dark. Without noticing me, or hearing my step, my sister was walking near a spreading old apple-tree, absolutely noiselessly as though she were a phantom. She was dressed in black, and was walking rapidly backwards and forwards on the same track, looking at the ground. An apple fell from the tree; she started at the sound, stood still and pressed her hands to her temples. At that moment I went up to her.

In a rush of tender affection which suddenly flooded my heart, with tears in my eyes, suddenly remembering my mother and our childhood, I put my arm round her shoulders and kissed her.

'What is the matter?' I asked her. 'You are unhappy; I have seen it for a long time. Tell me what's wrong?'

'I am frightened,' she said, trembling.

'What is it?' I insisted. 'For God's sake, be open!'

'I will, I will be open; I will tell you the whole truth. To hide it from you is so hard, so agonizing. Misail, I love...' she went on in a whisper, 'I love him...I love him...I am happy, but why am I so frightened?'

There was the sound of footsteps; between the trees appeared Dr. Blagovo in his silk shirt with his high top boots. Evidently they had arranged to meet near the apple-tree. Seeing him, she rushed impulsively towards him with a cry of pain, as though he were being taken from her.

'Vladimir! Vladimir!'

She clung to him and looked greedily into his face, and only then I noticed how pale and thin she had become of late. It was particularly noticeable from her lace collar which I had known for so long, and which now hung more loosely than ever before about her thin, long neck. The doctor was disconcerted, but at once recovered himself, and, stroking her hair, said:

'There, there.... Why so nervous? You see, I'm here.'

We were silent, looking with embarrassment at each other, then we walked on, the three of us together, and I heard the doctor say to me:

'Civilized life has not yet begun among us. Old men console themselves by making out that if there is nothing now, there was something in the forties or the sixties; that's the old: you and I are young; our brains have not yet been touched by *marasmus senilis*; we cannot comfort ourselves with such illusions. The beginning of Russia was in 862, but the beginning of civilized Russia has not come yet.'

But I did not grasp the meaning of these reflections. It was somehow strange, I could not believe it, that my sister was in love, that she was walking and holding the arm of a stranger and looking tenderly at him. My sister, this nervous, frightened, crushed, fettered creature, loved a man who was married and had children! I felt sorry for something, but what exactly I don't know; the presence of the doctor was for some reason distasteful to me now, and I could not imagine what would come of this love of theirs.

XV

MASHA and I drove to Kurilovka to the dedication of the school.

'Autumn, autumn, autumn...' said Masha softly, looking away. 'Summer is over. There are no birds and nothing is green but the willows.'

Yes, summer was over. There were fine, warm days, but it was fresh in the morning, and the shepherds went out in their sheepskins already; and in our garden the dew did not dry off the asters all day long. There were plaintive sounds all the time, and one could not make out whether they came from the shutters creaking on their rusty hinges, or from the flying cranes – and one's heart felt light, and one was eager for life.

'The summer is over,' said Masha. 'Now you and I can balance our accounts. We have done a lot of work, a lot of thinking; we are the better for it – all honour and glory to us – we have succeeded in self-improvement; but have our successes had any perceptible influence on the life around us, have they brought any benefit to anyone whatever? No. Ignorance, physical uncleanliness, drunkenness, an appallingly high infant mortality, everything remains as it was, and no one is the better for your having ploughed and sown, and my having wasted money and read books. Obviously we have been working only for ourselves and have had advanced ideas only for ourselves.' Such reasonings perplexed me, and I did not know what to think.

'We have been sincere from beginning to end,' said I, 'and if anyone is sincere he is right.'

'Who disputes it? We were right, but we haven't succeeded in properly accomplishing what we were right in. To begin with, our external methods themselves – aren't they mistaken? You want to be of use to men, but by the very fact of your buying an estate, from the very start you cut yourself off from any possibility of doing anything useful for them. Then if you work, dress, eat like a peasant you sanctify, as it were, by your authority, their heavy, clumsy dress, their horrible huts, their stupid beards.... On the other hand, if we suppose that you work for long, long years, your whole life, that in the end some practical results are obtained, yet what are they, your results, what can they do against such elemental forces as wholesale ignorance, hunger, cold, degeneration? A drop in the ocean! Other methods of struggle are needed, strong, bold, rapid! If one really wants to be of use one must get out of the narrow circle of ordinary social work, and try to act direct upon the mass! What is wanted, first of all, is a loud, energetic propaganda. Why is it that art – music, for instance – is so living, so popular, and in reality so powerful? Because the musician or the singer affects thousands at once. Precious, precious art!' she went on looking dreamily at the sky. 'Art gives us wings and carries us far, far away! Anyone who is sick of filth, of petty mercenary interests, anyone who is revolted, wounded and indignant, can find peace and satisfaction only in the beautiful.'

When we drove into Kurilovka the weather was bright and joyous. Somewhere they were threshing; there was a smell of rye straw. A mountain ash was bright red behind the hurdle fences, and all the trees wherever one looked were ruddy or golden. They were ringing the bells, they were carrying the ikons to the school, and we could hear them sing: 'Holy Mother, our Defender', and how limpid the air was, and how high the doves were flying.

The service was being held in the classroom. Then the peasants of Kurilovka brought Masha the ikon, and the peasants of Dubetchnya offered her a big loaf and a gilt salt cellar. And Masha broke into sobs.

'If anything has been said that shouldn't have been or anything done not to your liking, forgive us,' said an old man, and he bowed down to her and to me.

As we drove home Masha kept looking round at the school; the green roof, which I had painted, and which was glistening in the sun, remained in sight for a long while. And I felt that the look Masha turned upon it now was one of farewell.

XVI

IN the evening she got ready to go to the town. Of late she had taken to going often to the town and staying the night there. In her absence I could not work, my hands felt weak and limp; our huge courtyard seemed a dreary, repulsive, empty hole. The garden was full of angry noises, and without her the house, the trees, the horses were no longer 'ours'.

I did not go out of the house, but went on sitting at her table beside her bookshelf with the books on land work, those old favourites no longer wanted and looking at me now so shamefacedly. For whole hours together, while it struck seven, eight, nine, while the autumn night, black as soot, came on outside, I kept examining her old glove, or the pen with which she always wrote, or her little scissors. I did nothing, and realized clearly that all I had done before, ploughing, mowing, chopping, had only been because she wished it. And if she had sent me to clean a deep well, where I had to stand up to my waist in deep water, I should have crawled into the well without considering whether it was necessary or not. And now when she was not near, Dubetchnya, with its ruins, its untidiness, its banging shutters, with its thieves by day and by night, seemed to me a chaos in which any work would be useless. Besides, what had I to work for here, why anxiety and thought about the future, if I felt that the earth was giving way under my feet, that I had played my part in Dubetchnya, and that the fate of the books on farming was awaiting me too? Oh, what misery it was at night, in hours of solitude, when I was listening every minute in alarm, as though I were expecting someone to shout that it was time for me to go away! I did not grieve for Dubetchnya. I grieved for my love which, too, was threatened with its autumn. What an immense happiness it is to love and be loved, and how awful to feel that one is slipping down from that high pinnacle!

Masha returned from the town towards the evening of the next day. She was displeased with something, but she concealed it, and only said, why was it all the window frames had been put in for the winter, it was enough to suffocate one. I took out two frames. We were not hungry, but we sat down to supper.

'Go and wash your hands,' said my wife; 'you smell of putty.'

She had brought some new illustrated papers from the town, and we looked at them together after supper. There were supplements with fashion plates and patterns. Masha looked through them casually, and was putting them aside to examine them properly later on; but one dress, with a flat skirt as full as a bell and large sleeves, interested her, and she looked at it for a minute gravely and attentively.

'That's not bad,' she said.

'Yes, that dress would suit you beautifully,' I said, 'beautifully.'

And looking with emotion at the dress, admiring that patch of grey simply because she liked it, I went on tenderly:

'A charming, exquisite dress! Splendid, glorious, Masha! My precious Masha!'

And tears dropped on the fashion plate.

'Splendid Masha . . .' I muttered; 'sweet, precious Masha. . . .'

She went to bed, while I sat another hour looking at the illustrations.

'It's a pity you took out the window frames,' she said from the bedroom, 'I am afraid it may be cold. Oh, dear, what a draught there is!'

I read something out of the column of odds and ends, a receipt for making cheap ink, and an account of the biggest diamond in the world. I came again upon the fashion plate of the dress she liked, and I imagined her at a ball, with a fan, with bare shoulders, brilliant, splendid, with a full understanding of painting, music, literature, and how small and how brief my part seemed!

Our meeting, our marriage, had been only one of the episodes of which there would be many more in the life of this vital, richly gifted woman. All the best in the world, as I have said already, was at her service, and she received it absolutely for nothing, and even ideas and the intellectual movement in vogue served simply for her recreation, giving variety to her life, and I was only the sledge-driver who drove her from one entertainment to another. Now she did not need me. She would take flight, and I should be left alone.

And as though in response to my thought, there came a despairing scream from the garden.

'He-e-elp!'

It was a shrill, womanish voice, and as though to mimic it the wind whistled in the chimney on the same shrill note. Half a minute passed, and again through the noise of the wind, but coming, it seemed, from the other end of the yard:

'He-e-elp!'

'Misail, do you hear?' my wife asked me softly. 'Do you hear?'

She came out from the bedroom in her nightgown, with her hair down, and listened, looking at the dark window.

'Someone is being murdered,' she said. 'That is the last straw.'

I took my gun and went out. It was very dark outside, the wind was high, and it was difficult to stand. I went to the gate and listened, the trees roared, the wind whistled and, probably at the feeble-minded peasant's, a dog howled lazily. Outside the gates the darkness was absolute, not a light on the railway-line. And near the lodge, which a year before had been the office, suddenly sounded a smothered scream:

'He-e-elp!'

'Who's there?' I called.

There were two people struggling. One was thrusting the other out, while the other was resisting, and both were breathing heavily.

'Leave go,' said one, and I recognized Ivan Tcheprakov; it was he who was shrieking in a shrill, womanish voice: 'Let go, you damned brute, or I'll bite your hand off.'

The other I recognized as Moisey. I separated them, and as I did so could not resist hitting Moisey two blows in the face. He fell down, then got up again, and I hit him once more.

'He tried to kill me,' he muttered. 'He was trying to get at his mamma's chest. . . . I want to lock him up in the lodge for security.'

Tcheprakov was drunk and did not recognize me; he kept drawing deep breaths, as though he were just going to shout 'help' again.

I left them and went back to the house; my wife was lying on her bed; she had dressed. I told her what had happened in the yard, and did not conceal the fact that I had hit Moisey.

'It's terrible to live in the country,' she said. 'And what a long night it is. Oh dear, if only it were over!'

'He-e-elp!' we heard again, a little later.

'I'll go and stop them,' I said.

'No, let them bite each other's throats,' she said with an expression of disgust.

She was looking up at the ceiling, listening, while I sat beside her, not daring to speak to her, feeling as though I were to blame for their shouting 'help' in the yard and for the night's seeming so long.

We were silent, and I waited impatiently for a gleam of light at the window, and Masha looked all the time as though she had awakened from a trance and now was marvelling how she, so clever, and well-educated, so elegant, had come into this pitiful, provincial, empty hole among a crew of petty, insignificant people, and how she could have so far forgotten herself as ever to be attracted by one of these people, and for more than six months to have been his wife. It seemed to me that at that moment it did not matter to her whether it was I, or Moisey, or Tcheprakov; everything for her was merged in that savage drunken 'help' – I and our marriage, and our work together, and the mud and slush of autumn, and when she sighed or moved into a more comfortable position I read in her face: 'Oh, that morning would come quickly!'

In the morning she went away. I spent another three days at Dubetchnya expecting her, then I packed up all our things in one room, locked it, and walked to the town. It was already evening when I rang at the engineer's, and the street lamps were burning in Great Dvoryansky Street. Pavel told me there was no one at home; Viktor Ivanitch had gone to Petersburg, and Mariya Viktorovna was probably at the rehearsal at the Azhogins'. I remember with what emotion I went on to the Azhogins', how my heart throbbed and fluttered as I mounted the stairs, and stood waiting a long while on the landing at the top, not daring to enter that temple of the muses! In the big room there were lighted candles everywhere, on a little table, on the piano, and on the stage, everywhere in threes; and the first performance was fixed for the thirteenth, and now the first rehearsal was on a Monday, an unlucky day. All part of the war against superstition! All the devotees of the scenic art were gathered together; the eldest, the middle, and the youngest sisters were walking about the stage, reading their parts in exercise books. Apart from all the rest stood Radish, motionless, with the side of his head pressed to the wall as he gazed with adoration at the stage, waiting for the rehearsal to begin. Everything as it used to be.

I was making my way to my hostess; I had to pay my respects to her, but suddenly everyone said, 'Hush!', and waved me to step quietly. There was a silence. The lid of the piano was raised; a lady sat down at it screwing up her short-sighted eyes at the music, and my Masha walked up to the piano, in a low-necked dress, looking beautiful, but with a special, new sort of beauty not in the least like the Masha who used to come and meet me in the spring at the mill. She sang: 'Why do I love the radiant night?'

It was the first time during our whole acquaintance that I had heard her sing. She had a fine, mellow, powerful voice, and while she sang I felt as though I were eating a ripe, sweet, fragrant melon. She ended, the audience applauded, and she smiled, very much pleased, making play with her eyes, turning over the music, smoothing her skirts, like a bird that has at last broken out of its cage and preens its wings in freedom. Her hair was arranged over her ears, and she had an unpleasant, defiant expression in her face, as though she wanted to throw down a challenge to us all, or to shout to us as she did to her horses: 'Hey, there, my beauties!'

And she must at that moment have been very much like her grandfather the sledge-driver.

'You here too?' she said, giving me her hand. 'Did you hear me sing? Well, what did you think of it?' and without waiting for my answer she went on: 'It's a very good thing you are here. I am going to-night to Petersburg for a short time. You'll let me go, won't you?'

At midnight I went with her to the station. She embraced me affectionately, probably feeling grateful to me for not asking unnecessary questions, and she promised to write to me, and I held her hands a long time, and kissed them, hardly able to restrain my tears and not uttering a word.

And when she had gone I stood watching the retreating lights, caressing her in imagination and softly murmuring:

'My darling Masha, glorious Masha....'

I spent the night at Karpovna's, and next morning I was at work with Radish, re-covering the furniture of a rich merchant who was marrying his daughter to a doctor.

XVII

MY sister came after dinner on Sunday and had tea with me.

'I read a great deal now,' she said, showing me the books which she had fetched from the public library on her way to me. 'Thanks to your wife and to Vladimir, they have awakened me to self-realization. They have been my salvation; they have made me feel myself a human being. In old days I used to lie awake at night with worries of all sorts, thinking what a lot of sugar we had used in the week, or hoping the cucumbers would not be too salt. And now, too, I lie awake at night, but I have different thoughts. I am distressed that half my life has been passed in such a foolish, cowardly way. I despise my past; I am ashamed of it. And I look upon our father now as my enemy. Oh, how grateful I am to your wife! And Vladimir! He is such a wonderful person! They have opened my eyes!'

'That's bad that you don't sleep at night,' I said.

'Do you think I am ill? Not at all. Vladimir sounded me, and said I was perfectly well. But health is not what matters, it is not so important.... Tell me: am I right?'

She needed moral support, that was obvious. Masha had gone away. Dr. Blagovo was in Petersburg, and there was no one left in the town but me, to tell her she was right. She looked intently into my face, trying to read my secret thoughts, and if I were absorbed or silent in her presence she thought this was on her account, and was grieved. I always had to be on my guard, and when she asked me whether she was right I hastened to assure her that she was right, and that I had a deep respect for her.

'Do you know they have given me a part at the Azhogins'?' she went on. 'I want to act on the stage, I want to live – in fact, I mean to drain the full cup. I have no talent, none, and the part is only ten lines, but still this is immeasurably finer and loftier than pouring out tea five times a day, and looking to see if the cook has eaten too much. Above all, let my father see I am capable of protest.'

After tea she lay down on my bed, and lay for a little while with her eyes closed, looking very pale.

'What weakness,' she said, getting up. 'Vladimir says all city-bred women and girls are anæmic from doing nothing. What a clever man Vladimir is! He is right, absolutely right. We must work!'

Two days later she came to the Azhogins' with her manuscript for the rehearsal. She was wearing a black dress with a string of coral round her neck, and a brooch that in the distance was like a pastry puff, and in her ears earrings sparkling with brilliants. When I looked at her I felt uncomfortable: I was struck by her lack of taste. That she had very inappropriately put on earrings and brilliants, and that she was strangely dressed, was remarked by other people too; I saw smiles on people's faces, and heard someone say with a laugh: 'Kleopatra of Egypt.'

She was trying to assume society manners, to be unconstrained and at her ease, and so seemed artificial and strange. She had lost simplicity and sweetness.

'I told father just now that I was going to the rehearsal,' she began, coming up to me, 'and he shouted that he would not give me his blessing, and actually almost struck me. Only fancy, I don't know my part,' she said, looking at her manuscript. 'I am sure to make a mess of it. So be it, the die is cast,' she went on in intense excitement. 'The die is cast. . . .'

It seemed to her that everyone was looking at her, and that all were amazed at the momentous step she had taken, that everyone was expecting something special of her, and it would have been impossible to convince her that no one was paying attention to people so petty and insignificant as she and I were.

She had nothing to do till the third act, and her part, that of a visitor, a provincial crony, consisted only in standing at the door as though listening, and then delivering a brief monologue. In the interval before her appearance, an hour and a half at least, while they were moving about on the stage reading their parts, drinking tea and arguing, she did not leave my side, and was all the time muttering her part and nervously crumpling up the manuscript. And imagining that everyone was looking at her and waiting for her appearance, with a trembling hand she smoothed back her hair and said to me:

'I shall certainly make a mess of it.... What a load on my heart, if only you knew! I feel frightened, as though I were just going to be led to execution.'

At last her turn came.

'Kleopatra Alexyevna, it's your cue!' said the stage manager.

She came forward into the middle of the stage with an expression of horror on her face, looking ugly and angular, and for half a minute stood as though in a trance, perfectly motionless, and only her big earrings shook in her ears.

'The first time you can read it,' said someone.

It was clear to me that she was trembling, and trembling so much that she could not speak, and could not unfold her manuscript, and that she was incapable of acting her part; and I was already on the point of going to her and saying something, when she suddenly dropped on her knees in the middle of the stage and broke into loud sobs.

All was commotion and hubbub. I alone stood still, leaning against the side scene, overwhelmed by what had happened, not understanding and not knowing what to do. I saw them lift her up and lead her away. I saw Anyuta Blagovo come up to me; I had not seen her in the room before, and she seemed to have sprung out of the earth. She was wearing her hat and veil, and, as always, had an air of having come only for a moment.

'I told her not to take a part,' she said angrily, jerking out each word abruptly and turning crimson. 'It's insanity! You ought to have prevented her!'

Madame Azhogin, in a short jacket with short sleeves, with cigarette ash on her breast, looking thin and flat, came rapidly towards me.

'My dear, this is terrible,' she brought out, wringing her hands, and, as her habit was, looking intently into my face. 'This is terrible! Your sister is in a condition.... She is with child. Take her away, I implore you....'

She was breathless with agitation, while on one side stood her three daughters, exactly like her, thin and flat, huddling together in a scared way. They were alarmed, overwhelmed, as though a convict had been caught in their house. What a disgrace, how dreadful! And yet this estimable family had spent its life waging war on superstition; evidently they imagined that all the superstition and error of humanity was limited to the three candles, the thirteenth of the month, and to the unluckiness of Monday!

'I beg you...I beg,' repeated Madame Azhogin, pursing up her lips in the shape of a heart on the syllable 'you'. 'I beg you take her home.'

XVIII

A LITTLE later my sister and I were walking along the street. I covered her with the skirts of my coat; we hastened, choosing back streets where there were no street lamps, avoiding passers-by; it was as though we were running away. She was no longer crying, but looked at me with dry eyes. To Karpovna's, where I took her, it was only twenty minutes' walk, and, strange to say, in that short time we succeeded in thinking of our whole life; we talked over everything, considered our position, reflected. . . .

We decided we could not go on living in this town, and that when I had earned a little money we would move to some other place. In some houses everyone was asleep, in others they were playing cards; we hated these houses; we were afraid of them. We talked of the fanaticism, the coarseness of feeling, the insignificance of these respectable families, these amateurs of dramatic art whom we had so alarmed, and I kept asking in what way these stupid, cruel, lazy, and dishonest people were superior to the drunken and superstitious peasants of Kurilovka, or in what way they were better than animals, who in the same way are thrown into a panic when some incident disturbs the monotony of their life limited by their instincts. What would have happened to my sister now if she had been left to live at home?

What moral agonies would she have experienced, talking with my father, meeting every day with acquaintances? I imagined this to myself, and at once there came into my mind people, all people I knew, who had been slowly done to death by their nearest relations. I remembered the tortured dogs driven mad, the live sparrows plucked naked by boys and flung into the water, and a long, long series of obscure lingering miseries which I had looked on continually from early childhood in that town; and I could not understand what these sixty thousand people lived for, what they read the gospel for, why they prayed, why they read books and magazines. What good had they gained from all that had been said and written hitherto if they were still possessed by the same spiritual darkness and hatred of liberty, as they were a hundred and three hundred years ago? A master carpenter spends his whole life building houses in the town, and always, to the day of his death, calls a 'gallery' a 'galdery'. So these sixty thousand people have been reading and hearing of truth, of justice, of mercy, of freedom for generations, and yet from morning till night, till the day of their death, they are lying, and tormenting each other, and they fear liberty and hate it as a deadly foe.

'And so my fate is decided,' said my sister, as we arrived home. 'After what has happened I cannot go back *there*. Heavens, how good that is! My heart feels lighter.'

She went to bed at once. Tears were glittering on her eyelashes, but her expression was happy; she fell into a sound sweet sleep, and one could see that her heart was lighter and that she was resting. It was a long, long time since she had slept like that.

And so we began our life together. She was always singing and saying that her life was very happy, and the books I brought her from the public library I took back unread, as now she could not read; she wanted to do nothing but dream and talk of the future, mending my linen, or helping Karpovna near the stove; she was always singing, or talking of her Vladimir, of his cleverness, of his charming manners, of his kindness, of his extraordinary learning, and I assented to all she said, though by now I disliked her doctor. She wanted to work, to lead an independent life on her own account, and she used to say that she would become a school-teacher or a doctor's assistant as soon as her health would permit her, and would herself do the scrubbing and the washing. Already she was passionately devoted to her child; he was not yet born, but she knew already the colour of his eyes, what his hands would be like, and how he would laugh. She was fond of talking about education, and as her Vladimir was the best man in the world, all her discussion of education could be summed up in the question how to make the boy as fascinating as his father. There was no end to her talk, and everything she said made her intensely joyful. Sometimes I was delighted, too, though I could not have said why.

I suppose her dreaminess infected me. I, too, gave up reading, and did nothing but dream. In the evenings, in spite of my fatigue, I walked up and down the room, with my hands in my pockets, talking of Masha.

'What do you think?' I would ask of my sister. 'When will she come back? I think she'll come back at Christmas, not later; what has she to do there?'

'As she doesn't write to you, it's evident she will come back very soon.'

'That's true,' I assented, though I knew perfectly well that Masha would not return to our town.

I missed her fearfully, and could no longer deceive myself, and tried to get other people to deceive me. My sister was expecting her doctor, and I – Masha; and both of us talked incessantly, laughed, and did not notice that we were preventing Karpovna from sleeping. She lay on the stove and kept muttering:

'The samovar hummed this morning, it did hum! Oh, it bodes no good, my dears, it bodes no good!'

No one ever came to see us but the postman, who brought my sister letters from the doctor, and Prokovy, who sometimes came in to see us in the evening, and after looking at my sister without speaking went away, and when he was in the kitchen said:

'Every class ought to remember its rules, and anyone, who is so proud that he won't understand that, will find it a vale of tears.'

He was very fond of the phrase 'a vale of tears'. One day – it was in Christmas week, when I was walking by the bazaar – he called me into the butcher's shop, and not shaking hands with me, announced that he had to speak to me about something very important. His face was red from the frost and vodka; near him, behind the counter, stood Nikolka, with the expression of a brigand, holding a blood-stained knife in his hand.

'I desire to express my word to you,' Prokovy began. 'This incident cannot continue, because, as you understand yourself that for such a vale, people will say nothing good of you or of us. Mamma, through pity, cannot say something unpleasant to you, that your sister should move into another lodging on account of her condition, but I won't have it any more, because I can't approve of her behaviour.'

I understood him, and I went out of the shop. The same day my sister and I moved to Radish's. We had no money for a cab, and we walked on foot; I carried a parcel of our belongings on my back; my sister had nothing in her hands, but she gasped for breath and coughed, and kept asking whether we should get there soon.

XIX

AT last a letter came from Masha.

'Dear, good M. A.' (she wrote), 'our kind, gentle "angel" as the old painter calls you, farewell; I am going with my father to America for the exhibition. In a few days I shall see the ocean – so far from Dubetchnya, it's dreadful to think! It's far and unfathomable as the sky, and I long to be there in freedom. I am triumphant, I am mad, and you see how incoherent my letter is. Dear, good one, give me my freedom, make haste to break the thread, which still holds, binding you and me together. My meeting and knowing you was a ray from heaven that lighted up my existence; but my becoming your wife was a mistake, you understand that, and I am oppressed now by the consciousness of the mistake, and I beseech you, on my knees, my generous friend, quickly, quickly, before I start for the ocean, telegraph that you consent to correct our common mistake, to remove the solitary stone from my wings, and my father, who will undertake all the arrangements, promised me not to burden you too much with formalities. And so I am free to fly whither I will? Yes?

'Be happy, and God bless you; forgive me, a sinner.

'I am well, I am wasting money, doing all sorts of silly things, and I thank God every minute that such a bad woman as I has no children. I sing and have success, but it's not an infatuation; no, it's my haven, my cell to which I go for peace. King David had a ring with an inscription on it: "All things pass." When one is sad those words make one cheerful, and when one is cheerful it makes one sad. I have got myself a ring like that with Hebrew letters on it, and this talisman keeps me from infatuations. All things pass, life will pass, one wants nothing. Or at least one wants nothing but the sense of freedom, for when anyone is free, he wants nothing, nothing, nothing. Break the thread. A warm hug to you and your sister. Forgive and forget your M.'

My sister used to lie down in one room, and Radish, who had been ill again and was now better, in another. Just at the moment when I received this letter my sister went softly into the painter's room, sat down beside him and began reading aloud. She read to him every day, Ostrovsky or Gogol, and he listened, staring at one point, not laughing, but shaking his head and muttering to himself from time to time:

'Anything may happen! Anything may happen!'

If anything ugly or unseemly were depicted in the play he would say as though vindictively, thrusting his finger into the book:

'There it is, lying! That's what it does, lying does.'

The plays fascinated him, both from their subjects and their moral, and from their skilful, complex construction, and he marvelled at 'him', never calling the author by his name. How neatly *he* has put it all together.

This time my sister read softly only one page, and could read no more: her voice would not last out. Radish took her hand and, moving his parched lips, said, hardly audibly, in a husky voice:

'The soul of a righteous man is white and smooth as chalk, but the soul of a sinful man is like pumice stone. The soul of a righteous man is like clear oil, but the soul of a sinful man is gas tar. We must labour, we must sorrow, we must suffer sickness,' he went on, 'and he who does not labour and sorrow will not gain the Kingdom of Heaven. Woe, woe to them that are well fed, woe to the mighty, woe to the rich, woe to the moneylenders! Not for them is the Kingdom of Heaven. Lice eat grass, rust eats iron....'

'And lying the soul,' my sister added laughing.

I read the letter through once more. At that moment there walked into the kitchen a soldier who had been bringing us twice a week parcels of tea, French bread and game, which smelt of scent, from some unknown giver. I had no work. I had had to sit at home idle for whole days together, and probably whoever sent us the French bread knew that we were in want.

I heard my sister talking to the soldier and laughing gaily. Then, lying down, she ate some French bread and said to me:

'When you wouldn't go into the service, but became a house painter, Anyuta Blagovo and I knew from the beginning that you were right, but we were frightened to say so aloud. Tell me what force is it that hinders us from saying what one thinks? Take Anyuta Blagovo now, for instance. She loves you, she adores you, she knows you are right, she loves me too, like a sister, and knows that I am right, and I daresay in her soul envies me, but some force prevents her from coming to see us, she shuns us, she is afraid.'

My sister crossed her arms over her breast, and said passionately:

'How she loves you, if only you knew! She has confessed her love to no one but me, and then very secretly in the dark. She led me into a dark avenue in the garden, and began whispering how precious you were to her. You will see, she'll never marry, because she loves you. Are you sorry for her?'

'Yes.'

'It's she who has sent the bread. She is absurd really, what is the use of being so secret? I used to be absurd and foolish, but now I have got away from that and am afraid of nobody. I think and say aloud what I like, and am happy. When I lived at home I hadn't a conception of happiness, and now I wouldn't change with a queen.'

Dr. Blagovo arrived. He had taken his doctor's degree, and was now staying in our town with his father; he was taking a rest, and said that he would soon go back to Petersburg again. He wanted to study anti-toxins against typhus, and, I believe, cholera; he wanted to go abroad to perfect his training, and then to be appointed a professor. He had already left the army service, and wore a roomy serge reefer jacket, very full trousers, and magnificent neckties. My sister was in ecstasies over his scarf-pin, his studs, and the red silk handkerchief which he wore, I suppose from foppishness, sticking out of the breast pocket of his jacket. One day, having nothing to do, she and I counted up all the suits we remembered him wearing, and came to the conclusion that he had at least ten. It was clear that he still loved my sister as before, but he never once even in jest spoke of taking her with him to Petersburg or abroad, and I could not picture to myself clearly what would become of her if she remained alive and what would become of her child. She did nothing but dream endlessly, and never thought seriously of the future; she said he might go where he liked, and might abandon her even, so long as he was happy himself; that what had been was enough for her.

As a rule he used to sound her very carefully on his arrival, and used to insist on her taking milk and drops in his presence. It was the same on this occasion. He sounded her and made her drink a glass of milk, and there was a smell of creosote in our room afterwards.

'There's a good girl,' he said, taking the glass from her. 'You mustn't talk too much now; you've taken to chattering like a magpie of late. Please hold your tongue.'

She laughed. Then he came into Radish's room where I was sitting and affectionately slapped me on the shoulder.

'Well, how goes it, old man?' he said, bending down to the invalid.

'Your honour,' said Radish, moving his lips slowly, 'your honour, I venture to submit.... We all walk in the fear of God, we all have to die.... Permit me to tell you the truth.... Your honour, the Kingdom of Heaven will not be for you!'

'There's no help for it,' the doctor said jestingly; 'there must be somebody in hell, you know.'

And all at once something happened with my consciousness; as though I were in a dream, as though I were standing on a winter night in the slaughterhouse yard, and Prokofy beside me, smelling of pepper cordial; I made an effort to control myself, and rubbed my eyes, and at once it seemed to me that I was going along the road to the interview with the Governor. Nothing of the sort had happened to me before, or has happened to me since, and these strange memories that were like dreams, I ascribed to over-exhaustion of my nerves. I lived through the scene at the slaughter-house, and the interview with the Governor, and at the same time was dimly aware that it was not real.

When I came to myself I saw that I was no longer in the house, but in the street, and was standing with the doctor near a lamp-post.

'It's sad, it's sad,' he was saying, and tears were trickling down his cheeks. 'She is in good spirits, she's always laughing and hopeful, but her position's hopeless, dear boy. Your Radish hates me, and is always trying to make me feel that I have treated her badly. He is right from his standpoint, but I have my point of view too; and I shall never regret all that has happened. One must love; we ought all to love – oughtn't we? There would be no life without love; anyone who fears and avoids love is not free.'

Little by little he passed to other subjects, began talking of science, of his dissertation which had been liked in Petersburg. He was carried away by his subject, and no longer thought of my sister, nor of his grief, nor of me. Life was of absorbing interest to him. She has America and her ring with the inscription on it, I thought, while this fellow has his doctor's degree and a professor's chair to look forward to, and only my sister and I are left with the old things.

When I said good-bye to him, I went up to the lamp-post and read the letter once more. And I remembered, I remembered vividly how that spring morning she had come to me at the mill, lain down and covered herself with her jacket – she wanted to be like a simple peasant woman. And how, another time – it was in the morning also – we drew the net out of the water, and heavy drops of rain fell upon us from the riverside willows, and we laughed...

It was dark in our house in Great Dvoryansky Street. I got over the fence and, as I used to do in old days, went by the back way to the kitchen to borrow a lantern. There was no one in the kitchen. The samovar hissed near the stove, waiting for my father. 'Who pours out my father's tea now?' I thought. Taking the lantern I went out to the shed, built myself up a bed of old newspapers and lay down. The hooks on the walls looked forbidding, as they used to of old, and their shadows flickered. It was cold. I felt that my sister would come in in a minute, and bring me supper, but at once I remembered that she was ill and was lying at Radish's, and it seemed to me strange that I should have climbed over the fence and be lying here in this unheated shed. My mind was in a maze, and I saw all sorts of absurd things.

There was a ring. A ring familiar from childhood: first the wire rustled against the wall, then a short plaintive ring in the kitchen. It was my father come back from the club. I got up and went into the kitchen. Axinya the cook clasped her hands on seeing me, and for some reason burst into tears.

'My own!' she said softly. 'My precious! O Lord!'

And she began crumpling up her apron in her agitation. In the window there were standing jars of berries in vodka. I poured myself out a tea-cupful and greedily drank it off, for I was intensely thirsty. Axinya had quite recently scrubbed the table and benches, and there was that smell in the kitchen which is found in bright, snug kitchens kept by tidy cooks. And that smell and the chirp of the cricket used to lure us as children into the kitchen, and put us in the mood for hearing fairy tales and playing at 'Kings'....

'Where's Kleopatra?' Axinya asked softly, in a fluster, holding her breath; 'and where is your cap, my dear? Your wife, they say, has gone to Petersburg?'

She had been our servant in our mother's time, and used once to give Kleopatra and me our baths, and to her we were still children who had to be talked to for their good. For a quarter of an hour or so she laid before me all the reflections which she had with the sagacity of an old servant been accumulating in the stillness of that kitchen, all the time since we had seen each other. She said that the doctor could be forced to marry Kleopatra; he only needed to be thoroughly frightened; and that if an appeal were promptly written the bishop would annul the first marriage; that it would be a good thing for me to sell Dubetchnya without my wife's knowledge, and put the money in the bank in my own name; that if my sister and I were to bow down at my father's feet and ask him properly, he might perhaps forgive us; that we ought to have a service sung to the Queen of Heaven....

'Come, go along, my dear, and speak to him,' she said, when she heard my father's cough. 'Go along, speak to him; bow down, your head won't drop off.'

I went in. My father was sitting at the table

sketching a plan of a summer villa, with Gothic windows, and with a fat turret like a fireman's watch tower – something peculiarly stiff and tasteless. Going into the study I stood still where I could see this drawing. I did not know why I had gone in to my father, but I remember that when I saw his lean face, his red neck, and his shadow on the wall, I wanted to throw myself on his neck, and as Axinya had told me, bow down at his feet; but the sight of the summer villa with the Gothic windows, and the fat turret, restrained me.

'Good evening,' I said.

He glanced at me, and at once dropped his eyes on his drawing.

'What do you want?' he asked, after waiting a little.

'I have come to tell you my sister's very ill. She can't live very long,' I added in a hollow voice.

'Well,' sighed my father, taking off his spectacles, and laying them on the table. 'What thou sowest that shalt thou reap. What thou sowest,' he repeated, getting up from the table, 'that shalt thou reap. I ask you to remember how you came to me two years ago, and on this very spot I begged you, I besought you to give up your errors; I reminded you of your duty, of your honour, of what you owed to your forefathers whose traditions we ought to preserve as sacred. Did you obey me? You scorned my counsels, and obstinately persisted in clinging to your false ideas; worse still you drew your sister into the path of error with you, and led her to lose her moral principles and sense of shame. Now you are both in a bad way. Well, as thou sowest, so shalt thou reap!'

As he said this he walked up and down the room. He probably imagined that I had come to him to confess my wrong doings, and he probably expected that I should begin begging him to forgive my sister and me. I was cold, I was shivering as though I were in a fever, and spoke with difficulty in a husky voice.

'And I beg you, too, to remember,' I said, 'on this very spot I besought you to understand me, to reflect, to decide with me how and for what we should live, and in answer you began talking about our forefathers, about my grandfather who wrote poems. One tells you now that your only daughter is hopelessly ill, and you go on again about your forefathers, your traditions.... And such frivolity in your old age, when death is close at hand and you haven't more than five or ten years left!'

'What have you come here for?' my father asked sternly, evidently offended at my reproaching him for his frivolity.

'I don't know. I love you, I am unutterably sorry that we are so far apart – so you see I have come. I love you still, but my sister has broken with you completely. She does not forgive you, and will never forgive you now. Your very name arouses her aversion for the past, for life.'

'And who is to blame for it?' cried my father. 'It's your fault, you scoundrel!'

'Well, suppose it is my fault,' I said. 'I admit I have been to blame in many things, but why is it that this life of yours, which you think binding upon us, too – why is it so dreary, so barren? How is it that in not one of these houses you have been building for the last thirty years has there been anyone from whom I might have learnt how to live, so as not to be to blame? There is not one honest man in the whole town! These houses of yours are nests of damnation, where mothers and daughters are made away with, where children are tortured.... My poor mother!' I went on in despair. 'My poor sister! One has to stupefy oneself with vodka, with cards, with scandal; one must become a scoundrel, a hypocrite, or go on drawing plans for years and years, so as not to notice all the horrors that lie hidden in these houses. Our town has existed for hundreds of years, and all that time it has not produced one man of service to our country – not one. You have stifled in the germ everything in the least living and bright. It's a town of shopkeepers, publicans, counting-house clerks, canting hypocrites; it's a useless, unnecessary town, which not one soul would regret if it suddenly sank through the earth.'

'I don't want to listen to you, you scoundrel!' said my father, and he took up his ruler from the table. 'You are drunk. Don't dare come and see your father in such a state! I tell you for the last time, and you can repeat it to your depraved sister, that you'll get nothing from me, either of you. I have torn my disobedient children out of my heart, and if they suffer for their disobedience and obstinacy I do not pity them. You can go whence you came. It has pleased God to chastise me with you, but I will bear the trial with resignation, and, like Job, I will find consolation in my sufferings and in unremitting labour. You must not cross my threshold till you have mended your ways. I am a just man, all I tell you is for your benefit, and if you desire your own good you ought to remember all your life what I say and have said to you. . . .'

I waved my hand in despair and went away. I don't remember what happened afterwards, that night and next day.

I am told that I walked about the streets bareheaded, staggering, and singing aloud, while a crowd of boys ran after me, shouting:

'Better-than-nothing!'

XX

If I wanted to order a ring for myself, the inscription I should choose would be: 'Nothing passes away.' I believe that nothing passes away without leaving a trace, and that every step we take, however small, has significance for our present and our future existence.

What I have been through has not been for nothing. My great troubles, my patience, have touched people's hearts, and now they don't call me 'Better-than-nothing', they don't laugh at me, and when I walk by the shops they don't throw water over me. They have grown used to my being a workman, and see nothing strange in my carrying a pail of paint and putting in windows, though I am of noble rank; on the contrary, people are glad to give me orders, and I am now considered a first-rate workman, and the best foreman after Radish, who, though he has regained his health, and though, as before, he paints the cupola on the belfry without scaffolding, has no longer the force to control the workmen; instead of him I now run about the town looking for work, I engage the workmen and pay them, borrow money at a high rate of interest, and now that I myself am a contractor, I understand how it is that one may have to waste three days racing about the town in search of tilers on account of some twopenny-halfpenny job. People are civil to me, they address me politely, and in the houses where I work, they offer me tea, and send to enquire whether I wouldn't like dinner. Children and young girls often come and look at me with curiosity and compassion.

One day I was working in the Governor's garden, painting an arbour there to look like marble. The Governor, walking in the garden, came up to the arbour and, having nothing to do, entered into conversation with me, and I reminded him how he had once summoned me to an interview with him. He looked into my face intently for a minute, then made his mouth like a round 'o', flung up his hands, and said: 'I don't remember!'

I have grown older, have become silent, stern, and austere, I rarely laugh, and I am told that I have grown like Radish, and that like him I bore the workmen by my useless exhortations.

Mariya Viktorovna, my former wife, is living now abroad, while her father is constructing a railway somewhere in the eastern provinces, and is buying estates there. Dr. Blagovo is also abroad. Dubetchnya has passed again into the possession of Madame Tcheprakov, who has bought it after forcing the engineer to knock the price down twenty per cent. Moisey goes about now in a bowler hat; he often drives into the town in a racing droshky on business of some sort, and stops near the bank. They say he has already bought up a mortgaged estate, and is constantly making enquiries at the bank about Dubetchnya, which he means to buy too. Poor Ivan Tcheprakov was for a long while out of work, staggering about the town and drinking. I tried to get him into our work, and for a time he painted roofs and put in window-panes in our company, and even got to like it, and stole oil, asked for tips, and drank like a regular painter. But he soon got sick of the work, and went back to Dubetchnya, and afterwards the workmen confessed to me that he had tried to persuade them to join him one night and murder Moisey and rob Madame Tcheprakov.

My father has greatly aged; he is very bent, and in the evenings walks up and down near his house. I never go to see him.

During an epidemic of cholera Prokofy doctored some of the shopkeepers with pepper cordial and pitch, and took money for doing so, and, as I learned from the newspapers, was flogged for abusing the doctors as he sat in his shop. His shopboy Nikolka died of cholera. Karpovna is still alive and, as always, she loves and fears her Prokofy. When she sees me, she always shakes her head mournfully, and says with a sigh: 'Your life is ruined.'

On working days I am busy from morning till night. On holidays, in fine weather, I take my tiny niece (my sister reckoned on a boy, but the child is a girl) and walk in a leisurely way to the cemetery. There I stand or sit down, and stay a long time gazing at the grave that is so dear to me, and tell the child that her mother lies here.

Sometimes, by the graveside, I find Anyuta Blagovo. We greet each other and stand in silence, or talk of Kleopatra, of her child, of how sad life is in this world; then, going out of the cemetery, we walk along in silence and she slackens her pace on purpose to walk beside me a little longer. The little girl, joyous and happy, pulls at her hand, laughing and screwing up her eyes in the bright sunlight, and we stand still and join in caressing the dear child.

When we reach the town Anyuta Blagovo, agitated and flushing crimson, says good-bye to me and walks on alone, austere and respectable.... And no one who met her could, looking at her, imagine that she had just been walking beside me and even caressing the child.

THE DARLING

THE DARLING

OLENKA, the daughter of the retired collegiate assessor, Plemyanniakov, was sitting in her back porch, lost in thought. It was hot, the flies were persistent and teasing, and it was pleasant to reflect that it would soon be evening. Dark rain-clouds were gathering from the east, and bringing from time to time a breath of moisture in the air.

Kukin, who was the manager of an open-air theatre called the Tivoli, and who lived in the lodge, was standing in the middle of the garden looking at the sky.

'Again!' he observed despairingly. 'It's going to rain again! Rain every day, as though to spite me! I might as well hang myself! It's ruin! Fearful losses every day.'

He flung up his hands, and went on, addressing Olenka:

'There! that's the life we lead, Olga Semyonovna. It's enough to make one cry. One works and does one's utmost; one wears oneself out, getting no sleep at night, and racks one's brain what to do for the best. And then what happens? To begin with, one's public is ignorant, boorish. I give them the very best operetta, a dainty masque, first-rate music-hall artists. But do you suppose that's what they want!

They don't understand anything of that sort. They want a clown; what they ask for is vulgarity. And then look at the weather! Almost every evening it rains. It started on the tenth of May, and it's kept it up all May and June. It's simply awful! The public doesn't come, but I've to pay the rent just the same, and pay the artists.'

The next evening the clouds would gather again, and Kukin would say with an hysterical laugh:

'Well, rain away, then! Flood the garden, drown me! Damn my luck in this world and the next! Let the artists have me up! Send me to prison! – to Siberia! – the scaffold! Ha, ha, ha!'

And next day the same thing.

Olenka listened to Kukin with silent gravity, and sometimes tears came into her eyes. In the end his misfortunes touched her; she grew to love him. He was a small thin man, with a yellow face, and curls combed forward on his forehead. He spoke in a thin tenor; as he talked his mouth worked on one side, and there was always an expression of despair on his face; yet he aroused a deep and genuine affection in her. She was always fond of someone, and could not exist without loving. In earlier days she had loved her papa, who now sat in a darkened room, breathing with difficulty; she had loved her aunt who used to come every other year from Bryansk; and before that, when she was at school, she had loved her French master. She was a gentle, soft-hearted, compassionate girl, with mild, tender eyes and very good health. At the sight of her full rosy cheeks, her soft white neck with a little dark mole on it, and the kind, naïve smile, which came into her face when she listened to anything pleasant, men thought, 'Yes, not half bad', and smiled too, while lady visitors could not refrain from seizing her hand in the middle of a conversation, exclaiming in a gush of delight, 'You darling!'

The house in which she had lived from her birth upwards, and which was left her in her father's will, was at the extreme end of the town, not far from the Tivoli. In the evenings and at night she could hear the band playing, and the crackling and banging of fireworks, and it seemed to her that it was Kukin struggling with his destiny, storming the entrenchments of his chief foe, the indifferent public; there was a sweet thrill at her heart, she had no desire to sleep, and when he returned home at daybreak, she tapped softly at her bedroom window, and showing him only her face and one shoulder through the curtain, she gave him a friendly smile. . . .

He proposed to her, and they were married. And when he had a closer view of her neck and her plump, fine shoulders, he threw up his hands, and said:

'You darling!'

He was happy, but as it rained on the day and night of his wedding, his face still retained an expression of despair.

They got on very well together. She used to sit in his office, to look after things in the Tivoli, to put down the accounts and pay the wages. And her rosy cheeks, her sweet, naïve, radiant smile, were to be seen now at the office window, now in the refreshment bar or behind the scenes at the theatre. And already she used to say to her acquaintances that the theatre was the chief and most important thing in life, and that it was only through the drama that one could derive true enjoyment and become cultivated and humane.

'But do you suppose the public understands that?' she used to say. 'What they want is a clown. Yesterday we gave "Faust Inside Out", and almost all the boxes were empty; but if Vanitchka and I had been producing some vulgar thing, I assure you the theatre would have been packed. To-morrow Vanitchka and I are doing "Orpheus in Hell." Do come.'

And what Kukin said about the theatre and the actors she repeated. Like him she despised the public for their ignorance and their indifference to art; she took part in the rehearsals, she corrected the actors, she kept an eye on the behaviour of the musicians, and when there was an unfavourable notice in the local paper, she shed tears, and then went to the editor's office to set things right.

The actors were fond of her and used to call her 'Vanitchka and I', and 'the darling'; she was sorry for them and used to lend them small sums of money, and if they deceived her, she used to shed a few tears in private, but did not complain to her husband.

They got on well in the winter too. They took the theatre in the town for the whole winter, and let it for short terms to a Little Russian company, or to a conjurer, or to a local dramatic society. Olenka grew stouter, and was always beaming with satisfaction, while Kukin grew thinner and yellower, and continually complained of their terrible losses, although he had not done badly all the winter. He used to cough at night, and she used to give him hot raspberry tea or lime-flower water, to rub him with eau-de-Cologne and to wrap him in her warm shawls.

'You're such a sweet pet!' she used to say with perfect sincerity, stroking his hair. 'You're such a pretty dear!'

Towards Lent he went to Moscow to collect a new troupe, and without him she could not sleep, but sat all night at her window, looking at the stars, and she compared herself with the hens, who are awake all night and uneasy when the cock is not in the hen-house. Kukin was detained in Moscow, and wrote that he would be back at Easter, adding some instructions about the Tivoli. But on the Sunday before Easter, late in the evening, came a sudden ominous knock at the gate; someone was hammering on the gate as though on a barrel – boom, boom, boom! The drowsy cook went flopping with her bare feet through the puddles, as she ran to open the gate.

'Please open,' said someone outside in a thick bass. 'There is a telegram for you.'

Olenka had received telegrams from her husband before, but this time for some reason she felt numb with terror. With shaking hands she opened the telegram and read as follows:

'Ivan Petrovitch died suddenly to-day. Awaiting immate instructions fufuneral Tuesday.'

That was how it was written in the telegram – 'fufuneral', and the utterly incomprehensible word 'immate'. It was signed by the stage manager of the operatic company.

'My darling!' sobbed Olenka. 'Vanitchka, my precious, my darling! Why did I ever meet you! Why did I know you and love you! Your poor heart-broken Olenka is all alone without you!'

Kukin's funeral took place on Tuesday in Moscow, Olenka returned home on Wednesday, and as soon as she got indoors she threw herself on her bed and sobbed so loudly that it could be heard next door, and in the street.

'Poor darling!' the neighbours said, as they crossed themselves. 'Olga Semyonovna, poor darling! How she does take on!'

Three months later Olenka was coming home from mass, melancholy and in deep mourning. It happened that one of her neighbours, Vassily Andreitch Pustovalov, returning home from church, walked back beside her. He was the manager at Babakayev's, the timber merchant's. He wore a straw hat, a white waistcoat, and a gold watch-chain, and looked more like a country gentleman than a man in trade.

'Everything happens as it is ordained, Olga Semyonovna,' he said gravely, with a sympathetic note in his voice; 'and if any of our dear ones die, it must be because it is the will of God, so we ought to have fortitude and bear it submissively.'

After seeing Olenka to her gate, he said good-bye and went on. All day afterwards she heard his sedately dignified voice, and whenever she shut her eyes she saw his dark beard. She liked him very much. And apparently she had made an impression on him too, for not long afterwards an elderly lady, with whom she was only slightly acquainted, came to drink coffee with her, and as soon as she was seated at table began to talk about Pustovalov, saying that he was an excellent man whom one could thoroughly depend upon, and that any girl would be glad to marry him. Three days later Pustovalov came himself. He did not stay long, only about ten minutes, and he did not say much, but when he left, Olenka loved him – loved him so much that she lay awake all night in a perfect fever, and in the morning she sent for the elderly lady. The match was quickly arranged, and then came the wedding.

Pustovalov and Olenka got on very well together when they were married.

Usually he sat in the office till dinner-time, then he went out on business, while Olenka took his place, and sat in the office till evening, making up accounts and booking orders.

'Timber gets dearer every year; the price rises twenty per cent.,' she would say to her customers and friends. 'Only fancy we used to sell local timber, and now Vassitchka always has to go for wood to the Mogilev district. And the freight!' she would add, covering her cheeks with her hands in horror. 'The freight!'

It seemed to her that she had been in the timber trade for ages and ages, and that the most important and necessary thing in life was timber; and there was something intimate and touching to her in the very sound of words such as 'baulk', 'post', 'beam', 'pole', 'scantling', 'batten', 'lath', 'plank', etc.

At night when she was asleep she dreamed of perfect mountains of planks and boards, and long strings of waggons, carting timber somewhere far away. She dreamed that a whole regiment of six-inch beams forty feet high, standing on end, was marching upon the timber-yard; that logs, beams, and boards knocked together with the resounding crash of dry wood, kept falling and getting up again, piling themselves on each other. Olenka cried out in her sleep, and Pustovalov said to her tenderly: 'Olenka, what's the matter, darling? Cross yourself!'

Her husband's ideas were hers. If he thought the room was too hot, or that business was slack, she thought the same. Her husband did not care for entertainments, and on holidays he stayed at home. She did likewise.

'You are always at home or in the office,' her friends said to her. 'You should go to the theatre, darling, or to the circus.'

'Vassitchka and I have no time to go to theatres,' she would answer sedately. 'We have no time for nonsense. What's the use of these theatres?'

On Saturdays Pustovalov and she used to go to the evening service; on holidays to early mass, and they walked side by side with softened faces as they came home from church. There was a pleasant fragrance about them both, and her silk dress rustled agreeably. At home they drank tea, with fancy bread and jams of various kinds, and afterwards they ate pie. Every day at twelve o'clock there was a savoury smell of beetroot soup and of mutton or duck in their yard, and on fast-days of fish, and no one could pass the gate without feeling hungry. In the office the samovar was always boiling, and customers were regaled with tea and cracknels. Once a week the couple went to the baths and returned side by side, both red in the face.

'Yes, we have nothing to complain of, thank God,'

Olenka used to say to her acquaintances. 'I wish everyone were as well off as Vassitchka and I.'

When Pustovalov went away to buy wood in the Mogilev district, she missed him dreadfully, lay awake and cried. A young veterinary surgeon in the army, called Smirnin, to whom they had let their lodge, used sometimes to come in in the evening. He used to talk to her and play cards with her, and this entertained her in her husband's absence. She was particularly interested in what he told her of his home life. He was married and had a little boy, but was separated from his wife because she had been unfaithful to him, and now he hated her and used to send her forty roubles a month for the maintenance of their son. And hearing of all this, Olenka sighed and shook her head. She was sorry for him.

'Well, God keep you,' she used to say to him at parting, as she lighted him down the stairs with a candle. 'Thank you for coming to cheer me up, and may the Mother of God give you health.'

And she always expressed herself with the same sedateness and dignity, the same reasonableness, in imitation of her husband. As the veterinary surgeon was disappearing behind the door below, she would say:

'You know, Vladimir Platonitch, you'd better make it up with your wife. You should forgive her for the sake of your son. You may be sure the little fellow understands.'

And when Pustovalov came back, she told him in a low voice about the veterinary surgeon and his unhappy home life, and both sighed and shook their heads and talked about the boy, who, no doubt, missed his father, and by some strange connection of ideas, they went up to the holy ikons, bowed to the ground before them and prayed that God would give them children.

And so the Pustovalovs lived for six years quietly and peaceably in love and complete harmony.

But behold! one winter day after drinking hot tea in the office, Vassily Andreitch went out into the yard without his cap on to see about sending off some timber, caught cold and was taken ill. He had the best doctors, but he grew worse and died after four months' illness. And Olenka was a widow once more.

'I've nobody, now you've left me, my darling,' she sobbed, after her husband's funeral. 'How can I live without you, in wretchedness and misery! Pity me, good people, all alone in the world!'

She went about dressed in black with long 'weepers', and gave up wearing hat and gloves for good. She hardly ever went out, except to church, or to her husband's grave, and led the life of a nun. It was not till six months later that she took off the weepers and opened the shutters of the windows. She was sometimes seen in the mornings, going with her cook to market for provisions, but what went on in her house and how she lived now could only be surmised. People guessed, from seeing her drinking tea in her garden with the veterinary surgeon, who read the newspaper aloud to her, and from the fact that, meeting a lady she knew at the post-office, she said to her:

'There is no proper veterinary inspection in our town, and that's the cause of all sorts of epidemics.

One is always hearing of people's getting infection from the milk supply, or catching diseases from horses and cows. The health of domestic animals ought to be as well cared for as the health of human beings.'

She repeated the veterinary surgeon's words, and was of the same opinion as he about everything. It was evident that she could not live a year without some attachment, and had found new happiness in the lodge. In anyone else this would have been censured, but no one could think ill of Olenka; everything she did was so natural. Neither she nor the veterinary surgeon said anything to other people of the change in their relations, and tried, indeed, to conceal it, but without success, for Olenka could not keep a secret. When he had visitors, men serving in his regiment, and she poured out tea or served the supper, she would begin talking of the cattle plague, of the foot and mouth disease, and of the municipal slaughter-houses. He was dreadfully embarrassed, and when the guests had gone, he would seize her by the hand and hiss angrily:

'I've asked you before not to talk about what you don't understand. When we veterinary surgeons are talking among ourselves, please don't put your word in. It's really annoying.'

And she would look at him with astonishment and dismay, and ask him in alarm: 'But, Voloditchka, what *am* I to talk about?'

And with tears in her eyes she would embrace him, begging him not to be angry, and they were both happy.

But this happiness did not last long. The veterinary surgeon departed, departed for ever with his regiment, when it was transferred to a distant place – to Siberia, it may be. And Olenka was left alone.

Now she was absolutely alone. Her father had long been dead, and his arm-chair lay in the attic, covered with dust and lame of one leg. She got thinner and plainer, and when people met her in the street they did not look at her as they used to, and did not smile to her; evidently her best years were over and left behind, and now a new sort of life had begun for her, which did not bear thinking about. In the evening Olenka sat in the porch, and heard the band playing and the fireworks popping in the Tivoli, but now the sound stirred no response. She looked into her yard without interest, thought of nothing, wished for nothing, and afterwards, when night came on she went to bed and dreamed of her empty yard. She ate and drank as it were unwillingly.

And what was worst of all, she had no opinions of any sort. She saw the objects about her and understood what she saw, but could not form any opinion about them, and did not know what to talk about. And how awful it is not to have any opinions! One sees a bottle, for instance, or the rain, or a peasant driving in his cart, but what the bottle is for, or the rain, or the peasant, and what is the meaning of it, one can't say, and could not even for a thousand roubles. When she had Kukin, or Pustovalov, or the veterinary surgeon, Olenka could explain everything, and give her opinion about anything you like, but now there was the same emptiness in her brain and in her heart as there was in her yard outside. And it was as harsh and as bitter as wormwood in the mouth.

Little by little the town grew in all directions. The road became a street, and where the Tivoli and the timber-yard had been, there were new turnings and houses. How rapidly time passes! Olenka's house grew dingy, the roof got rusty, the shed sank on one side, and the whole yard was overgrown with docks and stinging-nettles. Olenka herself had grown plain and elderly; in summer she sat in the porch, and her soul, as before, was empty and dreary and full of bitterness. In winter she sat at her window and looked at the snow. When she caught the scent of spring, or heard the chime of the church bells, a sudden rush of memories from the past came over her, there was a tender ache in her heart, and her eyes brimmed over with tears; but this was only for a minute, and then came emptiness again and the sense of the futility of life. The black kitten, Briska, rubbed against her and purred softly, but Olenka was not touched by these feline caresses. That was not what she needed. She wanted a love that would absorb her whole being, her whole soul and reason – that would give her ideas and an object in life, and would warm her old blood. And she would shake the kitten off her skirt and say with vexation:

'Get along; I don't want you!'

And so it was, day after day and year after year, and no joy, and no opinions. Whatever Mavra, the cook, said she accepted.

One hot July day, towards evening, just as the cattle were being driven by, and the whole yard was full of dust, someone suddenly knocked at the gate. Olenka went to open it herself and was dumbfounded when she looked out: she saw Smirnin, the veterinary surgeon, grey-headed, and dressed as a civilian. She suddenly remembered everything. She could not help crying and letting her head fall on his breast without uttering a word, and in the violence of her feeling she did not notice how they both walked into the house and sat down to tea.

'My dear Vladimir Platonitch! What fate has brought you?' she muttered, trembling with joy.

'I want to settle here for good, Olga Semyonovna,' he told her. 'I have resigned my post, and have come to settle down and try my luck on my own account. Besides, it's time for my boy to go to school. He's a big boy. I am reconciled with my wife, you know.'

'Where is she?' asked Olenka.

'She's at the hotel with the boy, and I'm looking for lodgings.'

'Good gracious, my dear soul! Lodgings! Why not have my house? Why shouldn't that suit you? Why, my goodness, I wouldn't take any rent!' cried Olenka in a flutter, beginning to cry again. 'You live here, and the lodge will do nicely for me. Oh dear! how glad I am!'

Next day the roof was painted and the walls were whitewashed, and Olenka, with her arms akimbo, walked about the yard giving directions. Her face was beaming with her old smile, and she was brisk and alert as though she had waked from a long sleep. The veterinary's wife arrived – a thin, plain lady, with short hair and a peevish expression. With her was her little Sasha, a boy of ten, small for his age, blue-eyed, chubby, with dimples in his cheeks. And scarcely had the boy walked into the yard when he ran after the cat, and at once there was the sound of his gay, joyous laugh.

'Is that your puss, auntie?' he asked Olenka. 'When she has little ones, do give us a kitten. Mamma is awfully afraid of mice.'

Olenka talked to him, and gave him tea. Her heart warmed and there was a sweet ache in her bosom, as though the boy had been her own child. And when he sat at the table in the evening, going over his lessons, she looked at him with deep tenderness and pity as she murmured to herself:

'You pretty pet!...my precious!...Such a fair little thing, and so clever.'

'"An island is a piece of land which is entirely surrounded by water,"' he read aloud.

'An island is a piece of land,' she repeated, and this was the first opinion to which she gave utterance with positive conviction after so many years of silence and dearth of ideas.

Now she had opinions of her own, and at supper she talked to Sasha's parents, saying how difficult the lessons were at the high schools, but that yet the high school was better than a commercial one, since with a high school education all careers were open to one, such as being a doctor or an engineer.

Sasha began going to the high school. His mother departed to Harkov to her sister's and did not return; his father used to go off every day to inspect cattle, and would often be away from home for three days together, and it seemed to Olenka as though Sasha was entirely abandoned, that he was not wanted at home, that he was being starved, and she carried him off to her lodge and gave him a little room there.

And for six months Sasha had lived in the lodge with her. Every morning Olenka came into his bedroom and found him fast asleep, sleeping noiselessly with his hand under his cheek. She was sorry to wake him.

'Sashenka,' she would say mournfully, 'get up, darling. It's time for school.'

He would get up, dress and say his prayers, and then sit down to breakfast, drink three glasses of tea, and eat two large cracknels and half a buttered roll. All this time he was hardly awake and a little ill-humoured in consequence.

'You don't quite know your fable, Sashenka,' Olenka would say, looking at him as though he were about to set off on a long journey. 'What a lot of trouble I have with you! You must work and do your best, darling, and obey your teachers.'

'Oh, do leave me alone!' Sasha would say.

Then he would go down the street to school, a little figure, wearing a big cap and carrying a satchel on his shoulder. Olenka would follow him noiselessly.

'Sashenka!' she would call after him, and she would pop into his hand a date or a caramel. When he reached the street where the school was, he would feel ashamed of being followed by a tall, stout woman; he would turn round and say:

'You'd better go home, auntie. I can go the rest of the way alone.'

She would stand still and look after him fixedly till he had disappeared at the school-gate.

Ah, how she loved him! Of her former attachments not one had been so deep; never had her soul surrendered to any feeling so spontaneously, so disinterestedly, and so joyously as now that her maternal instincts were aroused. For this little boy with the dimple in his cheek and the big school cap, she would have given her whole life, she would have given it with joy and tears of tenderness. Why? Who can tell why?

When she had seen the last of Sasha, she returned home, contented and serene, brimming over with love; her face, which had grown younger during the last six months, smiled and beamed; people meeting her looked at her with pleasure.

'Good-morning, Olga Semyonovna, darling. How are you, darling?'

'The lessons at the high school are very difficult now,' she would relate at the market. 'It's too much; in the first class yesterday they gave him a fable to learn by heart, and a Latin translation and a problem. You know it's too much for a little chap.'

And she would begin talking about the teachers, the lessons, and the school books, saying just what Sasha said.

At three o'clock they had dinner together: in the evening they learned their lessons together and cried. When she put him to bed, she would stay a long time making the cross over him and murmuring a prayer; then she would go to bed and dream of that far-away misty future when Sasha would finish his studies and become a doctor or an engineer, would have a big house of his own with horses and a carriage, would get married and have children.... She would fall asleep still thinking of the same thing, and tears would run down her cheeks from her closed eyes, while the black cat lay purring beside her: 'Mrr, mrr, mrr.'

Suddenly there would come a loud knock at the gate.

Olenka would wake up breathless with alarm, her heart throbbing. Half a minute later would come another knock.

'It must be a telegram from Harkov,' she would think, beginning to tremble from head to foot. 'Sasha's mother is sending for him from Harkov.... Oh, mercy on us!'

She was in despair. Her head, her hands, and her feet would turn chill, and she would feel that she was the most unhappy woman in the world. But another minute would pass, voices would be heard: it would turn out to be the veterinary surgeon coming home from the club.

'Well, thank God!' she would think.

And gradually the load in her heart would pass off, and she would feel at ease. She would go back to bed thinking of Sasha, who lay sound asleep in the next room, sometimes crying out in his sleep:

'I'll give it you! Get away! Shut up!'

THE LADY WITH THE DOG

THE LADY WITH THE DOG

I

IT was said that a new person had appeared on the sea-front: a lady with a little dog. Dmitri Dmitritch Gurov, who had by then been a fortnight at Yalta, and so was fairly at home there, had begun to take an interest in new arrivals. Sitting in Verney's pavilion, he saw, walking on the sea-front, a fair-haired young lady of medium height, wearing a *béret*; a white Pomeranian dog was running behind her.

And afterwards he met her in the public gardens and in the square several times a day. She was walking alone, always wearing the same *béret*, and always with the same white dog; no one knew who she was, and everyone called her simply 'the lady with the dog'.

'If she is here alone without a husband or friends, it wouldn't be amiss to make her acquaintance,' Gurov reflected.

He was under forty, but he had a daughter already twelve years old, and two sons at school. He had been married young, when he was a student in his second year, and by now his wife seemed half as old again as he. She was a tall, erect woman with dark eyebrows, staid and dignified, and, as she said of herself, intellectual. She read a great deal, used phonetic spelling, called her husband, not Dmitri, but Dimitri, and he secretly considered her unintelligent, narrow, inelegant, was afraid of her, and did not like to be at home. He had begun being unfaithful to her long ago – had been unfaithful to her often, and, probably on that account, almost always spoke ill of women, and when they were talked about in his presence, used to call them 'the lower race'.

It seemed to him that he had been so schooled by bitter experience that he might call them what he liked, and yet he could not get on for two days together without 'the lower race'. In the society of men he was bored and not himself, with them he was cold and uncommunicative; but when he was in the company of women he felt free, and knew what to say to them and how to behave; and he was at ease with them even when he was silent. In his appearance, in his character, in his whole nature, there was something attractive and elusive which allured women and disposed them in his favour; he knew that, and some force seemed to draw him, too, to them.

Experience often repeated, truly bitter experience, had taught him long ago that with decent people, especially Moscow people – always slow to move and irresolute – every intimacy, which at first so agreeably diversifies life and appears a light and charming adventure, inevitably grows into a regular problem of extreme intricacy, and in the long run the situation becomes unbearable. But at every fresh meeting with an interesting woman this experience seemed to slip out of his memory, and he was eager for life, and everything seemed simple and amusing.

One evening he was dining in the gardens, and the lady in the *béret* came up slowly to take the next table. Her expression, her gait, her dress, and the way she did her hair told him that she was a lady, that she was married, that she was in Yalta for the first time and alone, and that she was dull there. . . . The stories told of the immorality in such places as Yalta are to a great extent untrue; he despised them, and knew that such stories were for the most part made up by persons who would themselves have been glad to sin if they had been able; but when the lady sat down at the next table three paces from him, he remembered these tales of easy conquests, of trips to the mountains, and the tempting thought of a swift, fleeting love affair, a romance with an unknown woman, whose name he did not know, suddenly took possession of him.

He beckoned coaxingly to the Pomeranian, and when the dog came up to him he shook his finger at it. The Pomeranian growled: Gurov shook his finger at it again.

The lady looked at him and at once dropped her eyes.

'He doesn't bite,' she said, and blushed.

'May I give him a bone?' he asked; and when she nodded he asked courteously, 'Have you been long in Yalta?'

'Five days.'

'And I have already dragged out a fortnight here.'

There was a brief silence.

'Time goes fast, and yet it is so dull here!' she said, not looking at him.

'That's only the fashion to say it is dull here. A provincial will live in Belyov or Zhidra and not be dull, and when he comes here it's 'Oh, the dulness! Oh, the dust!' One would think he came from Grenada.'

She laughed. Then both continued eating in silence, like strangers, but after dinner they walked side by side; and there sprang up between them the light jesting conversation of people who are free and satisfied, to whom it does not matter where they go or what they talk about. They walked and talked of the strange light on the sea: the water was of a soft warm lilac hue, and there was a golden streak from the moon upon it. They talked of how sultry it was after a hot day. Gurov told her that he came from Moscow, that he had taken his degree in Arts, but had a post in a bank; that he had trained as an opera-singer, but had given it up, that he owned two houses in Moscow. ... And from her he learnt that she had grown up in Petersburg, but had lived in S— since her marriage two years before, that she was staying another month in Yalta, and that her husband, who needed a holiday too, might perhaps come and fetch her. She was not sure whether her husband had a post in a Crown Department or under the Provincial Council – and was amused by her own ignorance. And Gurov learnt, too, that she was called Anna Sergeyevna.

Afterwards he thought about her in his room at the hotel – thought she would certainly meet him next day; it would be sure to happen. As he got into bed he thought how lately she had been a girl at school, doing lessons like his own daughter; he recalled the diffidence, the angularity, that was still manifest in her laugh and her manner of talking with a stranger. This must have been the first time in her life she had been alone in surroundings in which she was followed, looked at, and spoken to merely from a secret motive which she could hardly fail to guess. He recalled her slender, delicate neck, her lovely grey eyes.

'There's something pathetic about her, anyway,' he thought, and fell asleep.

II

A WEEK had passed since they had made acquaintance. It was a holiday. It was sultry indoors, while in the street the wind whirled the dust round and round, and blew people's hats off. It was a thirsty day, and Gurov often went into the pavilion, and pressed Anna Sergeyevna to have syrup and water or an ice. One did not know what to do with oneself.

In the evening when the wind had dropped a little, they went out on to the groyne to see the steamer come in. There were a great many people walking about the harbour; they had gathered to welcome someone, bringing bouquets. And two peculiarities of a well-dressed Yalta crowd were very conspicuous: the elderly ladies were dressed like young ones, and there were great numbers of generals.

Owing to the roughness of the sea, the steamer arrived late, after the sun had set, and it was a long time turning about before it reached the groyne. Anna Sergeyevna looked through her lorgnette at the steamer and the passengers as though looking for acquaintances, and when she turned to Gurov her eyes were shining. She talked a great deal and asked disconnected questions, forgetting next moment what she had asked; then she dropped her lorgnette in the crush.

The festive crowd began to disperse; it was too dark to see people's faces. The wind had completely dropped, but Gurov and Anna Sergeyevna still stood as though waiting to see someone else come from the steamer. Anna Sergeyevna was silent now, and sniffed the flowers without looking at Gurov.

'The weather is better this evening,' he said. 'Where shall we go now? Shall we drive somewhere?'

She made no answer.

Then he looked at her intently, and all at once put his arm round her and kissed her on the lips, and breathed in the moisture and the fragrance of the flowers; and he immediately looked round him, anxiously wondering whether anyone had seen them.

'Let us go to your hotel,' he said softly. And both walked quickly.

The room was close and smelt of the scent she had bought at the Japanese shop. Gurov looked at her and thought: 'What different people one meets in the world!' From the past he preserved memories of careless, good-natured women, who loved cheerfully and were grateful to him for the happiness he gave them, however brief it might be; and of women like his wife who loved without any genuine feeling, with superfluous phrases, affectedly, hysterically, with an expression that suggested that it was not love nor passion, but something more significant; and of two or three others, very beautiful, cold women, on whose faces he had caught a glimpse of a rapacious expression – an obstinate desire to snatch from life more than it could give, and these were capricious, unreflecting, domineering, unintelligent women not in their first youth, and when Gurov grew cold to them their beauty excited his hatred, and the lace on their linen seemed to him like scales.

But in this case there was still the diffidence, the angularity of inexperienced youth, an awkward feeling; and there was a sense of consternation as though someone had suddenly knocked at the door. The attitude of Anna Sergeyevna – 'the lady with the dog' – to what had happened was somehow peculiar, very grave, as though it were her fall – so it seemed, and it was strange and inappropriate. Her face dropped and faded, and on both sides of it her long hair hung down mournfully; she mused in a dejected attitude like 'the woman who was a sinner' in an old-fashioned picture.

'It's wrong,' she said. 'You will be the first to despise me now.'

There was a water-melon on the table. Gurov cut himself a slice and began eating it without haste. There followed at least half an hour of silence.

Anna Sergeyevna was touching; there was about her the purity of a good, simple woman who had seen little of life. The solitary candle burning on the table threw a faint light on her face, yet it was clear that she was very unhappy.

'How could I despise you?' asked Gurov. 'You don't know what you are saying.'

'God forgive me,' she said, and her eyes filled with tears. 'It's awful.'

'You seem to feel you need to be forgiven.'

'Forgiven? No. I am a bad, low woman; I despise myself and don't attempt to justify myself. It's not my husband but myself I have deceived. And not only just now; I have been deceiving myself for a long time. My husband may be a good, honest man, but he is a flunkey! I don't know what he does there, what his work is, but I know he is a flunkey! I was twenty when I was married to him. I have been tormented by curiosity; I wanted something better. "There must be a different sort of life," I said to myself. I wanted to live! To live, to live!...I was fired by curiosity...you don't understand it, but, I swear to God, I could not control myself; something happened to me: I could not be restrained. I told my husband I was ill, and came here....And here I have been walking about as though I were dazed, like a mad creature;...and now I have become a vulgar, contemptible woman whom anyone may despise.'

Gurov felt bored already, listening to her. He was irritated by the naïve tone, by this remorse, so unexpected and inopportune; but for the tears in her eyes, he might have thought she was jesting or playing a part.

'I don't understand,' he said softly. 'What is it you want?'

She hid her face on his breast and pressed close to him.

'Believe me, believe me, I beseech you...' she said. 'I love a pure, honest life, and sin is loathsome to me. I don't know what I am doing. Simple people say:

"The Evil One has beguiled me." And I may say of myself now that the Evil One has beguiled me.'

'Hush, hush!...' he muttered.

He looked at her fixed, scared eyes, kissed her, talked softly and affectionately, and by degrees she was comforted, and her gaiety returned; they both began laughing.

Afterwards when they went out there was not a soul on the sea-front. The town with its cypresses had quite a deathlike air, but the sea still broke noisily on the shore; a single barge was rocking on the waves, and a lantern was blinking sleepily on it.

They found a cab and drove to Oreanda.

'I found out your surname in the hall just now: it was written on the board – Von Diderits,' said Gurov. 'Is your husband a German?'

'No; I believe his grandfather was a German but he is an Orthodox Russian himself.'

At Oreanda they sat on a seat not far from the church, looked down at the sea, and were silent. Yalta was hardly visible through the morning mist; white clouds stood motionless on the mountain-tops. The leaves did not stir on the trees, grasshoppers chirruped, and the monotonous hollow sound of the sea, rising up from below, spoke of the peace, of the eternal sleep awaiting us. So it must have sounded when there was no Yalta, no Oreanda here; so it sounds now, and it will sound as indifferently and monotonously when we are all no more. And in this constancy, in this complete indifference to the life and death of each of us, there lies hid, perhaps, a pledge of our eternal salvation, of the unceasing movement of life upon earth, of unceasing progress towards perfection. Sitting beside a young woman who in the dawn seemed so lovely, soothed and spellbound in these magical surroundings – the sea, mountains, clouds, the open sky – Gurov thought how in reality everything is beautiful in this world when one reflects: everything except what we think or do ourselves when we forget our human dignity and the higher aims of our existence.

A man walked up to them – probably a keeper – looked at them and walked away. And this detail seemed mysterious and beautiful, too. They saw a steamer come from Theodosia, with its lights out in the glow of dawn.

'There is dew on the grass,' said Anna Sergeyevna, after a silence.

'Yes. It's time to go home.'

They went back to the town.

Then they met every day at twelve o'clock on the sea-front, lunched and dined together, went for walks, admired the sea. She complained that she slept badly, that her heart throbbed violently; asked the same questions, troubled now by jealousy and now by the fear that he did not respect her sufficiently. And often in the square or gardens, when there was no one near them, he suddenly drew her to him and kissed her passionately. Complete idleness, these kisses in broad daylight while he looked round in dread of someone's seeing them, the heat, the smell of the sea, and the continual passing to and fro before him of idle, well-dressed, well-fed people, made a new man of him; he told Anna Sergeyevna how beautiful she was, how fascinating. He was impatiently passionate, he would not move a step away from her, while she was often pensive and continually urged him to confess that he did not respect her, did not love her in the least, and thought of her as nothing but a common woman. Rather late almost every evening they drove somewhere out of town, to Oreanda or to the waterfall; and the expedition was always a success, the scenery invariably impressed them as grand and beautiful.

They were expecting her husband to come, but a letter came from him, saying that there was something wrong with his eyes, and he entreated his wife to come home as quickly as possible. Anna Sergeyevna made haste to go.

'It's a good thing I am going away,' she said to Gurov. 'It's the finger of destiny!'

She went by coach and he went with her. They were driving the whole day. When she had got into a compartment of the express, and when the second bell had rung, she said:

'Let me look at you once more... look at you once again. That's right.'

She did not shed tears, but was so sad that she seemed ill, and her face was quivering.

'I shall remember you... think of you,' she said. 'God be with you; be happy. Don't remember evil against me. We are parting for ever – it must be so, for we ought never to have met. Well, God be with you.'

The train moved off rapidly, its lights soon vanished from sight, and a minute later there was no sound of it, as though everything had conspired together to end as quickly as possible that sweet delirium, that madness. Left alone on the platform, and gazing into the dark distance, Gurov listened to the chirrup of the grasshoppers and the hum of the telegraph wires, feeling as though he had only just waked up. And he thought, musing, that there had been another episode or adventure in his life, and it, too, was at an end, and nothing was left of it but a memory.... He was moved, sad, and conscious of a slight remorse. This young woman whom he would never meet again had not been happy with him; he was genuinely warm and affectionate with her, but yet in his manner, his tone, and his caresses there had been a shade of light irony, the coarse condescension of a happy man who was, besides, almost twice her age. All the time she had called him kind, exceptional, lofty; obviously he had seemed to her different from what he really was, so he had unintentionally deceived her....

Here at the station was already a scent of autumn; it was a cold evening.

'It's time for me to go north,' thought Gurov as he left the platform. 'High time!'

III

AT home in Moscow everything was in its winter routine; the stoves were heated, and in the morning it was still dark when the children were having breakfast and getting ready for school, and the nurse would light the lamp for a short time. The frosts had begun already. When the first snow has fallen, on the first day of sledge-driving it is pleasant to see the white earth, the white roofs, to draw soft, delicious breath, and the season brings back the days of one's youth. The old limes and birches, white with hoar-frost, have a good-natured expression; they are nearer to one's heart than cypresses and palms, and near them one doesn't want to be thinking of the sea and the mountains.

Gurov was Moscow born; he arrived in Moscow on a fine frosty day, and when he put on his fur coat and warm gloves, and walked along Petrovka, and when on Saturday evening he heard the ringing of the bells, his recent trip and the places he had seen lost all charm for him. Little by little he became absorbed in Moscow life, greedily read three newspapers a day, and declared he did not read the Moscow papers on principle! He already felt a longing to go to restaurants, clubs, dinner-parties, anniversary celebrations, and he felt flattered at entertaining distinguished lawyers and artists, and at playing cards with a professor at the doctor's club. He could already eat a whole plateful of salt fish and cabbage....

In another month, he fancied, the image of Anna Sergeyevna would be shrouded in a mist in his memory, and only from time to time would visit him in his dreams with a touching smile as others did. But more than a month passed, real winter had come, and everything was still clear in his memory as though he had parted with Anna Sergeyevna only the day before. And his memories glowed more and more vividly. When in the evening stillness he heard from his study the voices of his children, preparing their lessons, or when he listened to a song or the organ at the restaurant, or the storm howled in the chimney, suddenly everything would rise up in his memory: what had happened on the groyne, and the early morning with the mist on the mountains, and the steamer coming from Theodosia, and the kisses. He would pace a long time about his room, remembering it all and smiling; then his memories passed into dreams, and in his fancy the past was mingled with what was to come. Anna Sergeyevna did not visit him in dreams, but followed him about everywhere like a shadow and haunted him. When he shut his eyes he saw her as though she were living before him, and she seemed to him lovelier, younger, tenderer than she was; and he imagined himself finer than he had been in Yalta. In the evenings she peeped out at him from the bookcase, from the fireplace, from the corner – he heard her breathing, the caressing rustle of her dress. In the street he watched the women, looking for someone like her.

He was tormented by an intense desire to confide his memories to someone. But in his home it was impossible to talk of his love, and he had no one outside; he could not talk to his tenants nor to anyone at the bank. And what had he to talk of? Had he been in love, then? Had there been anything beautiful, poetical, or edifying or simply interesting in his relations with Anna Sergeyevna? And there was nothing for him but to talk vaguely of love, of woman, and no one guessed what it meant; only his wife twitched her black eyebrows, and said: 'The part of a lady-killer does not suit you at all, Dimitri.'

One evening, coming out of the doctors' club with an official with whom he had been playing cards, he could not resist saying:

'If only you knew what a fascinating woman I made the acquaintance of in Yalta!'

The official got into his sledge and was driving away, but turned suddenly and shouted:

'Dmitri Dmitritch!'

'What?'

'You were right this evening: the sturgeon was a bit too strong!'

These words, so ordinary, for some reason moved Gurov to indignation, and struck him as degrading and unclean. What savage manners, what people! What senseless nights, what uninteresting, uneventful days! The rage for card-playing, the gluttony, the drunkenness, the continual talk always about the same thing. Useless pursuits and conversations always about the same things absorb the better part of one's time, the better part of one's strength, and in the end there is left a life grovelling and curtailed, worthless and trivial, and there is no escaping or getting away from it – just as though one were in a madhouse or a prison.

Gurov did not sleep all night, and was filled with indignation. And he had a headache all next day. And the next night he slept badly; he sat up in bed, thinking, or paced up and down his room. He was sick of his children, sick of the bank; he had no desire to go anywhere or to talk of anything.

In the holidays in December he prepared for a journey, and told his wife he was going to Petersburg to do something in the interests of a young friend – and he set off for S—. What for? He did not very well know himself. He wanted to see Anna Sergeyevna and to talk with her – to arrange a meeting, if possible.

He reached S— in the morning, and took the best room at the hotel, in which the floor was covered with grey army cloth, and on the table was an inkstand, grey with dust and adorned with a figure on horseback, with its hat in its hand and its head broken off. The hotel porter gave him the necessary information; Von Diderits lived in a house of his own in Old Gontcharny Street – it was not far from the hotel: he was rich and lived in good style, and had his own horses; everyone in the town knew him. The porter pronounced the name 'Dridirits'.

Gurov went without haste to Old Gontcharny Street and found the house. Just opposite the house stretched a long grey fence adorned with nails.

'One would run away from a fence like that,' thought Gurov, looking from the fence to the windows of the house and back again.

He considered: to-day was a holiday, and the husband would probably be at home. And in any case it would be tactless to go into the house and upset her. If he were to send her a note it might fall into her husband's hands, and then it might ruin everything. The best thing was to trust to chance. And he kept walking up and down the street by the fence, waiting for the chance. He saw a beggar go in at the gate and dogs fly at him; then an hour later he heard a piano, and the sounds were faint and indistinct. Probably it was Anna Sergeyevna playing. The front door suddenly opened, and an old woman came out, followed by the familiar white Pomeranian. Gurov was on the point of calling to the dog, but his heart began beating violently, and in his excitement he could not remember the dog's name.

He walked up and down, and loathed the grey fence more and more, and by now he thought irritably that Anna Sergeyevna had forgotten him, and was perhaps already amusing herself with someone else, and that that was very natural in a young woman who had nothing to look at from morning till night but that confounded fence. He went back to his hotel room and sat for a long while on the sofa, not knowing what to do, then he had dinner and a long nap.

'How stupid and worrying it is!' he thought when he woke and looked at the dark windows: it was already evening. 'Here I've had a good sleep for some reason. What shall I do in the night?'

He sat on the bed, which was covered by a cheap grey blanket, such as one sees in hospitals, and he taunted himself in his vexation:

'So much for the lady with the dog... so much for the adventure.... You're in a nice fix....'

That morning at the station a poster in large letters had caught his eye. 'The Geisha' was to be performed for the first time. He thought of this and went to the theatre.

'It's quite possible she may go to the first performance,' he thought.

The theatre was full. As in all provincial theatres, there was a fog above the chandelier, the gallery was noisy and restless; in the front row the local dandies were standing up before the beginning of the performance, with their hands behind them; in the Governor's box the Governor's daughter, wearing a boa, was sitting in the front seat, while the Governor himself lurked modestly behind the curtain with only his hands visible; the orchestra was a long time tuning up; the stage curtain swayed. All the time the audience were coming in and taking their seats Gurov looked at them eagerly.

Anna Sergeyevna, too, came in. She sat down in the third row, and when Gurov looked at her his heart contracted, and he understood clearly that for him there was in the whole world no creature so near, so precious, and so important to him; she, this little woman, in no way remarkable, lost in a provincial crowd, with a vulgar lorgnette in her hand, filled his whole life now, was his sorrow and his joy, the one happiness that he now desired for himself, and to the sounds of the inferior orchestra, of the wretched provincial violins, he thought how lovely she was. He thought and dreamed.

A young man with small side-whiskers, tall and stooping, came in with Anna Sergeyevna and sat down beside her; he bent his head at every step and seemed to be continually bowing. Most likely this was the husband whom at Yalta, in a rush of bitter feeling, she had called a flunkey. And there really was in his long figure, his side-whiskers, and the small bald patch on his head, something of the flunkey's obsequiousness; his smile was sugary, and in his buttonhole there was some badge of distinction like the number on a waiter.

During the first interval the husband went away to smoke; she remained alone in her stall. Gurov, who was sitting in the stalls, too, went up to her and said in a trembling voice, with a forced smile:

'Good-evening.'

She glanced at him and turned pale, then glanced again with horror, unable to believe her eyes, and tightly gripped the fan and the lorgnette in her hands, evidently struggling with herself not to faint. Both were silent. She was sitting, he was standing, frightened by her confusion and not venturing to sit down beside her. The violins and the flute began tuning up. He felt suddenly frightened; it seemed as though all the people in the boxes were looking at them. She got up and went quickly to the door; he followed her, and both walked senselessly along passages, and up and down stairs, and figures in legal, scholastic, and civil service uniforms, all wearing badges, flitted before their eyes. They caught glimpses of ladies, of fur coats hanging on pegs; the draughts blew on them, bringing a smell of stale tobacco. And Gurov, whose heart was beating violently, thought:

'Oh, heavens! Why are these people here and this orchestra!...'

And at that instant he recalled how when he had seen Anna Sergeyevna off at the station he had thought that everything was over and they would never meet again. But how far they were still from the end!

On the narrow, gloomy staircase over which was written 'To the Amphitheatre', she stopped.

'How you have frightened me!' she said, breathing hard, still pale and overwhelmed. 'Oh, how you have frightened me! I am half dead. Why have you come? Why?'

'But do understand, Anna, do understand...' he said hastily in a low voice. 'I entreat you to understand....'

She looked at him with dread, with entreaty, with love; she looked at him intently, to keep his features more distinctly in her memory.

'I am so unhappy,' she went on, not heeding him. 'I have thought of nothing but you all the time; I live only in the thought of you. And I wanted to forget, to forget you; but why, oh why, have you come?'

On the landing above them two schoolboys were smoking and looking down, but that was nothing to Gurov; he drew Anna Sergeyevna to him, and began kissing her face, her cheeks, and her hands.

'What are you doing, what are you doing!' she cried in horror, pushing him away. 'We are mad. Go away to-day; go away at once.... I beseech you by all that is sacred, I implore you.... There are people coming this way!'

Someone was coming up the stairs.

'You must go away,' Anna Sergeyevna went on in a whisper. 'Do you hear, Dmitri Dmitritch? I will come and see you in Moscow. I have never been happy; I am miserable now, and I never, never shall be happy, never! Don't make me suffer still more! I swear I'll come to Moscow. But now let us part. My precious, good, dear one, we must part!'

She pressed his hand and began rapidly going downstairs, looking round at him, and from her eyes he could see that she really was unhappy. Gurov stood for a little while, listened, then, when all sound had died away, he found his coat and left the theatre.

IV

AND Anna Sergeyevna began coming to see him in Moscow. Once in two or three months she left S—, telling her husband that she was going to consult a doctor about an internal complaint – and her husband believed her, and did not believe her. In Moscow she stayed at the Slaviansky Bazaar hotel, and at once sent a man in a red cap to Gurov. Gurov went to see her, and no one in Moscow knew of it.

Once he was going to see her in this way on a winter morning (the messenger had come the evening before when he was out). With him walked his daughter, whom he wanted to take to school: it was on the way. Snow was falling in big wet flakes.

'It's three degrees above freezing-point, and yet it is snowing,' said Gurov to his daughter. 'The thaw is only on the surface of the earth; there is quite a different temperature at a greater height in the atmosphere.'

'And why are there no thunderstorms in the winter, father?'

He explained that, too. He talked, thinking all the while that he was going to see *her*, and no living soul knew of it, and probably never would know. He had two lives: one open, seen and known by all who cared to know, full of relative truth and of relative falsehood, exactly like the lives of his friends and acquaintances; and another life running its course in secret. And through some strange, perhaps accidental, conjunction of circumstances, everything that was essential, of interest and of value to him, everything in which he was sincere and did not deceive himself, everything that made the kernel of his life, was hidden from other people; and all that was false in him, the sheath in which he hid himself to conceal the truth – such, for instance, as his work in the bank, his discussions at the club, his 'lower race', his presence with his wife at anniversary festivities – all that was open. And he judged of others by himself, not believing in what he saw, and always believing that every man had his real, most interesting life under the cover of secrecy and under the cover of night. All personal life rested on secrecy, and possibly it was partly on that account that civilized man was so nervously anxious that personal privacy should be respected.

After leaving his daughter at school, Gurov went on to the Slaviansky Bazaar. He took off his fur coat below, went upstairs, and softly knocked at the door. Anna Sergeyevna, wearing his favourite grey dress, exhausted by the journey and the suspense, had been expecting him since the evening before. She was pale; she looked at him, and did not smile, and he had hardly come in when she fell on his breast. Their kiss was slow and prolonged, as though they had not met for two years.

'Well, how are you getting on there?' he asked. 'What news?'

'Wait; I'll tell you directly. . . . I can't talk.'

She could not speak; she was crying. She turned away from him, and pressed her handkerchief to her eyes.

'Let her have her cry out. I'll sit down and wait,' he thought, and he sat down in an arm-chair.

Then he rang and asked for tea to be brought him, and while he drank his tea she remained standing at the window with her back to him. She was crying from emotion, from the miserable consciousness that their life was so hard for them; they could only meet in secret, hiding themselves from people, like thieves! Was not their life shattered?

'Come, do stop!' he said.

It was evident to him that this love of theirs would not soon be over, that he could not see the end of it. Anna Sergeyevna grew more and more attached to him. She adored him, and it was unthinkable to say to her that it was bound to have an end some day; besides, she would not have believed it!

He went up to her and took her by the shoulders to say something affectionate and cheering, and at that moment he saw himself in the looking-glass.

His hair was already beginning to turn grey. And it seemed strange to him that he had grown so much older, so much plainer during the last few years. The shoulders on which his hands rested were warm and quivering. He felt compassion for this life, still so warm and lovely, but probably already not far from beginning to fade and wither like his own. Why did she love him so much? He always seemed to women different from what he was, and they loved in him not himself, but the man created by their imagination, whom they had been eagerly seeking all their lives; and afterwards, when they noticed their mistake, they loved him all the same. And not one of them had been happy with him. Time passed, he had made their acquaintance, got on with them, parted, but he had never once loved; it was anything you like, but not love.

And only now when his head was grey he had fallen properly, really in love – for the first time in his life.

Anna Sergeyevna and he loved each other like people very close and akin, like husband and wife, like tender friends; it seemed to them that fate itself had meant them for one another, and they could not understand why he had a wife and she a husband; and it was as though they were a pair of birds of passage, caught and forced to live in different cages. They forgave each other for what they were ashamed of in their past, they forgave everything in the present, and felt that this love of theirs had changed them both.

In moments of depression in the past he had comforted himself with any arguments that came into his mind, but now he no longer cared for arguments; he felt profound compassion, he wanted to be sincere and tender....

'Don't cry, my darling,' he said. 'You've had your cry; that's enough.... Let us talk now, let us think of some plan.'

Then they spent a long while taking counsel together, talked of how to avoid the necessity for secrecy, for deception, for living in different towns and not seeing each other for long at a time. How could they be free from this intolerable bondage?

'How? How?' he asked, clutching his head. 'How?'

And it seemed as though in a little while the solution would be found, and then a new and splendid life would begin; and it was clear to both of them that they had still a long, long way to go, and that the most complicated and difficult part of it was only just beginning.

ABOUT THE TRANSLATOR

CONSTANCE GARNETT (1862–1946) was a distinguished translator responsible for introducing many of the great Russian classics to English readers. As well as Chekhov she translated Tolstoy, Dostoevsky, Turgenev, Gogol and Herzen. She was married to the author Edward Garnett and mother of the novelist and critic David Garnett.

ABOUT THE INTRODUCER

CRAIG RAINE, formerly poetry editor at Faber & Faber, is now Fellow of New College, Oxford. He is the author of *A Martian Sends a Postcard Home* (poems) and *Haydn and the Valve Trumpet* (essays).

TITLES IN EVERYMAN'S LIBRARY

CHINUA ACHEBE
Things Fall Apart

THE ARABIAN NIGHTS
(2 vols, tr. Husain Haddawy)

MARCUS AURELIUS
Meditations

JANE AUSTEN
Emma
Mansfield Park
Northanger Abbey
Persuasion
Pride and Prejudice
Sanditon and Other Stories
Sense and Sensibility

HONORÉ DE BALZAC
Cousin Bette
Eugénie Grandet
Old Goriot

SIMONE DE BEAUVOIR
The Second Sex

SAUL BELLOW
The Adventures of Augie March

WILLIAM BLAKE
Poems and Prophecies

JORGE LUIS BORGES
Ficciones

JAMES BOSWELL
The Life of Samuel Johnson

CHARLOTTE BRONTË
Jane Eyre
Villette

EMILY BRONTË
Wuthering Heights

MIKHAIL BULGAKOV
The Master and Margarita

SAMUEL BUTLER
The Way of all Flesh

ITALO CALVINO
If on a winter's night a traveler

ALBERT CAMUS
The Outsider

MIGUEL DE CERVANTES
Don Quixote

GEOFFREY CHAUCER
Canterbury Tales

ANTON CHEKHOV
My Life and Other Stories
The Steppe and Other Stories

KATE CHOPIN
The Awakening

CARL VON CLAUSEWITZ
On War

S. T. COLERIDGE
Poems

WILKIE COLLINS
The Moonstone
The Woman in White

JOSEPH CONRAD
Heart of Darkness
Lord Jim
Nostromo
The Secret Agent
Typhoon and Other Stories
Under Western Eyes
Victory

THOMAS CRANMER
The Book of Common Prayer

DANTE ALIGHIERI
The Divine Comedy

DANIEL DEFOE
Moll Flanders
Robinson Crusoe

CHARLES DICKENS
Bleak House
David Copperfield
Dombey and Son
Great Expectations
Hard Times
Little Dorrit
Martin Chuzzlewit
Nicholas Nickleby
The Old Curiosity Shop
Oliver Twist
Our Mutual Friend
The Pickwick Papers
A Tale of Two Cities

DENIS DIDEROT
Memoirs of a Nun

JOHN DONNE
The Complete English Poems

FYODOR DOSTOEVSKY
The Brothers Karamazov
Crime and Punishment

GEORGE ELIOT
Adam Bede
Middlemarch
The Mill on the Floss
Silas Marner

WILLIAM FAULKNER
The Sound and the Fury

HENRY FIELDING
Joseph Andrews and Shamela
Tom Jones

F. SCOTT FITZGERALD
The Great Gatsby
This Side of Paradise

GUSTAVE FLAUBERT
Madame Bovary

FORD MADOX FORD
The Good Soldier
Parade's End

E. M. FORSTER
Howards End
A Passage to India

ELIZABETH GASKELL
Mary Barton

EDWARD GIBBON
The Decline and Fall of the Roman Empire
Vols 1 to 3: The Western Empire
Vols 4 to 6: The Eastern Empire

J. W. VON GOETHE
Selected Works

IVAN GONCHAROV
Oblomov

GÜNTER GRASS
The Tin Drum

GRAHAM GREENE
Brighton Rock
The Human Factor

THOMAS HARDY
Far From the Madding Crowd
Jude the Obscure
The Mayor of Casterbridge
The Return of the Native
Tess of the d'Urbervilles
The Woodlanders

JAROSLAV HAŠEK
The Good Soldier Švejk

NATHANIEL HAWTHORNE
The Scarlet Letter

JOSEPH HELLER
Catch-22

ERNEST HEMINGWAY
A Farewell to Arms
The Collected Stories

GEORGE HERBERT
The Complete English Works

HERODOTUS
The Histories

HINDU SCRIPTURES
(tr. R. C. Zaehner)

JAMES HOGG
Confessions of a Justified Sinner

HOMER
The Iliad
The Odyssey

VICTOR HUGO
Les Misérables

HENRY JAMES
The Awkward Age
The Bostonians
The Golden Bowl
The Portrait of a Lady
The Princess Casamassima
The Wings of the Dove
Collected Stories (2 vols)

JAMES JOYCE
Dubliners
A Portrait of the Artist as a Young Man
Ulysses

FRANZ KAFKA
Collected Stories
The Castle
The Trial

JOHN KEATS
The Poems

SØREN KIERKEGAARD
Fear and Trembling and The Book on Adler

RUDYARD KIPLING
Collected Stories
Kim

THE KORAN
(tr. Marmaduke Pickthall)

CHODERLOS DE LACLOS
Les Liaisons dangereuses

GIUSEPPE TOMASI DI LAMPEDUSA
The Leopard

D. H. LAWRENCE
Collected Stories
The Rainbow
Sons and Lovers
Women in Love

MIKHAIL LERMONTOV
A Hero of Our Time

PRIMO LEVI
If This is a Man and The Truce
The Periodic Table

NICCOLÒ MACHIAVELLI
The Prince

THOMAS MANN
Buddenbrooks
Death in Venice and Other Stories
Doctor Faustus

KATHERINE MANSFIELD
The Garden Party and Other Stories

GABRIEL GARCÍA MÁRQUEZ
Love in the Time of Cholera
One Hundred Years of Solitude

ANDREW MARVELL
The Complete Poems

HERMAN MELVILLE
The Complete Shorter Fiction
Moby-Dick

JOHN STUART MILL
On Liberty and Utilitarianism

JOHN MILTON
The Complete English Poems

YUKIO MISHIMA
The Temple of the Golden Pavilion

MARY WORTLEY MONTAGU
Letters

THOMAS MORE
Utopia

TONI MORRISON
Song of Solomon

MURASAKI SHIKIBU
The Tale of Genji

VLADIMIR NABOKOV
Lolita
Pale Fire
Speak, Memory

V. S. NAIPAUL
A House for Mr Biswas

THE NEW TESTAMENT
(King James Version)

THE OLD TESTAMENT
(King James Version)

GEORGE ORWELL
Animal Farm
Nineteen Eighty-Four

THOMAS PAINE
Rights of Man
and Common Sense

BORIS PASTERNAK
Doctor Zhivago

PLATO
The Republic

EDGAR ALLAN POE
The Complete Stories

ALEXANDER PUSHKIN
The Collected Stories

FRANÇOIS RABELAIS
Gargantua and Pantagruel

JOSEPH ROTH
The Radetzky March

JEAN-JACQUES ROUSSEAU
Confessions
The Social Contract and the Discourses

SALMAN RUSHDIE
Midnight's Children

WALTER SCOTT
Rob Roy

WILLIAM SHAKESPEARE
Comedies Vols 1 and 2
Histories Vols 1 and 2
Romances
Sonnets and Narrative Poems
Tragedies Vols 1 and 2

MARY SHELLEY
Frankenstein

ADAM SMITH
The Wealth of Nations

ALEXANDER SOLZHENITSYN
One Day in the Life of
Ivan Denisovich

SOPHOCLES
The Theban Plays

CHRISTINA STEAD
The Man Who Loved Children

JOHN STEINBECK
The Grapes of Wrath

STENDHAL
The Charterhouse of Parma
Scarlet and Black

LAURENCE STERNE
Tristram Shandy

ROBERT LOUIS STEVENSON
The Master of Ballantrae and
Weir of Hermiston
Dr Jekyll and Mr Hyde
and Other Stories

HARRIET BEECHER STOWE
Uncle Tom's Cabin

JONATHAN SWIFT
Gulliver's Travels

JUNICHIRŌ TANIZAKI
The Makioka Sisters

W. M. THACKERAY
Vanity Fair

HENRY DAVID THOREAU
Walden

ALEXIS DE TOCQUEVILLE
Democracy in America

LEO TOLSTOY
Anna Karenina
Childhood, Boyhood and Youth
The Cossacks
War and Peace

ANTHONY TROLLOPE
Barchester Towers
Can You Forgive Her?
Doctor Thorne
The Eustace Diamonds

ANTHONY TROLLOPE *cont.*
Framley Parsonage
The Last Chronicle of Barset
The Small House at Allington
The Warden

IVAN TURGENEV
Fathers and Children
First Love and Other Stories
A Sportsman's Notebook

MARK TWAIN
Tom Sawyer
and Huckleberry Finn

JOHN UPDIKE
Rabbit Angstrom

GIORGIO VASARI
Lives of the Painters, Sculptors
and Architects

VIRGIL
The Aeneid

VOLTAIRE
Candide and Other Stories

EVELYN WAUGH
The Complete Short Stories
Brideshead Revisited
Decline and Fall
The Sword of Honour Trilogy

EDITH WHARTON
The Age of Innocence
The Custom of the Country
The House of Mirth
The Reef

OSCAR WILDE
Plays, Prose Writings and Poems

MARY WOLLSTONECRAFT
A Vindication of the Rights of
Woman

VIRGINIA WOOLF
To the Lighthouse
Mrs Dalloway

W. B. YEATS
The Poems

ÉMILE ZOLA
Germinal

This book is set in Old Style. Throughout the first half of the nineteenth century, modern typefaces were predominant in all areas of publishing. In 1852, however, Miller and Richard, who had been in the forefront of modern face production, set a new trend when they issued specimens of a regularized old face which was named Old Style. Types of this kind became popular in the second half of the nineteenth century.

OSCAR WILDE
Plays, Prose Writings and Poems

MARY WOLLSTONECRAFT
A Vindication of the Rights of Woman

VIRGINIA WOOLF
To the Lighthouse
Mrs Dalloway

WILLIAM WORDSWORTH
Selected Poems

W. B. YEATS
The Poems

ÉMILE ZOLA
Germinal